St Peter Port

1680-1830

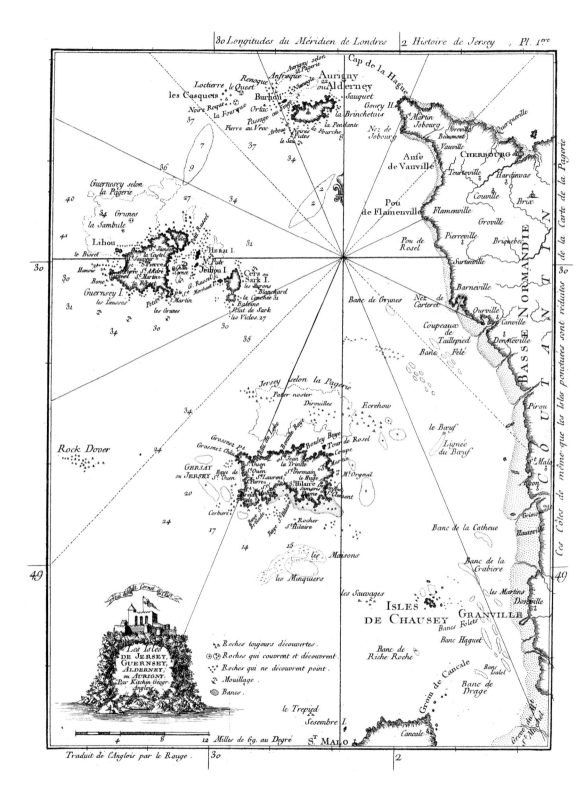

The Channel Islands, a French version of a map by Thomas Kitchin. Modern authorities
locate St Peter Port ('St Pierre') at 49°27'N, 2°32'W

St Peter Port

1680-1830

The history of an international entrepôt

Gregory Stevens Cox

BOYDELL PRESS

First published 1999

Published by the Boydell Press
an imprint of Boydell & Brewer Ltd
PO Box 9, Woodbridge, Suffolk IP12 3DF, UK
and of Boydell & Brewer Inc.
PO Box 41026, Rochester, NY 14604-4126, USA
website: http://www.boydell.co.uk

ISBN 085115 758 0

A catalogue record for this book is available
from the British Library

Library of Congress Cataloguing-in-Publication Data

This publication is printed on acid-free paper

Printed in Great Britain by
St Edmundsbury Press Ltd, Bury St Edmunds, Suffolk

In piam memoriam

et matris meae et patris mei

qui in hoc oppido sepulti sunt.

Requiescant in pace.

Helen Hilson Stevens Cox (*nata* Whitton, *vidua* Hotchkiss) 1918–1971

James Stevens Cox FSA 1910–1997

CONTENTS

COLOUR ILLUSTRATIONS
between pages 74 and 75

BLACK AND WHITE ILLUSTRATIONS
between pages 138 and 139

Guernsey (London, 1815). Built in 1811, at a cost of eleven thousand pounds. By the late Georgian era it had become impractical to detain prisoners in Castle Cornet. [Brett, p. 36]

Plate 30:   St James' Church. Built in 1818, as a cost of approximately seven thousand pounds; John Wilson was the architect. The church was intended as a place where worship would be held in English, to serve the large number of migrants in the town. 'An extremely important and handsome specimen of the neo-classical style'. [Brett, p. 42. Lithograph by Paul Jacob Naftel, 1844]

Plate 31:   The Arcades and the New Meat Market. The Arcades were built in 1830 as a fish market. 'Both in its accommodation and the abundance of its supply is admitted to be unrivalled in any place in Europe.' The architect was John Wilson who was also responsible for the New Meat Market built in 1822. The cost of the New Meat Market was £4,222. [Brett, p. 32. Lithograph published by Moss, c.1830]

Plate 32:   Plans for the modernisation of Fountain Street, John Wilson architect, 1828. 'Both sides of this excellent street were very deliberately designed as part of the same conception as Les Arcades' [Brett, p. 33]. (© States of Guernsey Heritage Committee)

Plate 33:   Le Manoir de Markham – 'a very pretty Gothick villa'. [Brett, p. 80]

Plate 34:   Grange Lodge, built by 1830. [Brett, p. 45]

Plate 35:   An embryonic spa town. The Strand Baths, an advertisement in the *Mercure de Guernesey, et Publiciste de St Pierre-Port*, 20 May 1820; and Mr Greenslade's new baths, an advertisement in the *Gazette de Guernesey*, 27 May 1820. In the years following the Napoleonic Wars the merchants of St Peter Port tried to transform the town into a tourist resort. Baths were opened. In 1820 Mr Greenslade fitted up new baths 'in a very handsome and elegant manner, equal, if not superior to any at the most fashionable bathing places in England'. The architect was Mr Wilson and he was praised for his 'very judicious plan, which embraces warm and cold baths; fresh and salt water; also shower baths, plunging baths, &c.; when these, with other advantages are made known to the invalid, the valetudinarian, the gay, and fashionable; strangers of every denomination will resort to us.' *Gazette de Guernesey*, 27 May 1820, p 3b (and see C. Aptel *et al.*, *Thomas Dobrée Un homme un musée* (Nantes, 1997), p. 73, for the project of Thomas Dobrée to construct baths at the Tourgant in the Pollet)

Plate 36:   London to the Channel Islands in twelve hours, 1848. (Reproduced by kind permission of the Borough of Poole Museums Service)

Plate 37:   The quay and harbour, St Peter Port, Victorian era

Plate 38:   Continuity and change – The Truchot, 1999. Many of the modern banks of St Peter Port stand on the site of the Georgian warehouses

FIGURES

TABLES

PREFACE

On 13 May 1986 I delivered a lecture entitled *Commerce, class and culture in Georgian Guernsey* to the Société Guernesiaise. Following this a don from the University of London encouraged me to formalise my research and suggested that I should approach the centre for Urban History at the University of Leicester. In due course I was accepted at the university as a postgraduate. I herewith thank Professor Peter Clark and his colleagues at the Centre for their unfailing help and encouragement over the years.

During the course of my research I have received generous help from many institutions and individuals. The Education Council of the States of Guernsey awarded me a bursary towards my research costs and I thank the Council for this very practical assistance. I extend similar thanks to the Royal Historical Society for a travel grant to check archives in London. Canon Foster and the Very Reverend J. R. Fenwick, Dean of Guernsey, granted me permission to consult the Town Church archives and the Ecclesiastical Court records. Mr Richings kindly gave access to the Royal Court Library. Mr K. H. Tough, Her Majesty's Greffier, gave permission to study the archives at the Greffe and patiently answered many questions. His assistants, Stephen Francis, James Beale and Keith Robilliard, have been diligent in finding documents and anticipating my requests. The staff of the Constables' Office – Mr Jehan, Mrs Mitchell and Mrs Wesom – have been unfailingly helpful and I thank the Constables past and present for their kind permission to research the parochial records. At the Priaulx Library Dr Tomlinson and his staff – Mrs M. Eddie, Miss E. Gallienne, Mrs G. Martel, Mrs J. Vidamour, Mr B. Hassall and Mrs Howitt – have been helpful beyond the call of duty. At the Island Archives Service Hugh Lenfestey answered several questions about the topography of St Peter Port and made available the records of the Town Hospital. His successor, Dr Ogier, has been equally obliging. I thank the staff of the Guille-Allès Library – Eric Stevens, sometime Chief Librarian, and his successor, Maggie Falla, Sarah Fletcher, Ann Goulding, Susan Laker, Laura Milligan and Helen Paul in particular – for numerous kindnesses, not least the securing of several scarce volumes through the inter-library loan scheme. At Candie Museum the late Rona Cole and her successor Peter Sarl, together with Brian Owen and Alan Howell, showed me relevant pictures and prints.

Peter de Sausmarez made available all his archives at Sausmarez Manor and also granted me permission to consult the de Sausmarez papers lodged on loan at the Greffe. I have received similar generosity from several other Guernsey inhabitants. To Mrs Grant, Mrs Cormack and Mr Richard Hocart I owe my awareness of family papers in private hands. I thank Canon V. J. Collas for a Huguenot reference; Mrs Moore has supplied helpful references to Guernsey trade at Barcelona and Salou; Mrs Marie Holland has helped to clarify some biographical details.

Peter Tagart has illuminated many aspects of sea transport through the ages, in particular with his explanations about *cabotage* and *charter parties.* James Marr gave useful cartographic advice. With patience, skill and ingenuity Paul Fernando has guided masses of my raw data through computers; I am deeply grateful to him for the many hours that he has spent thus. Brian Green, Graham Jackson and Peter Izat have equally helped with photographs. I remember here, with a sad sense of loss, the late Thomas Tudor Loveday who encouraged my earliest efforts in the field of economic history. Having studied economics at Princeton, Cambridge and Oxford, Tom was always happy to offer three rival explanations of any economic phenomenon – and then knock them down. Another friend, the late Ian Harris, gave quiet encouragement (more, perhaps, than he realised). I owe thanks to many other colleagues in the teaching world: to Sister Mary Stanislaus and Sister Mary Gertrude of Blanchelande College; to Jurat Alan Bisson, sometime headmaster of Guernsey Grammar School, and to his staff – Dennis Balls (now headmaster), Audrey Bisson, David Fletcher, John Nicolle, Jennie Falla and Eric Grimsley; and to Lesley Le Page, Principal of Blanchelande Girls' College.

I have received equal kindness outside Guernsey. I thank the archivists, librarians and staff of the British Library; Cambridge University Library; Guildhall Library, London; Hampshire Record Office, Winchester; Poole Museums Service, Dorset; Public Record Office, London; Northamptonshire Record Office; Scottish Record Office, Edinburgh; United Grand Lodge of England, Freemasons' Hall, London; Archives Municipales, Nantes; Musée Dobrée, Nantes; National Portrait Gallery of Sweden, Stockholm; the Landsarkivet, Gothenburg, Sweden. Sue Beckett of the Borough of Poole Museums Service gave timely help over a transport query. Mrs Kitchen of Kew has provided excellent accommodation and food on my many expeditions to the Public Record Office.

Scholars from several countries have answered my importunate questions; I thank in particular Professor Cullen, Professor Mathias, Dr Keith Marshall, Dr Nicholas Rodger and Dr Lars Holm for their time and trouble. Mr Hobday kindly compared some demographic enumerations. At Leicester University Alastair Milne ran baptismal and burial data through a computer programme. There were other scholars whom I met at historical conferences held at the universities of Leicester, London, Uppsala, Leiden and Louvain; their contributions are acknowledged – directly and obliquely – in the end notes and bibliography.

My family and relations have lived with my research for many years. I thank Mrs Adèle Stevens Cox for help with several of the illustrations; Mr and Mrs Gerald Smith who have frequently provided accommodation on my visits to England; Rosemary, Emma, Naomi and Andrew who have given constant encouragement and who have survived amidst my mountain of files (and fluctuating moods) for more years than I care to contemplate; and Advocate Howitt, my son-in-law, who has answered questions on Guernsey law. My interest in the past started when I was three years old and I accompanied my father to an archaeological excavation; he always encouraged my efforts and lived to see my doctoral thesis presented. In my researches I have scanned several thousand books and manuscripts in French; I remember with gratitude those who taught me that language in my schooldays in Dorset: the late Major Porter; the late N. Hepburn; and the late Major Thackthwaite.

Dr Borsay and Dr Rodger examined my doctoral thesis and made some kindly suggestions. I thank the Royal Historical Society for accepting the thesis for publication in one of their monograph series and Messrs Boydell and Brewer for taking over the volume so that it might be more lavishly illustrated. It has been a great joy to work with Dr Barber and his staff at Boydell and Brewer – Ellie Ferguson, Vanda Andrews, Pru Harrison, Joan Jordan and the rest of the team; I have much appreciated their thoughtful advice and professionalism. Kathleen Halson of Messrs Creeds (Broadoak, Bridport) cheerfully and efficiently typeset a text not made easier by the author's bad writing. Dr Arnold Harvey read the galley proofs with an eagle eye and made numerous helpful comments. There are many others to whom I owe a variety of thanks. I trust that they will forgive me if I here include them in a general 'thank you'. I conclude where I started, by acknowledging my gratitude to Professor Peter Clark; it has been a privilege to explore aspects of urban history with him. He has saved me from numerous errors; any that remain are my fault alone.

Gregory Stevens Cox

ABBREVIATIONS

Actes	*Actes des Etats de l'ile de Guernesey, 1605* (Guernsey, 1851–)
BL	British Library
Brett	C.E.B. Brett, *Buildings in the Town and Parish of St Peter Port* (Guernsey, 1975)
BSJ	Bulletin of the Société Jersiaise
COf	Constables' Office, St Peter Port
Duncan	J. Duncan, *The History of Guernsey* (London, 1841)
Dupont	G. Dupont, *Histoire du Cotentin et de ses Iles* 4 vols (Caen, 1885)
E C	Ecclesiastical Court archives (housed in the Greffe, St Peter Port)
Le Roy	*Notebook of Pierre Le Roy*, ed. by G. E. Lee (Guernsey, 1893)
l .t.	livre(s) tournois (approx 14 l. t. = £1 sterling in the 18th century)
Ordonnances	*Recueil d'Ordonnances de la cour Royale de l'Isle de Guernesey 1553–* (Guernsey, 1852 –)
PP	Parliamentary Papers
PRO	Public Record Office, London
QRGS	*Quarterly Review of the Guernsey Society*
TC	The Town Church, St Peter Port
TC DdCdF	Town Church, Délibérations des Chefs de Famille
TSG	Transactions of La Société Guernesiaise (*Guernsey Society of Natural Science and Local Research* before 1922)
Tupper	F. B. Tupper, *The History of Guernsey and its Bailiwick* (Guernsey, 1854)

Conventions

Dates are rendered as in manuscripts (i.e. old style before 1752).

Maps are to be found as Frontispiece, Plate I, and in Appendix 28.
        Appendix 28, map 1 indicates the location and names of the island parishes.

Place names are usually rendered as in their documentary source
        Glatigny = Glateny = Glatney = Glategny
        L'Hyvreuse = New Ground = Cambridge Park
        la rue des forges = Smith Street
        Ville Neuve = New Town
        Cette = Sète (France)

Personal names: It should be noted that there were two branches of the *(de) Sausmarez* family, one branch spelling the name *Saumarez*.

GLOSSARY

abjuration	renunciation/recantation of Roman Catholicism, made by Huguenots
acte	law created by the States of Guernsey
armateur	ship-owner; organiser of a privateering venture
barrière	the boundaries of the town; see pp. 14, 129-130
cabotage	coasting trade
disette	dearth of food; see p. 64 and Appendix 13
douzaine ⎱ *douzeniers* ⎰	group, originally twelve in number, that ran the parish; see p. 14
Gemeinschaft	community, based on close personal ties
Gesellschaft	organisation, based on impersonal ties
hogshead	measure of wine, half a pipe [q.v.]
jurat	permanent 'judge' sitting in the Royal Court; see p. 14
livre tournois	the standard money system of Tours, used in Guernsey from the medieval era. In the 18th century there were approximately 14 l.t. to the pound sterling; the livre, like the pound sterling, was subdivided into sols (= shillings) and deniers (= d., pence)
marchand	merchant, usually retailing to the public; see p. 52
négociant	merchant operating at national and international level; see p. 52
ordonnance	regulation; see p. 14
pipe	a wine cask, equivalent to two hogsheads; a measure of 105–132 gallons. See p. 153
préciput	a preference legacy, regularly the principal dwelling house; see p. 80
reconnaissance	profession of faith, made by Huguenots
rente	rent; see pp. 129–130
tod	a measure of wool, regularly of 32 lbs
tun	a measure, equal to four hogsheads [q.v.] or two pipes [q.v.]
venelle	a narrow lane
vingtaine	subdivision of the parish; see p. 14

1

The Background

I Urban history and St Peter Port

St Peter Port has not been well served by historians. Very little research has been conducted into the history of St Peter Port since 1935 when the late Professor Le Patourel analysed the mediaeval development of the town.[1] The topography and architecture of St Peter Port have received some attention. Edith Carey presented extracts from the notes of the Victorian antiquary F. C. Lukis which clarified aspects of the town lay-out in the early nineteenth century.[2] C. E. B. Brett's inventory of historic buildings catalogued the wealth of late Georgian and Regency architecture in St Peter Port[3]; and John McCormack's study threw light on vernacular building traditions in the island and town.[4] But the focus of these works was such that they had little to say about the economy, society and culture of the town and their relation to building forms. One reason for the lack of research into the history of St Peter Port has been the general understanding that there is little relevant evidence, especially for the eighteenth century.[5] It is true that St Peter Port lacked many of the institutions regularly found in English towns (e.g. guilds) and the corresponding records have never existed. It is also true that the port records were destroyed in 1940.[6] Nevertheless, there are good collections of parochial, ecclesiastical and insular archives which provide the foundations for an urban study.

The publication in 1986 of *A People of the Sea* offered a wealth of information about the maritime history of the Channel Islanders. However it contained strangely little about St Peter Port as a port town. In fact there is a subtle but profound difference between the maritime activities of the islanders and the history of the port. The trading of a Guernsey-owned vessel from port to port in the Pacific fell within the terms of reference of Dr Jamieson's work; the arrival of Baltic and Mediterranean vessels to trade in St Peter Port in the eighteenth century did not. *A People of the Sea* contains three chapters – nearly 90 pages – describing the privateering ventures of the islanders in the eighteenth century; but includes just one paragraph about St Peter Port as an entrepôt.[7] Furthermore, Dr Jamieson's work did not consider the volume and value of trade transacted through the port, nor the significance of the entrepôt trade in the policies of the islanders.[8]

There is scope, then, for a study which attempts to quantify the volume and value of the maritime trade of St Peter Port; and which relates these economic data to an examination of the town and its demographic, social and physical evolution. In writing about 'Lisbon as a port town in the eighteenth century' Stephen Fisher has commented that while that city's commerce and shipping have attracted reasonable attention, 'relatively little has been written on the general character, physical, social and so on, of this celebrated port town'. He has observed that such studies of European ports during the era of the Commercial Revolution do exist 'but are still unusual'. He has also argued that a study of the structure and articulation of European ports is helpful in promoting an understanding of their differing success as trading centres.[9]

It would be possible to study St Peter Port as a port town and to a considerable extent that is the agenda of the present work. However, this monograph attempts to be an *urban* rather than just a port history. A full understanding of St Peter Port demands an examination of its relationship – economic and cultural – with its insular hinterland just as much as its links with the proximate forelands of Normandy and Brittany and more distant horizons. St Peter Port was both a market town and administrative centre serving the nine rural parishes of Guernsey as well as being a port engaged in local and international trading. To be understood fully the town needs to be considered in its own insular setting *and* as a link in networks of French, English and international urban systems.

This study explores the identity of St Peter Port in the 'long' eighteenth century, focusing on seven areas: overseas trade; internal economy; demography; migration; social structure and residential patterns; sociability and culture; and the physical transformation of the town. These represent the themes that currently concern the growing number of British urban historians.[10] At this juncture it may be useful to survey the theoretical and methodological ideas that underpin the current study of eighteenth century towns.

Much work on urban history earlier this century was predicated on theories that reified the town and presented it as a social reality, an *explanans*. Subsequently Philip Abrams and other urban historians repudiated the assumptions of this approach. Abrams, for example, argued that 'the ramparts of the town identify an enterprise not an entity'.[11] He believed that the most effective attempts to understand towns were those which studied the power relationships which towns embody. 'On inspection many of the best case studies and many of the most convincing general commentaries in the field of urban history prove to be, often implicity, studies of and commentaries on action and relationships within a complex of domination.' This had been the approach of Max Weber in *Economy and Society*; and was the understanding of Abrams' co-authors.[12]

Scepticism about the validity of reifying the town has extended to theories about industrialisation and urbanisation. Martin Daunton, for example, has urged that the level of urbanisation should be seen as a reflection of other variables rather than as an independent factor. He concedes that towns acted 'as a solvent of social norms and traditional consumption patterns' and that they had an independent role on the side of modernisation. However, he does not see eighteenth century towns as 'useful analytical tools in explaining economic growth'; rather, he considers that it would be wiser to take the level of urban population as given and to concentrate on a different range of questions. The provisioning of cities, the building processes, the adjustment to the new urban environment and the control of society are the themes that he advocates for study. Daunton, like Abrams, denies the town a causal significance. During a period of economic growth it was not the town itself which was the independent factor, but rather the merchants whose investments happened 'to be in that particular location'.[13]

Professor Daunton's view is easily harmonised with recent economic theories about entrepreneurial culture. In the past economists often concentrated on theories of rational choice in the market and neglected 'the dimensions of personality'. Now, however, Mark Casson and other economists are becoming increasingly aware of the significance of culture in determining commercial success. Great cities and ports are viewed as 'the theatre for the various trading cultures ... where merchants competed for trade'.[14] This approach can have its own problems. The comment of Peter Borsay is relevant in this context: 'towns are treated as the accidental spaces in which interesting processes and incidents happen to occur; not as a special type of place which, by virtue of its generic qualities, moulded experiences and instigated events'. The corrective to this error is, in part, he argues, the study of towns as part of a system rather than as 'solitary entities'.[15]

Scholars have suggested a variety of theoretical frameworks for systems analysis. Jan de Vries has maintained that during the early modern period an integrated network of towns linked by economic forces emerged in Europe.[16] The thesis postulates an era of general urban stagnation during the seventeenth and early eighteenth centuries, with urban regeneration in the later eighteenth century. The schema of de Vries appears to fit the continental experience but sits uneasily with the English data. While de Vries' model is essentially economic, Immanuel Wallerstein has postulated a European 'world economy' integrated by political and economic factors.[17] Cities played an important role in his model which has subsequently been adapted and elaborated by P. M. Hohenberg and L. H. Lees. Much of their analysis is based on central place and network systems, each system being characterised by structural, functional and evolutionary features. Hohenberg and Lees have argued that as an analytical tool their system's approach has a validity for more than one era.[18]

The analysis of English towns has often been conceptualised in hierarchical terms. However Penelope Corfield has urged that by the eighteenth century English towns were talked of 'in terms of their leading economic functions'. Places became identified as 'dockyard towns, manufacturing towns, spas, holiday resorts, university towns, as well as "thoroughfare towns" on the main roads'. These she has denominated 'the mutable terms of a dynamic urban world' and her study of English towns between 1700 and 1800 is based on analyses of the dynamics of urban growth.[19] The most obvious aspect of English urban growth in the eighteenth century was population increase. In 1700 sixty-seven towns with a population of between 2,500 and 100,000 inhabitants accounted for 7½% of the nation's population; a century later there were 187 such towns and they housed 20% of the national population.[20] Altogether some 31% of the population lived in an urban centre by 1801. Eighteenth century towns and cities have traditionally been seen as graveyards, with mortality rates consistently running ahead of birth rates. Immigration has been understood to be 'the principal locomotive of demographic urbanization'.[21] Caution is necessary, however. Studies of English provincial towns have demonstrated that some experienced natural population increase.[22]

A. M. van der Woude has expressed reservations about the conventional theories of urban natural decrease. He has hypothesised that rural-urban migration rates varied and that they directly influenced the urban birth rate. Urban natural decrease was not inevitable, it was merely the result of variation in migration flows. But whereas van der Woude views rural-urban immigration as a positive factor, Allan Sharlin has postulated that temporary migrants in urban centres depressed the birth rate. Sharlin's model is internally consistent but empirical evidence from Amsterdam and elsewhere does not seem to support it.[23] This is not to minimise the impact of migration. Even when there was natural increase in towns and cities, immigration provided a vital flow of new town dwellers. Earlier demographic studies tended to discuss net balances of migrants in a somewhat impersonal and statistical manner. Recently new methodologies have been developed to distinguish between the different cohorts of migrants and their motivation. The wealthy merchant moving a few miles to a better residence had little in common with the poor artisan travelling from a distant region in search of a living.[24] The analysis of church depositions and similar archives is progressively shedding light on migration processes. Simple 'push' and 'pull' interpretations are no longer sufficient. Scholars increasingly are examining the impact of migrants on the receiving community and the agencies that helped to integrate them into their new urban environment.[25]

Urban growth was particularly to be found in towns that were expanding as centres of commerce, industry, trade, defence (the dockyards and naval centres) and leisure pursuits. Many port towns flourished during the eighteenth century thanks to the expanding volume of overseas trade. Peter Borsay has characterised ports and market towns as the 'engines of the commercial system, pumping goods to and fro along the arteries of trade'.[26] There has been a lively debate about the relationship between national economic growth and urbanization. As has been seen above, Martin Daunton has questioned whether urbanization can be regarded as an independent factor and views it more as a reflection of other variables.[27]

What is abundantly clear is that many county gentry and 'pseudo-gentry' took to living in town. This stimulated the growth of the service sector; and the professionals, retailers, artisans and domestics busy in the tertiary sector themselves became part of the new urban army of consumers. The growing number of doctors, lawyers and other professionals have been represented as part of the rising middle classes. They were more conscious of fashion than their country cousins and spent more lavishly. The wealthy, with an even greater surplus of cash, indulged in conspicuous consumption. In that sense the urban way of life was an important dynamic in the national economy. Moreover, the taste for civilized standards led directly to the improvement of the urban fabric.[28]

There has been considerable debate about the extent to which urban society became more polarised during the course of the long eighteenth century. The traditional view maintained that there was an increasing divide between the cultural patterns of patricians and plebeians; and that this was re-inforced by physical segregation as the wealthy moved from town centre to suburb. Jonathan Barry has challenged this thesis in his study of Bristol, arguing that the upper ranks, on the one hand, continued to enjoy traditional popular customs; and, on the other hand, that the new forms of urban culture were available to more people than just the urban élite. It is not clear whether the experience of Bristol was typical or exceptional.[29]

Peter Borsay and others have redefined the debate by drawing attention to sub-cultures and minority cultures, and to the tensions occasioned by religion and politics. To concentrate on the divide between élite and plebeian is perhaps too simplistic. There is also a danger in paying too much attention to division, and too little to what united townspeople.[30] This latter is a theme that has attracted the attention of Professor Peter Clark. He has contended that the mushrooming of clubs and societies in towns in the post-Restoration era helped to promote social integration and that the new forms of urban sociability generated 'a renewed consciousness and pride in the urban community'.[31]

The present study attempts to explore the history of St Peter Port against the background of these approaches and debates. It has been remarked earlier that the town should be studied in the context of its hinterland. Recent research suggests that this is too limited. Professor King has argued in *Urbanism, Colonialism, and the World Economy* that the colonial city should be viewed first in relation to its colonized territory; secondly in its links with the metropolitan power; thirdly in the context of its region; fourthly as part of an empire; fifthly in the world system; and finally as a colonial city *per se*. 'Which of these levels we choose to examine … will depend on the problem to be investigated.'[32] Whether St Peter Port should be regarded as a colonial town is a question that will be addressed a little later. That apart, Professor King's multi-dimensional approach is eminently appropriate for placing St Peter Port in a series of persectives. In the second part of this chapter there is a rapid review of the experience of English, French and American port towns belonging to the local, regional and international networks within which the Guernsey merchants operated. The chapter then considers whether St Peter Port should be viewed as a colonial town – fundamental for an understanding of the relationship between the islanders and the British government. After this synchronic approach – which is intended to set eighteenth century St Peter Port in its geographical, economic and constitutional context – there is a short diachronic survey which traces the historical development of St Peter Port from the Roman period to the late seventeenth century. Finally there is an outline of the workings of the insular and urban government to provide an institutional framework for the discussion of the demographic, economic and social development of the town.

II Port towns in the eighteenth century

Table 1.1 Urban growth in eighteenth century England

	% growth	
	1750/1700	1801/1750
England	14	50
London	17	42
10 historic regional centres	18	21
8 established ports *	58	48
8 ports + Liverpool	72	82
4 'new' manufacturing towns	159	274

* Bristol, Hull, Colchester, Newcastle, Ipswich, Great Yarmouth, King's Lynn, Southampton.
Source: E. A. Wrigley, 'Urban growth and agricultural change: England and the Continent in the early modern period' in P. Borsay (ed.), *The Eighteenth-Century Town* (Harlow, 1990), pp. 49, 50

Significant among the rising towns and cities of England in the eighteenth century were the ports, their growth stimulated by the expansion of English trade overseas. Initially the growth of foreign trade was slow; during the period 1700–45 the average growth rate was only 0.5% per annum. This picked up to 2.8% p.a. between 1745 and 1771 and fast growth of 4.9% came in the closing two decades of the century.[33] Not all ports shared equally in this expansion of trade. Those that grew fastest were 'coal' ports such as Newcastle and Sunderland and those involved in Atlantic trade – Bristol and Liverpool in particular. During the course of the eighteenth

Table 1.2: Merchant shipping owned in some English ports (000s tons)

	1709 [Tons burden]	1792 [Measured tons]	Multiplier
Newcastle	11.5	121.2	10.5
Hull	7.5	58.0	7.7
King's Lynn	6.5	16.8	2.6
Great Yarmouth	11.4	35.8	3.1
Ipswich	1.5	4.4	2.9
Colchester	1.9	4.0	2.1
Southampton	1.6	9.2	5.8
Bristol	15.5	43.9	2.8
Liverpool	6.4	92.1	14.4
All outports	179.8	812.3	4.5
Total (London and outports)	319.8	1186.5	4.7

Notes and sources: Ports arranged from north-east around to north-west. Subsequent to 1786 tonnage was measured by a different method; consequently the 1792 figures are not strictly comparable with the 1709 figures. Nevertheless, the multiplier gives a crude index of the growth. P. Corfield, *The Impact of English Towns 1700–1800* (Oxford, 1982), p. 37 (Reproduced by kind permission of Oxford University Press). See also S. Chapman, *Merchant Enterprise in Britain* (Cambridge, 1992), p. 41

century foreign trade became increasingly concentrated in a smaller number of the larger provincial ports. By 1772 out of seventy-four listed ports only sixteen had more than five hundred registered tons active in foreign trade.[34] The medium and smaller sized ports tended to concentrate on coastal shipping, fishing and, in some cases, smuggling. An approximate index of the growth of shipping trade at the ports is afforded by a comparison of the shipping tonnages for the year 1709 and 1792 (Table 1.2).

The successful ports shared some, if not all, of the following characteristics. First, they were able to handle larger vessels either because of topographical advantages or thanks to dock improvement schemes.[35] Secondly, they were geographically well situated to engage in a major branch of overseas trade. Thus Hull on the east coast was well placed to trade with the Baltic, while Liverpool, Whitehaven and Bristol on the west coast found good markets in Ireland and America. Thirdly, they were able to achieve a reasonable balance in the volume of import and export trade. This led to the optimum use of shipping capacity. Merchants in ports that traded in bulky one-way commodities could experience difficulties.[36] Fourthly, successful ports served – and were served by – an extensive hinterland. Bristol became the 'metropolis of the west', while Liverpool served Lancashire and the industrialising Midlands.[37] Fifthly, the ports contained a merchant community with the entrepreneurial ability to create and develop trading opportunities.[38] The lack of one or more of these factors tended eventually to arrest port development.

Because of their rapid growth the port towns frequently displayed a high population density. Housing was packed around the dock areas with lodging houses, inns and brothels catering to the needs of the sailors and dock workers.[39] But the port towns also displayed a statelier aspect. The wealthy merchants of Bristol enjoyed 'sumptuous mansions, luxurious living, liveried menials'[40] and Professor Minchinton has guardedly portrayed the city as being 'in some slight way, a centre of conspicuous consumption'.[41]

Such luxury was not confined to Bristol. Southampton enjoyed some commercial prosperity and became popular as a spa. In the 1760s and 1770s residences were fitted up 'in the neatest and genteelest manner'; the promenade was enhanced; and the paving, lighting and the watch were improved. The years 1773–74 saw Southampton at its zenith as a spa. Among the amenities available to residents and visitors were dancing in the Long Rooms, plays at the theatre, companionship in the coffee houses, the latest novels at the circulating library, and shops with representatives from London.[42] The nearby port of Weymouth enjoyed a similar urban transformation in the late eighteenth century, mainly thanks to the fashion for sea-bathing and the summer visits of George III and his court.[43]

In this study we shall be examining how far such developments also affected St Peter Port. Certainly the improvements in English towns such as Southampton did not pass unnoticed by the residents of St Peter Port. Members of the de Sausmarez family, for example, received catalogues and advertising sheets from Southampton and London traders.[44] There were other cultural ties which bound Guernsey to the port towns in the south of England. Theatrical troupes regularly travelled from Plymouth and Southampton to St Peter Port to play for a season; there were links between the masonic lodges of Guernsey and those of English ports; and the children of St Peter Port merchants were frequently educated at academies in the port towns of Hampshire, Dorset and Devon.[45]

French ports

Among French towns it was ports that experienced the greatest expansion in the eighteenth century. This was due to dynamic growth in overseas trade.[46] In fact French trade expanded even more vigorously than that of England. Kriedte has observed that it grew three-fold between 1716–20 and 1784–88, as compared to a 2.4-fold growth of English foreign trade.[47] However, the average annual growth rates of French trade were higher in the early years of the eighteenth century and decreased later in the century – the reverse of the English pattern.

Of the port towns those situated on the Atlantic coast grew most vigorously.[48] Bordeaux specialised in the handling of colonial produce such as sugar, indigo, cocoa, coffee, silk and cotton, much of which was re-exported to Holland and the north. The port also exported wine from its hinterland. Between 1717 and 1789 the total value of the trade of Bordeaux increased twenty-fold and incomes in the city kept ahead of prices, a rare occurrence in France at that time.[49] Nantes experienced a similar boom, initially thanks to the wine trade and then by dealing in slaves, sugar and coffee. By 1780 the value of international trade to the port was in the region of 65 million livres tournois. In 1725 there were some 230 *négociants* in Nantes; by 1790 there were 400.[50] In Nantes, as in Bordeaux, many handsome public and private buildings were erected in neo-classical styles.

Table 1.3: Vessels registered at, or departing from, French ports 1664–1787

	Bordeaux	La Rochelle	Lorient	Nantes	St Malo
1664	11	18		12	48
1686		93		84	117
1704	29	45		151	90
1730		34	18		
1787	245	34	85	116	18

Source: J. G. Clark, *La Rochelle and the Atlantic Economy during the Eighteenth Century* (Baltimore, 1981), p. 27

Table 1.4: Population of some Atlantic and Channel ports, 1650–1800

	Bordeaux	La Rochelle	Lorient	Nantes	St Malo	Dunkirk
1650	40	17	0	40	15	?
1700	50	14	0	42	25	11
1750	67	16	0	57	15	15
1800	88	18	15	74	17	21

Notes and source: J. de Vries, *European Urbanization 1500–1800* (London, 1984), Appendix 1. Populations rounded to the nearest thousand. 0 = less than 10,000

There was prosperity in other towns. La Rochelle was involved in French colonial trade and its economy depended upon that sector to 'a degree unmatched at other ports'. The port of Lorient for many years enjoyed a monopoly of the French East India trade. Coffee, India cloths, Bengal silks, Chinese porcelain and spices from the Dutch East Indies were regularly offered at the auction sales of *La Compagnie Française des Indes* held at Lorient. Subsequent to the demise of the old company, a new Company of the Indies was founded there in 1785.[51]

St Malo participated in a range of Atlantic trades. From the sixteenth century she traded wheat and textiles to the Iberian peninsula from where her vessels returned with gold and silver. The Malouins integrated their commercial ventures by trading Newfoundland cod to the Mediterranean. The treaty of the Pyrenees (1659) consolidated the opportunities open to St Malo *négociants* and by 1682 some two million écus of silver were being exported from Spain to St Malo. This helped to finance other enterprises. From c. 1695 the Malouins engaged in an ambitious series of voyages to the South Seas. The voyages were discontinued c. 1724 because St Malo lost both government backing and the necessary investment capital. Nevertheless, the town maintained its links with Newfoundland, Spain, England and Holland and continued to trade in wheat, textiles, cod and silver.[52]

These major ports were involved in three complementary economic systems. First, there were local links with small French port towns, *le petit cabotage*. Secondly, there was traffic with Britain, Holland and Scandinavia, *le grand cabotage*. Thirdly, there was long distance oceanic trading conducted by *vaisseaux de long cours*.[53] St Peter Port was geographically well situated to participate in some of the trade of all three systems.

The Guernsey merchants traded regularly with the French ports that we have just discussed. But the port that came nearest *in function* to St Peter Port in the eighteenth century was Dunkirk. It had interests in fishing (both in local waters and off Newfoundland) and in short-distance coastal trading. It was a frontier town situated close to the maritime powers of England and Holland; during wartime it served as a centre for French privateers. Dunkirk's status as a free-port made it a rendez-vous for smugglers and an entrepôt for handling colonial produce. The port sustained two important industries: the processing of tobacco and the handling of spirits. Manufacturing attracted workers to the town, whose population grew rapidly from 15,944 in 1770 to 27,106 in 1789.[54] There was little *direct* trade between Dunkirk and St Peter Port. Their activities were complementary rather than inter-dependent. For example, Dunkirk supplied cargoes to smugglers from the south-east of England, while St Peter Port served the south-west counties.

The Atlantic economy

Having examined the English and French ports, it is time to turn to more distant towns involved in the 'Atlantic economy'. In the eighteenth century St Peter Port was integrated into an international network of seaborne commerce which embraced the port towns of north-west Europe and North America. The merchants of Philadelphia, Boston, New York, Bordeaux, Nantes, London and Amsterdam were linked in shared commercial purposes. 'Investment capital, goods, information, and people flowed between these centres'.[55] These flows were more important to merchants than the demands of patriotism. Mark Gregory, a London merchant with extensive interests in St Peter Port trade, explained to Lord Hawkesbury: 'The first object of a merchant is his interest, all attempts of governments to lead him from that will be in vain.'[56]

The growth of the North American ports was rapid. In 1690 Boston had a population of 6,000; New York and Philadelphia counted 14,000 and 12,000 respectively.[57] Buoyed up by an economic boom, and drawn further into international commercial networks, the three ports had populations between thirteen and sixteen thousand by the mid-eighteenth century.[58] The ports were tied to London by political and commercial links; and they also formed part of a colonial network of towns and cities that consistently reflected the culture and fashions of the metropolitan capital.[59]

III St Peter Port

At this juncture it is relevant to examine whether St Peter Port should be considered a colonial town. Superficially such a classification seems surprising; a colony is commonly understood to involve the imposition of imperial rule on a native people. In the eighteenth century some Englishmen viewed Guernsey as part of Hampshire, an understandable mistake as the island fell within the diocese of Winchester.[60] In fact Guernsey was not part of the realm of England but was a dominion, like the other Channel Islands, Ireland and the Isle of Man. These British islands, although dependencies of the Crown, enjoyed considerable political autonomy. Professor Fieldhouse has observed that these dominions 'supplied a ready-made constitutional pattern into which the new American colonies were fitted without difficulty'.[61] Consequently there were many similarities between the polity of Guernsey and those of the American colonies. They each had their own political institutions, assemblies and legal systems; and the Crown and Westminster exercised little control over their internal administration. It was only in the economic sphere that the British government sought to impose rigid controls (with the Navigation Acts). Edmund Burke summarised the system of the first British Empire as a 'state of commercial servitude and civil liberty'.[62] Although there is a distinction *de jure* between a dominion and a colony, in practice the constitutional and economic relationships between Guernsey and Britain in the eighteenth century were very similar to those of the American colonies with the mother country. When in 1780 the British government started to construct a new fort near St Peter Port to defend the island against a French invasion, the Royal Court of Guernsey obstructed the work. The island leaders feared that the French would impose a harsher occupation if they had to overcome stiff opposition; they also suspected that with the return of peace the fort would be used by the British to suppress the smuggling trade.[63] This and similar episodes betray the *mentalité* of a 'colony'. It seems probable that some aspects of the urban development of St Peter Port are best understood in a 'colonial' context.

The early development of St Peter Port

Recent archaeological excavations suggest that in the Roman period there was a trading post at the Plaiderie, near the centre of modern St Peter Port. This may have constituted the nucleus of the original settlement that was later to develop into the town of St Peter Port. In the 10th century Guernsey was assimilated into the Duchy of Normandy. The island was thoroughly integrated into the feudal polity of the duchy and Guernsey became Norman in its laws, customs, language and institutions. By virtue of military conquest Duke William of Normandy became King of England in 1066; this created the political link between the Channel Islands and England. In the early thirteenth century King John lost control of mainland Normandy to the French king but managed to retain the islands. Subsequent English monarchs have ruled the islands not in their capacity as English sovereigns but rather as descendants of the Norman dukes.

At some point in the thirteenth or fourteenth century St Peter Port developed into a town. There has been considerable debate about the definition of the term 'town' as scholars have attempted to compile lists of criteria applicable universally to towns in different societies and at varying dates. Professor Hilton has recently suggested three criteria for defining mediaeval English and French towns.[64] They are: first, the existence of a permanent market; secondly, occupational heterogeneity in 'an economy which produced, bought and sold commodities other than those necessary for subsistence'; and, thirdly, an institutional dimension.

These were, essentially, the aspects considered by Professor Le Patourel in his essay on the early history of St Peter Port.[65] Professor Le Patourel demonstrated that by the fourteenth century the king's administration of Guernsey was centralised in St Peter Port, that being the location of the king's castle, the king's court and the king's grange. There was a market in St Peter Port serving the garrison and the island. The harbour of St Peter Port was a port of call for foreign shipping engaged in the exchange of the corn, cloth and salted fish of north-west Europe for the wine and spices of Bordeaux and the south. Moreover, Guernsey merchants were actively trading abroad, co-operating together as 'socii mercatores'. There was a concentration of population in St Peter Port, with the inhabitants enjoying a very considerable degree of personal and tenurial freedom. The town was referred to 'quasi burgum' and there are traces of burgage tenure. By many standards fourteenth century St Peter Port was a town.

However, Professor Le Patourel could find no trace of the municipal institutions characteristic of the fully developed mediaeval town – the council, the self-administration, the community of burgesses, the gild-merchants. Even the existence of a town wall was doubtful. By the criteria of Professor Pirenne mediaeval St Peter Port was *not* a town. Professor Le Patourel concluded that there were two possible theories. Either St Peter Port found its municipal institutions in the institutions of the island and therefore had no need to evolve separate institutions for itself; or St Peter Port should be examined in the context of neighbouring Normandy and Brittany, a region 'where towns did not evolve important urban institutions, and seem to have got on very well without them'.[66]

In the fifteenth century St Peter Port suffered some setbacks. The loss of Gascony to the French disrupted the Anglo-French wine trade; and the Channel Island waters became infested with pirates. The situation improved when, in the 1480s, Pope Sixtus IV promulgated a bull conferring neutrality on the islands during wartime. This privilege lasted for just over two centuries and brought major benefits to St Peter Port. English and French merchants were able to trade in safety in St Peter Port during wartime. By the late sixteenth century William Camden observed that the town was well provided with fortifications 'and the merchants abound as soon as there is war'.[67]

In 1629 Heylyn found that the Guernseymen were 'masters of stout barks' in which they ventured 'unto all these nearer ports of Christendom', selling abroad the works 'of the poorer sort' such as waistcoats, stockings and other manufactures of wool.[68] The town suffered somewhat, though, during the English Civil War. Castle Cornet was held until 1651 by Royalist forces, while the town and island declared for Parliament. The Royalists bombarded the town and some damage was done to the area around the town church. In a declaration to Oliver Cromwell the islanders complained that they had lost their ships, their traffic and their trading because their harbour and port had been 'closed and shut up' by Sir Peter Osborne, the commander of Castle Cornet. The population of the island stood at eight thousand and many were in want and poverty.[69] The declaration may contain some exaggerations but the general picture appears to be reasonably accurate. Though the town had grown considerably in the sixteenth and early seventeenth centuries its economic state at the Restoration was hardly strong – a situation not unlike that of many English provincial towns.

Insular and urban government

The economic and social history of St Peter Port is not intelligible without some understanding of the constitution of the island. What follows is a simple outline which explains the significance of certain technical terms used throughout the monograph. It is possible to analyse the workings of the constitution at three levels: the national, the insular and the parochial.

At the national level the government of Guernsey came under the crown which appointed a governor, lieutenant-governor, procureur, comptroller and the bailiff. In the seventeenth and eighteenth centuries the governors rarely, if ever, resided in the island. Instead, a lieutenant-governor took up the post in the island and regularly reported to the governor and to various departments of state in England. The Home Office and Privy Council took a direct interest in the administration of the island. Orders-in-Council emanating from the Privy Council gave laws to the island. Occasionally Acts of Parliament relating to foreign affairs or trade applied to the island (e.g. the Navigation Acts).

At the insular level the government of Guernsey was guided by the bailiff. By tradition a Guernseyman, the bailiff presided as chief judge of the court and had custody of the seal of the island. The bailiff also presided at the meetings of the States of Guernsey, an assembly that had the power to legislate by passing *actes*. The States constituted a form a parliament but its powers were, in practice, relatively limited. Regulations were frequently introduced not through *actes* passed by the States but by *ordonnances* passed by the twelve jurats. The jurats, sitting with the bailiff, judged all causes criminal and civil (except cases of treason, coining and assault on the bailiff and jurats). The jurats, having the power both to create regulations and to exercise judicial control, ruled Guernsey as oligarchs. In the sixteenth century the schoolmaster Adrian Saravia observed that the jurats 'lord it over them like dumb cattle'.[70] The jurats were able to frustrate even the Crown. Any dispute affecting the Crown was heard before the Royal Court in St Peter Port where the jurats enjoyed a number of advantages. They could cite ancient privileges and baffle English officials who were unfamiliar with Norman law (the juridical basis of Guernsey law) and island practice. The jurats were not trained lawyers and did not have 'the restraint of a professional conscience'.[71]

The ten ecclesiastical parishes of the island constituted the parochial divisions for administrative purposes. The parish of St Peter Port included the town but no distinction was made between town and parish except in the case of the administration of wills, when a different set of rules applied to property within the *barrières* of the town.[72] Business relating to the parish was considered and administered by the *douzaine*. In principle there were twelve *douzeniers* in each parish. The *douzeniers* were chosen from the wealthiest men of the parish. They assessed tax contributions; measured the king's fiefs; enquired after the names of tenants who owed chief rents; and decided differences over meets and bounds. Apart from the meetings of the *douzaine* there were occasionally larger parochial gatherings attended by the 'family heads'. In St Peter Port the deliberations of the *chefs de famille* were held in the town church.

Each parish was sub-divided into *vingtaines*. Originally every twenty families made a *vingtaine* but with the passage of time and population growth the size of the *vingtaines* varied. One man from each *vingtaine* served for a year as a *vingtenier*. Apart from collecting taxes the *vingteniers* summoned men to arms (for muster or to keep watch); organised the repair of the highways; and could destrain goods of any who defaulted. The *vingteniers* were responsible for most of the day-to-day administration of the parish and worked closely with the constable. He maintained the peace, set the watch at night, kept an eye on strangers, prevented begging, inspected taverns, tasted beer, cider and wine, and ensured that bakers gave correct weight. The constable received from *vingteniers* all taxes raised by order. As St Peter Port grew in size the office of constable became increasingly onerous. By the nineteenth century the town required two constables and a number of assistant constables. The office of constable was frequently held by wealthy men from merchant families and corresponded in some respects to the mayoralty of an English town.[73] In parochial administration, as in insular government, the machinery of control lay in the hands of landowners and merchants, the local aristocracy.[74]

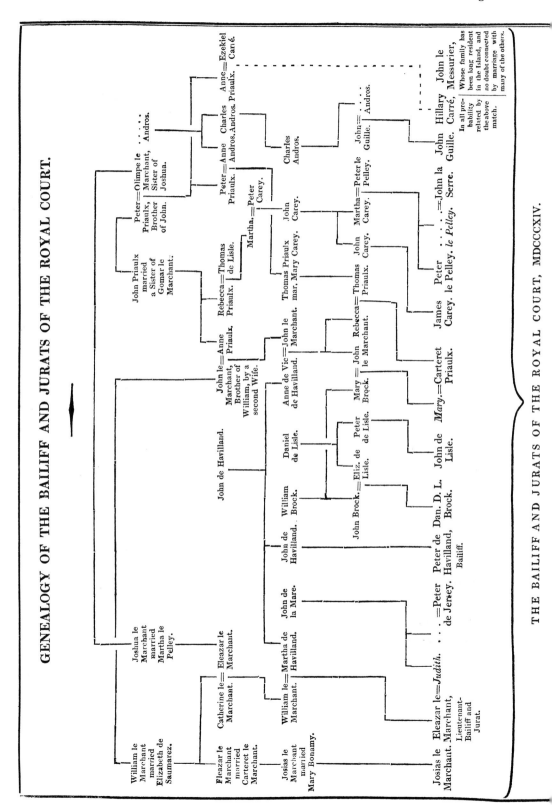

GENEALOGY OF THE BAILIFF AND JURATS OF THE ROYAL COURT.

THE BAILIFF AND JURATS OF THE ROYAL COURT, MDCCCXIV.

2

Foreign Trade

During the course of the eighteenth century the population of St Peter Port grew over threefold and its taxable wealth increased sixfold. This growth was largely sustained by foreign trade without which, according to an eighteenth century bailiff of Guernsey, two-thirds of the islanders would have been compelled to emigrate.[1] This chapters opens with a simple model of Guernsey's economy and traces the development of St Peter Port, the only port serving the island. (The harbour of St Sampson began to be developed in the late eighteenth century but the foreign trade of Guernsey was controlled by St Peter Port.)

Thanks to a conjuncture of geographical, political, mercantilist and entrepreneurial factors St Peter Port developed as a major entrepôt in the years between 1660 and 1750. Initially the trade was predominantly Anglo-French, St Peter Port acting as a mart for the trading of high tariff goods; but by the second half of the eighteenth century the entrepôt was handling a wide variety of goods (mostly destined for England) from a dozen or more countries. The entrepôt was part of an international trading complex, playing the rôle of 'node in a network of linked cities'.[2] The merchants of St Peter Port successfully established agents and factors in major ports throughout the world of the 'Atlantic economy'.

The port books of St Peter Port were destroyed by enemy action in 1940 and so the quantification of the town's trade is difficult. The problem is compounded by the fact that the St Peter Port merchants often engaged in clandestine trade. Two strategies have been employed to try to illuminate the volume and value of St Peter Port's trade. First, fragmentary evidence from a wide number of sources is presented to illustrate the quantity of specific commodities traded by the St Peter Port merchants. Secondly, the customs records of the import and export trade between Guernsey and England, Scotland and Ireland are analysed. These complementary approaches establish a number of parameters which demonstrate the importance of the town as a trading port. The chapter continues with a short examination of the re-organisation of foreign trade that took place in the nineteenth century. When the British government suppressed the smuggling trade in 1805–1810, the St Peter Port merchants looked for new markets. They succeeded in developing a considerable trade with South America.

Apart from its ordinary commerce St Peter Port was also a base for privateering during wartime. It was long considered that profits from privateering were responsible for rapid capital accumulation in St Peter Port in the eighteenth century. Recently that view has been challenged but the debate has been inconclusive. New evidence is   presented below which suggests that although privateering was often profitable, especially for the agents, trade was the real engine of economic growth.

The Guernsey economy

Guernsey was not well endowed with land or capital and there was a constant threat that agricultural output would fail. Fishing increased the supply of food and left a surplus for export. During the mediaeval period Salerie, just to the north of St Peter Port, was developed as an éperquerie for the drying and curing of conger.[3] Guernsey conger, mackerel and herring were regularly sold in France. In the mid-fourteenth century Parisian fishmongers were shouting out 'leur hareng de Garnisi, de Saffaire, d'Escone ou de Frainclais' (= herring from Guernsey, Suffolk, Scanie, or Pas-de-Calais).[4] Fishing was further developed in the sixteenth century when the merchants of St Peter Port participated in a triangular trade. They sent vessels to fish off Newfoundland; the catches of cod were shipped to Portugal, Spain and France; and the Guernsey vessels returned home with cargoes such as wool and iron. The Newfoundland fish paid for the imports. The balance of trade of the island further improved when the St Peter Port merchants developed a stocking export industry.[5]

Had its fortune been dictated solely by the factors of production, the economic history of Guernsey might well have been limited to small-scale trading exchanges. However, the island profited from a favourable geographical location and from political decisions made by foreign powers. Guernsey, situated close to the coast of France, was well placed to engage in Anglo-French trade. Such opportunities were enhanced when a papal bull of 1481 confirmed an Anglo-French agreement that Guernsey would be regarded as neutral in any future conflict. This was advantageous to the islanders and to English and French merchants. The Queen of Hungary (as regent of the Netherlands) complained in 1544 that the English made use of the neutrality of Guernsey for bartering freely with the French as often as they liked without hindrance or restriction of any sort. In 1544 the import of French goods into England was prohibited; but, as the interdiction did not apply to the Channel Islands, French wine could be shipped to Guernsey and re-exported to England.[6]

The development of St Peter Port as an entrepôt

The trade of Guernsey with foreign ports was seriously disrupted by the English Civil War.[7] From c.1660, however, the merchants of St Peter Port were able to benefit from a number of factors which, in combination, led to the rapid growth of St Peter Port as a major international entrepôt. These factors were: the development of the Atlantic economy; the location of

Guernsey; the trading privileges enjoyed by the islanders; and the high tariffs associated with mercantilism.

In the late seventeenth and eighteenth centuries British and French trade increased considerably, thanks in part to a growing demand for American and Asian colonial products. This was accompanied by a demand in Europe for British re-exports of colonial produce. Britain also found an expanding market in her American colonies for British manufactures and re-exports of Asian and European goods. In this developing Atlantic economy major British ports, led by Bristol and Liverpool, as well as port cities of northern and western France, found opportunities for trading on a greatly increased scale.[8] St Peter Port was excellently situated in relation to the principal shipping lanes of this Atlantic economy. First, the town was well located on the north-south axis to serve as an entrepôt in Anglo-French trade. Secondly, being at the western end of the Channel, St Peter Port was ideally positioned to engage in the Atlantic trade. In contrast to London the western outports were one or two weeks 'closer' to the West Indies and during wartime these outports benefited even more.[9]

Traditionally Guernsey had enjoyed considerable privileges in its trade with England. Relying on ancient practice the islanders saw themselves as free and discharged from all customs, tolls and subsidies, 'as well in the Island, as elsewhere, in Her Majesty's Dominions'.[10] Apart from 'some trifle for keeping their piers and harbours in repair' goods could enter Guernsey as into a free-port.[11] This was of considerable significance during the age of mercantilism, when national economies were protected by high tariff barriers.

The Guernsey merchants were well placed to ignore the provisions of the Navigation Acts. Under this legislation the Channel Islanders' shipping was regarded as English built, but no exception was made in regard to their commerce. Although the islanders could trade directly with any of the ports of Spain and Portugal or with those of the Azores, Madeira or the Canaries, they were not supposed to deal directly with the English colonies, or to bring colonial raw materials into English ports.[12] In practice the St Peter Port merchants ignored the Navigation Acts and invoked customary privileges. The customs authorities at the English ports were often confused. In 1744 the Treasury cleared up some of the misunderstandings by ruling that 'no one should bring from the Channel Islands into any port of the kingdom products from the English colonies, because not first taken on at the place of their origin'.[13] The implementation of this ruling led to an increase in the amount of colonial produce smuggled from Guernsey to England.

Throughout the eighteenth century the English authorities found it practically impossible to enforce the Navigation Acts in Guernsey. The regulations relating to the nationality of carrying vessels were regularly ignored. In 1777 (during the American War of Independence) John Guille of St Peter Port commented: 'We have had part of our brandy in French bottoms from Spain to avoid the high insurance & the Americans; tho' it is against the Act of Navigation no one has taken any notice of it. The bills [of] lading were made for Dunkirk.'[14]

The importance of St Malo to the Guernsey merchants

The rise of St Peter Port as a significant entrepôt in the second half of the seventeenth century was linked to the flourishing commerce of the nearby French port of St Malo. Writing from Guernsey in 1667 Colonel J. Atkins commented: 'It is a rare thing now to hear from England, and 'tis as hard a matter to send thither, for St Malos is the place they all send to'.[15] This observation is confirmed by a 1678 listing of sailings from St Peter Port.[16] Of the 149 sailings recorded [28 August 1678 – 11 December 1678] 95 were to France and of these nearly a quarter were specifically identified as being to St Malo (no other named port, French or English, had a higher ranking).

St Malo was enjoying its golden age. To the south the Malouins made fortunes in Cadiz, trafficking in silver.[17] There was also an extensive trade between St Malo and England. Textiles, lace, oil, soap, port, hemp, cordage and honey were exported from St Malo to England; in return the Malouins imported draperies, tin, lead, coal, slate, hides, beef, herring, sardine and other fish, and tallow. Most of this Anglo-French trade was conducted by strangers as the Malouins distrusted the English 'qu'ils disent estre infidels'.[18] Analyses of the port movements of St Malo demonstrate that many vessels arrived in ballast in St Malo and left with merchandise, especially for the Channel Islands.[19] The shipping patterns of St Peter Port and St Malo in the second half of the seventeenth century suggest that the Guernsey merchants were established as trusted middlemen in the St Malo – England trade.

Malouins visited St Peter Port where they spent gold and silver on contraband goods, tobacco in particular.[20] Trading links were maintained with the French even during wartime and despite British acts specifically forbidding such trade.[21] In September 1712 Mr John Sherwood reported to the English customs: 'the French merchants are here in great numbers ... bring in wine, brandy, linen, cloth, salt and wares of diverse sorts ... They carry from us coal, soap, rosin, wool, tobacco, East India goods and what not.'[22]

Trade with the Malouins flourished with the restoration of peace. In 1713 we find that le sieur Thomas le Mesurier of Guernsey made accord with Jean Heilly to command *l'Aigle* of St Malo, a vessel of 220 tons. Thirty-five men were engaged in Guernsey to serve as crew. The projected journey was a triangular voyage to Guinea – Jamaica – Guernsey.[23] It is not clear whether the expedition took place but there is good evidence of a joint venture soon afterwards. In 1716 a Guernsey ship at St Pierre, Newfoundland, had Malouins as its principal officers and crew fishing from its sixteen boats.[24]

The Malouins were active in developing trade with South America from where some cargoes reached St Peter Port. C.1716 a Frenchman from St Malo 'lately arrived from the South-Sea' came to Guernsey 'to traffic', bringing with him 'three small branches of a tree which he said was the tree that bore the Balsam of Peru'.[25] When St Malo declined as a great port in the 1720s, the St Peter Port merchants continued to trade there but they increasingly developed their links with Nantes and other ports involved in international commerce. For their part French merchants were attracted to St Peter Port where they could buy British colonial produce, principally tobacco and East India goods.[26] Between c.1720 and c.1750 the Guernsey merchants developed St Peter Port as an entrepôt. In the next section we shall examine the ways in which they improved the facilities of the port.

The improvement of port facilities

As there were no bonded warehouses in England in the early eighteenth century for the storage of wine, English merchants found it convenient to have cargoes shipped to Guernsey in bulk and then sent across to England in smaller consignments. In this way they avoided having to pay down one large sum in English duty.[27] Thus in 1719 we find Abraham Eyre and his partners in Southampton explaining that they did not have the cash to pay the duty down for the whole cargo of Bordeaux wine shipped to Guernsey and so they let part of the cargo remain in the island until they were 'more in cash'.[28]

Eyre complained that 'by the hotness of the weather and the badness of their cellars which are above ground' his wines in St Peter Port had turned and were hardly fit for distilling. Between 1719 and 1747 new – and, apparently, better – warehouses were built. Several young men of the island sold their small estates 'and turned the money into building of warehouses for wine and brandy'. They regarded those who had it in their power but did not follow this method of trade as 'slothful and stupid'.[29] By c.1747 the merchants and 'the monied men' of the island had built some twenty or thirty 'magazines' (i.e. warehouses) which could be reckoned 'among the most magnificent and spacious in England'.[30] In 1751 Dicey eulogised St Peter Port as having 'the best vaults in Europe'. He claimed 'that all wines (especially Lisbon or white wines) kept at Guernsey but a very few months, do actually imbibe, or receive a peculiar flavour, and are mended in quality, to what the same species of wines have, when immediately imported here from Portugal or any part of Spain'.[31] The new warehouses represented a significant improvement in the entrepôt facilities. The St Peter Port merchants could handle large consignments of wine for English merchants *and* trade extensively on their own behalf.

The status of St Peter Port as an entrepôt was enhanced by harbour improvements. In the late seventeenth century the harbour consisted of a single pier which could shelter 'about 20 or 30 sail of small vessels'.[32] In 1684 the States decided to enclose the harbour by building a north pier. The work was started but there were interruptions and financial difficulties. In 1724/5 the leading merchants of St Peter Port and other inhabitants raised six to seven thousand livres tournois by a voluntary subscription. There were further grants in 1728 and by 1730 the pier was almost complete.[33] Altogether the townsfolk subscribed about twelve thousand livres tournois to the project. It was money well invested. St Peter Port harbour was rendered 'more easy of access'; its shipping was sheltered from storms; and trade considerably increased. Prior to the improvements the farm of the pier had been reckoned at six to seven hundred livres tournois per annum; by the 1750s it was valued at three thousand livres tournois.[34] The pride that Guernsey merchants took in their harbour improvement was soundly based. By the 1750s more – and larger – ships were visiting St Peter Port from European and American ports.[35]

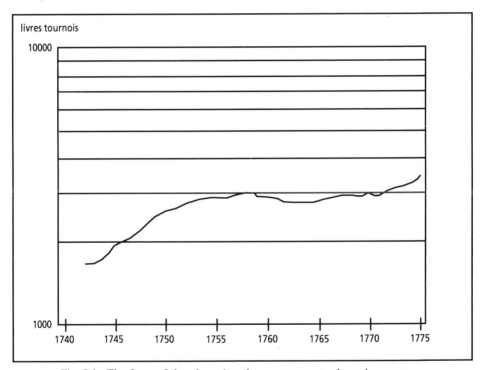

Fig. 2.1: The farm of the *chaussée* – eleven year centred moving average
(Source: Greffe, Commonplace book)

The waters around Guernsey posed navigational hazards, especially to foreigners. This problem was solved in part when in 1746 Nicholas Dobrée (senior), a St Peter Port merchant, published charts of Guernsey and the other Channel Islands based on his own survey. The charts were considered 'very accurately done' and were issued with an accompanying booklet of sailing directions printed in French and English. The maps were republished in 1779, 1786 and 1794.[36]

The St Peter Port entrepôt at its zenith

From the mid-eighteenth century, and especially after the suppression of smuggling from the Isle of Man (1765), St Peter Port became one of the principal commercial entrepôts in the Atlantic economy.[37] The merchants enjoyed a good reputation among the French who saw them as 'riches marchands qui font un grand commerce'. They were like the merchants in Jersey, but traded on a greater scale and were 'plus honnêtes'.[38] St Peter Port, with its improved harbour and purpose-built warehouses, had become an entrepôt in the fullest sense of the word.[39] Cargoes, generally of goods that attracted high tariffs in the normal course of international trade, were brought to St Peter Port, which served as a storage centre, distribution point and mart.

The supplies came to St Peter Port directly from colonies; via major ports engaging in *le grand commerce*; and from the sales of East India goods in England, France, Holland, Denmark and Sweden. The Guernsey merchants sometimes acted for overseas clients and handled goods on a commission basis; but much of the cargo landed in St Peter Port had been bought by the St Peter Port merchants and was intended for re-sale either in bulk, wholesale, to another merchant (*négociant*) or in smaller lots to retailers (*marchands*). Some cargoes (e.g. wines) were held in St Peter Port for a considerable length of time before being forwarded; and wine and tobacco were often 'processed' in St Peter Port.[40]

Many cargoes were sold in St Peter Port. Spirits and tobacco were bought by smugglers who sailed across to the town. A wide variety of goods was sold to vessels sailing for Newfoundland: tea, silks, muslins, calicoes, India goods of all kinds, French brandy, molasses, French and Dutch linens and woollens, French nets and lines for fishing, Dutch cordage, utensils, provisions and all sorts of wines.[41] Some English vessels bound for New England and Quebec, after clearing in Great Britain, took on 'great quantities' of goods in St Peter Port contrary to the Navigation Acts.[42] British naval vessels departing on voyages similarly stocked up in St Peter Port.[43] During wartime 'considerable purchases' of British manufactures were frequently made by neutrals who touched at the island.[44]

Some of the entrepôt goods were shipped openly and legally to their next destination. This was generally the case with bulky cargoes such as wine and fruit. Some cargoes were shipped openly to the British Isles but were furnished with false bills of lading. For example, French wine was described as of Spanish origin to evade the high duties on goods of French origin.[45] 'Considerable quantities' of tea, brandy, gin, wine and tobacco were shipped from Guernsey to Alderney. That island, being a little closer to England, was more convenient for English smugglers.[46] Sometimes Guernsey mariners ran contraband cargoes across to the English coast; but it was more commonly the case that the cross-channel smuggling was conducted by the English.

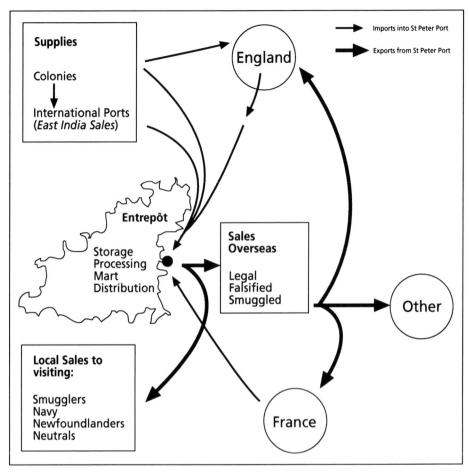

Fig 2.2: The working of the entrepôt

By the second half of the eighteenth century many commodities were handled in the St Peter Port entrepôt (fig 2.3). The major items were spirits, wine, tobacco, East India goods, tea and fruit. The volume of cargoes handled by the St Peter Port merchants is discussed below.

A network of agents and factors

Underpinning the development of St Peter Port as an international entrepôt was the establishment of a network of connections at strategic commercial points throughout the world of the Atlantic economy. As the nineteenth century historian Lukis observed: 'Parents, whose sons were intended for commercial pursuits, would send them to Spain, France, Holland and other countries, and there they established themselves as agents for their Guernsey relations.'[47] An example of one such son is Pierre Frédéric Dobrée. Sent to France in 1775, he settled in Nantes where his father was known to many of the *négociants*. In 1779 he married Rose-Marie Schweighauser, the daughter of a protestant merchant of Swiss origin. The

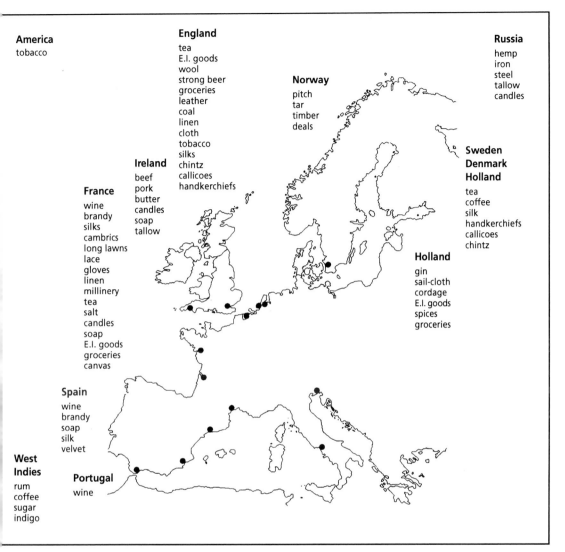

America
tobacco

England
tea
E.I. goods
wool
strong beer
groceries
leather
coal
linen
cloth
tobacco
silks
chintz
callicoes
handkerchiefs

Ireland
beef
pork
butter
candles
soap
tallow

France
wine
brandy
silks
cambrics
long lawns
lace
gloves
linen
millinery
tea
salt
candles
soap
E.I. goods
groceries
canvas

Norway
pitch
tar
timber
deals

Russia
hemp
iron
steel
tallow
candles

Sweden
Denmark
Holland
tea
coffee
silk
handkerchiefs
callicoes
chintz

Holland
gin
sail-cloth
cordage
E.I. goods
spices
groceries

Spain
wine
brandy
soap
silk
velvet

West Indies
rum
coffee
sugar
indigo

Portugal
wine

Fig 2.3: Commodities sent to the entrepôt and the location of Guernsey agents in Europe
(see Appendix 2)

marriage alliance was cemented by a formal business partnership between Pierre Frédéric and his father-in-law. Soon afterwards Pierre Frédéric wrote to his Guernsey cousins, the merchants Le Mesurier and Jean Carey junior, offering to supply French brandy, taffia, rice, tobacco, sugar, coffee, indigo, cocoa and other items. Pierre Frédéric also corresponded regularly with his father in St Peter Port, exchanging mercantile news and arranging business.[48]

The Guernsey merchants enjoyed good business relations with a number of foreign *négociants*. The excellent links with the merchant houses of St Malo have already been mentioned.[49] Other important contacts included the Swedish, Danish, Dutch and French merchants who acted as agents at the various European sales of East India goods each year. Examples of such agents were Arfwidson & Sons at Gothenburg who bought for their Guernsey clients at the Swedish India sales; Fabritius & Wever of Copenhagen, who attended the Danish India sales; and Chenard, Giraudais & LePage who attended the sales of *La Compagnie Française des Indes* at Lorient.[50]

For much of the eighteenth century there were several merchant bankers of Guernsey origin working in London – Bonamy & Samuel Dobrée, Dobrée & Aubin, Perchard & Brock and Paul Le Mesurier. These merchant bankers handled many financial transactions for their fellow islanders, negotiating bills of exchange, investing money, acting as shipping and insurance agents, securing letters of marque during wartime, and collecting rents from land held in England.[51] The Guernsey connection gave these merchant-bankers an unrivalled understanding of the entrepôt trade, privateering and French trade. Paul Le Mesurier set up a commercial house in Normandy in 1785 in partnership with his brother Havilland (based in Guernsey) with a view to developing trade with Tobago.[52] Paul was elected Lord Mayor of London in 1793, the first Guernseyman to achieve this distinction. He was also a Member of Parliament and was active in arguing in defence of the Channel Islands' interests.[53] Another English MP, Mark Gregory, although not an islander by birth, was a friend of the St Peter Port merchant family of Guille and was part of the Guernsey 'connection' in London.[54] Gregory was a merchant and belonged to the governing body of Lloyds.[55] He had interests in Turkey and Spain and set up a trading house in Barcelona in partnership with Guille. Much of the brandy shipped from Catalonia to Guernsey in the second half of the eighteenth century was handled by the partnership of Gregory & Guille.[56]

The shipping of the cargoes

Despite the growing importance of British shipping, many imports to St Peter Port continued to be carried in foreign shipping throughout the second half of the eighteenth century. Much of the gin, coffee, tea, silk, handkerchiefs, calicoes and chintz from Holland and Sweden arrived in ships belonging to the Danes, Swedes and Dutch.[57] This is independently confirmed by cases heard in the Cour d'Amirauté at St Peter Port[58] and by depositions recorded in the Dobrée protest book.[59] Baltic shipping brought goods from the north on the outward voyage and sometimes carried southern produce to St Peter Port on return voyages from the Mediterranean. The true destination – St Peter Port – was frequently concealed, a policy dictated through a desire to thwart the Navigation Acts; to deceive insurers; or to protect the cargo during wartime. In 1778, for example, the St Peter Port merchant John Guille ordered a cargo of tea from John George Ekman of Gothenburg and gave instructions that the captain and crew were not to know 'they are to unload here'. If the vessel was seized,

Ekman was to claim from the insurers, representing the cargo as his property.[60]

The fact that foreign vessels regularly delivered cargoes to St Peter Port had important implications for the Guernsey merchants. They were able to handle a greater volume of commodities than could have been carried by the island's shipping. The merchants employed their own vessels in a variety of profitable trades that served the entrepôt. Guernsey shipping carried wine, brandy, cottons and linens from France; rum from the West Indies; tobacco from Maryland and Virginia; and traded to Newfoundland and Africa.[61] A clear pattern emerges. The Guernsey vessels concentrated on the Channel and transatlantic trades which were sheltered from foreign competition by the Navigation Acts.[62] The northern trade with the Baltic – which demanded shipping with excellent manning ratios because of Dutch competition – was essentially left to foreigners. Guernsey vessels also participated in 'bulk-breaking', a characteristic activity at entrepôts. The cargoes brought in large foreign ships to St Peter Port were re-shipped in the smaller island vessels to London and the English outports.[63]

Trade with Newfoundland, Africa and the West Indies

From the late sixteenth century Guernsey fishermen went to Newfoundland to fish for cod. This developed into a triangular trade, the fish being taken from Newfoundland and sold in Spanish and Portuguese ports; cargoes such as wine were loaded there and transported back to Guernsey. In the late seventeenth century some four to six Guernsey vessels were engaged in the trade.[64] Although several of the St Peter Port merchants maintained interests in Newfoundland during the eighteenth century, the level of activity was relatively low. It is possible that the competition of the West Country and Jersey 'Newfoundlanders' had some influence. Also, other mercantile ventures probably proved more profitable to the Guernsey merchants.

In the mid-eighteenth century some St Peter Port merchants participated in the notorious 'triangular trade', taking slaves from West Africa to the West Indies and returning to Europe with Caribbean cargoes. It is difficult to assess the extent to which the Guernsey merchants were involved in the trade. Nineteenth century Guernsey historians denied that the islanders had ever participated in slaving voyages.[65] However, a number of cases heard in the *Cour d'Amirauté* in St Peter Port provide evidence of several such voyages. In November 1740, for example, James Seaborn, sometime master of the *Charles*, was actioned by the ship's owners for final returns on the voyage that he had made to the coast of Africa; in a counter-action Seaborn claimed ten casks of rum from Mr Charles Mauger.[66] Seaborn was again involved in litigation in August 1742, this time over the commission 'sur le produit de 6200lbs pez d'yvoire à 5 p cent'.[67] The year 1742 also witnessed a long series of court cases involving le Sieur Thomas

Ebsworthy [Elsworthy], master of the *Anne Galley*, a vessel owned by Mr Pierre Dobrée. Ebsworthy bought 241 negroes in Africa, some of whom died, apparently on the middle passage. In Barbados Ebsworthy misappropriated the money from the sale of eight of the slaves. During the course of the litigation Dobrée demanded delivery of twenty-five elephants' tusks and a piece of camwood and Ebsworthy counter-claimed for a butt of rum.[68]

There is little evidence of Guernsey merchants participating in the slave trade after c.1750, possibly because of the competition from Liverpool and London merchants. Most voyages of Guernsey ships to the West Indies in the second half of the eighteenth century appear to have been either direct or via Madeira (where wine cargoes were delivered), the raison d'être of the voyages being the return cargo of rum from Barbados, Jamaica or Santa Cruz. On the West Indies run the Guernsey merchants used their own vessels[69] which tended to be lightly manned. Slaving voyages required greater capital investment.[70]

The principal commodities handled in the entrepôt

It is time to turn away from the discussion of the general patterns of trade to consider the volume and value of the principal commodities handled in the St Peter Port entrepôt.

Spirits

The late seventeenth and early eighteenth centuries witnessed a rapid acceleration in the production of distilled drinks in the western world. This was partly production-led, thanks to the improvement of distilling techniques and the increasing availability of raw materials, and partly consumer-led, as urban society acquired a taste for new tipples. Guernsey merchants in France took an active part in developing the Cognac brandy trade. Professor Cullen observes that in the second decade of the eighteenth century these Guernseymen were the main impetus behind shipments destined for London, the largest and most discriminating spirits market in England.[71] St Peter Port merchants supplied brandy to the English market throughout the eighteenth century. They imported principally from Nantes, La Rochelle, Bordeaux and Sète in France; and, later, from Barcelona in Spain. Small quantities of the brandy were shipped openly to England but most of the sales were to smugglers.

The St Peter Port merchants appear to have become interested in the rum trade c.1730.[72] In 1738 the quantity of rum shipped from Guernsey to Southampton was 1,724 gallons; in 1740 it amounted to 5,062 gallons. When the British government gained greater control over the Isle of Man in the 1760s, Manx traders shipped rum from the Danish West Indies to Guernsey.[73]

The scale of the spirit trade at the end of the eighteenth century can be quantified with some precision. In the eight months from January to August 1796 some 6,975 pipes of French brandy, 2,354 pipes of Spanish brandy, 1,507 pipes of gin and 88 pipes of rum were brought into Guernsey. This

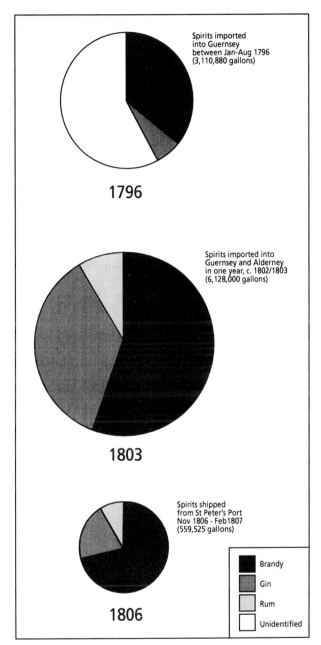

Fig 2.4: Spirits traded through the St Peter Port entrepôt

amounted to 10,924 pipes and was all for British accounts. It was not possible for a precise figure to be given of the imports for the accounts of island merchants but it was estimated that they had received about 15,000 pipes.[74]

An estimate made c.1802/3 suggested that annually 60 vessels from Holland imported 2,268,000 gallons of gin to Guernsey and Alderney. The quantity of brandy imported was reckoned at 28,000 pipes (3,360,000 gallons) and the rum imported was estimated at 5,000 puncheons (500,000 gallons). According to the calculations the alcohol was increased at least one sixth in volume by water added in Guernsey. The British allowed one million gallons for what was consumed on the island, or shipped elsewhere, or lost. This left an estimated 6,150,000 gallons which entered Britain from Guernsey, mostly illegally.[75]

In the four months from November 1806 to February 1807 the vessels observed clearing Guernsey carried cargoes which totalled 400,560 gallons of brandy, 49,570 gallons of rum and 109,395 gallons of gin. Had all of this been smuggled into England the lost excise duties would have amounted to £411,367/18/1½, the lost custom duties £39,145/18/4.[76]

Wine

It has been mentioned earlier that St Peter Port merchants were involved in the shipping of French wine to England from the mediaeval period onwards. During the eighteenth century the island merchants continued to trade in French wines (from the Bordeaux area in particular) but they increasingly dealt in Portuguese and Spanish wines, especially port. This reflected the swing in English fashion away from French wines towards Iberian produce. British legislation and tariffs were directed against French goods on the one hand; and trade links with Portugal were strengthened on the other.[77] In 1762 the Consul and Committee of the British Oporto Factory complained to the Earl of Egremont that the Portuguese were shipping 'several thousand pipes' of wine to Guernsey, Plymouth and Portsmouth in their own vessels: 'large quantities of their wines are deposited in the Island of Guernsey which are afterwards fraudulently introduced into England as British property'.[78]

In 1763, in the exceptional conditions of wartime, the Guernsey merchants shipped 1,869 tuns 2 hogsheads 15 gallons of Portuguese wine to the English outports and 718 tuns 2 hogsheads 29 gallons to London.[79] The following year Warren Lisle reported to the London Customs Board that many of the merchants had laid out great sums of money in making vaults and magazines 'for receiving of port wines which is now at an end and greatly lessens the business here'.[80] In fact the Guernsey merchants continued to handle considerable quantities of Portuguese wine. Thanks to a British concession Guernsey merchants were allowed 12% 'leakage' on foreign wines that they handled for English accounts. A certificate was required and the shipper in the island had to declare *inter alia*, that the wines had received no mixture since their landing in the island, that the wines had been imported in British bottoms only, and that the wine was the property of British subjects only.[81] During the following two decades quantities of between three to six hundred tuns of Iberian wine were shipped annually from Guernsey to England.[82] Considerable quantities of French wines were traded by the St Peter Port merchants, particularly during the years of the French revolutionary wars.[83]

Tobacco

Tobacco was an important commodity to the St Peter Port entrepôt from the late seventeenth century onwards. Some was smuggled back into England[84] but the main customers were the French. The establishment of the tobacco monopoly in 1674 in France made smuggling an attractive proposition. Professor Jacob Price has remarked that from the Channel Islands 'every variety of tobacco, even that of St Domingue, could be smuggled into France'.[85] Price's calculations suggest that perhaps 25,000lb of tobacco were required per annum for the needs of the islanders of Guernsey and for legitimate sales to visiting ships. The quantity of tobacco exported from England to Guernsey frequently ran far above this level and, by inference, was sold mainly to French smugglers. During the War of the Spanish Succession the annual average export from England to Guernsey was approximately 75,000lbs.[86] The volume rose considerably in the decade 1713–22 to an annual average of 357,768lbs.[87] Tobacco continued to be exported from England to Guernsey in quantities larger than necessary for island consumption. On the eve of the American Revolution (from 1769–76) the annual average re-export from England to Guernsey was 291,438lbs.[88] The quantity shipped from England fell after the American War of Independence.[89] However, in the *post bellum* era the Guernsey merchants imported not only from England but also intermittently from Scotland[90] and directly from the U.S.A.[91]

After the defection of the American colonies the relevance of the Navigation Acts to trade between America and Guernsey was not clear. The island merchants profited from this uncertainty and imported much greater quantities. A total of 5,198 hogsheads were brought into the island in 1789 and 3,144 hogshead in 1790. The bailiff calculated in 1791 that the island was handling five thousand hogsheads of tobacco annually, and that this earned above one hundred thousand pounds sterling 'on a moderate computation'. The French came in small craft to buy the tobacco, taking 15 to 30 hogsheads per vessel.[92] C.1802 it was estimated that the amount of tobacco imported into Guernsey was five thousand hogsheads (the hogshead measuring 1,200lbs); this gives a total of six million lbs of tobacco.[93] During the four winter months of 1806–07 it was assessed that 350,300lbs of tobacco had been shipped out of Guernsey.[94]

India goods

East India goods were traded by the St Peter Port merchants in some quantity after the Treaty of Utrecht. In the years 1713–16 forty-five different types of East India fabrics were exported from England to Guernsey, the principal varieties being chintz, chelloes, cuttanees, romals, soosays and 'Stuffs Guiney'.[95] In the 1720s and 1730s tea consumption in Europe increased following the development of direct trade between Europe and China.[96] In 1732 Henry Mauger reported that several merchants had imported into Guernsey large quantities of tea from France; a quantity weighing 150lbs had been found hidden in a barn.[97] In 1734 Mauger complained that the St Peter Port merchants daily imported all sorts of India goods both from Holland and France: 'within these few days several of them are gone to Nants to be at a sale, so that in all likelihood many cargoes of Tea & other foreign commiditys will soon be imported here to the great detriment of the trade of Great Britain'.[98]

Tea and East India goods were frequently despatched from London to Guernsey via Southampton.[99] A 'very great quantity' of the tea (and some coffee) exported to the Channel Islands was run back to England.[100] The year 1744 saw an exceptionally large volume of tea exported officially from England to Guernsey (90,724lbs from London, 73,482lbs from the outports).[101]

Customs reports in 1764 refer to East India goods 'of all sorts' imported into Guernsey from England, France and Holland.[102] The merchants in Guernsey 'have India goods from Port L'Orient and Holland and have agents that attend the sales at these places'.[103] Teas were bought from England, France, Denmark and Holland[104] and shipped in Dutch, Danish and Swedish vessels 'from which countries they used to buy them during the war'.[105] As late as 1790 tea smuggling from Guernsey was considered 'an enormous evil'.[106]

Fruit

The Guernsey merchants frequently dealt in fruit from France and the Mediterranean. There were particularly good opportunities during the War of the Austrian Succession (see Appendix 3.2) and the Seven Years War for profitable trade in this sector. The year 1763 was exceptional (see Table 2.1 below), with over two and a half thousand tons of fruit being imported into London and the English outports from Guernsey. The fruit was shipped in bulk to Guernsey and then carried in smaller vessels to England. Entries in the Bristol port books illustrate the Guernsey – England stage of the trade (see Table 2.2).

Table 2.1 The quantity of fruit imported into England from Guernsey, 1763

	to London quantity cwts/qu/lbs	to the English outports quantity cwts/qu/lbs
currants	6973-3-14	1644-2-8
prunes	1518-3-10	
raisins		
denial	30229-2-11	3775-2-11
lyord	1297-3-5	
Malaga	8-0-20	
Solis	4803-2-23	2395-3-6

Source: PRO CUST 3/63

Table 2.2 Shipping from Guernsey to Bristol, June 1763

June	Vessel	tons	master	crew	cargo
1	Elizabeth	20	John Little	m + 2	wine, raisins, cork
8	"		Thomas Hammong	m + 3	raisins, oil, cork
9	Mary	25	Andrew Morell	m + 2½	raisins, wine, oil, cork
15	Jenny & Mary	12	John Snow	m + 2	wine, cork &c
17	Nancy	30	Nicholas Enuf	m + 3½	raisins, cork

m = master, ½ = boy

Source: W. Minchinton, *The Trade of Bristol in the Eighteenth Century* (Bristol Record Society, 1957) pp. 43–45

Large quantities of cargoes are not easy to visualise. How much trade was St Peter Port handling in relation to other ports? It must be stressed that as an entrepôt St Peter Port had a specific and narrow function. The total of cargo traded through the port was smaller in volume and value than that handled in many of the great international ports such as Bordeaux and Liverpool. However, in certain commodity sectors the St Peter Port entrepôt trade rivalled that of many of the leading British ports. For example, during the years 1771–81 on average 1,330 tuns of wine were imported annually into Bristol. This was lower than the average for the preceding two centuries but affords a yardstick for comparison.[107] As we have seen, in 1763 just over two and a half thousand tuns of wine from Portugal alone were shipped from the island to England. This was, admittedly, an exceptional year but the figure illustrates the fact that the Guernsey merchants were playing a significant rôle in England's foreign trade.[108] The scale of trading in wine in St Peter Port was even greater by the end of the century. In 1795 a single Guernsey merchant received 2,491 hogsheads and 17 cases (= approx 623 tuns) of Claret and Hermitage from Bordeaux for the account of just one London firm.[109] The volume of spirits handled in St Peter Port was even more impressive. In 1802 the quantity of brandy imported legally into Britain was the equivalent of about half the quantity of brandy shipped through St Peter Port in that year.[110]

By national standards the quantity of tobacco traded by the St Peter Port merchants was relatively modest for much of the century. On the eve of the American War of Independence the Scottish merchants imported nearly 46 million lbs of tobacco, while the Guernsey import was not much greater than a quarter of a million lbs. However, the position altered significantly after the war. By 1795 the total Scottish import of tobacco amounted to 2,731,091lbs and in 1800 to 4,074,919lbs, whereas the Guernsey merchants were handling some five to six million lbs of tobacco annually by this time.[111]

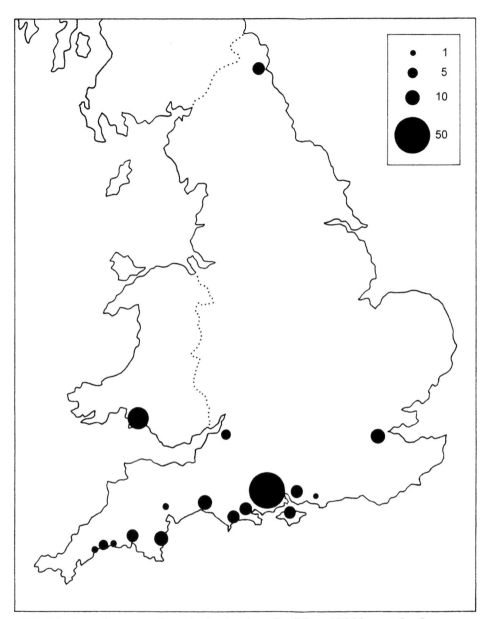

Fig. 2.5: Annual average of vessels clearing from English and Welsh ports for Guernsey
1710–1717 (see Appendix 5)

Trade with England and Wales

Trade between the island and British ports was clearly of great
importance in all aspects of St Peter Port's economy and this is considered in
more detail now. In the late seventeenth and eighteenth centuries
Guernsey's trade with England and Wales was based on London, the ports of
the South West, and the coal ports of Newcastle, Sunderland, Swansea and
Llanelli. Southampton handled a great deal of Guernsey's trade. During the

war years 1710–12 nearly half of the vessels clearing from English ports for Guernsey sailed from Southampton. With the return of peace [1713–17] the total volume of traffic between England and Guernsey increased and Southampton's share dropped to just below 30%, although the number of sailings from Southampton actually rose during those years.[112] Southampton continued to serve as a 'staple port' to Guernsey throughout the eighteenth century. High priced goods from London were frequently despatched to the island via Southampton, especially during wartime, when the London – Guernsey voyage was endangered by enemy privateers. By 1807 Southampton was forwarding goods from London, Manchester, Birmingham and Sheffield to the island.[113]

The port books record a large number of vessels sailing from Newcastle and Swansea to the island. These statistics in part represent the fact that the Guernsey merchants were involved in the export of coal to France. English and Welsh coal transported by sea to the west coast of France was 'cheaper there than French coal, which had to be carried great distances overland'.[114]

From 1697 onwards official figures exist for Guernsey's trade with England.[115] These have to be interpreted with care as commodities were valued at fixed prices selected at the beginning of the eighteenth century. The statistics therefore suggest the physical *volume* of foreign trade rather than the *value*.[116] Moreover the figures make no allowance for smuggled goods. Nevertheless, if analysed with caution the statistics do reveal the growth and changing patterns of Guernsey's trade.

English imports from Guernsey consisted principally of:

[a] island produce: cider, cattle, salt, lobsters, stone and knitwear;
[b] entrepôt goods: wine, fruit, salt (French), textiles, iron and a variety of other goods.

During the early eighteenth century the major constituent in the value of imports into England from Guernsey consisted of the woollen garments knitted on the island. The stockings alone sometimes accounted for almost half of the total value of all imports. By the second half of the century this had changed. A much larger volume of entrepôt goods was being imported into England, while the volume of island produce rose only slightly. Although less Guernsey knitwear was imported into England, there was a big increase in the quantity of granite shipped from the island to London.

The exports from England to Guernsey can be classified as follows:

(a) goods for the Guernsey domestic market (principally food, textiles, building materials);
(b) goods destined for the international entrepôt trade (including colonial re-exports such as tobacco);
(c) materials required to operate the entrepôt trade (glass, timber, iron).

During the course of the century the quantity of commodities required by the Guernsey domestic market rose. This was due, first, to the increase in population which needed more food, clothing and heating (= more flour, textiles and coal). Secondly, the growth in prosperity stimulated a demand for more fashionable luxuries (= more expensive textiles). Thirdly, a building boom in the last quarter of the century led to the shipping of more limestone, bricks, pantiles, slabs, steps, quoins and slates. Larger quantities of goods were also sent from England for the entrepôt market. Moreover the merchants and coopers needed more glass, bottles, wooden staves and hoops to package their alcohol and tobacco. The busier the harbour became, the greater was the demand for sailcloth, cordage and the ironmongery of the chandler's trade.

Having broadly characterised the nature of England's trade with Guernsey, it remains to examine the trade statistics, always bearing in mind that we are dealing with *volume* rather than *value*, and that the trade figures represent only the legal trade. Between 1697 and 1801 the volume of exports from England to Guernsey was commonly in excess of the volume of imports into England from Guernsey. There were 37 years in which this was not the case: 1701–11, 1746–48, 1755–59, 1761–63, 1770–73, 1777, 1779–81, 1783, 1796–1801. The terms of trade improved for Guernsey in these years because the volume of her exports to England increased. It is immediately apparent that these were almost all war years. The merchants of St Peter Port benefited because, with the disruption of international trading patterns, they were able to take over some lucrative business. The exports from Guernsey to England during wartime also included some prize cargoes. During the course of the eighteenth century the aggregate volume of legal trade between England and Guernsey (i.e. imports + exports) increased tenfold.

Trade with Scotland

During the eighteenth century the Scots greatly enjoyed drinking French claret; for some it was a rejection of port – the English drink – and hence an affirmation of Scottish independence. French wines, however, were subject to heavy duties and so the Scots looked to entrepôts such as St Peter Port for their supplies. French wine could be shipped from Guernsey to Scotland as Spanish or Portuguese wine, Iberian produce attracting a smaller duty than French at the Scottish port of entry. In 1751–52 and 1760–61 almost all of the French wine landed at Leith was from Guernsey. Other produce imported from Guernsey included French prunes and, occasionally, walnuts, chestnuts and salt. There are some rare references to Scottish exports to Guernsey. Between 1741 and 1744 James Watson, merchant of Greenock, shipped roll and leaf tobacco in trusses on board the *Endeavour* of Wexford and the *Mary* of Waterford to the island. However, the total quantity of tobacco shipped to Guernsey seems to have been relatively small.[117]

In general it is very difficult to quantify the scale of trade between Guernsey and Scotland in the first half of the eighteenth century. There is

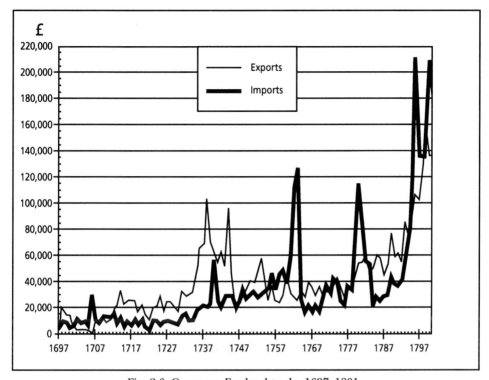

Fig. 2.6: Guernsey–England trade, 1697–1801
(exports from England to Guernsey, imports from Guernsey into England)

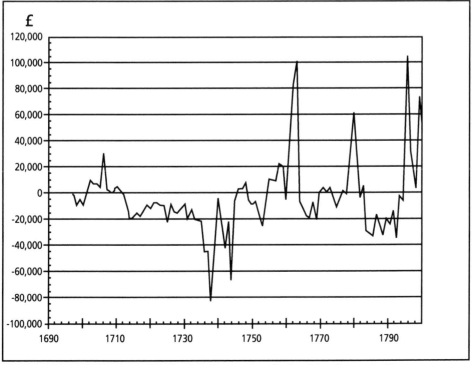

Fig. 2.7: Guernsey–England, balance of trade (positive figures indicate
a balance in Guernsey's favour)

better evidence for the volume of trade in the second half of the century. Customs returns show that generally the volume of imports into Scotland from Guernsey was greater than the volume of exports from Scotland to Guernsey. The imports into Scotland included small quantities of a considerable number of goods, some of Guernsey origin, the rest foreign. In 1775 the list of imports included anchovies, apples, capers, cork, nuts, oil of cloves, olives, pickles, rosin, brandy, vinegar and wine.[118] During the French revolutionary wars large quantities of wine were imported from Guernsey (e.g. 412 tuns 1 hogshead 23 gallons of Spanish wine and 41 tuns 2 hogsheads 45 gallons of French wine in 1799).[119] There was a regular export from Scotland to Guernsey of small quantities of coal, bottles and green glass. In some years large quantities of tobacco were exported to Guernsey and this altered the terms of trade in Scotland's favour (e.g. 1766: 490,400lbs of tobacco to Guernsey; 1789: 238,477lbs).[120]

Trade with Ireland

There was considerable trade between Guernsey and Ireland in the eighteenth century but it is not easy to quantify before 1782–83. In 1765 the parliament of Bordeaux forbade the mixing of Spanish wine with local claret, a mixture esteemed in Ireland and previously exported there in great volume. About 8,000 tuns of claret were shipped yearly from Bordeaux to Ireland, according to William Le Marchant. In consequence of the ban on the mixing of wines, the claret and Spanish wines were shipped separately to Guernsey, mixed in the island and forwarded to Ireland. The St Peter Port merchants made a profit of above £3,000 on this transaction; and in 1766 the Bordeaux parliament reversed its ban on mixing.[121]

Trade between Guernsey and Ireland seems to have been stimulated during the American War of Independence. In February 1782 Henry Budd complained to the Lieutenant Governor about the considerable quantities of salted beef and pork brought from Ireland to Guernsey by Captain Cullen, master of a brigantine from Waterford. These shipments were for Mr Khae, an Irish merchant who had been resident in the island for some months. Some of the provisions were destined for the 'iniquitous traffick of conveying from hence salt provisions for the equipment of the enemy's fleet'.[122]

It was possibly this episode that led to the recording of Irish – Guernsey trade separately (rather than aggregated with Jersey).[123] In the last two decades of the eighteenth century Irish exports to Guernsey consisted principally of meat and dairy products (beef, pork, ham, bacon, butter) together with items manufactured from animal fats (candles, soap, tallow). Irish exports were usually shipped from the ports of south-east Ireland (from Dublin round to Cork), but there were occasional shipments of linen from Belfast.[124]

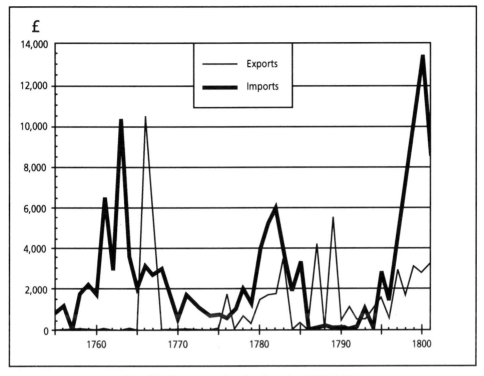

Fig. 2.8: Guernsey–Scotland trade, 1755–1801
(exports from Scotland to Guernsey, imports from Guernsey into Scotland)

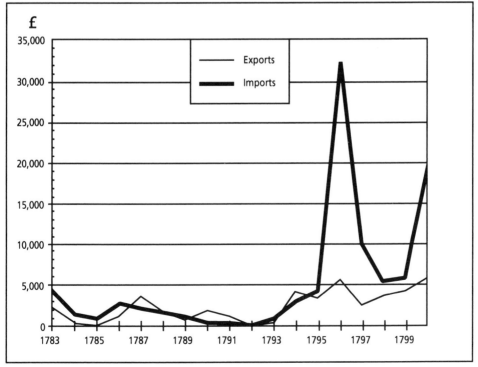

Fig. 2.9: Guernsey–Ireland trade, 1783–1800
(exports from Ireland to Guernsey, imports from Guernsey into Ireland)

Guernsey exports to Ireland consisted of a variety of goods but the main value resided in wines. The volume of trade increased during the French wars, with 966 tuns 1 hogshead 33 gallons of French wine being exported from Guernsey to Ireland in the year ending 25 March 1796; just over 90% of this was for the Dublin market.[125] Exports from Ireland to Guernsey also ran at a higher level during the war years 1793–1800.

The South American trade in the nineteenth century

During the Napoleonic Wars the British government could no longer afford to forego the excise and customs dues evaded by smugglers. Acts were introduced in 1805 and 1807 to suppress smuggling and the Guernsey merchants soon found themselves in difficulties.[126] The function of St Peter Port as an entrepôt was greatly reduced and there was considerable unemployment. The merchants looked for new markets and turned towards Brazil and St Domingo 'where most of the low articles of India goods' found 'a ready sale'.[127] In fact the Guernsey merchants discovered that in South America they could sell a diversity of cargoes from Northern Europe and the Mediterranean. Their trade centred on Rio de Janeiro. In the eighteen months from January 1825 to June 1826 there were forty-three arrivals in Rio of twenty-six Guernsey vessels. The usual return cargoes from Brazil consisted of coffee, hides and sugar. On return to Europe the vessels touched at Gibraltar where they received instructions about their port of unloading.[128]

This trade represented a significant shift from the eighteenth century pattern. Although some of the voyages originated from, or ended in, St Peter Port, many of the voyage 'legs' were between foreign ports. The South American trade involved the St Peter Port merchants in a carrying tade rather than in a home-based entrepôt business. Although organised from St Peter Port, the commercial centre of the new trade was Rio de Janeiro. There were profits for the ship owners but the harbour and town of St Peter Port slowly lost out.

Shipping

Having reviewed the development of Guernsey's trade, it is appropriate to take a short look at the evolution of the island's fleet. It will be seen that the shipping reflected the changing pattern of foreign trade handled by the St Peter Port merchants.

In 1680 there were eighteen vessels based in St Peter Port. The commonest type of vessel was the bark, of which there were eight. The pink was the second favourite type of vessel. Whereas the barks were mainly French built, all five of the pinks were of English construction. These were larger than the barks, ranging in size from 50 to 120 tons. Vessels described as pinks were very often of the fly-boat type with hull forms of the Dutch fashion. This achieved 'a high carrying capacity in relation to the ship's main

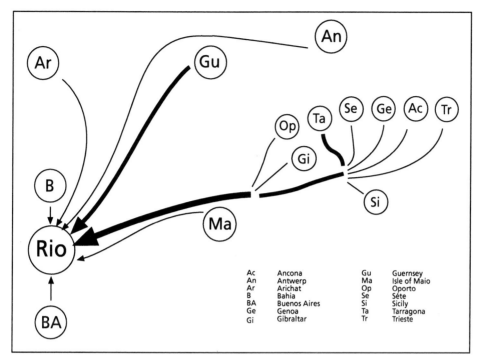

Fig. 2.10: Ports of departure of Guernsey vessels sailing to Rio de Janeiro,
January 1825 to June 1826

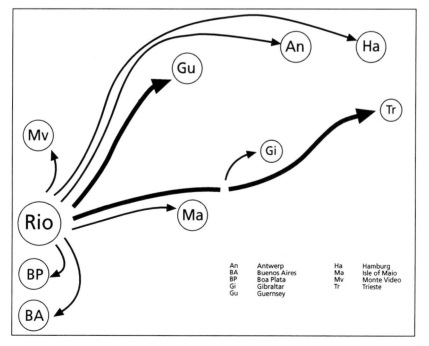

Fig. 2.11: Ports of destination of Guernsey vessels clearing from Rio de Janeiro,
January 1825 to June 1826

measurements'.[129] The barks and pinks were particularly well suited to the carrying of cargoes between St Malo and England.

Table 2.3 Ships belonging to St Peter Port, 1680

	N	tons	avg. tonnage	
Pinks	5	410	82	all English built
Ketches	2	65	32.5	" "
Barks	8	223	27.9	2 English, 6 French built
Double-shallop	1	8	8	English built
Small hoy	1	8	8	" "
Ship	1	7	7	French built

Source: Royal Court, Legge Survey

Between 1680 and 1701 the number of Guernsey's ships nearly doubled. This can be attributed to successes in trading and in privateering. In 1701 Guernsey owned thirty-two vessels, of 1,260 tons; the crew strength was 180 men. This represents an average tonnage for Guernsey vessels of 39.4 tons, somewhat lower than the average for the shipping of all outports (62.0 tons). In comparison with the shipping owned by English ports the fleet of St Peter Port was relatively modest. London boasted 140 thousand tons, Liverpool nine thousand and Whitehaven seven thousand. Southampton's fleet, however, with 1.6 thousand tons was not much larger.[130]

Aggregate details for the mid-eighteenth century are lacking. In 1788 Guernsey is listed as possessing sixty-nine vessels of 5,074 tons.[131] The 1788 record may be incomplete as the island was credited with seventy-seven vessels of 5,861 tons in 1789.[132] These figures suggest that the size of the island fleet was approximately 4.7 times greater in 1789 than it had been in 1701. This is in line with the average growth of the fleets belonging to the English outports. In 1788 London possessed 315 thousand tons of shipping, Liverpool 76 thousand tons, Whitehaven 52 thousand tons, Southampton 9 thousand tons.[133]

Much of the Guernsey fleet consisted of relatively small vessels suitable for bulk-breaking. In 1788 six vessels (8.7%) were under twenty tons; twenty-four vessels (34.8%) were between twenty to forty tons; and twelve (17.4%) were between forty to sixty tons. Thus, over half of the shipping was made up of vessels of 60 tons and below. Only seventeen ships (24.6%) were over one hundred tons.

There was some shipbuilding in Guernsey during the eighteenth century but most vessels were English or plantation built.[134] Vessels suitable for privateering were bought on the outbreak of war.[135] After a period of successful privateering there were captured enemy ships for sale in St Peter Port; these could sometimes be bought cheaply.[136] In 1788 nine out of Guernsey's sixty-nine vessels were identified as prize ships.[137]

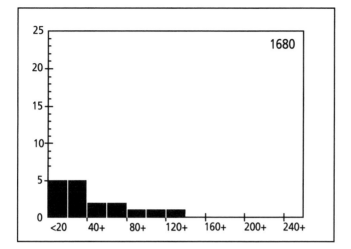

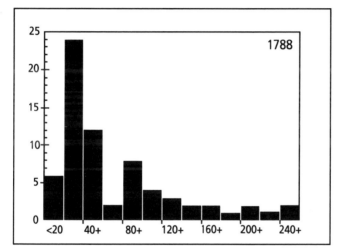

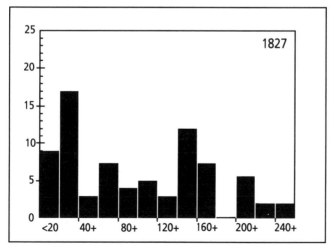

Fig. 2.12: The composition of the Guernsey fleet, 1680, 1788 and 1827
(vertical axis = number of ships; horizontal axis = tonnage)

The number of Guernsey vessels increased from seventy-seven to eighty-eight between 1789 and 1801; and then from eighty-eight to one hundred and twelve between the years 1801-1803. With the decline of the entrepôt trade (1805–10), the island fleet grew smaller. The decline was arrested, however, by the development of the trade with South America. From 1812 onwards there was considerable shipbuilding in and near St Peter Port. Many of the vessels were designed specifically for the requirements of local merchants – the brigs for voyages to South America, the cutters for Channel trading. In 1827 the Guernsey fleet numbered seventy-seven vessels (7,723 aggregate tons) and one pleasure vessel.[138]

Table 2.4 Ships belonging to St Peter Port, 1827

	Total	
	vessels	tonnage
Ships	6	1,328
Brigs	29	4,586
Schooners	6	515
Sloops and cutters	36	1,294
Pleasure vessel	1	14
	78	7,737

Source: J. Jacob, *Annals of Some of the British Norman Isles* (Paris, 1830), pp. 459–461

Privateering

So far this chapter has been concerned with the trade of the Guernsey merchants and in particular with their development of St Peter Port as an entrepôt. It has been argued that from the mid-eighteenth century St Peter Port was one of the principal commercial entrepôts in the Atlantic economy and that this generated considerable profits. By the beginning of the nineteenth century the British government was losing so much excise and customs duty on goods smuggled from St Peter Port into England that it introduced legislation which crippled the entrepôt trade. However, the Guernsey merchants soon found a profitable new venture by trading with the newly opened markets in South America. It remains to re-assess one of the more notable aspects of the port economy – privateering. This has often been represented as the source of St Peter Port's wealth. C. E. Brett argued that there was only very moderate prosperity until the American, Revolutionary and Napoleonic wars. 'Vast fortunes were made, still pretty much legally, by privateering; one merchant, John Le Mesurier, brought in £212,000 with eight ships in the course of 1779 alone.'[139] The value of privateering and the relative importance of trade are central issues which need to be resolved.

In 1689 King William allowed the neutrality of the Channel Islands to lapse. This meant, *inter alia*, that it became legitimate in wartime for lapse. This meant, *inter alia*, that it became legitimate in wartime for Guernseymen to operate as privateers both in local waters and further away. Furnished with letters of marque issued by the High Court of Admiralty in London the Guernsey privateers were able to cruise in armed traders or private men-of-war and capture enemy merchant vessels. As Great Britain was frequently at war with the Bourbon powers during the 'long' eighteenth century, there were frequent opportunities for the islanders to engage in privateering. Professor Bromley has observed that at first 'the Islands were extremely slow to commission privateers'.[140] This reluctance is probably to be attributed to a desire to continue trading with the French. However, from c.1696 the islanders committed themselves more energetically to attacking the enemy. Professor Bromley estimated that the Guernsey captors received at least £200,000 gross in the Spanish Succession War alone. Later wars were also, apparently, profitable. The value of the prizes taken during the American War of Independence [£981,300] has commonly been regarded as the source of the wealth that led to the urban improvement of St Peter Port.[141]

Peter Wickins has urged that the profits from privateering were widely dispersed 'enough to thwart rather than promote capital accumulation'.[142] He does allow that 'the dispersion was less than would appear at first sight from the number of beneficiaries entitled to participate in the rewards';[143] and in the third stage of his essay he does present material that can be used to qualify his initial thesis.

Assessing two earlier wars Professor Bromley established the impressive extent of Guernsey privateering in the period 1689–97 and 1702–12 but concluded by agreeing with the seventeenth century Jersey historian who commented that 'Privateering, which, tho' gainful to some particular Persons, could not make us amends for the loss of peaceable open Trade, the Benefit whereof is more general and diffusive.'[144] Dr Jamieson, examining the period 1739–1783, opined that trade 'whether in peace or war, was the main source of capital in the Islands and brought prosperity to the widest section of the population. Privateering ... brought wealth to only a handful of investors.'[145]

The concern of this study is with the impact of privateering on the economy of St Peter Port. In the immediate context of the urban economy privateering appears to have been beneficial. First, it should be noted that much of the money invested in fitting out and maintaining privateering voyages came from outside the town and, indeed, from outside the island.[147] The *négociants* in St Peter Port who acted as agents and armateurs were cushioned against failure. Even if a privateer made no captures, the agent could set expenses against the shares of the investors. It was the *marginal* investor who stood to lose; those operating the system had a good chance of covering their expenses, at the least.

Secondly, privateering had a wider impact on the urban economy than is implied by a study that concentrates exclusively on the analysis of prize values. The total equation should take into account the stimulus to the St Peter Port economy resulting from the arrival in the town of adventurers and seamen. The prospect of prizes attracted mariners from far and wide. Peter Carey estimated that in the War of the Spanish Succession some 1,700 men were employed in privateering, half from Guernsey, the remainder being English, Irish, Dutch and others.[148] These men ate, drank, lodged and fornicated in St Peter Port, both while looking for employment and in the intervals between voyages. Moreover while crews were ashore the ships laid in copious supplies of victuals from the St Peter Port market in preparation for the next cruise; at times this led to scarcities and high prices.[149]

Thirdly, the auctions of prize cargoes attracted foreign merchants to St Peter Port. During the period 1777–82 there were over 150 such sales in Guernsey, some of which were advertised in *Lloyd's Evening Post*. The issue of that newspaper for 31 March – 2 April 1779 carried six advertisements for forthcoming Guernsey sales.[150] Apart from the prize cargoes there were captured vessels for sale. In the autumn of 1778 there were vessels of all sizes available in Guernsey 'from 80 tons to 300, mostly French built new and old, selling cheaply' and the Dutch came over to buy them.[151] These contacts may well have borne other commercial fruit; in that sense the value of privateering is unquantifiable.

This analysis suggests that there should be a measured appreciation of the rôle of privateering in the generation of wealth in St Peter Port. It is mistaken to see privateering in the late eighteenth century as the sudden source of urban wealth (*pace* C. E. Brett); but it would be equally misleading to discount the significance of privateering to the urban economy (*pace* P. L. Wickins). There is, happily, some completely independent evidence which illuminates the rate at which St Peter Port grew wealthier during the eighteenth century. This is now discussed.

In nearly every year from the 1720s onwards the inhabitants of St Peter Port were assessed for tax purposes. Throughout the eighteenth century income served as the basis for these assessments. Those engaged in privateering had their assessments revised upwards relatively quickly after any success.[152] Consequently the aggregate tax assessments reflect the economic fortunes of the town and provide independent evidence about the impact of privateering (see Fig. 2.13). The graph reveals that St Peter Port became increasingly wealthy during the eighteenth century and analysis suggests that *trade*, not privateering, was the crucial factor in generating this urban prosperity. The rapid rise in the aggregate assessments in the early 1720s corresponds with the prosperous years of the St Malo trade. There was no growth during the 1730s but the economy picked up again in the 1740s, precisely at the time when the merchants were building their spacious warehouses and developing the entrepôt trade. From then onwards the town grew wealthier at a relatively constant rate during years of war and of peace.

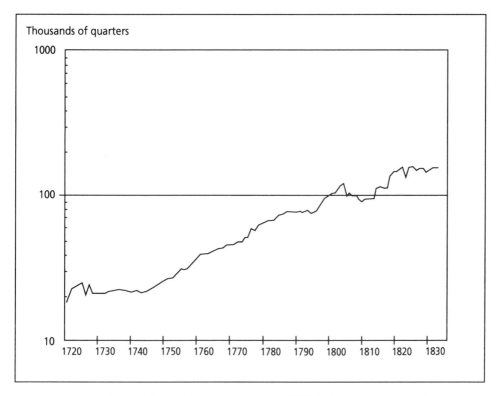

Fig. 2.13: The taxable wealth of St Peter Port, 1722–1834, in quarters of wheat,
semi-logarithmic graph (Source: COf, Livres de Taxe)

The fortunes of privateering and the influx of wealth during the American War are discernible but hardly exceptional. The economy 'peaked' in the early years of the Napoleonic War but then suffered a setback when the British government suppressed the smuggling trade. This affected the poor much more seriously than the rich who, by this time, were protected by their extensive savings in the British funds. In the post 1814 era many taxpayers prospered by switching to the French funds and the merchants reaped profits from the trade with South America.[153]

The tax assessments indicate that during the eighteenth century the *rate* of growth of urban wealth was marginally greater during some war years. Privateering did make its contribution; but it was as an entrepôt that St Peter Port annually grew richer. Even during war years commercial success was due as much to trade as to privateering. The island merchants happily traded with the enemy. During the American War the French sent orders to Guernsey by way of Amsterdam; and the St Peter Port merchants used neutral shipping to deliver cargoes.[154]

Finally, privateering was not always what it seemed to be. Although Guernsey privateers captured French vessels, the enemy did not lose: 'Malgré que les corsaires & fregates prennent les Français ils n'y perdent rien parce qu' ils sont assurés à Londres'.[155] The island merchants and the French waged war at the expense of the English: 'en pareil cas c'est faire la guerre aux depens des Anglais', commented Guille.[156] The islanders ostentatiously paraded their success at privateering. However, their exploits demand closer scrutiny. During the years 1780–83 some fifty letters-of-marque were issued to commanders of Alderney and Guernsey vessels to proceed against Dutch shipping. This resulted in the condemnation of just four Dutch prizes. Meanwhile the commanders of vessels based at Penzance were granted fifteen similar letters-of-marque and secured seven Dutch prizes.[157] *Either* the islanders were not very successful at privateering against the Dutch; *or* they placed trade ahead of privateering.

Conclusion

In the late seventeenth century the St Peter Port merchants profited from the prosperity of St Malo. As the Malouins did not trust the English, the islanders were able to play a major rôle in the carrying trade between St Malo and England. In the first half of the eighteenth century the Guernsey merchants transformed the port facilities of St Peter Port. They improved the harbour and built some twenty or thirty commodious warehouses. These entrepreneurial initiatives, coupled with the traditional trading privileges claimed by the islanders, underpinned the growth of St Peter Port as an entrepôt. The merchants educated their sons for trade; and sent them out to European and American ports to serve as agents.[158] This created a network through which orders, credit and commercial intelligence flowed easily. The merchants of St Peter Port grew progressively wealthier thanks to the entrepôt trade. The British government did not recognise St Peter Port as a free port *de jure*; but *de facto* the port functioned as such.

By the second half of the eighteenth century St Peter Port was a major commercial centre in the world of the Atlantic economy. Trade was the central concern of the *négociants*. In wartime privateering offered a partial substitute for lost trade. Privateering brought profits to some individuals, particularly to the *armateurs* who organised the speculative enterprises. However, war also offered opportunities for profitable trade. The *négociants* were not unanimously in favour of privateering; their *métier* was international trade. The principal value of privateering was constitutional. The Guernsey merchants regularly defended their privileges (and the entrepôt) by extolling their value as privateers; Guernsey was a nursery of seamen, a front-line against the French.[159] The British government tolerated these arguments until the era of the Napoleonic Wars. Then, impatient with the scale of smuggling from the island to England (and the lost excise revenue), it compelled the Guernsey merchants to abandon supplying smugglers.[160] The *négociants* weathered the crisis and re-adjusted their trading patterns. They found a new way to exploit the commercial potential of their international network of agents and developed a carrying trade between

Europe and Rio de Janeiro. This was a profitable new venture for the Guernsey *négociants* but one in which the town of St Peter Port played a much reduced rôle; its days as a major international entrepôt were at an end.

Fig. 2.14: An eighteenth century warehouse; converted in the 1960s into *The Cellar Club*, and now demolished

3

The Internal Economy of the Town

St Peter Port was both a port and a market town. These functions fashioned the structure of its internal economy. As a market town it was a central place offering services and marketing to the island; as a port it linked the island economy to a wider trading network.[1] The first section of this chapter studies the rôle of St Peter Port as a market centre. This leads onto an analysis of the internal structure of the town's economy in the seventeenth and early eighteenth centuries. We shall see that merchants dominated the urban hierarchy and regulated the work of the town. Below the merchants there were a few professionals and a large number of labourers. The merchants controlled both the urban and rural economies as they operated a putting-out industry which tied the country parishes tightly to the town economy.

The second section of the chapter examines the impact of the entrepôt on the urban economy in the eighteenth century. The merchants invested in the port infrastructure, developed harbour-related industries and fostered crafts. Then, the success of the entrepôt created surplus wealth that was available, in part, for conspicuous consumption. This encouraged the growth of services and the opening of specialist retail shops. The trend was accelerated in the 1780s when a larger British garrison was stationed at Fort George (in the town parish).

The final section of the chapter analyses the economic readjustment that occurred in the early nineteenth century when the entrepôt trade declined and the garrison was reduced in size. The shipbuilding industry was expanded and St Peter Port enjoyed quiet prosperity as a market town and minor resort.

I The market centre for the island

During the mediaeval period St Peter Port emerged as the market centre for the island. The town became the location of a fish market in the thirteenth century 'for the sustenance and convenience of the lord king's castles and garrison and of all the people of the island', the market days being established as Tuesdays, Thursdays and Saturdays. Next, in 1309, the general market of the island was moved from the Câtel parish to St Peter Port. Three reasons were given for the transfer. First, St Peter Port was a sort of borough ('quasi-burgum') whereas the other parishes were country vills with houses dispersed in the fields. Secondly, there was 'a far greater concourse' of people, both countrymen and strangers, at St Peter Port than in any other parish. Thirdly, in practice there already was buying and selling in St Peter Port on Sundays when, during service, they held a market 'to the great scandal of Christianity'. It was decided before the king's justices in 1309 that thenceforth the market should be held exclusively in the vill of St Peter Port every Thursday.[2] In some respects St Peter Port was not as convenient a location for the island market as the more central Câtel parish; but with its inhabitants, soldiers and strangers the town was the natural destination for islanders with agricultural surplus to sell. The decision of 1309 confirmed an economic reality.

The fact that marketing in St Peter Port was conducted next to the church was not unusual in the mediaeval world. In England buying and selling took place wherever there were regular assemblies; churches provided good opportunities 'for they attracted people every Sunday and especially on festivals'.[3] From the fourteenth century onwards the Guernsey markets continued to be held near the town church. The principal markets were located in the High Street. Fish was displayed for sale on mats near the juncture of the Grande Rue and the Carrefour; lower down the street countrywomen displayed vegetables; and butchers hung, carved and sold their meat at the junction of Grande Rue and Cow Lane.[4] The market brought countryfolk into St Peter Port throughout the year. The town was also the location of a great fair held annually just before Christmas.[5] On this occasion countryfolk brought to the merchants of St Peter Port garments that they had knitted during the course of the year. Having sold their handicraft, the countryfolk bought supplies from the town traders.

In 1758 William Le Marchant, jurat and merchant, calculated the annual profits made by the country in supplying the town:

'900 oxen, at £10 each, one with the other £9000
2500 sheep and lambs, at 15s. each 1875
1000 calves, at 25s. each 1250
2500 hhds of cider, at 10s. per hhd 1250
150000lb of butter, at 8d. per lb 5000
800 hogs, at 40s. each 1600
To geese, ducks, fowls, and eggs 600
In furze for breaming ships and heating the ovens 225
In lobsters and other fish 400
In potatoes, carrots and greens, &c 800
                                        Total sterling   £22,000 '[6]

Le Marchant estimated that the country spent £4,000 on 'such things as it takes from the town' and concluded that there remained a balance of £18,000 'which the country inhabitants profit upon those of the town yearly during the war'. But Le Marchant wanted to rebut the idea that the town inhabitants should pay a larger proportion of the island taxation and that the effects in trade of merchants in town should be valued for taxation purposes. Consequently his audit was selective and biased. He dismissed the *rentes* paid by country inhabitants to town dwellers with the sophistry that the former grew every year more wheat upon their grounds than was necessary to pay the *rentes*. Nevertheless, despite the bias, Le Marchant's calculation throws a valuable light on the nature and volume of trade between the country parishes and St Peter Port.

The internal economy of the town

In the early modern period the shape of the urban hierarchy of St Peter Port seems, as in many English towns, to have resembled a pyramid with a narrow élite of merchants at the apex and large numbers of poor people at the base. The élite controlled both the urban and insular economies. As merchants operating in the port they managed foreign trade. Those serving as jurats were able to implement pro-trade policies in their *ordonnances* and court judgments. Although the merchants were not great landowners in the fashion of their English contemporaries, many owned small farms in the country parishes. The English term *merchant* in fact translates two French words – *négociant* and *marchand*. The *négociant* operated on a grander scale, he was like a wholesaler, trading with other merchants and selling his commodities 'in bales, cases or full lots'.[7] The *marchand* on the other hand operated in the retail market, selling commodities to consumers. In the early eighteenth century there were approximately sixty leading '*marchants et négocians*' working in St Peter Port.[8] Apart from trading, this mercantile élite financed shipping and privateering and organised the putting-out of a knitting industry.[9]

Below the élite came a small number of professionals such as the rector, doctors and advocates. As late as 1775 there were only three medical practitioners serving the whole island.[10] It is not possible to calculate the number of people working in other sectors of the St Peter Port economy because scarcely any relevant source material has survived. However, church registers, wills, *actes* and *ordonnances* sometimes refer to occupations and this makes it possible to sketch in outline the rest of the structure of the urban economy. A certain number of the inhabitants of the parish of St Peter Port were occupied in agriculture and fishing, the town providing an immediate market for their produce. The provision of food and drink involved millers, bakers, fishmongers, butchers and brewers. Innkeepers, sometimes styled 'taverniers' but usually known as 'cabaretiers', supplied drink and, by an ordonnance of 1611, were required to keep beds ready to accommodate travellers. In 1683 there were 24 licensed *cabaretiers* in St Peter Port and they probably gave employment to a number of servants.[11] The building and clothing trades were other important sectors of the urban economy. In metalworking St Peter Port could boast blacksmiths, pewterers and a few silversmiths.[12] The port sector required ships' carpenters, sailmakers, block makers, porters, carriers and boatmen; and suppliers of cordage, pitch, tar and other equipment. Part of the urban population was made up of seamen and captains; at the beginning of the eighteenth century the thirty-two vessels of Guernsey were crewed by 180 men, many, if not all of whom, had lodgings in St Peter Port.[13]

An *ordonnance* of 1605 regulating the wages of artisans and manual labourers ('travailleurs de bras') provides some insights into the structure of the economy.[14] The passing of this *ordonnance* may possibly have been caused by a shortage of skilled manual labour.

Table 3.1 The wages of artisans, Guernsey, 1605

	To artisan d. (English pence)
Ships' carpenters	18
Common carpenters	10
Stone dressers and master masons	10
Common masons	8
Slaters	10
Thatchers	8
Woolcombers	10
Harvesters	12
Woodcutters	8
Gardeners	8
Common labourers	6

Source: *Ordonnances* vol. 1 pp 67-68 (abbreviated)

The regulations reveal a labour hierarchy, ships' carpenters being permitted to earn three times the amount fixed for common labourers. Of the eleven occupations regulated, five were immediately connected with the construction sector. Some evidence suggests that building craftsmen were in short supply in Guernsey in the early modern period. For example, when building work was undertaken by James de Havilland in the mid-seventeenth century craftsmen were brought across from England.[15]

Retailing was poorly developed in the town in the seventeenth century and there are frequent references to Frenchmen visiting the island to sell commodities. In 1658, for example, a Norman doctor arrived with three assistants. They erected a theatre in front of Jean Bord's house, played some tricks and sold medicines for all sorts of diseases. After six weeks they returned to France 'having made much money ... for the time they were here'.[16] Complaints were made from time to time about strangers retailing their goods 'en chambres' and in the street.[17]

There was little specialisation in the retail shops that did exist in St Peter Port. Nathaniel Carey's account book, kept between 1737 and 1747, shows that he dealt in a wide range of goods including wine, spirits, groceries, shoes and textiles.[18] In the mid-eighteenth century the Misses Rivoueres stocked drugs, spices, chintz and china at their shop in Fountain Street. Shops were of the simplest 'lock up' variety, a lowered shutter at a window offering an outside counter (see Plate IV). Window decoration was unusual, although not unknown. In 1763, to celebrate the end of the Seven Years War, the shops of St Peter Port 'assumed a gayer appearance than usual'. Esther Neho's shop displayed 'an astonishing variety' of nuts, almonds, penny whistles and purple-dyed eggs 'at uncommonly low prices'.[19]

Women constituted an essential part of the urban economy as they supplied a large reserve of cheap or 'free' labour. Female work was used as a substitute for male work, allowing men to be released for other occupations. While merchants travelled abroad their wives looked after their commercial interests in St Peter Port. Some wives continued in business when widowed. Most of the women working in the town seem, like their English counterparts, to have been predominantly of the middling and lower ranks and employed either in occupations connected with textiles, petty retailing and the provision of food and drink or in domestic service.[20] Details of these women and their work are usually lacking but documents occasionally provide what may be glimpses of typical situations. For example, in 1707 Jean Gruchy and his wife Marthe sold their partnership interest in a shop in St Peter Port to the third partner, their mother, Marie Bonamy, because they found that they were called to be more in the fields than in town. Not having the time to help in the shop as they would have wished, they sold their share of the stock to their mother for 400 l.t.[21]

At the 'base' of the economic pyramid there was a large pool of poor people. These constituted a cheap urban workforce and provided the common labourers needed in the port and construction trades. But much of that work was seasonal and it is probable that underemployment was a frequent problem. It was in these circumstances that the merchants were able to operate a putting-out industry.

The knitting industry

Until the mid-eighteenth century the knitting industry was of major economic significance to St Peter Port and Guernsey. It provided employment for at least a quarter of the population of the island and produced valuable export commodities. The industry was organised on a 'putting-out' basis. This employed many rural workers who combined the by-employment of knitting with their farm work. Putting-out was also an important part of the economy of St Peter Port. The town merchants organised the industry; and many urban workers found employment either in preparing the wool or in knitting.[22]

The industry probably arose in a Ricardian manner as a response to population pressure and land scarcity. This created a supply of labour surplus to the requirements of agriculture. Moreover, even amongst those engaged in agriculture there was seasonal underemployment which made by-employment a useful extra source of income. Finally, the system of partible inheritance practised in Guernsey meant that small land holdings were the rule rather than the exception. As a consequence farms were frequently too small to provide a family with more than a subsistence living. Combined, these factors produced the classic conditions for the establishment of a putting-out system. A pool of underemployed rural workers was available to the owners of circulating capital looking for cheap labour. Merchants were in an ideal position to benefit from putting-out as they controlled both the purchase and distribution of the wool *and* organised the export of the finished goods.

There were several ways in which production was organised. Two German words neatly categorise the two main branches: *Kaufsystem* and *Verlagsystem*. The *Kaufsystem* was a form of production characterised by familial production units which were subjected to the dominance of merchant capital; while the *Verlagsystem* was characterised by large scale production units, with significant division of labour, dominated by the 'marchand-fabricant'.[23] Both the *Kaufsystem* and the *Verlagsystem* appear to have been practised in Guernsey. In 1677 Charles Trumbull described St Peter Port as being inhabited by 'stocking merchants as they will call themselves, those that buy all the stockings that are made in the island and barter or sell them away by wholesale in France'.[24] This implies a *Kaufsystem*, as does a petition of 1716.[25] The merchant John Guille, on the other hand, seems to have been operating something closer to a *Verlagsystem* in the 1770s.[26] The evidence is not clear-cut. It is possible that the *Kaufsystem* developed through time into a *Verlagsystem*; or, the *Verlagsystem* may have been the characteristic form of production in the town.

Whether *Kaufsystem* or *Verlagsystem*, the merchants in St Peter Port controlled the whole operation for it was they who imported the wool under licence from England. The licences were crucial. In January 1685 Mary Major, widow, and Peter Major, her son, sent a petition to Lord Hatton pointing out that formerly she had received 60 tods of wool 'which was but a small quantity, and not able to suffice us who keep both the combing and the stocking trade'; as they had an allowance now of only thirty tods they had 'been constrained to buy licences at a very dear rate to our very great prejudice and of the poor people which we employ'.[27] By the second half of the eighteenth century the island knitting industry was dominated by just a few merchants. This situation seems to have come about through the practice of buying licences. The shift towards oligopoly may represent the transition from *Kaufsystem* to *Verlagsystem*.

The quantity of wool exported from England was regulated by an Act of Parliament passed in Charles II's reign which permitted the export of 1,000 tods annually to Guernsey.[28] However, the knitting industry on the island increased to such an extent that during the reign of James II the allowance was raised to 2,000 tods.[29] The supply of wool from England was supplemented occasionally by cargoes imported from other countries. In October 1687 le Sieur Samuel Dobrée was actioned by Pierre Vallet, part owner of the ship *le Content*, for 12 livres tournois for the freight on four 'pouchées de laine' brought from Bilbao to Guernsey.[30] On the other hand, not all of the wool exported from England to Guernsey reached its destination as some cargoes were illegally 'owled' to France.[31] It follows that we should understand that *approximately* two thousand tods of wool were imported annually into Guernsey.

Most of the wool was used to make stockings, but smaller quantities of other garments were also knitted. The exports from Guernsey to London in 1699 included nineteen dozen pairs of breeches; three dozen pairs of gloves; thirty-one petticoats; fourteen dozen pairs of sleeves (for women); $1,751^1/_3$ dozen pairs of stockings; and fifty-one $^1/_3$ dozen waistcoats. The exports to the English outports included blankets, coarse, five parcels; breeches 104 pairs; gloves knit seven dozen 1 pair; petticoats three; stockings $1,273^1/_2$ dozen pairs; ditto, women's six dozen; worst caps five $^1/_3$ dozen; worst drawers twelve pairs; worst waistcoats 213 dozen; and a small quantity of serge and worsted stuff.[32]

Some tentative calculations can be made about the volume and value of the industry. A knitter could produce one or two pairs of stockings per week. In England the aulnage collectors in 1595 reckoned that one knitter made two pairs of stockings per week.[33] However, a more relevant indicator may be that in 1687 six thousand knitters in Jersey reputedly made six thousand pairs of stockings weekly, using one hundred tods of uncombed wool.[34] If the Guernsey knitters worked at the same rate as their Jersey counterparts, it would have taken approximately 2300 people to transform the whole of the two thousand tods into one hundred and twenty thousand pairs of stockings. But this leaves out of the reckoning the people needed to clean, comb and spin the wool preparatory to the knitting. It is not easy to find reliable figures for these processes but clearly the whole operation – from tods of raw wool to finished stockings – could easily have involved three thousand islanders. Joan Thirsk calculated that the English domestic market employed somewhere between 90,000 and 220,000 knitters.[35] Her figures suggested that somewhere between 1.6% and 4.9% of the English population were involved in knitting stockings and she concluded that the industry was a substantial employer of labour. The Guernsey figures suggest that at least a quarter of the total population of the island was engaged, whole time or part time, in the industry in the late seventeenth century.

The knitters were badly paid. In the early eighteenth century they earned no more than 4d a week by their knitting 'but can hardly subsist thereby'.[36] In 1759 it was reckoned that there were very few who could earn one shilling per week 'and the others not that sum'.[37] The merchants, on the other hand, seem to have made a relatively good profit. In the late seventeenth century – at a time when there was parity between market prices and the prices recorded by the English customs – Guernsey stockings imported into England were entered as worth 24 to 30 shillings per dozen pairs (i.e. approximately 2s 3d per pair). The St Peter Port merchants often dealt in high quality knitting. In 1677 Charles Trumbull recorded that the stockings manufactured in Guernsey were 'generally of a finer sort than those in Jersey, some of them so curiously knit and so fine that they may be drawn through a ring, and worth 20 shillings or 30 shillings'.[38]

de Vries has argued that this type of industrial activity was characterised by its 'co-ordination by urban merchants and its dependence on distant markets'.[39] The St Peter Port merchants competed successfully in foreign markets by manufacturing stockings of high quality. In the second half of the seventeenth century the merchants regularly exported knitted goods to Paris where fellow Guernseymen acted as agents. Success depended in part in reacting swiftly to the transient fads of fashion. The correspondence of the merchants Matthew and Michael de Sausmarez illustrates this. While Michael collected orders in Paris, Matthew organised the knitting in Guernsey. The cousins used some 33 code numbers to identify different designs and colours. Among those available were 'marbled, fine marbled, very fine marbled, striped with a fiery red colour, plain white, white striped with blue, greyish white, greyish white striped, greyish brown, iron-grey, blue and white, and black'.[40]

Whereas France was the major export market in the seventeenth century, England became the principal market in the eighteenth century. However, as the entrepôt and its more profitable commerce developed, the knitting industry went into decline. In 1771 William Le Marchant observed 'we do not so much as import two thirds of the two thousand tods yearly allowed us from England'.[41] Eventually the Guernsey industry was unable to compete with the cheaper textiles produced in English mills and the island manufactory died away.

II The impact of the entrepôt

During the seventeenth century there was little scope for growth in the urban or insular economies, the factors of production being relatively limited. In the eighteenth century the town economy was transformed by the development of the entrepôt. As St Peter Port became increasingly important in the world of the Atlantic economy its population and wealth grew. Maritime commerce stimulated shipping-related occupations and led to the development of commodity-related industries such as tobacco-working and coopering. The merchants accumulated more capital and underwrote more ambitious ventures; these, in turn, enhanced the prosperity of the entrepôt. The earnings of those employed in the new industries fed back directly into the urban economy. The commercial success of the port attracted immigration; and the larger urban population required better 'maintenance industries', especially for the provision of food and drink. As the inhabitants became wealthier they increasingly sought luxuries. This stimulated the retail sector. In short the development of the entrepôt set in train a series of economic 'multipliers'. The tertiary sector was further stimulated in 1780 by the arrival in St Peter Port of a much larger British garrison. The officers required tailors and a wide range of goods and services.

Shipping-related occupations

The entrepôt and its shipping sustained a variety of specialist occupations such as sail-making and piloting. There was also a regular need for the repairing, modifying and fitting-out of vessels.[42] As we have seen in Chapter Two, in the late seventeenth and eighteenth centuries the Guernsey merchants usually operated vessels that had been built in France, England or, occasionally, the American colonies.[43] However a certain number of vessels were built locally. British colonial records show that the 40 ton sloop *Two Brothers* was built in Guernsey in 1739 and the 50 ton snow *Charming Nancy* in 1746; and there were others.[44] Shipbuilding was further developed towards the end of the eighteenth century. Typical of the vessels constructed was the *Alarm*, a lugger measuring '90 feet upon deck from stem to stern – 24 feet beam' which, like many others, had been built 'in a field … and when ready for launching was removed by screws to temporary slips on the beach'.[45] By 1804 there were 103 shipwrights working in local yards.[46]

The entrepôt involved not just the trading of cargoes but also the working and preparation of certain commodities. Some of these ancillary services were labour intensive and played an important rôle in the urban economy. Tobacco leaf, for example, was regularly turned into roll or snuff. By the end of the eighteenth century there were nine tobacco manufactories employing a workforce of approximately eleven hundred.[47] In 1800 Stiles observed that 'many indigent boys and girls' were employed in this sector.[48] In the early eighteenth century the St Peter Port merchants had prevented non-islanders setting up tobacco manufactories in the island; but later in the century one of the large snuff manufactories was owned by George Watson of Bristol.[49]

The transporting and distribution of large volumes of wine, spirits and tobacco required a ready supply of barrels of all sizes. Indeed, St Peter Port may, in part, have owed its development as an entrepôt to the fact that many English smugglers were driven to the island from France in the 1720s when the *directeur des aides* banned barrels below thirty pots in size in the administrative élection of Valognes.[50] At more or less the same time a certain number of English coopers settled in St Peter Port and helped to develop the craft locally. By the early nineteenth century there were some seven hundred coopers working in the St Peter Port entrepôt.[51]

There were two branches of this trade – that of the dry-cooper and that of the wet-cooper. The dry-cooper made casks for solid materials such as flour and tobacco. His work was far less exacting than that of the wet-cooper who had to construct water-tight casks that could 'withstand the strain of fermenting liquids and rough handling during transport'.[52] Further, the cask had frequently to be of an exact capacity and the quality of the wood employed was critical. When ordering from a Guernsey merchant in 1768 the Scottish firm of Alexander Oliphant & Co. requested that their wine should be shipped in pipes 'in order to be more favourably dealt with in the gauge here so its no matter how large they are, but please take care they be good casks & sweet'.[53] In addition to understanding the woods the wet-cooper required a mastery of nine skills: preparing the staves, raising the cask, trussing and bending, topping, cleaning down, bunging, heading, caulking, and fitting the hoops.[54]

Coopers were involved not just in making new barrels but also in attending to the storage of wine and the modification of existing barrels. As the St Peter Port wine merchant Guille explained to Thos. and R. Shuffield of Norwich: 'Port wine is generally lodged in a vault or in a close cellar over a vault on the ground floor according to the directions we receive. When it is to remain some time in a vault we take off the wooden hoops and put additional iron hoops in their place which it is not so necessary to do when in a cellar'.[55] Guille's letter outlined the services offered by the wine merchants (see Appendix 19). One of the most important operations carried out in the cellars was racking, the transferring of wine from one cask to another, usually about once every three months. This was a process that could significantly affect the quality of the wine.[56]

The coopers constituted a skilled section of the urban workforce and were essential to the working of the entrepôt. When the smuggling trade was suppressed (1805–1810) the coopers were under-employed. It was this, probably, that encouraged local merchants to develop the island shipbuilding industry in the early nineteenth century.

The development of retailing and service industries

There was rapid capital accumulation in St Peter Port in the second half of the eighteenth century, especially among the *négociants*. The increase in sales of entrepôt commodities such as tobacco, tea and spirits brought larger profits to the St Peter Port merchants. These profits were partly re-invested in maritime speculations and some money was invested in the British funds.[57] There still remained a surplus of wealth which was spent on induced imports.[58] During the second half of the eighteenth century there was an increasing demand in St Peter society for English goods. This phenomenon was analogous to the consumer boom in England identified by McKendrick, Brewer, Plumb and others. Their thesis has been criticised but most historians have accepted that this era witnessed growing conspicuous consumption among the wealthiest classes and patterns of increased spending in the middle classes.[59]

Economic development, with increased *per capita* purchasing power, brought about changes in the supply of services and in the organisation of retailing. Artisans and professionals were engaged to cater for a more fashionable style of life; entertainers and actors amused the leisure hours of the affluent bourgeoisie. But these new specialists themselves became consumers. 'In part, the producers of manufactured goods and the providers of urban services were the market.'[60]

A retailing 'revolution' took place during the late eighteenth century with the opening of many new shops in the principal streets of St Peter Port. Typical of these shops were the perfumery of James Grellier (opened in the High Street in 1794) and the chemist shop of John Hill & Co (opened in the Pollet in 1794).[61] These were specialist shops, run by immigrants, and they catered for the affluent members of Guernsey society. In the new environment of consumerism shopkeepers exploited a variety of techniques to promote their goods and to increase their turnover. Bow windows replaced the pentices of the early modern period and facilitated displays.[62] Advertisements were published in the newly established *Gazette de Guernesey* and customers were educated about the latest fashions and styles. The description 'from London' was regularly employed in advertisements not just to designate the origin of goods, but also to indicate excellence and metropolitan fashionability. Edward Draper in the Pollet advertised 'best quality London hats just in'.[63] Other traders advertised 'carpets from London', 'best plate gilted looking glasses from London', and 'dwarf trees from London'.[64] Metropolitan expertise was similarly prized. Solovin, a tailor in the High Street, boasted that he employed a young man from London whom he would challenge against any workman in the island.[65] Shops carried larger stocks and offered a wider range of choice. In July 1796 Cowan's (watchmakers in the High Street) held a sale in which they offered '100 dozen gloves, 600 fans 100 hats &c &c'.[66] The sale itself constituted one of the new retailing techniques.

Sometimes the locals helped visiting tradesmen to display their goods. Pitter from Bath advertised that he had on sale at Miss Marston's, Pollet, 'an assortment of articles in Silk, Gold and Silver, Laces, Bugle, Trimmings in black, white and colours, Gold Earrings, Broaches, Necklaces, Beads in Patent Pearls, Lustre, Cornelian and Coral, Fans in Ivory, Wood, Silk and Spangl'd, and a number of articles too numerous for an advertisement'. Pitter made at least two visits from fashionable Bath to St Peter Port, which suggests that he found a good market in Guernsey.[67] Other tradespeople visiting the island included Hine, a staymaker from London; Mrs Synger from Nottingham with an assortment of black and white lace; Strickland from London, selling cambrics; Mrs Farmer, a corset-maker from London, and S. Baster, a milliner and dressmaker from Hoblyn's of Bath and Weymouth.[68] Some travelling merchants offered goods for sale by public auction.[69]

The service trades expanded to sustain the new style of public sociability. Hairdressers and wigmakers established themselves in the town and provided the aristocratic ladies of St Peter Port with the latest London hair styles. Fencing, dancing, music and art masters gave tuition to the fashionable. Miniature painters executed correct likenesses. And, as we shall see in Chapter Eight, architects were increasingly commissioned to design elegant new buildings for private and public sociability.[70]

Entrepreneurs introduced new facilities for leisure pastimes. Entertainment and the theatre flourished. The actor-impressario John Bernard made the town theatre 'Royal' (1795). He also established 'a Vauxhall' close to the town. This project failed despite 'two very pretty singers; supper-boxes and summer-houses; some thousands of variegated lamps; a loyal French band ... fireworks, patronage, and other fanciful matters'.[71] But commercial failure was unusual at this time. The urban economy was flourishing and consumer demand outstripped supply. Even the world of children became a market. Schoolmasters, mostly from England, opened a host of academies and private schools in St Peter Port in the 1790s. Some schools capitalised on the requirements of the entrepôt and promised sound instruction in arithmetic and accounting. Others taught accomplishments and catered for parents with social aspirations.[72]

III Early nineteenth century problems and re-adjustments

In the early nineteenth century the urban economy suffered two major setbacks. The entrepôt declined when the British government suppressed smuggling (1805–1810); and at the end of the Napoleonic Wars the British garrison in Guernsey was greatly reduced in size (1815). The slump in the entrepôt particularly hurt the port workers and coopers. However, new jobs were created when the town merchants expanded the shipbuilding industry. The majority of the shipyards were located in or near St Peter Port, although a few vessels were built at St Sampson's or in Sark. Between 1812 and 1827 the island yards built four ships, twenty-six brigs, three schooners and thirty-five cutters. Many of these vessels were used in the newly established trade with South America; the St Peter Port merchants were commissioning purpose-built boats for their own trading ventures.[73]

Between 1805 and 1820 the upper classes in the town were sufficiently wealthy to weather the economic recession. Indeed there is plenty of evidence that they continued to enjoy a life of conspicuous consumption. Their servants also prospered; a correspondent writing in 1815 was so shocked by the sight of domestic servants decked in silk and lace that he wished to introduce sumptuary laws. 'Hardly do I dare to walk a yard, but I meet a greasy-fisted, red-elbowed wench, tricked out in her *silks*, her *point*, or *mechlin lace*, with a straw bonnet of the newest fashion, ornamented with rows of artificial flowers'.[74] By the late Georgian era St Peter Port was essentially a market town with an affluent gentry element. The latter provided enough business to sustain the retailing and the service sectors. From c.1820 St Peter Port slowly developed as a resort and spa town. Initially there appear to have been only a small number of visitors but as transport links with England improved tourism acquired a growing importance in the urban economy. With its low cost of living and pleasant climate St Peter Port also became attractive to impecunious English gentlemen and invalids as a retirement town.

The census conducted in 1831 recorded the occupational structure of St Peter Port.[75] The classification was very simple and tended to reflect social class rather than economic status. At the top of the hierarchy were 'capitalists' and professional men who formed one fifth of the number of employed males in the parish. There were very few manufacturers (nine); but those engaged in the retail trade and handicraft accounted for almost half of the total. There were only 74 male servants, but 917 female servants. English visitors were surprised when, in the absence of male butlers, they were served by females.[76]

Conclusion

The internal economy of St Peter Port was shaped by the merchants engaged in foreign trade. In the seventeenth century the *négociants* employed hundreds of urban poor in a putting-out industry; the export of knitted goods to France and England neatly complemented the carrying trade of the island merchants. In the eighteenth century the *négociants* developed the entrepôt and fostered ancillary crafts; by c.1800 they were employing some seven hundred coopers and eleven hundred tobacco workers. When the entrepôt trade declined the *négociants* expanded the shipbuilding industry; in this way the merchants created a fleet of vessels purpose-built for their new trade with South America.

In each of these three stages the merchants harnessed the domestic labour force to the requirements of foreign trade. There were three factors which facilitated their management of the economy. First, in the seventeenth and eighteenth centuries the merchants dominated the urban and insular government; they were not opposed by any other interests. The merchants could consistently pursue pro-trade policies. Secondly, as will be seen in

Chapter Five, they had the power to encourage – or discourage – migration flows. Consequently they could regulate the size and composition of the workforce, probably to a greater extent than was possible in English towns. Finally, in a small island the clique of wealthy merchants enjoyed more monopoly and monopsony power than merchants in England or France. They did not initially have to compete for labour. This gave them an advantage over some of their rivals abroad.

The entrepôt trade created a host of ancillary jobs. The coopers and tobacco workers alone accounted for approximately 16% of the urban population in 1800. It may reasonably be conjectured that at least a quarter of the town's population was involved in port-related activities. The experience of St Peter Port was similar to that of other ports. Various estimates have been made for London, one of which suggests that by the eighteenth century one quarter of the capital's population depended directly on employment in the port trades.[77] At Dunkirk in 1789 tobacco-working employed about five thousand and distilling was also labour intensive.[78] At Bordeaux in the late eighteenth century shipbuilding employed between seven and eight hundred workers; sugar-refining three hundred; tobacco-working about five hundred. Glass and pottery factories employed another four hundred. Finally, the two hundred and fifty vessels of Bordeaux required at least five thousand sailors.[79]

The entrepôt created new forms of work organisation in St Peter Port. In the seventeenth and early eighteenth centuries the putting-out system involved the merchants in fact-to-face encounters with the stocking makers. The tobacco industry, however, of the late eighteenth century was organised on a factory basis with eleven hundred workers located in some nine manufactories. It would be a mistake to characterise this as a shift to capitalism; the putting-out system was no less capitalist than factory production. However, the factory system increased the managerial control of the merchants and eroded traditional societal patterns.[80]

4

Demography

Guernsey was not included in the United Kingdom census until 1821 and there has been very little research into the population history of the island or its capital St Peter Port. This chapter tries to establish a more secure understanding of the demography of St Peter Port, fundamental for an examination of the economic and social history of the town.

It will be seen that enumerations and estimates suggest that the population of St Peter Port grew from about 3,000 in the second half of the seventeenth century to about 11,000 at the end of the eighteenth century. An aggregate analysis of the baptisms and burials recorded in the parish church registers reveals the underlying dynamics. Growth was achieved mainly through natural increase until the mid-eighteenth century; migration then became progressively more significant. St Peter Port did not suffer many mortality crises. The population density of Guernsey was high throughout the eighteenth century; but prompt action by the insular authorities effectively averted subsistence crises. St Peter Port enjoyed a healthier history than many other towns thanks to a variety of environmental, social and economic factors.

Contemporary population estimates

The earliest census figures available for Guernsey and St Peter Port date from 1800. The population of the island then amounted to 16,155 and the parish of St Peter Port numbered 8,450 inhabitants 'exclusive of sailors in his majesty's service, privateers, and merchant vessels; also of strangers not permanently settled, who may amount to 2,000 or 3,000'.[1] These figures, based upon 'an exact census', were supplied by the Royal Court, Guernsey, to Mr Stiles, a commissioner sent by the British government to enquire into the smuggling carried on from the island. The two or three thousand strangers 'not permanently settled' were principally to be found in St Peter Port. It follows that the aggregate population (permanent population + temporary population) of St Peter Port in 1800 was approximately eleven thousand; and that of Guernsey eighteen and a half thousand.

Some rough enumerations were made by the parochial authorities in the eighteenth century. There were also government estimates and militia returns. Such estimates are liable to error but have some evidential value and are now examined. On several occasions Guernsey experienced serious corn shortage. During times of dearth (*disette*) the authorities imported extra corn into the island. In 1727, during such an emergency, the inhabitants of the island were enumerated as being 10,246 of whom 4,350 lived in St Peter Port. Two quarters of wheat were required to sustain each inhabitant for one year; the island therefore needed 21,000 quarters.[2] During a later corn crisis in 1765 it was calculated that 3,580 quarters of corn were needed to supply the St Peter Port population from May until September.[3] *If* the calculations were based on the same assumptions as those of 1727, the town population in 1765 was approximately 5,370.

From 1780 the strength of the British garrison on Guernsey increased. This led to the import of larger quantities of corn into the island. Officials in Guernsey writing to the Home Office sometimes discussed this. For example, in 1789 H. Brown explained that the native population of the island was eighteen thousand but that allowance had also to be made for the garrison, their women and children, and 'the vast concourse of strangers'.[4] In 1794 John Small estimated the island population at twenty thousand; and in 1807 General Doyle calculated the civilian population of the island as being twenty thousand, the garrison four thousand, and the garrison women and children 'not overrated' at a thousand, giving a grand total of twenty-five thousand altogether.[5] Most of the garrison soldiers were stationed at Fort George, in the parish of St Peter Port; army families regularly lodged in the town.

Guernsey militia returns provide some demographic insights. In 1656 the island could muster 1,418 men, of whom St Peter Port supplied 340. Using a multiplier of seven, and ignoring the fact that the male/female ratio probably varied between town and country, Tupper concluded that the population of the island was 'fully 9,926 souls' and that the population of St Peter Port was probably about 3,000.[6] In 1680 the island mustered 1,902 men, the town 521 men.[7] Tupper found this number 'in a population of less than 10,000 souls' incredible. The militia returns are in fact comparable to the English muster rolls for which a multiplier of between 4 to 7 has been argued.[8] These multipliers suggest that in 1680 the island population was somewhere between 7,608 and 13,314 and the town population between 2,084 and 3,647.

Ecclesiastical records contain some evidence. Details for Guernsey are not to be found in the Compton Census but St Peter Port rectors occasionally estimated the size of their parish.[9] In 1735 Elie de Fresne told the Bishop of Winchester 'we are near 6000 souls in this parish'.[10] This was almost certainly an exaggeration, prompted by the fact that some English families had complained about de Fresne. The greater the size of his parish (and the greater the number of island-born parishioners), the smaller appeared the size of the 'English' problem.

The Royal Court letter book contains estimates of the island population in 1756 (twelve thousand) and of the town population in 1781 (at least eight thousand).[11] These figures may be considered well informed. Despite their limitations these estimates provide a good picture of the demographic

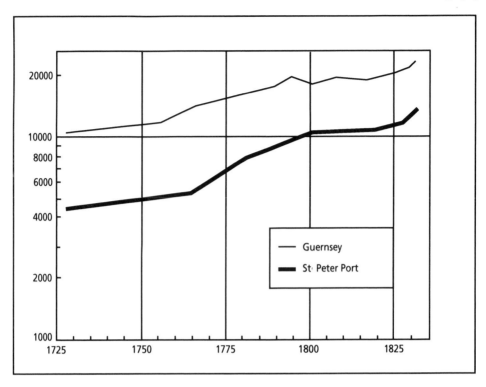

Fig. 4.1: The population of Guernsey and St Peter Port, 1727–1831,
based on contemporary estimates and enumerations.
(Semi-logarithmic graph to illustrate the *rate* of population increase)

trends. Between 1656 and 1727 the total island population increased gradually. There was a faster rate of growth in St Peter Port, whose population rose from approximately 3,000 to 4,350 (a growth of 45%). Between 1727 and 1800 the island population increased from 10,246 to 18,655 (a growth of 82.1%), while the population of St Peter Port rose from 4,350 to approximately 11,000 (a growth of 152.9%).[12]

St Peter Port grew at a faster rate than the other island parishes. St Sampson's developed rapidly at the end of the eighteenth century when the harbour took some of the shipping that could no longer be accommodated in St Peter Port harbour. The growth of the remaining parishes was considerably smaller. Câtel would appear to be an exception, but a hospital for the poor of the nine country parishes was built here in the mid-eighteenth century; this 'distorted' the population figure. The population of Torteval in the south-west actually declined.[13] Some parish registers which are currently being analysed demonstrate that there was considerable out-migration from the Guernsey countryside in the eighteenth century. The population increase in St Peter Port was achieved, in part, through a rural-urban shift. During the course of the eighteenth century St Peter Port moved into the position of housing over half the island population. This urban growth generated friction between St Peter Port and the nine rural parishes.

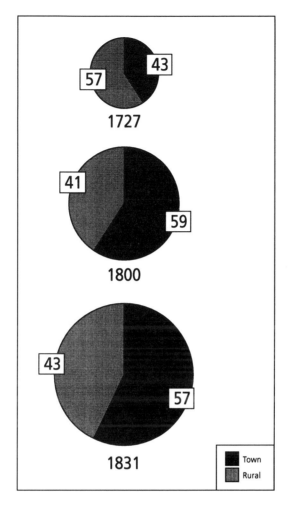

Fig. 4.2: Town and country – the population of Guernsey in 1727, 1800 and 1831
(expressed in percentages). By the late eighteenth century more than half the population
of the island lived in St Peter Port

For a long time the countryfolk argued that the town should contribute
more to the States taxation; the town dwellers counter-claimed that they
were under-represented in the States.[14]

Baptismal, marriage and burial records

The census figures and estimates supply isolated 'snap-shots' of the
population but fail to identify the underlying demographic patterns. A study
of baptisms and burials reveals the extent of natural increase and
inmigration, the frequency of mortality crises and the relation between birth
and death rates. Such a study is feasible because the parish church of St Peter
Port possesses a continuous series of baptismal, marriage and burial registers
dating from the sixteenth century. For the eighteenth century these registers
satisfy the preliminary requirements for a demographic study: there are over

one hundred entries per year and there are only two small gaps. Evidence of under-registration is slight. A small volume listing baptisms and burials 'administered in English' (1757–1761) contains a few records based upon pieces of paper found in the consistory in 1821. There may also have been under-recording in the late eighteenth century when nonconformity was introduced into the island.

Throughout the period of study there were British soldiers, sometimes accompanied by wives and children, garrisoned in the parish of St Peter Port. From the late seventeenth century until c. 1780 the size of the garrison was small. Had the registers been kept consistently, with members of the garrison always identified, it would have been possible to isolate the military presence in the aggregate analysis. But this was not possible. During the years 1794–1810 a separate register of garrison baptisms and burials was kept.[15] Some of these military entries were also recorded in the town church registers. Because of this double registration the garrison register has *not* been included in the aggregate analysis.

Marriages are not considered in this thesis because the records cannot yield sound statistical evidence. Inhabitants of the town regularly married outside the parish, St Andrew's being a particularly popular location. Moreover English couples eloped to St Peter Port; it is impossible to distinguish between migrants and elopers.[16]

The discussion of problems involved in this aggregate analysis should not obscure the fact that the registers compare well with many of their English counterparts; and they do provide a solid foundation for examining population trends. The aggregate baptismal and burial data have been

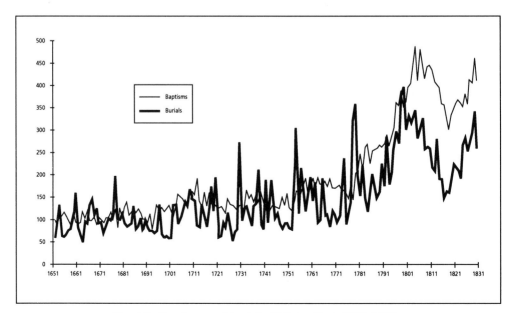

Fig. 4.3: Baptisms and burials, St Peter Port, 1651–1831

checked by the Leicester version of computer programmes devised by the Cambridge Group for the History of Population and Social Structure. The analysis suggested that the baptismal and burial data were consistent.

The aggregate analysis shows that during the eighteenth century the baptismal (= birth) rate generally remained higher than the burial (= death) rate. The population growth of St Peter Port was consequently due in part to natural increase. But change in population size can also be influenced by migration. The aggregate analysis can be used in conjunction with population figures to determine the relative contributions of natural increase and migration to population change. This is done by using the well established demographic equation:

Pt2 = Pt1 + (B–D) + net balance of migration
(i.e. inmigration *minus* outmigration)

where P = population, t2 = second date, t1 = first date,

B = number of baptisms [= births], D = number of burials [= deaths].

This equation acknowledges that changes of population size in a given community are brought about not just by births and deaths but also by migration inwards and outwards. When re-arranged the equation reveals the net balance of migration: net balance = Pt2 – {Pt1 + (B–D)}.

Table 4.1   The relative contribution of migration and natural increase to the population growth of St Peter Port, 1727–1831

	Population		balance of migration	migration	natural increase
	t1	t2			
1680–1727	3000?	4500?	+ 214?	14.3%	85.7%
1727–1765	4500	5370	+ 251	28.9%	71.1%
1765–1800	5370	11000	+ 4136	73.5%	26.5%
1800–1821	11000	11173	–	–	–
1821–1827	11173	12132	+ 189	19.7%	80.3%
1827–1831	12132	13893	+ 1287	73.1%	26.9%

[+ = inmigration into St Peter Port

These figures should not be allowed to assume a spurious precision. Their accuracy is determined by the census returns and the registration of baptisms and burials. Moreover, as Dr Corfield comments, such a study 'cannot yield precise figures because the subsequent offspring (and indeed the eventual mortality) of the migrants themselves are counted as part of the urban vital statistics'.[17] Nevertheless, the figures do show major trends. The population increase of St Peter Port in the first half of the eighteenth century was predominantly due to natural increase, the scale of migration being relatively limited. However migration was of cardinal importance between 1765–1800. During the years 1800–1821 there was significant natural increase [+2440]; but its impact was cancelled by an almost equal flow of emigration between 1814–1821. The emigration flow was reversed in the 1820s and inmigration contributed significantly to population growth in the years between 1827 and 1831. We shall examine these migration trends in greater detail in Chapter Five.

The church register evidence can be used alongside the independently attested population figures to calculate crude birth and death rates.

Table 4.2 Crude birth and death rates, St Peter Port, 1680–1831

year	population	crude birth rate	crude death rate
1680	2800	45.4	36.1
	3000	42.3	33.7
	3200	39.7	31.6
1727	4350	30.8	18.6
1765	5370	33.3	18.6
1800	11000	31.7	35.8
1814	11000	36.1	25.4
1821	11173	30.7	20.0
1827	12132	29.3	20.7
1831	13893	29.5	18.3

Most of the crude birth rates are comfortably within the parameters anticipated by Wrigley and Schofield. They have observed that in most pre-industrial European populations the crude birth rate fell in the range 28–40 per 1,000.[18] As the population for the year 1680 is not certain, the figures have been worked three times to show the possible range. High birth rates are not necessarily suspect; they do occur and 'are often associated with populations with high proportions of young adults acquired through immigration'.[19]

According to Wrigley and Schofield 'death rates in pre-industrial England are unlikely to have been as extreme as twenty or thirty-five per thousand except fleetingly in unusual circumstances'.[20] The death rate in St Peter Port seems to have been rather low in several years. This is perhaps to be explained by the observations of Jan de Vries about the loss of sailors at sea. He notes that Wrigley and Schofield treat such loss 'as a form of migration rather than a form of mortality.'[21] If St Peter Port sailors lost at sea are considered 'missing deaths', the crude death rates given above require adjustment. The degree of error will be greatest for those periods when St Peter Port inhabitants were particularly involved in sea-faring.

There were twenty-five years in the eighteenth century in which the number of deaths in St Peter Port appear to have exceeded the number of births; but the deficit was usually slight and demographic recovery was swift. The birth/death ratios suggest that natural increase was reasonably secure for most of the eighteenth century.

Crisis mortality

St Peter Port experienced only a limited number of years of crisis mortality. This is remarkable as seaports are popularly considered to have been unhealthy. Writing in 1805 Doyle said that there had never been a plague or contagious disorder in the island but this was clearly an exaggeration.[22] The years of crisis mortality can be detected by the analysis of the burial records. There have been numerous attempts to devise indices for measuring the intensity of crises, each methodology having idiosyncratic virtues and problems. The St Peter Port figures have been analysed using the computer programme of the University of Leicester (based on the programme of the Cambridge Group for the History of Population and Social Structure). This gives a month-by-month quinquennial analysis with a centred moving average.

The application of these statistical approaches to an analysis of the burial records of St Peter Port yields the following table:

Table 4.3 Crisis mortality in St Peter Port, 1654–1800

Start year	Start month	End year	End month	Severity factor*
1654	Sept	1654	Nov	3.4
1661	Sept	1662	Feb	2.9
1667	Nov	1668	Jan	3.9
1678	May	1678	Jun	3.4
1703	Jan	1703	Apr	2.9
1707	Dec	1708	Mar	3.4
1710	Nov	1711	Mar	4.1
1721	Jun	1721	Sep	2.6
1731	May	1732	Mar	3.8
1738	Nov	1739	May	2.8
1742	Jan	1742	Apr	3.4
1744	Oct	1745	Jan	3.4
1755	Jul	1755	Nov	5.9
1757	Nov	1758	Jan	3.0
1775	Apr	1775	Jul	3.5
1778	Dec	1780	Jun	2.9
1780	Sep	1780	Nov	4.5
1783	Aug	1783	Oct	3.5
1787	Jan	1787	Mar	3.1
1799	Dec	1800	Mar	2.2

* *The severity factor is the number of times by which the actual average monthly total is greater than the predicted total*

Table 4.3 lists only crisis mortality. In many years there were seasonal epidemics which sometimes affected particular sections of the community. In 1770, for example, a letter-writer recorded the death of several dignataries '& many children of the small Pox' and in April 1778 Guille mentioned 'spring and autumn fevers which reign greatly with the poor people of this island'.[23] Such epidemics inflicted numerous deaths without becoming crises.

The identity of some of the crisis epidemics in St Peter Port can be established. The last outbreak of the plague suffered in Guernsey occurred in the years 1629–1630.[24] The epidemic of 1661–1662 was an outbreak of smallpox and other complaints.[25] The epidemic of 1731 (cause unidentified) was still dimly remembered almost a century later as having 'nearly depopulated the island'.[26] The crisis in 1755 was a smallpox epidemic. In July of that year the 'chefs de famille' decided to inoculate the children in the town hospital (poorhouse) provided that the parents did not object and that the children acquiesced with 'bon coeur'.[27]

The epidemic in 1775 was introduced by soldiers garrisoned at Fort George. Jeremie recorded that a dissentry or bloody flux broke out in a regiment of highlanders quartered there. 'The corps was nearly destroyed, and the malady spreading in the neighbouring parishes made considerable ravages.'[28]

The epidemic of 1778–1779 was recorded in some detail by Nicholas de Garis. From the end of 1778, and throughout 1779, scarlatina was prevalent throughout the island. The illness was characterised by an unbearable pain in the throat. Almost everyone experienced an attack and those who survived took a long while to convalesce. The epidemic was exacerbated by other illnesses – measles, smallpox, purpura and military fever *inter alia.*[29]

The epidemic in the early months of 1787 was smallpox. On 9 December 1786 the town authorities decided to raise 1,500 livres tournois to inoculate the children of the poor and other poor people. On 15 January 1787 Thomas Dobrée recorded that about 700 had been inoculated, three or four at most having died. He observed that those who had taken the disease in the natural way died very fast and he found it strange that people could be so weak and foolish as not to accept inoculation.[30]

By 1805 Jennerian vaccination had reached the island. In July of that year Ann Grut wrote to her husband (who was in Ireland on business): 'Our dear little Peter was carried to him (*Dr Paul*) last Tuesday, to be inoculated with the cowpox, for the natural smallpox infects the whole island and sweeps away many of the inhabitants.'[31] There was some opposition to the Jennerian method and a lively correspondence was published in the Guernsey press. In April 1808 S. M. Taylor 'Member of the Royal Jennerian Society' advertised that he would vaccinate on Wednesday and Saturday mornings from 10 to 12 o'clock at No. 11 High Street; the poor would receive free treatment.[32] Vaccination won the day; at the session of Chief

Pleas held on 3 October 1808 the Royal Court prohibited inoculation with smallpox unless specific permission had been granted by the Court.[33]

The next significant outbreak of smallpox appears to have been in 1824–1825. On 1 February 1825 the Royal Court enforced rigorous rules. The *ordonnance* of 3 October 1808 was activated; smallpox victims were forbidden to walk about in public before making a complete recovery; and buildings which housed a smallpox victim were to display a notice saying 'La Petite Vérole est dans cette Maison.' The constables were to enforce the regulations and to encourage vaccination.[34] A contemporary writer commented that these ordinances 'if zealously enforced' would tend to check the further progress of the disease which was understood to be strictly contagious. The writer regretted that there was still a bias in the country parishes in favour of inoculation and that numbers of children in the country had not been vaccinated. By April 1825 the progress of the disease had slowed: 'a solitary case or two has appeared in some of the thickly-inhabited houses of the town, but as most of the individuals residing in them had been vaccinated, it has been confined to the persons originally affected'. A month later smallpox was still 'about the country' but 'not prevalent' in town.[35]

Vaccination seems to have proved successful in St Peter Port; but smallpox was only one of the diseases prevalent in 1824–1825 as the following table shows:

Table 4.4 Diseases and illnesses in Guernsey, July 1824 – June 1825

1824	
July	Diarrhoea, dysenteric symptoms [p. 62].
August	Derangements in the hepatic and digestive functions; a few straggling cases of cholera morbus; measles [p. 95].
September	Bowel complaints; diarrhoea; measles [p. 128].
October	Croup [p. 174].
November	Croup [p. 224].
December	Low nervous fever; croup; smallpox [p. 262].
1825	
January	Smallpox; colds; children affected by slight continued fevers [pp. 301–303].
February	Erysipelas; eruptive disorders; colds; coughs [p. 344].
March	Pulmonic complaints; several phthisical patients dead [p. 383].
April	Smallpox; diseases of the eye; an anomalous kind of eruption among children, neither scarlet fever nor measles [p. 421].
May	Smallpox [p. 464].

[Source: *The Monthly Selection* (Guernsey, 1824–1825)]

The young were particularly at risk. The medical report mentions that the town children were the first to suffer from the measles – 'imported by persons coming from Jersey' – in August 1824; and in the following month diarrhoea was affecting 'children principally'.[36]

In October 1832 cholera entered St Peter Port from Jersey. In a detailed analysis of this epidemic Dr Kellett-Smith has identified '369 (?371) cases with 103 (105?) deaths; which works out at a mortality rate of 28%. This compares creditably with the rate in England, of the order of 37%, and of Jersey which was around 40%.'[37] The relatively low mortality rate in Guernsey may perhaps be attributed to the wide range of measures taken by the island authorities. Although the epidemiology of cholera was imperfectly understood, some of the measures taken to combat the disease were fortuitously effective. The importation of bedding was forbidden; a strict quarantine was imposed; the roadways were washed; tar was burnt and vitriol and chloride of lime were sprinkled; Sunday schools were cancelled; the drinking of red currant juice to combat dehydration was recommended; blankets and clothes were distributed to the needy; and the town poor were moved from the hospital to the Vale. Dr Kellett-Smith argues that many of these measures were directly or indirectly valuable in helping to control the spread of the disease. Of the fatalities a large proportion seem to have been English migrants residing in the poorer parts of the town, close to contaminated water-supplies.[38]

Jacques Dupâquier has argued that the chronology of crisis mortality differed between France and England in the seventeenth century; great crises in one country had no echo in the other. After 1705, on the other hand, the 'two countries marched in step' – crises were experienced in common. He conjectures that seventeenth century crises were 'national' and eighteenth century crises 'international'. But after testing this hypothesis he rejects it in favour of regional, rather than national or international, analysis.[39] It is not easy to fit St Peter Port into such an analysis. The temporal co-incidence of a crisis in Guernsey with a crisis in France does not *in itself* prove that there was a causal linkage. As a port town St Peter Port was exposed to infection from many quarters. Nevertheless, St Peter Port traded extensively with St Malo and other French ports and was vulnerable to French epidemics. It is possible that the St Peter Port crisis of 1661–1662 was related to 'la crise de l'Avènement' of 1660–1662.[40] The epidemics of 1710, 1738–1739 and 1742 may also form part of the history of French crisis mortality. The crisis of 1740–1742 particularly affected the Atlantic and north-western coast of France, directly opposite Guernsey.[41] However, June 1741 to October 1742 was also a period of local crises in England;[42] as Dupâquier remarked, some of the epidemics of the eighteenth century can be termed 'international'.[43]

As an island Guernsey was, in one respect, insulated from epidemics. But the population needed to trade abroad and shipping frequently threatened to 'import' disease. A quarantine was regularly established. In 1711 'when Bremen & other parts in the North were infected' the Royal

I. Map of St Peter Port, 1680

II. Urban networks: Old House – shipyard and outhouses – at Trinity, Newfoundland, c.1770

III. Urban networks: Weymouth in the late Georgian era

IV. View of St Peter Port, watercolour by Joshua Gosselin, 1790s

V. The brig *St George*, 1825

VI. Cow Lane, St Peter Port

VII. Market place in 1809

VIII. Market Square, Assembly Rooms and Arcade, 1838

IX. Boat-building yards, South Beach, St Peter Port

X. 'Hunting the hare in Guernsey', c.1733

XI. Matthew de Sausmarez (d. 1697)

XII. Michael de Sausmarez (1655-1689)

XIII. Nicolas Dobrée (1678-1751)

XIV. Pierre Frédéric Dobrée (1757-1801)

XV. Marie-Rose Dobrée (1757-1781)

XVI. Paul Le Mesurier (1755-1805)

XVII. Antoine Rosetti

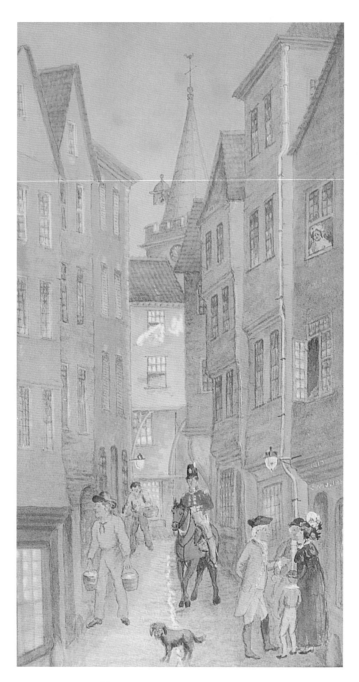

XVIII. Lower Fountain Street

XIX. Old Fountain Street

XX. The Quay, St Peter Port

XXI. Elizabeth College

Court of Guernsey made regulations 'under severe penalties' which proved 'effectual and sufficient'.[44] Nine years later, when the plague was raging at Marseilles, a quarantine boat was arranged.[45] English quarantine regulations were regularly extended to the island by means of Orders-in-Council.[46]

Food provision and subsistence crises

Historians have paid increasing attention to the links between demography and nutrition. It has been suggested that mortality crises were closely linked to subsistence crises. This idea was popularised by Pierre Goubert in his study on Beauvais and the Beauvaisis. However, Chaunu has objected that there were instances of mortality crises without high prices, and high prices without corresponding mortality crises.[47]

To understand the story of food crisis in Guernsey and St Peter Port it is necessary to examine the whole picture of the island's food provision. In 1841 Jonathan Duncan calculated that the territorial surface of Guernsey was twenty-four square miles i.e. 15,366 English acres [= approx. 62 square kilometres]. He estimated that 10,240 English acres were fit for cultivation.[48] There may have been slightly more land available for agriculture in the eighteenth century, prior to the suburban sprawling of St Peter Port.

The density of population on the island was high. Already by 1727 – when the island population was calculated as being 10,500 – there were approximately one hundred and seventy inhabitants per square kilometre. Guernsey fell into the third and highest level of population density identified by A. P. Usher in which forty to forty-four inhabitants per square kilometre already corresponded to 'demographic tension'.[49] By the early nineteenth century the population density of Guernsey had risen to approximately three hundred and ninety-five people per square kilometre.

How large a population could be sustained by the produce of the island? In England Daniel Defoe estimated that three acres of good land or four acres of average land were required to support one man. If these figures are applied to Guernsey, it suggests that the island could support a population of between three and four thousand inhabitants. This calculation sits comfortably with another estimate that in the pre-modern period a town of three thousand inhabitants needed to be served by the lands of ten villages (or approximately 8.5 km^2) in order to live.[50] This model is strikingly similar to the reality of St Peter Port in the seventeenth century – the town parish of approximately three thousand inhabitants being served by nine rural parishes in an island approx. 8 km^2. Guernsey, with a population of 10,500 in 1727 increasing to 24,500 in 1836, experienced 'demographic tension' throughout the eighteenth century. The islanders coped with this by operating an intensive form of farming; by eating a lot of fresh fish, and less meat than the English; and by importing food.[51]

When did Guernsey cease to be self-sustaining in corn production? Some clues are provided by examining Guernsey's sister island of Jersey. In the early seventeenth century Jersey was able to feed its population by its own production and export surplus for barter at St Malo with the Spanish merchants.[52] However, by the late seventeenth century Falle was observing that the island did not produce sufficient for the inhabitants, who were often supplied with corn from England, or (in time of peace) from France; and that the islanders often went as far as Danzig because of the cheapness of the market there.[53] It seems reasonable to infer from this that Guernsey, a smaller island than Jersey and with a higher population density, was probably importing supplementary corn supplies by the end of the seventeenth century. This policy was encouraged by the falling grain prices in England in the late seventeenth and early eighteenth centuries. By the second half of the eighteenth century the island could not produce above two thirds of the provisions required by the inhabitants and was importing from the west of England 'but principally from the neighbouring provinces of Brittany and Normandy'.[54]

Having established the general pattern of the food supply of Guernsey and St Peter Port, it remains to examine the correlation, if any, between subsistence crises and mortality crises. References to food shortages are scattered throughout a variety of sources and the list in Appendix 13 is almost certainly not complete. However, there is an independent source of information about the island harvests for this period. Yearly, at Michaelmas, the medium annual price of a quarter of wheat was fixed by the Royal Court to provide a basis for the calculation of *rentes*.[55] The valuations established by the court appear to reflect accurately the state of the harvest and of the wheat market on the island. A statistical test can demonstrate those years in which the price fixed for wheat was more than one standard deviation higher than the mean price for the preceding ten years. There were many years when Guernsey experienced subsistence crises. Yet few of these years coincided with years of crisis mortality; and in those cases of coincidence it is not clear whether there was a direct or indirect causal link between the food shortage and the deaths, or, indeed, whether there was *any* link. Undernourishment may have led to more deaths; but Massimo Livi-Bacci has shown that it is a mistake to jump too readily to such conclusions.[56]

When the Guernsey harvest failed, the island and parish authorities acted energetically. In the late winter and early spring they arranged the import of corn from overseas. Until c.1750 supplies were often available from England, a major grain exporter in the first half of the eighteenth century. After c.1750 the islanders sometimes had to look further abroad.[57] By corresponding with Guernseymen established as factors in foreign ports the island authorities found it relatively easy to arrange shipments of cereals to St Peter Port, sometimes from markets as distant as Danzig and Quebec.[58] When the grain reached the island, care was taken to ensure that the poor could afford it. The States and constables regulated the sale and arranged subsidies.[59] An *ad hoc* tax made good any financial deficit.[60] There were bread riots in Jersey in the eighteenth century but there seem to have been none in Guernsey.[61]

Conclusion

It has been seen that throughout the eighteenth century the birth rate in St Peter Port was generally higher than the death rate. It has also been demonstrated that there were few years of crisis mortality. Some explanation of the relatively healthy nature of St Peter Port is necessary. There does not appear to be any single reason, but rather a complex mixture of environmental, social and economic factors. Some of these have been mentioned earlier but it will be convenient to bring them together.

First, Guernsey enjoys a climate which is – and was – relatively mild compared to the climate of central France and mainland Britain. The islanders were subjected rarely, if ever, to the full rigours of a bad winter. The climate of Guernsey was similar to that of Brittany, a province that escaped largely unaffected even in the great winter of 1709 thanks to its mild, wet climate.[62] Secondly, St Peter Port may have had a better quality water supply than many towns. Some of the inhabitants collected rain water in their own tanks. This conferred a double advantage. The water was unlikely to become contaminated by the seepage of drains; and the risks of mass infection associated with public pumps were avoided. The outbreak of cholera (a water-borne disease) in 1832 was principally located in the poor quarter of the town by the harbour; the inhabitants here may have been more dependent on communal pumps.[63] Thirdly, throughout the eighteenth century a rigorous quarantine was imposed whenever there was the risk of a disease-ridden vessel entering the harbour. A similar system was operated in England but it is possible that it was easier to administer the quarantine effectively in a small island like Guernsey. Fourthly, in the last third of the eighteenth century there were considerable efforts to inoculate the town population against smallpox, and then, in the nineteenth century, to vaccinate. Razzell conjectured that the control of smallpox was one of the decisive factors in bringing down mortality rates in the second half of the eighteenth century.[64] His thesis has been criticised but is not discredited. Furthermore, his conclusion may be correct in respect of some areas, even if not universally true. Fifthly, throughout his period there seems to have been adequate provision for the poor. The church and the parish authorities organised poor relief;[65] and when the harvest failed sufficient corn was imported for the *whole* population. Finally, it is possible that nutritional standards were better in St Peter Port than in some other eighteenth century towns. The poorhouse diet furnishes a clue to the diet of the urban poor in general. According to Thomas Dicey the inmates of the town hospital (workhouse) were fed at dinner on fresh beef, salt pork, pease soup 'and now and then fish and parsnips'; breakfast and supper consisted of bread and butter. They received about a pint of small beer at every meal, except the little children who drank out of a spring 'remarkable for the soft milky quality of its water'. Dicey's account is confirmed by the hospital accounts. During the six months from July to December 1766 the 136 to 150 inmates were provisioned with beans, turnips, potatoes, carrots, cucumbers, herbs, fresh fish, 'conger to refresh the poor', 112½lbs of lard and 2,411½lbs of bacon (= approximately twelve ounces of bacon *per caput* each week).[66]

It is instructive to compare the experiences of St Peter Port with those of St Malo and Dunkirk. St Malo suffered plague attacks in 1606–1622 and in 1663. It also experienced crisis mortality in 1693, in common with the rest of France. But in the great crisis of 1709 St Malo was unaffected. The Malouins benefited from the mild climate of Brittany and from their ability to ship corn from ports as distant as Bergen and Danzig. The demographic history of St Malo was essentially a happy one.[67] The story at Dunkirk was dramatically different. Between 1695 and 1789 the average annual number of deaths was ninety-eight higher than the number of births, despite there being a high birth rate. Between a third and a half of the mariners of Dunkirk perished at sea. Yet this was not the reason for Dunkirk's high death rate. Cabantous draws attention to the poor urban environment, portraying the marshy, fever-ridden land around the town as the cause of the high death rate. The population growth of Dunkirk (from 10,515 in 1685 to 27,106 in 1789) was achieved by large flows of migrants into the town.[68]

It seems legitimate to conclude that it is rash to make generalisations about the unhealthiness of port towns. St Peter Port and Dunkirk both experienced corn shortages and epidemics, often in the same years. But *local* factors were decisive in shaping the favourable birth/death ratio in St Peter Port and in producing the dismal statistics at Dunkirk.

5

Migration

It has been demonstrated in the previous chapter that migration was a critical factor in the population growth of St Peter Port. Aggregate analysis, however, is purely quantitative and tends to produce 'an impersonal, dehumanized approach' to migration studies.[1] Recent research has emphasised the need for studies which attempt to explore the migration process 'as it affected the society in which migration occurred' and relating migration to 'regional economic prosperity, variations in wage rates and employment opportunities, the availability and cost of transport and the topography over which a move took place, the availability of information through kin, friendship networks or propaganda, social and cultural barriers which may have inhibited movement, and political controls on movement and inmigration'.[2] This is a challenging programme. Eighteenth-century documentation for migration in England is limited and for Guernsey the situation is even more problematical. There are no archives like the English ecclesiastical court deposition papers. Nevertheless, the dynamic factors influencing migration field and flow can be discerned, and the migration process can be illustrated with limited biographical data.

During the eighteenth century rural 'push' and urban 'pull' brought many islanders into St Peter Port. Analysis reveals a diversity of motives and patterns. Migration from the country was not solely an escape from Malthusian pressures; and movement into St Peter Port was induced not only by the entrepôt-oriented economy but also by the developing service sector. As St Peter Port became larger and wealthier it attracted migrants from more distant horizons.

Endogenous factors determined the patterns of migration throughout the century and were of first importance. There were also, however, waves of immigration into St Peter Port occasioned by external pressures. War and privateering brought merchants and mariners to the town. In 1739 Carey asserted that during the War of the Spanish Succession the Guernsey privateers alone employed 'not less than 1700 men, whereof about the one half belonged to the Island, & the remainder were English and Irish with some Dutch & other Foreigners'.[3] These were essentially temporary migrants who made little immediate impact on the town except as consumers. Religious persecution in France (c.1681–c.1727) drove Huguenots to Guernsey; and towards the end of the eighteenth century French Royalists and Catholics sought refuge on the island. An effort will be made to quantify the extent and nature of French settlement during these periods.

With the decline of the entrepôt trade in the early nineteenth century the economy of St Peter Port changed. There was considerable emigration during the difficult years between 1815 and 1820. This was followed by a phase of quiet urban improvement which attracted a considerable number of labourers and artisans from the south-west of England and from Normandy. The rate of immigration into the town was accelerated by the improvement of transport links across the Channel. The census returns of 1821 and 1831, together with enumerations of 1827 and 1830, afford the opportunity for statistical analysis. It can be demonstrated that migration significantly affected the demographic profile and social geography of St Peter Port. By the second decade of the nineteenth century approximately one third of the town population was of English origin.

Rural 'push' factors

There is a good case for arguing that demographic pressure (intensified by the small land area of Guernsey) was necessarily bound to lead, via Malthusian forces, to rural out-migration. It might be argued that whatever the system of land tenure and agricultural production, the country parishes could sustain only a certain level of population density before migration became inevitable. However, it is necessary to examine the island customs of inheritance because these structured the forms of rural life and employment, which in turn shaped migration patterns.

The laws and customary practice of Guernsey were founded on those of the duchy of Normandy – of which the island formed a constituent part from the tenth to the thirteenth century. In matters of inheritance Guernsey essentially conformed with the system of Normandy and of the west of France – one of egalitarianism. It is true that the Guernsey tradition contained a contradictory element because the eldest son enjoyed the right to *préciput*. In this respect the Guernsey tradition resembled that of the Caux district in Normandy 'where there obtains, even among the commonalty, an English-style right of primogeniture that constitutes *ipso facto* an enormous disadvantage for younger sons'.[4] But despite the advantage conferred on the eldest son by *préciput* in Guernsey, the fundamental principle of the insular system was partible inheritance. When the eldership had been taken, the real property was divided, two thirds among the sons, one third among the daughters. Land could not be devised by will; and all the children had a right to a share in the inheritance.[5]

Under this system Guernsey landed property became extremely subdivided. In 1815 Thomas Quayle observed that the proprietor who occupied an estate from forty-five to sixty vergées (= approx. eighteen to twenty-five acres) was deemed 'a capital farmer'[6] and in 1844 Duncan calculated that on average each house in the country had approximately five English acres attached to it; many houses had only two or three acres attached to them.[7] In brief, the system of partible inheritance could lead to a form of rural pauperization, the land holdings being scarcely large enough to support a small nuclear family, let alone a family with dependants and/or servants. In 1815 Berry commented that few persons were able to grow more than for their own existence and the payment of their rents.[8] The inheritance rules had the further consequence that daughters, although acknowledged, were disadvantaged; and that few labourers were employed.[9]

It can be urged that this system of inheritance, land tenure and payment of *rentes* (often owed to seigneurs living in the town) encouraged more intensive agricultural practices. The landholdings were so small that the cultivators had the opportunity to work more like horticulturalists than farmers. But the law of diminishing returns meant that there could be no escape from Malthusian factors. Too many younger siblings and children could not be supported on the small farms; surplus population was driven away from the country to St Peter Port, and elsewhere, in search of work.

The case of Nicholas Blondel was probably quite typical. When his father married again, and a large second family was born, Nicholas saw no prospect in remaining at home; 'wherefore, after staying until he was of age, conscientiously discharging his duty to his father, he left him and came to town with a very small sum in his pocket, and having some knowledge in spoon and buckle making he hired a small shop, where he cooked his victuals, &c., and from one mechanism to another lived pretty comfortable, and after a few years married'.[10]

Others just left the land and sought alms in town. In 1759, for example, the inhabitants of St Peter Port complained that the streets of the town were 'daily crowded by the poor of the country, who do not subsist but by the alms which they receive from charitable persons of the town'.[11] This was the most basic form of rural out-migration, one prompted by subsistence needs. The town merchants relieved some of the pressure of rural unemployment by harnessing surplus labour in two ways. The shipowners recruited islanders to serve as crew on vessels sent to the fisheries off Newfoundland. This was a form of seasonal migration. Secondly, the town merchants organised a stocking knitting industry which created rural by-employment. This allowed a larger number of people to subsist in the country parishes and slowed down the rate of rural out-migration.[12]

So far our analysis has been concerned primarily with Malthusian forces as a 'push' factor. There were other forces at work. People living in the country parishes were born into a rural society that acknowledged at least three status ranks. In the parish of St Pierre du Bois, for example, although there were no gentlemen there were yeoman farmers designated *le Sieur*, master craftsmen and tenant farmers designated *Maître*, and labourers and the poor known simply by their name. 'Legally a man was known as the son of his father "Nicholas So-and-so, fils Nicolas" ... A woman was simply known by her men-folk "Elizabeth or Marthe, wife, widow or daughter of Nicolas, fils Nicolas".'[13] A consequence of this social structure was that descent rather than market forces determined what work each individual did. One way of avoiding a predestined occupation was to migrate to town where employers were more interested in aptitude. Sometimes parents living in the country parishes arranged for their children to be apprenticed in St Peter Port, the classic route of 'career' migration. Daniel Quertier from the parish of St Martin's was formally apprenticed to Peter Le Cocq, gunsmith and locksmith of St Peter Port, commencing 25 April 1737. Some four years later Daniel left that employment and was turned over to Stephen Mourant, mariner.[14] Daniel in effect engaged in a form of 'step migration', from the Guernsey countryside to St Peter Port in stage one, and from St Peter Port to the sea in stage two. Such 'step migration' may well have been relatively frequent in the early modern period, especially when the urban economy was in a phase of economic recession. In the seventeenth century a number of islanders served their apprenticeships in England; and there was a constant 'leakage' of population from the island and town to sea-faring careers.[15]

Work in progress on the church registers of the country parishes of Guernsey suggests that between 1727 and 1800 there was a steady outmigration from the countryside. At the same time the sex ratios at birth and death in St Peter Port differed; the 'skew' suggests that the town was gaining females as inmigrants. It is highly probable that there was a significant movement of girls and young women into St Peter Port where they found employment as domestics and widened their marriage horizons.

Urban 'pull' factors

Hitherto the examination of migration has been centred on factors essentially endogenous to the island. Rural emigration has been seen as a response to Malthusian forces; as a means of escaping from 'ascribed status'; as a quest for improvement through apprenticeship; as part of a sequence in step migration; as a form of employment and marriage opportunity for females. It has also been seen that in many cases, although not all, rural 'push' factors brought countryfolk to St Peter Port. In this sense the town was a 'passive' receiver of migrants who had been motivated by extra-urban factors. The town was often able to assimilate these newly arrived workers; but at other times the rural migrants proved a burden to the townsfolk and legislation was invoked to drive them back to their native parishes.[16]

The population increase of the town resulted in part from rural 'push' factors; equally important was the growth induced by the entrepôt sector of the St Peter Port economy. Professor Williamson has recently discussed the relationship between dynamic sectors of the urban economy and migration. He has drawn attention to the significance of the price elasticities of demand for urban output and has argued that city growth and migration rates are likely to be higher 'the more open is the economy to foreign trade.'[17]

Port-based enterprise constituted the dynamic modern sector of St

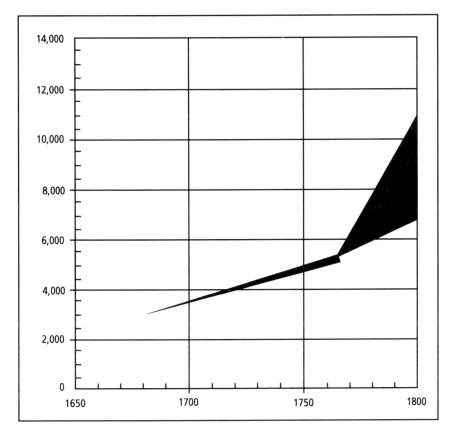

Fig. 5.1: The contribution of migration to the population increase of St Peter Port
in the eighteenth century

Peter Port in the eighteenth century. The handling and processing of
commodities in the international market created new types of employment
and required a larger workforce. Job creation and wage differentials led to
inmigration and town growth. The entrepôt and its allied industries in part
required *skilled* labour. This constituted a problem in the early days and led
to the employment of foreign migrants. The English ropemaker David
Aldridge pointed out in 1727 that he had been encouraged to settle in the
island to establish a *corderie* as there was none then existing in Guernsey. At
the same time shipbuilders, coopers and sailmakers came from England to
work in St Peter Port.[18]

When St Peter Port became increasingly important as a trading centre
foreign merchants settled in the town. In 1738 Philip Durrell wrote to John
de Sausmarez explaining that Mr Trawton (?Taunton) and his family
planned to settle in Guernsey soon. 'He is in the wine trade and intends to
keep large quantities of wines in the island in order to send them over to
England to his brother who is in partnership with him ... if the widow Guerin
could make room in her house for seven or eight people [I] believe it would
be a good lodging for them.'[19] A number of British and foreign merchants

settled in the town, frequently on a temporary basis, sometimes permanently.[20] It is instructive to study the migration history of one such merchant who settled in St Peter Port. William Bell was born in Leith in 1726. On his father's death in 1736 he went to Archibald Stewart's counting house in Edinburgh and occasionally attended the wine vaults in Leith. In 1742 he went to Boulogne where he worked in the vaults and counting house of Charles Smith until 1744. He returned to Scotland; then went to London and on to Zealand, later returning to England. In 1748 he travelled from London to Guernsey where he stayed for five weeks. He returned to London and then in September 1748 he toured France. He travelled via Paris – Rheims – Beaune – Lyons – Avignon – Montpellier – Sète and Toulouse to Bordeaux. There he took ship for Guernsey, arriving in May 1749. He settled in St Peter Port and in 1755 married Mary Le Marchant, daughter of one of the most influential merchants in Guernsey. Bell prospered as a wine merchant and left off business in 1792 in favour of his sons William and George.[21] Bell's long series of moves from childhood in Leith to his final settlement in St Peter Port represents 'career' migration that brought him from humble obscurity at the age of ten to the centre of the Guernsey élite by the age of 29. He was one of the leading wine merchants for many years.[22] It may reasonably be inferred that through career migration Bell acquired a good understanding of the international wine trade and that this underpinned his commercial success.

The Guernsey merchants on occasion took legal action to curb the competition of foreign merchants engaged in industry in Guernsey.[23] But generally there seems to have been no prejudice against immigrant merchants such as Bell settling in St Peter Port. He brought a wealth of knowledge about the European wine trade in general and Scottish trade in particular. Archibald Stewart of Edinburgh had trading connections with Isaac Dobrée and Jean Cornelius in St Peter Port.[24] Through Stewart and his other commercial acquaintances Bell would have had access to an extensive network of mercantile contacts. This was essential for success in trading as it secured credit and reduced risks. Bell's arrival in St Peter Port conferred an advantage on the entrepôt just as he in return derived a benefit from being able to operate from St Peter Port.

The entrepôt trade generated capital accumulation in the merchant class. This in turn led to the growth of the tertiary sector which also drew in immigrants. Although the evidence is fragmentary, it seems possible to distinguish two phases in this development. In the first phase the immigrants belonged, in the main, to long established crafts and trades associated with food distribution, clothing and building. We find English butchers and bakers; tailors and shoemakers; a seamstress and a staymaker; joiners and a glazier.[25] These migrants were joining a workforce which was serving a larger and *wealthier* urban population. More butchers imply more meat consumption. As the inhabitants of St Peter Port grew wealthier their appetites and diets altered. Similarly, the presence of an immigrant staymaker can be construed as denoting the existence in St Peter Port of ladies wishing to dress fashionably.[26] In the second phase – from c.1760 onwards – the merchant class grew even wealthier, and their tastes correspondingly more sophisticated. This sustained the development of a tertiary sector that became increasingly specialised as it catered for the leisure interests and luxury tastes of an affluent bourgeoisie. Thus we find the arrival of confectioners, cabinet-makers, musicians, dancing-masters, actors and printers. The taste of the bourgeoisie for fine new houses and more urban amenities (such as a new market, assembly rooms, chapels, a theatre and a court house) stimulated the building industry which employed immigrant builders, masons, sawyers, carpenters, joiners and labourers.[27]

Urban attitudes to immigration

Migrants were a mixed blessing to the town. Newcomers with relevant skills were welcome, especially when the economy was expanding; but vagrants and vagabonds represented a burden – actual or potential – on the resources of the urban taxpayers. The English Poor Law regulations and the Settlement Act were not operative in Guernsey but the island authorities exercised a similar system. A long series of *ordonnances* controlled and regulated the migrant flow. An *ordonnance* of 1685 concerning strangers and vagabonds in St Peter Port and Guernsey required islanders to return to their native parishes and specified that, unless permission had been granted, marriages involving foreigners were thenceforth prohibited.[28] An *ordonnance* issued in 1726 developed the legislation by setting out the conditions and qualifications for being received as an 'habitant' and the procedure for changing parish. This legislation required lodging-house keepers to inform the Crown officials about strangers.[29] Throughout the century *cabaretiers* were often required to keep check list of strangers. From this it may be inferred that on their arrival in St Peter Port immigrants regularly put up at the *cabarets* (wine shops/taverns) which seem to have played a rôle similar to that of the English alehouse. By the 1780s there were just over a hundred *cabarets* in St Peter Port, many by the harbourside.[30]

Much legislation controlling migrants dates from the second half of the eighteenth century, when the expanding entrepôt economy was drawing many artisans and retailers into St Peter Port. These *ordonnances* strengthened earlier legislation. By 1786 the urban and island authorities had developed a system which gathered *intelligence* about newcomers; kept *surveillance* on immigrants' behaviour; maintained *control* over their activities; and exercised *sanctions* and expulsions. Ships' masters were required to give details of arriving foreigners to the town authorities[31] and passenger lists had to be submitted within 24 hours of arrival in the island.[32] *Cabaretiers* and lodging-house keepers were instructed to submit lists of migrants and their professions to the parish constables.[33] Certain occupations were subject to restrictions; migrants practising medicine and surgery, actors and charlatans needed permission to pursue their vocations.[34] Immigrants were required to produce papers about their native legal settlement.[35] Parish constables were empowered to produce before the courts any immigrants suspected of being liable to become a charge on the parish.[36] The regulations about settlement in the island were re-iterated and strengthened.[37] The court had the power to caution strangers and, if necessary, to expel them from the island. The *ordonnances* were issued when there were high levels of immigration. The insular authorities had several fears. Street disorder was blamed on the migrants; and some foreigners constituted a threat during wartime. But the deepest anxiety was that immigrants might become a charge on the community, particularly if they acquired the status of *habitants*.

External pressures causing migration to St Peter Port

Guernsey, being close to the coast of France, offered a convenient asylum to migrants during troubled times. St Peter Port witnessed two such waves of migration during the period 1680–1830: Huguenots fleeing from the persecution of Louis XIV's régime; and Catholics and Royalists fleeing from the French Revolution.

The Revocation of the Edict of Nantes in 1685 is popularly seen as the beginning of the persecution of the Huguenots in France. In fact harassment and flight had started well before that date. In 1681 le Sieur Papin, 'ci-devant lecteur au preche', fled with his family from their home in the parish of St Saviour at La Rochelle and found exile in Guernsey.[38] But what started as a trickle was soon to become a flood. Valuable evidence of this is contained in the *abjurations* and *reconnaissances* entered in the Ecclesiastical Court registers. These records suggest that there were three main 'waves' of refugees. The first 'wave' fell immediately after the Revocation (1685) and lasted until 1690; the second fell during the years of peace of 1699–1700; the third was less concentrated and lasted some ten years, from 1717–1727. Many of the refugees in the first and second 'waves' came from Saintonge and Aunis; the third 'wave' included exiles from the South of France.[39]

St Peter Port proved a welcome residence for some of the refugees. The town already housed several families of French origin (e.g. the Dobrées and Fautrarts) who had sought refuge during the wars of religion in the sixteenth century. And the islanders were decidedly anti-Catholic. Writing in 1715 on the foiling of a Jacobite threat, Guille, a Guernsey landowner and merchant, referred to 'les Papistes nos Ennemis Jurés', a sentiment with which more than one Huguenot could have concurred.[40]

It is not easy to determine how many Huguenots settled in St Peter Port. The *abjurations* and *reconnaissances* do not in themselves prove more than temporary domicile in the island. Many refugees stayed in Guernsey for a

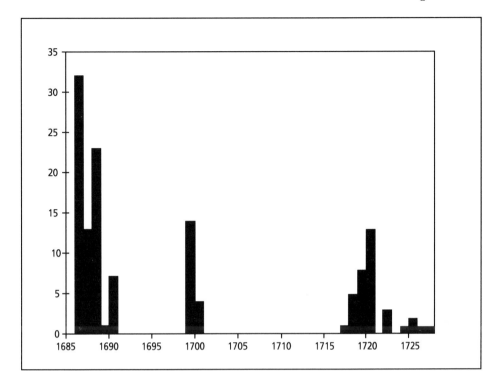

Fig. 5.2: *Abjurations* and *reconnaissances* of Huguenots recorded in the Ecclesiastical Court Register, St Peter Port

matter of just days or weeks until they could find an opportunity to travel further. Typical of these was David Garrick, a wine merchant from Bordeaux, who left everything, even his wife and a four month old son, and travelled via St Malo to Guernsey where he remained for the space of a month. Garrick arrived in London on 5 October 1685 where he was shortly joined by his wife and son who travelled by boat from Bordeaux.[41] St Peter Port, with its protestant, French-speaking merchants and its trade routes leading to England and the New World, proved an excellent *temporary* asylum for the refugees.

The baptisms, marriages and burials recorded in the Town Church registers cast some light on the number who settled permanently. During the years 1703–1724 two or more baptisms were recorded for some thirty Huguenot families. Of these families it can with some assurance be asserted that they were permanently settled in St Peter Port. There were at least a further eight families credited with one baptism apiece. During the period 1701–1724 some sixty-two burials of Huguenots are recorded; forty-five of these surnames are additional to the family names of the baptismal list. Some of the burials may have been of celibates; but a high proportion of the Huguenots fleeing from France consisted of families. The evidence suggests that eighty to a hundred Huguenot families had settled in St Peter Port by the early eighteenth century, and that they represented somewhere between 4%–7% of the urban population. This is consistent with estimates of the size of the Huguenot settlements in some of the Devon ports.[42]

Huguenots settling in St Peter Port included surgeons, an apothecary, schoolmasters and mariners.[43] At least three Huguenot refugees commanded island privateers in the wars against the French; but it is not easy to determine how many Huguenots served as ordinary sailors because there were those who employed *noms-de-guerre*.[44] Some of the settlers were families of standing and substance. There were four such households in the Grande Rue – those of le Sieur Pierre Tyrand, Mr Simon Rivoire, Mr Lauga and Mr Condamine.[45] There were poor Huguenots as well. Wills registered in the Ecclesiastical Court record bequests made to the 'pauvres françois réfugiez de cette isle' but it is difficult to calculate the precise number of these indigents.[46]

French émigrés [*tempore* French Revolution]

A considerable number of royalist and Catholic refugees found political asylum in Guernsey from 1789. Some settled. Antoine Rosetti, a musician and composer, fled from Normandy and found employment for many years running the Assembly Rooms in St Peter Port.[47] However, most of the émigrés remained in the island for only a short while. In 1796 the Catholic priests were moved from the island to England.[48] Some émigrés eked out a precarious existence by giving lessons in dancing, fencing and drawing; other copied music, carved ivory, worked hair as ornaments, or kept a billiard table. There were families of distinction 'some of whom had come over with small remnants of their property, but many comparatively resourceless'.[49]

British military analyses of 1805 identified three groupings of émigrés in Guernsey. First, there were the foreigners, principally Frenchmen, who had been many years in the island, 'several of them being married & settled and in some degree identified with the inhabitants'. Some of these had settled in the island long before the French Revolution broke out. Secondly, there were the Frenchmen formed into 'La Compagnie des Français à Guernsey' under the surveillance of the Baron de la Garde. The officers were all emigrants of long standing who appeared 'to have given up all idea of returning to France'. The privates were mostly 'mechanics or peasants'. The 'mechanics' included coopers, labourers, servants, shoemakers, smiths, a baker, joiner, knife-grinder and gun-smith. There were forty-six in the Compagnie, of whom about half lived in town. Thirdly, there were the Royalists who had served under General George in La Vendée, fifty-one in number, under the charge of Mr De Vossey. These were 'accustomed to an irregular warfare', 'tired of an inactive life' and 'impatient of control'. They were 'exceedingly troublesome' and potentially dangerous, both militarily and politically.[50] The evidence suggests that although *at moments* there were large numbers of émigrés in St Peter Port and Guernsey, the number of refugees who *settled* in St Peter Port was relatively very small and had only a marginal impact on town life.[51]

Immigration in the nineteenth century

The patterns of migration in the nineteenth century differed from those of the eighteenth century in various ways. The urban economy was depressed by the collapse of the entrepôt trade (1805–14) and by a reduction in the size of the garrison (c.1815). This, combined with bad harvests and high food prices, prompted many islanders to emigrate to America and Canada.[52] The emigrants were predominantly from the poorer classes. The wealthy were not adversely affected by the economic difficulties because many of their foreign investments were flourishing.[53]

After 1821 the urban economy improved. There was a change in the flow of migration, with an increasing volume of immigration *into* St Peter Port. There were several reasons for this. A number of English gentlemen settled in the town, attracted either by the relatively low levels of taxation or by the salubrious climate.[54] In Guernsey they could maintain a certain standard of living on a modest income. These settlers, and the prosperous natives of the town, continued to require domestics. The retail trade and other branches of the tertiary sector prospered, drawing into St Peter Port a host of skilled and semi-skilled artisans, some with a knowledge of new technologies (e.g. gas-workers).[55] A large number of craftsmen were needed to build fashionable new houses on the outskirts of St Peter Port. In the centre of the town the demolition of the mediaeval *rue Tanquoel* and the construction of a commercial arcade (c.1830) was carried out by French labourers 'at a wage of only one franc each day – living being then very cheap in Guernsey'.[56]

Immigration into St Peter Port became considerably easier from the mid-1820s thanks to the development of steam-shipping links between Guernsey and Plymouth, Southampton and Cherbourg.[57] Between 1 Jan. 1826 and 1 Nov. 1826 there were 1,896 ship arrivals in Guernsey, with 39,350 persons landing.[58] Some of these were visitors, others were islanders returning home, but many were seasonal migrants. They came principally from Normandy and Wessex. These were regions experiencing demographic and economic pressures.[59]

In December 1830 the Guernsey authorities became anxious about the unrest in the south of England (the 'Swing' riots) and feared that the hundreds of unknown strangers in their midst constituted a threat. Spurred by this worry, they compiled a survey of male migrants in St Peter Port. The records are detailed but require careful handling as it can be demonstrated that many English residents were omitted (presumably on the grounds that they were well known and 'safe'). The clearest understanding of the

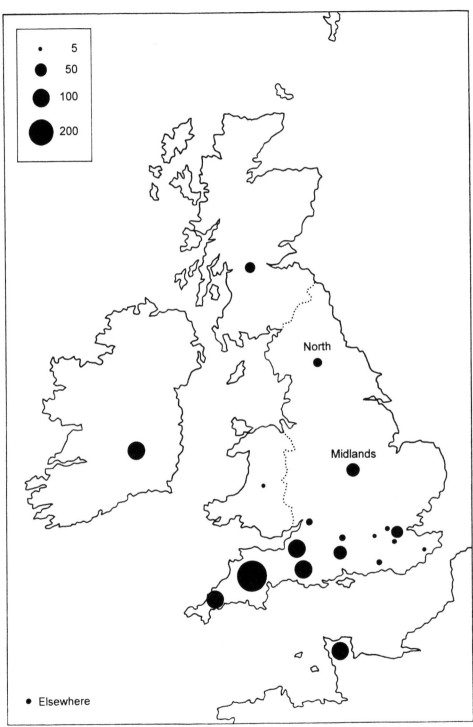

Fig. 5.3: The origin of male migrants resident in St Peter Port, December 1830

migration patterns is achieved by an analysis of the cohort of migrants who arrived during 1830. This shows that the typical male migrant was English, in his twenties and single. It is hazardous to judge social and economic status by occupation, but the majority of these immigrants appear to have been of the lower middle or working class.[60]

Many of the newcomers arrived through *chain migration*. For example, the following migrated from Modbury in Devon to St Peter Port: John Wyatt, a schoolmaster, and his family in 1825; George Prout, founder, in 1827; John Pike, a cordwainer, and his brother, a carpenter, in 1827; Richard Pike, a mason, and his wife in 1828 (three months after John and Josh Pike); George Avery, a labourer, in 1830.[61] Chain migration was probably instrumental in the formation in St Peter Port of the clusters of specialists all from one particular area in England (e.g. stone-cutters and stone-dressers from Swanage in Dorset).[62] At the same time regional and local affinities may have helped the migrants to find their feet. Thus in 1830 at Saundry's (on the south beach) there were to be found six miners, all from Cornwall.[63]

The social and economic impact of migration in the early nineteenth century

Migration had a profound impact on St Peter Port society in the early nineteenth century. First, it skewed the sex ratio. There were 75.0 males per 100 females in 1821; 79.5 in 1827; and 75.3 in 1831.[64] The impact was particularly exaggerated in the cohorts of those aged between twenty and thirty. A note appended to the 1821 census explained the phenomenon as due to 'the absence of the seamen abroad in registered vessels, of the men at Gaspée, &c, in the Cod Fishery, of the young men settled elsewhere; and to the many English servant-maids employed in town'.[65] The emigration of *males* combined with the immigration of *females* produced the very low sex ratio of 48.7 in the cohort of those in their twenties.

Secondly, migrants were not spread evenly throughout the town; patterns of segregation developed in the residential distribution of migrant sub-groups. These patterns are revealed by the analysis of a census conducted in 1827. Statistical tests establish the indices of segregation and dissimilarity and the location quotients of the town streets (Appendix 15). The degree of segregation must not be exaggerated but most streets possessed their own idiosyncratic character. The following generalisations underline the most significant trends. Recently arrived migrants were particularly over-represented in Berthelot Street, Church Street, Market Street, Fountain Street, Bordage Street, Cornet Street, Beauregard, and Glategny (see Fig. 5.5 and Appendix 15.4). These streets lay in the old quarter of the town, near the harbour, and offered cheap lodging houses, taverns and slum accommodation for labourers and poorer artisans. These streets also housed a certain number of migrants, male and female, of longer standing. Clusters of *settled* migrants, male and female, were to be found in

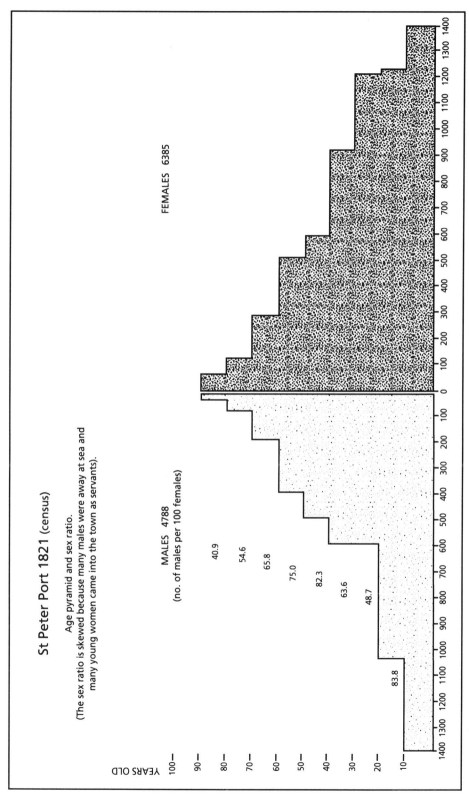

St Peter Port 1821 (census)

Age pyramid and sex ratio.
(The sex ratio is skewed because many males were away at sea and many young women came into the town as servants).

FEMALES 6385

MALES 4788
(no. of males per 100 females)

40.9
54.6
65.8
75.0
82.3
63.6
48.7
83.8

YEARS OLD

Fig. 5.4: An age/sex pyramid of the St Peter Port population, 1821 (based on census figures, *The Star*, 7 Aug. 1821)

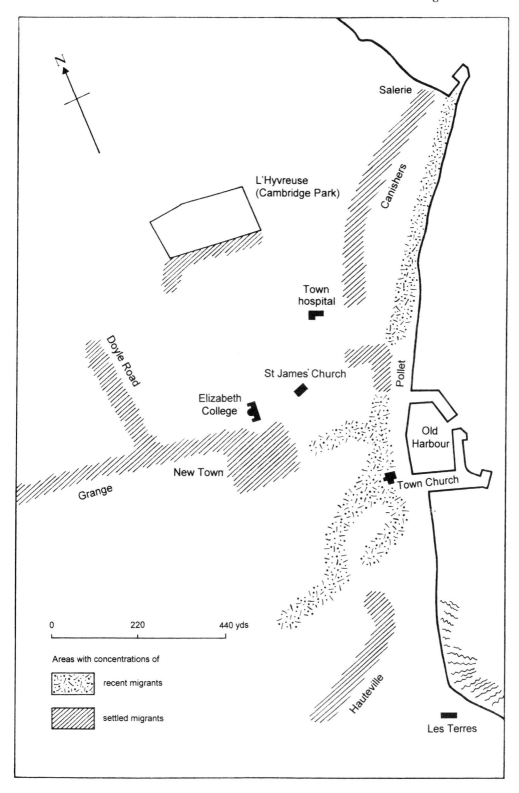

Fig. 5.5: The location of immigrants in St Peter Port, 1827

some of the more salubrious suburbs – L'Hyvreuse, Doyle Road and New Town. Many of these migrants were English settlers of the 'middle class'. The settled migrant females displayed the greatest degree of residential dissimilarity and segregation (see Appendices 15.2 and 15.3). The reason for this is that there were concentrations of English women and migrant servants in wealthier areas (and an absence of such females in poorer localities).

Conclusion

'The great Multitudes of People requisite for Manufactories, Sea-Ports, etc. proves the Necessity of In-Comers', observed Dr Short in 1750.[66] 'In-Comers' were no less necessary to St Peter Port than to the English ports. Throughout the 'long' eighteenth century migrants swelled the town population. The settlement of Huguenot refugees in the late seventeenth and early eighteenth centuries re-inforced the French culture of the town. But thereafter the main flows of migration were from England. The English migrants changed the demographic, economic and cultural character of St Peter Port. By the second decade of the nineteenth century it was calculated that approximately one third of the town population was English.[67] In some areas of St Peter Port native (i.e. Guernsey) residents constituted less than half the population. Migration flows skewed age/sex ratios to such an extent that in 1821 among the young adults there were approximately two females for every one male. English immigrants brought occupational skills which expanded and enriched the urban economy. But the volume of immigration amounted to informal colonisation and this revolutionised the societal patterns and culture of St Peter Port. These themes are explored in the following chapters.

6

The Structure of Society

This chapter examines the class structure, distribution of wealth and social geography of St Peter Port (changing patterns of sociability are analysed in Chapter Seven). It will be demonstrated that in the early modern period the social and economic structures of St Peter Port had affinities with those of French towns. The vocabulary of status (*Monsieur, le Sieur*) was identical and helped to divide urban dwellers into four ranks. As in many other towns in France and England, the merchant élite tended to live in the centre of the town, the poorer on the periphery.

The commercial prosperity of St Peter Port in the second half of the eighteenth century created social tensions. The merchants competed in displays of conspicuous consumption and squabbled for the designation *écuyer*, some energetic craftsmen climbed to higher status ranks; the lower orders jeered at the gentry entering the assembly rooms; and some strangers failed to show deference to the town constables. The island authorities tried to contain the situation with a variety of measures. They developed strategies to cope with the problems of poverty and vagrancy. However, they were not able to arrest the transformation of social attitudes. By the late eighteenth century the town parish housed many English immigrants and a sizeable British garrison. These newcomers arrived lacking the status titles of the Guernsey tradition and arrogated the titles they desired. As the old system of status crumbled, the St Peter Port élite discovered a new form of social stratification in physical segregation. By 1831 most of the wealthy inhabitants had moved from the centre of St Peter Port to the periphery. The wealthy were now physically more segregated from other sections of society than they had been in the early eighteenth century.

The analysis that follows is based on the tax records kept by the town constables from 1715 onwards. Three years have been selected to provide a framework for analysis: 1727, 1800 and 1831. Reliable population figures are available for these years; and these dates correspond to significant stages in the economic history of the town. The year 1727 stands at the threshold of the development of the entrepôt; the year 1800 witnesses the entrepôt at its zenith; and 1831 presents St Peter Port in its post-entrepôt era. The analyses start with a lengthy 'static' examination of the structure of society and residential geography in 1727. This is necessary, first, to establish the significance of the vocabulary of rank used in St Peter Port in the eighteenth century; and secondly, to provide a foundation for comparative purposes. After this 'static' snapshot there are two diachronic analyses. The first examines the changes that occurred between 1727 and 1800; the second analyses the years 1800–31. These diachronic surveys are 'anchored' by the data for 1727, 1800 and 1831. Finally, St Peter Port in 1831 is compared and contrasted with St Peter Port in 1727.

The tax ledgers list assessments of individuals, expressed in quarters of wheat. When the authorities had established the tax-paying capacity of the town, they were able to determine the rate at which the tax should be levied. For example, in 1715 the town tax payers were assessed at 16,531 quarters. By levying 7½ deniers (about one half-penny) per quarter the constables were able to raise five hundred livres tournois. Until 1824 tax was raised on income; thereafter it was based on capital.[1] Between 1715 and 1830 the wealth of the town increased nearly ten times (from 16,531 quarters to 152,930). Allowing for inflation and changes in the mode of living, Tupper estimated that the income assessed at five hundred quarters in 1715 was fully equal to that assessed at one thousand five hundred quarters in 1840. However, it is not clear that Tupper fully appreciated the economic implications of the system. In 1780 thirty pounds a year interest in the English funds was estimated at forty quarters (i.e. one quarter = 15 shillings); but in the nineteenth century one quarter was reckoned as equalling £1 annual income. The quarter had a rôle analogous to that of gold in the past; it held its value against money.[2]

The structure of St Peter Port society, 1727

Some 394 people were assessed in 1727.[3] Approximately a quarter of these were widows or the guardians of minors; the rest were adult males. No assessment was lower than five quarters, which represented a 'threshold', the poorer ranks of society being exempted from the tax burden. The town population at this date was about 4,350, and so approximately 9% of all the inhabitants were being taxed. But some of the tax-paying females belonged to the families/households of male tax-payers; there is a risk of either underestimating the accumulation of wealth in a few families or of overestimating the spread of wealth if the figure of 9% is given undue weight. What gives a better indication of the structure of society is to observe the proportion of adult males who were being taxed. The sex-ratio and age composition of the town at this date are not accurately known but militia figures and analyses of burial sex-ratios provide a rough guide. Tentative estimates suggest that in 1727 there may have been about six hundred and fifty adult males in St Peter Port. It follows that over half of the adult males were not being taxed.

At the bottom of society were the untaxed poor, with an annual income of less than £2-10-0 (£2.50). Many of these knitted stockings, for which they received 4d a week. These urban poor corresponded to the cottagers and paupers of Gregory King's England who had an average income per head of £2 sterling per annum.[4] Some clue to the standard of living of the Guernsey

Table 6.1 Male taxpayers in St Peter Port, 1727

Assessment in quarters	= Income p.a. £ sterling *	% of male taxpayers	% of adult males
100 +	50 +	18	8 ?
20 +	10 +	42	19 ?
5 +	2.5 +	40	18 ?
not taxed			55 ?

Notes: the estimate 'income p.a. £ sterling' is based on the fact that in 1727 a quarter was valued for rente purposes at £7-10-0 tournois, approximately 10 shillings sterling.

poor is provided by the bread rates laid down in 1727. A loaf of the low quality 'pain à tout' costing one sol (approximately three farthings) had to weigh 1lb 1¹/₈oz. when corn was 5 l.t. a quarter.[5] It would have cost a pauper approximately eighteen and a quarter l.t. (approx. £1-6-8 sterling) to purchase one such loaf each day of the year. It seems that the poor of St Peter Port depended upon occasional labour and charity to survive.

Above the poor was a labouring class assessed as worth between five and twenty quarters. In English terms they had an annual income of between £2-10-0 and £10. An index of the meaning of such a sum is provided by the fact that some fifteen years later it cost 50 to 55 shillings sterling apiece to maintain the poor in the town hospital 'their whole charges and expense included'.[6] In terms of income these tax payers can be compared to the labouring people and outservants of Gregory King's England with an average income per head of £4-10-0 (£4.50) sterling per annum.[7]

Above these, and assessed at twenty quarters up to (but not including) one hundred quarters, were 42% of the tax payers. These people enjoyed the equivalent of an annual income of £10 to just under £50 per annum and were in easier circumstances. Finally, at the top of the pyramid were those assessed at one hundred quarters and more, some 18% of the tax payers, the wealthy with an income of £50 and more per annum.

In making the above analysis twenty quarters and one hundred quarters were used as dividing points. The reason for this is that the distribution of assessments seems to indicate that those levels were considered significant by contemporaries. In *practice* one hundred quarters marked the dividing line between those designated *le Sieur* and their social betters styled *Monsieur*. In this connection it should be noted that there was a correlation between income and status in 1727.[8] Again twenty quarters in *practice* marked the dividing line between those designated *le Sieur* (usually twenty quarters and above) and those designated simply by their name (usually under twenty quarters). Some confirmation for the significance of twenty quarters as a 'boundary' is to be found in a parish decision of 1758 when, during a time of food shortage, it was decided that those assessed at less than twenty quarters should receive assistance. Those assessed at twenty quarters and above were clearly deemed to be able to fend for themselves.[9]

The tax assessments suggest that there was a pyramid of wealth in St Peter Port very similar to that found in early modern English towns, the base very broad, then rising sharply to a narrow peak. Cumulative analysis reveals a concentration of wealth in a relatively few hands.

Table 6.2 Cumulative contribution of all taxpayers, St Peter Port, 1727

		% of tax payers	% of tax
Tax payers assessed	10 qu.	33.2	4.6
up to, and including	15 qu.	40.1	6.3
	20 qu.	51.8	10.0
	50 qu.	73.9	23.3
	90 qu.	82.2	32.8
	160 qu.	90.1	48.7

9.9% of the tax payers were contributing 51.3% of the tax; more approximately, one tenth of the tax payers were contributing half of the tax. The tax assessments reflected income and can be used as indices of income distribution. The St Peter Port figures can be compared with the English estimates of King [1688] and Massie [1759]. King calculated that the top 10% of income recipients accounted for 45.1% of the gross total of income; Massie calculated the same 10% as receiving 40.5% of the gross total of income.[10] The St Peter Port figures suggest a greater concentration of wealth among fewer people. This is not surprising as the distribution of wealth was likely to be particularly uneven in a port town, with its rich *négociants*.[11]

A Lorenz curve showing the cumulative percentage of taxpayers and the cumulative percentage of tax assessments (= incomes) illustrates the unequal distribution (see Fig. 6.1). If distribution were equal, all the points would lie on the diagonal. The nearer the curve is to the rectangular boundary, the more unequal the distribution. This graph can be expressed in terms of a single figure – the Gini coefficient. This measures the area enclosed between the curve and the diagonal as a percentage of the whole triangular area. It varies, therefore, between zero, in the case of complete equality, and unity, at the extreme of inequality. The Gini coefficient for the Lorenz curve representing the 1727 St Peter Port tax assessments is 0.643, which represents considerable inequality.[12] In fact the income distribution in St Peter Port in 1727 was actually more unequal than is suggested by the Gini coefficient because the graph represents solely the *taxpayers* and takes no account of the exempted townsfolk. Were they to be aggregated, the curve would come closer to the rectangular boundary (and the Gini co-efficient closer to 1).

Three status ranks were recognised in the 1727 tax assessments. The lowest designation was simply the taxpayer's name, with no title. Above this

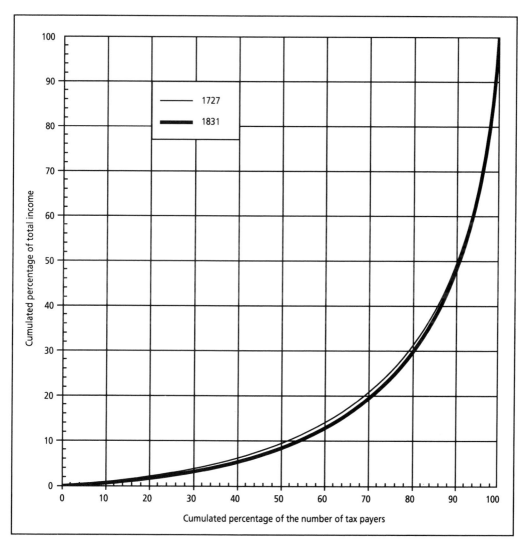

Fig. 6.1: Lorenz curves to illustrate the distribution of income amongst St Peter Port
taxpayers in 1727 and 1831. The Lorenz curve for 1800 is almost precisely the same as that
for 1831

were those styled *le Sieur*. The highest rank was that of *Monsieur/Mr.* Where appropriate, advocates, clergymen and captains were styled with their professional ranks, sometimes with status and professional rank (e.g. *Monsieur l'avocat –*). The frequency of the different designations was as follows:

Table 6.3 The status designation of male taxpayers, St Peter Port, 1727

	As % of male taxpayers
Mr/Mons	23
le Sieur	26
Name only	51
[not taxed]	

The titles given to women in part reflected social standing, in part marital status (no title, dame, madame, demoiselle, veuve; and combinations thereof, e.g. Madame veuve …). As in France under the ancien régime there was often a consciousness of the maiden names of females.[13] With widows it is not always immediately apparent whether their status was determined by birth or by marriage. In this respect an analysis of status in the male sector is less ambiguous. The correlation between wealth and status was as follows:

Table 6.4   The correlation between the status and the income of male taxpayers, St Peter Port, 1727

	Per capita assessment of income in quarters			
Status	Mode	Median	Mean	S. Deviation
Mr/Mons	200	120	181.1	170.0
le Sieur	10	40	55.1	54.1
Name only	10	10	14.2	9.7

It should be noted that the designation Mr/Mons was dependent on lineage and that there were a few relatively poor gentlemen. On the other hand the acquisition of wealth appears to have translated the poor into the realms of le Sieur and so there were no wealthy taxpayers designated by name alone. The following chart attempts to summarise the correlation between tax assessments, status designations and occupations; and to give some idea of the composition and structure of St Peter Port society in 1727.

Table 6.5 Wealth, status and occupations in St Peter Port, 1727

Quarters	Status designation	Occupations represented
500 +		gentlemen
400 +		merchants
300 +	Mr/Monsieur	shipowners
200 +		captain
100 +		church minister
90 +		
80 +		
70 +		
60 +		advocate
50 +	le Sieur	
40 +		church minister
30 +		
25 +		
20 +		shipwright
15 +		
10 +		captain, carrier,
	No title	cooper,
		master carpenter
5 +		sailmaker

This table initially suggests that there were three ranks in St Peter Port society in 1727. However, it needs to be remembered that the analysis above represents the taxed section of the community. Below the taxpayers designated by name alone were those exempted from paying tax. It is more accurate to consider St Peter Port society of the early eighteenth century as having four, not three, ranks. Such a social and economic structure has affinities with that found in eighteenth century French towns. At the top of the third estate in that society were gentlemen and *négociants*, 'l'élite roturière'. Below those came 'la classe moyenne', advocates, doctors, notaries and bourgeois, designated *le Sieur*. The third rank was comprised of the 'petite bourgeoisie', an artisanat referred to by name alone. In the fourth and lowest rank were 'le menu peuple' who were inadequately clothed and lived on bread, soup and water. In *ancien régime* Paris 'le menu peuple' formed some 53% of the total population, while in Lyons they comprised 39%.[14]

Residential patterns in St Peter Port, 1727

An analysis of the tax assessments reveals a concentration of wealth – aggregate and individual – in the centre of the town, with over half of the wealthiest inhabitants living in the three vingtaines of Carrefour, La Grande Rue and Rue du Pilori (Pillory). Several of the houses in these vingtaines were insured for five hundred to a thousand pounds, sometimes the contents being insured for a sum equal to that of the house.[15] The poorer vingtaines generally lay on the periphery of the town. It should be noted, however, that there were some poorer areas near the heart of the town, rue de l'Eglise in particular.

The wealthiest vingtaine was the Carrefour, situated halfway between the town church to the south and the Plaiderie (court house) to the north, and close to the harbour to the east. This vingtaine boasted sixteen tax assessments of one hundred quarters or more and was inhabited by some of the great *négociants* – Daniel de Lisle, Nicolas Dobrée and Thomas Le Marchant. The next concentration of wealth was in La Grande Rue, the site of the street market. Here there were thirteen tax assessments of one hundred quarters or more. Rue du Pilori was the third wealthiest vingtaine in terms of aggregate wealth and second in terms of per capita wealth but the neighbouring vingtaine of rue de l'Eglise was relatively poor, ranking eighth. The combined vingtaines of Cimetière-Beauregard had just three inhabitants assessed above one hundred quarters, of whom one was Mr Pierre Carey 'de la brasserie', assessed at five hundred and fifty quarters. This Mr Carey was not only a brewer but also a *négociant* and shipowner. Most of the other residents of this area seem to have been 'classe moyenne' or 'petite bourgeoisie'. Fountain Street housed a few merchant-shipowners together with a number of artisans. The vingtaines Contrée Mansell- Hauteville- Mt Durand-de Putron, and St Jacques-Couture- Bouet, and Truchot lay outside the 'barrières' of the old town; they were still essentially rural and were relatively poor. It is essential, however, to stress that there were some wealthy individuals who lived in the 'poor' vingtaines; and, conversely, some less wealthy artisans were to be found in the 'rich' vingtaines. Thus, the 'poor' vingtaine of the Truchot could also boast three inhabitants assessed at three hundred quarters or above. Nonetheless, a pattern emerges: a higher than average number of wealthy townspeople lived in the three central vingtaines. Here there was a concentration of merchants and gentlemen, together with some artisans. The 'outer' vingtaines were relatively poorer and contained more *petite bourgeoisie* and probably many of the unassessed *menu peuple*. The picture suggested by the data is similar to that argued by Schwarz in his analysis of social class and social geography in London and one has to recognise, as Peter Borsay suggests, that 'any tendency towards segregation was only a tendency, *since all parishes accommodated a significant sprinkling of the various tax-paying categories*'.[16]

Changes between 1727 and 1800

As we have seen, the period between 1727 and 1800 saw considerable growth in population (from 4,350 to approximately 11,000) and assessed wealth (from 24,415 quarters to 94,455 quarters). The number of taxpayers

The vingtaines
arranged in rank
order of wealth
(based on mean
per caput assessment)
1. Carrefour
2. Pilori
3. Grande Rue
4. Truchot
5. St Jacques –
   Couture – Bouet
6. Berthelot
7. Fontaine
8. Eglise
9. Cimètiere –
   Beauregard
10. Contrée-Mansell –
    Hauteville –
    Mt Durand
11. Pollet
12. de Putron

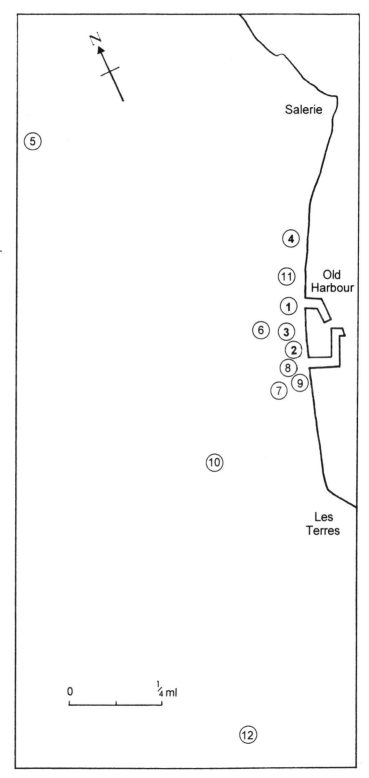

Fig. 6.2: The ranking of the *vingtaines* in St Peter Port, 1727 (see Appendix 23)

rose from 394 in 1727 to 696 in 1800. The population was 2.5 times larger and the taxed urban wealth 3.9 greater. The Lorenz Curve representing the tax assessments of 1800 has a Gini coefficient of 0.660 as against 0.643 in 1727. This demonstrates that among the taxpayers of St Peter Port in 1800 there was marginally greater inequality of distribution of tax assessments – and therefore of income – in 1800 than there had been in 1727. Initially this seems to confirm Professor Hoskins' hypothesis that 'as the average wealth of a community rises ... the inequality in the distribution of that wealth itself increases.'[17] And yet on closer inspection the shift was minimal – as may easily be seen from a graphical representation (see Fig 6.1).

Table 6.6   The six highest St Peter Port tax assessments, 1780

	quarters	x 20 = capital, in sterling	x 14 = capital in livres t.
John Carey	1950	£39,000	546,000
Elizée Tupper	1850	37,000	518,000
Nicolas Maingy senr	1650	33,000	462,000
John Brock's heirs	1420	28,400	397,600
Pierre Mourant	1400	28,000	392,000
Richard de Beauvoir	1020	20,400	285,600

Source: COf A24

Between 1727 and 1800 the merchant families of St Peter Port prospered; by 1780 there were six taxpayers assessed at over one thousand quarters. A note in the tax book for that year indicates that £30 a year interest in the English funds was estimated at forty quarters and £1,000 capital at fifty quarters. Whereas the leading merchants of St Peter Port in the early eighteenth century compared with the 'second class' English merchants of King (1688), the leading St Peter Port merchants of the late eighteenth century came close to the 'first class' English merchants of Massie (1759).[18] The St Peter Port fortunes are not comparable with those of some of the East India Company merchants in London, nor with those of the millionaires (livres tournois) of Nantes. Nevertheless, they do represent considerable wealth. In some instances it needs to be noted that there were other highly assessed members of the family, in addition to the chief taxpayer, and that the combined wealth of some families was very great. Marriages created wealthy partnerships. Jean Carey's success was due in part to his alliance with 'Madame veuve Mr James Le Ray', the widow of one of the town's most successful *négociants* of the 1760s. The characteristic of St Peter Port in the eighteenth century is that there was no one family of enormous wealth that totally dominated the mercantile scene but rather a cluster of wealthy families. By 1800 there were fourteen persons rated at 1,000 quarters or higher, the wealthiest being the *négociant* Elisha Tupper, assessed at 2,450 quarters (nearly £50,000 in capital by the 1780 criteria).

The fact that there was a grouping of wealthy families is of significance as it led to conspicuous consumption of a competitive nature. Such behaviour stimulated the urban economy and benefitted the ranks of the bourgeois and artisans who supplied goods and services to the upper ranks. This was a commercial world in which the hard-working craftsman could rise. Guillaume Henri, a silversmith, appeared in the tax books in the 1720s with no title and assessed at twenty quarters. By the 1740s he was rated at forty quarters and by 1755 he had achieved the designation *le Sieur*. Between 1757 and 1763 his assessment rose from fifty quarters to one hundred quarters and he had changed residence from the Cimetière-Beauregard area to Fountain Street. He clearly did well during the Seven Years War, perhaps thanks to the nature of wartime trade or to profitable investment in privateering.[19]

Guillaume Henri's rise was not unique. The flourishing nature of the port trades helped other craftsmen. Peter Lihou the cooper held £150 worth of 3% Consols in 1784, the Dobrées of London acting as his agent/banker.[20] Jean Guerin, cooper, was assessed at ten quarters in 1757 but by 1761 was designated *le Sieur* and was assessed at fifteen quarters. Similarly, Daniel Delisle, carpenter, rose from an assessment of ten quarters in 1756 to an assessment of twenty-five quarters in 1761.[21]

The rising wealth of the inhabitants of St Peter Port was accompanied by, and probably helped to cause, phases of social tension as sectors of the community worried about their status designation. One such phase occurred shortly after the Seven Years War. In 1765 a member of the Le Marchant family complained that he should receive the designation *écuyer* when his name was written in the tax book. On 15 June 1765 the Royal Court issued instructions that the jurats, Procureur and Controle du Roi should be accorded the designation *écuyer* (the bailiff was already so styled). The constables and douzaine of St Peter Port resisted the instruction of the Royal Court, arguing that the latter was arrogating to itself a power that properly belonged to the Crown and not to the Court.[22] Eventually the parish authorities capitulated and entered the designation *écuyer* as instructed.

This manifestation of 'gentrification' was accompanied by an ordonnance of the Royal Court in 1766 which forbade 'mécaniques et gens de basse condition' to participate in cockfights, on the grounds that the gambling losses, waste of time and drunkenness associated with the sport were detrimental to family life.[23] However, gentlemen and those assessed at fifty quarters and above were allowed to attend cockfights. This *ordonnance* can be construed as having established a boundary between the *peuple* and the 'public', the 'haves' and the 'have nots'.[24]

As St Peter Port became busier with its entrepôt trade and larger garrison, the town constables and island authorities found it harder to maintain law and order. The authorities were confronted by a series of problems. Some strangers had little respect for the constables and were quite prepared to engage in altercations.[25] Some of the disorderliness had undertones of class tensions. For example, in December 1797 troublesome boys hurled 'immondices & saletés' at the gentry who were entering the assembly rooms.[26]

The presence in the town from the 1780s of large numbers of soldiers and sailors encouraged the running of disorderly houses and brothels.[27] Wartime prizes in the harbour attracted thieves; and shops became the target of 'smash and grab' raids.[28] The 1790s were particularly difficult because, in addition to the usual crowd of English smugglers, sailors and soldiers milling around the town, there were also companies of French royalists and Russian soldiers garrisoned temporarily on the island. Tempers sometimes ran high, with duel and death ensuing.[29] The authorities reacted to these difficulties by trying to make the streets safer. They had installed oil-lamps by 1799.[30]

The provision of assistance to the poor was another urban problem. It has already been remarked that the poorest inhabitants of St Peter Port lived on the breadline.[31] The price of bread cereals and the state of the urban economy determined the number who were in need. In the late 1720s and the 1730s St Peter Port experienced some economic difficulties; for over a decade the aggregate taxable wealth of the town did not increase.[32] During these years the parish frequently had nearly two hundred poor people to support. A weekly allowance was paid, sometimes amounting annually to upwards of £500 sterling. This provision was funded partly from contributions made at the church, partly by legacies, partly by bequests of *rentes*, and finally by a tax specifically for the maintenance of the poor in St Peter Port. In addition taxes were raised in several years to pay for the importation of corn and to subsidise the feeding of the poor.[33]

Different strategies were employed to try to reduce the growing burden of supporting the poor. In March 1730 the 'chefs de famille' decided in favour of 'badging'. Youths and men up to forty years old were to be provided with 'un bonnet, un casaquir, une paire de culote le tout fait de carisett bleu, & une chemise blanche', bearing the mark of the parish to distinguish them ('St Pierre Port'). The design of clothes for those above forty was different and was not to carry the badging. Girls and women to the age of forty were to be provided with 'une coiffe blanche, un corset, une jupe, de carisett bleu, & une chemise blanche' badged in a manner similar to the men's outfit. Women over forty were excused the badging. Material was to be ordered from England sufficient to clothe twelve or fourteen of each sex.[34]

Badging sought to stigmatise the poor and it may have controlled the situation for a limited period.[35] But from 1734 onwards the problem seems to have increased and the parish had to raise 4,000 livres tournois annually for poor relief. Part of the problem was that insufficient alms were being collected in the church. There were complaints that the poor misspent their relief money in drunkenness and riotous living, instead of maintaining their families. It was asserted that 'the children were usually left by their parents destitute about the streets, and brought up to all manner of vices, without any care taken of their education'.[36]

In the late 1730s the town merchants initiated a more ambitious plan to control the problem of the poor and founded a hospital (i.e. workhouse). The terms for entrance were sufficiently rigorous that of the two hundred who received the alms of the parish 'not above seventy' decided to enter the hospital when it was opened.[37] In 1751 Dicey recorded that the one hundred and twenty inmates then lodged in the hospital included 'mad, naturals, lame, sick, bed-ridden, lying-in women, infirm old people, and destitute poor children, left by sailors and soldiers, besides the children belonging to the parish (whereof several are bastards)'. The hospital gave relief to the poor *and* served as an instrument of control: 'several lewd women, incapable of subsisting honestly' were also detained there in 1751.[38]

Much of the money subscribed for the building of the hospital came from merchants and the hospital had a work ethic. The initial regulations [1741] envisaged a daily régime as follows:

Table 6.7 The daily régime of the Town Hospital

	Summer	Winter
Rise:	6 a.m.	7 a.m.
Breakfast:	7 a.m.	8 a.m.
Work:	7 a.m. – 7 p.m.	8 a.m. – 6 p.m.
Lunch:	1 p.m.	1 p.m.
Supper:	7 p.m.	6 p.m.
Bed:	9 p.m.	8 p.m.

Source: Priaulx 29121/408C, Watkins Ms vol 3, Town Hospital rules

The inmates were assigned work that was useful to the town economy and, in particular, to the merchants. The men and boys picked oakum, made twine, laid cordage and cast lead. The women spun wool and the girls knitted stockings; in the 1750s Mr Jacques Combeau, a master weaver from Cherbourg, organised textile manufacture in the hospital. Depending on the season, the inmates helped at haymaking, apple-picking and grave-digging.[39] Children of an appropriate age were farmed out to town tradesmen. Between 1743 and 1757 some 83 were apprenticed as coopers, tailors, smiths, servants, gardeners, carpenters, stone-cutters and, most frequently, as sailors.[40] Eleven girls and five boys were taken from the hospital in March 1752 by Captain James Flight to be indentured in Boston (America).[41]

The town hospital eased the problem of poverty but could not entirely solve it. Further measures that assisted were the foundation of a similar workhouse for the rural poor in the Câtel parish (1751); and the deportation back to England (or France) of any stranger who seemed likely to become a burden on the Guernsey taxpayer. Finally, the problem of poverty became less burdensome as the town became richer. The entrepôt trades created employment which reduced the pool of the underemployed. Referring to the number admitted to the hospital in the late eighteenth century Berry commented that 'the Island being prosperous, the number had been on the decline, and was little more than one hundred and forty-four'.[42] Moreover, the wealthier the town grew, the lighter became the burden of supporting the poor. In 1740 the authorities raised nearly four thousand livres tournois for the poor on inhabitants assessed at 21,894 quarters; in 1790 over seven thousand livres tournois were raised for the hospital on 77,100 quarters. In 1740 it was necessary to levy 3 sous 6 deniers per quarter; but in 1790 nearly twice as much money could be raised by a tax set at 2 sous per quarter – almost half the rate imposed in 1740.[43]

Thomas Dicey, writing in 1751, was very impressed by the hospital. He felt that it was 'a very laudable undertaking brought to perfection within these few years' and he accordingly devoted a supplement of fourteen pages to a description of it. He hoped that the St Peter Port hospital might be 'regularly imitated' in every county in England.[44] The standard of administration of the hospital fell in the late eighteenth century and reforms were implemented in the early nineteenth century.[45] In general, however, the hospital seems to have been an effective institution in the eighteenth century.

Changing residential patterns, 1727–1800

Between 1727 and 1800 the status of the town vingtaines changed considerably. In 1727 the Pollet contributed only 2.2% towards the town taxes and in this respect ranked eleventh among the vingtaines. The Pollet taxpayers were among the least wealthy of the town, approximately half being assessed at ten quarters. But this vingtaine (together with the Truchot) was developed by the merchants in the 1740s and 1750s and by 1800 the Pollet ranked third in the order of aggregate wealth, fourth in per capita tax assessment.[46]

Extensive growth occurred in the 'peripheral' vingtaines in the latter part of the eighteenth century. As late as the 1760s Hauteville was one of the poorest vingtaines. Yet by 1800 it had become the residence of several merchants and had risen to fourth in terms of aggregate wealth. Berthelot Street, with its new urban developments to the west of the old town, had emerged by 1800 as the vingtaine with the highest mean tax assessment. This was the area to which the rich were gravitating. From the 1780s onwards there was a shift of wealthy inhabitants away from the mediaeval town centre

The vingtaines
arranged in rank
order of wealth
(based on mean
per caput
assessment)
1. Berthelot
2. Grande Rue
3. Carrefour
4. Pollet
5. Cimetière –
    Beauregard
6. Truchot –
    Glatney
7. Hauteville –
    de Putron
8. Eglise – Pilori
9. Fontaine
10. Contrée-
    Mansell –
    Mt Durand
11. St Jacques –
    Couture

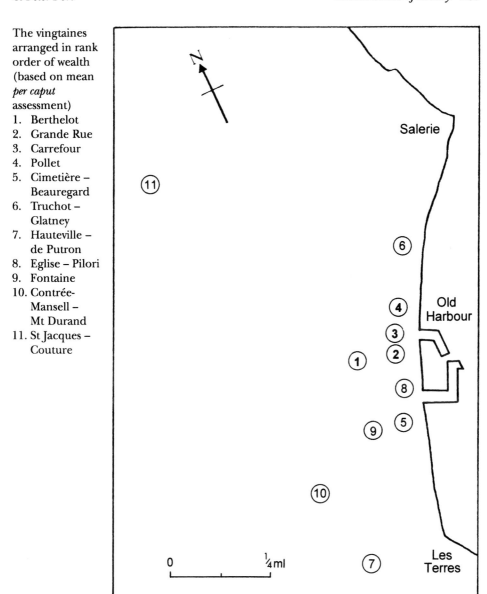

Fig. 6.3: The ranking of the vingtaines in St Peter Port, 1800 (see Appendix 24)

to the periphery, a process similar to the suburbanisation that occurred in many contemporary English towns. As the periphery became wealthier, so the Carrefour and Grande Rue became relatively poorer. These vingtaines had contributed 37.6% of the tax revenue raised in 1727 and 41.9% in 1766 but by 1800 they contributed only 26.7%. An even greater decline occurred in the central vingtaines of Eglise and Pilori.

Changes between 1800 and 1831

Between 1800 and 1831 the population of St Peter Port increased from approximately 11,000 to 13,893; the aggregate tax assessment rose from 94,455 quarters to 143,025 quarters; and the number of tax assessments in 1831 was 824. The mean assessment in 1831 was 173.6 quarters as compared to 135.7 quarters in 1800, but the mode remained constant at twenty quarters. The Lorenz curve for the tax assessments of 1831 has a Gini coefficient of 0.658, almost identical to that for 1800 (0.660).

The values of the old seigneurial world continued to be challenged by the wealth of the *nouveaux riches*. Success in trade elevated some ordinary men to the ranks of the wealthy. This was resented by the 'old families' and led to exclusion strategies. In 1815 Berry, an English resident, observed that the self-made man unable to boast of the 'dignified ancestry of jurat, douzainier, or constable' could scarcely ever join 'what is called the first class'. The divisions were repeated at every level in society. Below the merchant came the tradesman. Then, 'sinking in gradations that might almost puzzle an able mathematician to define, the lower orders of people degenerate into a state of abject servility'.[47]

The tensions of the era 1800–31 are precisely those adumbrated by de Tocqueville in his analysis of the status anxiety engendered by the fading of aristocracy and the challenge of money and democracy. 'Secret hostilities then arise in the community.' The same individual simultaneously seeks to raise himself into a higher circle and to defend himself 'against the intrusion of those below him'.[48] A correspondent to *The Star* grumbled that persons in Guernsey 'arrogate to themselves titles, with impunity, to which they are not in the least entitled' and that whereas rich and well bred farmers and tradesmen were called *le Sieur*, others of mean and low birth were honoured by the title *Monsieur*. The correspondent hoped that the Royal Court would establish proper rules or abolish the custom of admitting titles altogether to diminish 'that spirit of discontent which, on this subject, is so very prevalent'.[49]

Changing residential patterns in the early nineteenth century

After 1800 the status of taxpayers was no longer inscribed in the parochial tax registers. With the disintegration of the traditional structure and vocabulary of rank, the élite felt compromised. They found a new form

The vingtaines
arranged in rank
order of wealth
(based on mean
per caput
assessment)
1. Grange
2. Hauteville
3. Rue des
    Forges
4. Ville-Neuve
5. Vauvert
6. Pollet
7. Glatney
8. St Jacques
9. Marché
10. Eglise

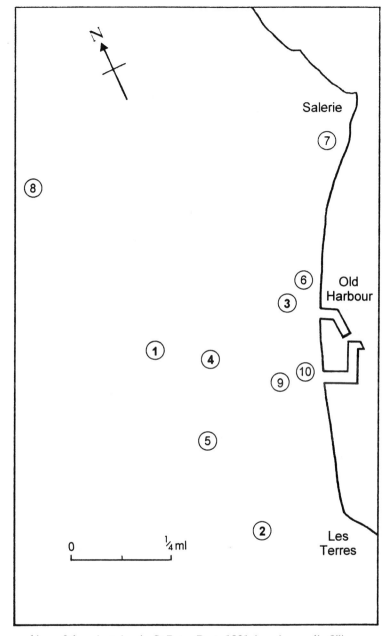

Fig. 6.4: The ranking of the *vingtaines* in St Peter Port, 1831 (see Appendix 25)

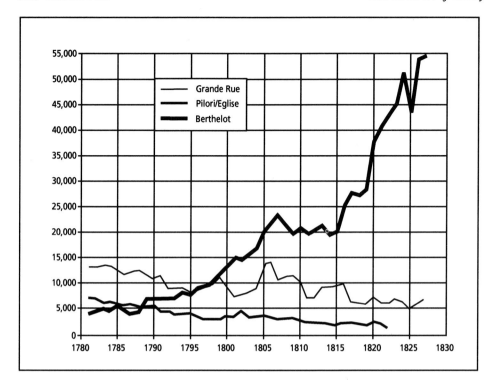

Fig. 6.5: The aggregate tax assessments of three vingtaines, 1781–1827. The central
vingtaines of Grande Rue and Pilori/Eglise slowly declined as the élite moved to peripheral
vingtaines such as Berthelot. (After 1822 Pilori/Eglise were aggregated with other
vingtaines. A different principle of tax assessment was used in 1825.)

of social stratification in physical segregation. Between 1800 and 1831 they
moved in increasing numbers from the mediaeval centre of St Peter Port to
the Grange, New Town and Hauteville. It would be mistaken to interpret this
move as solely a quest for social segregation; there were good health reasons
for seeking the suburbs.[50] Nevertheless, by 1831 the élite enjoyed greater
isolation than they had in 1727. This can be demonstrated by an
examination of the indices of dissimilarity and segregation [Appendix 23
and Appendix 25]. By 1831 there was a concentration of high income
residents in the Grange, New Town and Hauteville. Only two low income
taxpayers were to be found in the Grange, and fewer than 10% of the
taxpayers in New Town and Hauteville fell within that category.

Conclusion

Between 1727 and 1831 St Peter Port society re-organised itself. The
traditional vocabulary of rank collapsed; and the élite moved from the town
centre to the suburbs. This re-arrangement of spatial structure occurred in
other eighteenth century towns. Dr Baigent has suggested that residential
patterns in Bristol in the 1770s were transitional between the pre-industrial

and the modern. 'The central parishes were wealthy and housed many commercial and professional men as they always had done, but they were being eclipsed as the highest status areas of the city by the new residential suburbs.'[51] Dr Baigent has discussed the Bristol evidence in terms of a shift from *Gemeinschaft* to *Gesellschaft*. Like several other urban studies the work on Bristol is based on a single source of information and cannot capture the dynamic forces. The St Peter Port data are of interest precisely because they furnish material for *une histoire sérielle* in which spatial re-organisation can be related to economic and social developments.

It was in the 1760s that the commercial success of the entrepôt really disturbed the traditional order. As artisans prospered, the upper ranks asserted their superiority by employing a dichotomous classification of society rather than the traditional 'four rank' model. As we have seen, the community was divided by *ordonnance* into those who could legally engage in cock-fighting and those who could not. The legislation emphasised the divide between the rich and the poor, between élite and plebeian. At the same time the upper ranks re-inforced their status by arrogating the title *écuyer* (Esquire).

The Carrefour and Grande Rue continued to be the most select residential areas during the 1760s and 1770s. Le Sieur Pierre Mourant, assessed at 160 quarters, moved from the Pollet to the Grande Rue in 1772 in what seems to have been a 'betterment' step. In 1776 he was wealthier and his designation was revised upwards from *le Sieur* to *Ecuyer*. Mourant remained in the Grande Rue until the 1780s. He then moved to his newly built house at Candie, on the outskirts of the town. Mourant's move marks a watershed for he was one of the first of the wealthy *négociants* to leave the town centre. Unlike many of the *négociants* Mourant had no ties to an ancestral home in the Grande Rue. A house move was easier for a 'new man'. His motives are not known. He may have wished to escape the crowds of working people thronging the Grande Rue; or he may have wished to demonstrate his commercial success by a show of conspicuous consumption. In one sense his motives are unimportant; it was his *deed* that was significant. His handsome new house and extensive gardens constituted – deliberately or accidentally – a challenge to the other *négociants*.

The influx of English migrants in the 1780s and 1790s accelerated the collapse of the traditional *schema* of ranks. There was no automatic congruence between the migrants' perception of their own status and the islanders' evaluation of the '*gastarbeiter*'. These social frictions were exacerbated by economic changes. The migrants were working in a booming port town in which factories established new forms of organisation.

Societal changes in St Peter Port were contemporaneous with transformations elsewhere. The *ancien régime* vocabulary of ranks was abolished by the revolutionaries in France in the 1790s. After 1800 the constables of St Peter Port followed suit, listing just the names of taxpayers.

Distinction was no longer proclaimed by the vocabulary of status. The only way in which the town élite could now assert superiority was by the public display of wealth. The building of grand new houses on the outskirts of the town was the ultimate expression of economic power. It also offered the aristocracy the opportunity to avoid the urban proletariat. From c.1810 onwards the wealthy moved in increasing numbers to the new residential suburbs and by 1831 they were living in greater segregation than they had in 1727. Their move may have been accelerated by two factors. First, with the collapse of the entrepôt trade, harbour-side houses lost some of their economic significance. Secondly, the development between 1790 and 1820 of the New Town, with neat houses for the middling classes, may have spurred the élite to modernise.

The town taxpayers were much wealthier in 1831 than they had been in 1727. And yet curiously the Gini co-efficient remained virtually constant throughout this era. The pattern of distribution of wealth had not appreciably altered over the century despite the rapid economic changes that had occurred. This does not fit easily with the prevailing theory about urban development in the eighteenth century. It is generally understood that in the early modern period (sixteenth–seventeenth centuries) urban society resembled an inverted T – 'a low podium containing some 95% of the population, while balanced on top of this was a thin skyscraper of more wealthy people'. That contrasted with the modern structure of society – a 'lozenge or diamond in its general shape'. Dr McInnes viewed early eighteenth century society 'as being about half way between these two models'. The change occurred because the middle sections of society were growing; this altered the inverted T into a 'pyramidal or conical' shape. 'The middle band was thicker ... but not so broad as in the lozenge shaped society'.[52]

The St Peter Port data reveal no shift in the structure of wealth distribution between 1727 and 1831. The number of those belonging to the middle sections of society did increase; but as there were also more wealthy taxpayers the profile of societal structure did not alter. It is possible that the greater occupational specialisation of the late eighteenth century has created the mirage of a disproportionately larger middle class. Peter Borsay has commented: 'A larger and more diverse middling stratum would seem to fill the space between rich and poor, and lead to the emergence of a less polarised society. *Whether in reality this was the case is debatable.*'[53]

In the following chapters the development of sociability and the physical transformation of the town will be examined in greater detail. Chapter Seven explores, *inter alia*, the ways in which new forms of sociability mitigated the disruptive impact of the entrepôt economy. Chapter Eight sets the spatial re-organisation of St Peter Port society against the background of topographical, legal and environmental determinants.

7

The Growth of Sociability

In the sixteenth and seventeenth centuries the social life of St Peter Port was relatively simple and integrated. However, with the development of the entrepôt in the eighteenth century, the town became more sophisticated. With its clubs, promenade, assembly, theatre and circulating libraries St Peter Port increasingly resembled English provincial towns in the expression of its forms of sociability. Three inter-related factors promoted change: greater wealth; immigration; and the increasing influence of English manners. The establishment of a larger garrison at Fort George in the 1780s accentuated the impact of English culture. In St Peter Port, as in other colonial towns of the nascent British Empire, the officer class set a certain style and standard to the local population.

Change engendered social tensions and problems. Seigneurial traditions were dissolved in the entrepôt economy; cultural differentiation emphasised the divide between rich and poor; and immigrants brought different creeds. By the nineteenth century St Peter Port's population was divided by linguistic, religious and cultural differences. There was little cohesion between such disparate groups as the English labourers lodged in slums near the harbour, the patois-speaking Guernsey women working in the markets, the Guernsey élite living on the outskirts of the town, and the English gentry, sometimes of reduced means, living in New Town. Challenged by colonial dominance from above, and by English immigrants below, the élite of St Peter Port tried to assert its hegemony in religion and education. In a reaction against English culture it resurrected the feudal chevauchée and explored antiquarian byways of island history; but even in this the Guernsey gentry were imitating the English cult of the gothic.

Social life in St Peter Port c.1700–c.1750

At the end of the seventeenth century the institutions of St Peter Port society seem to have been working together with a degree of harmony. The apparent absence of overt conflict can be attributed to the oligarchic hegemony of the merchants who simultaneously enjoyed political power, economic strength and the prestige of high status[1] *Ordonnances* summarily made by jurats in their capacity as legislators were subsequently enforced by the very same jurats in their capacity as judges. The jurats were merchants or from the families of merchants; thus political, legal and economic decisions were made by, and for, the same interest group. This power was legitimised by an ideology based on traditional practice and it was reasonably easy for the ruling élite to preserve its authority.

Apart from the small English garrison and a few immigrants, the vast majority of the town inhabitants were francophone. There was just one established (Anglican) parish church and it enjoyed a spiritual monopoly as there were no Nonconformist or Catholic groups resident in St Peter Port in the early modern period. As late as 1749 Samuel Bonamy was able to write that 'the Church of England is the only communion among us, there being not one dissenter to my knowledge, either protestant or papist'.[2] The church maintained morality both directly, by condemning sinners on Sundays, and indirectly, by exercising control over the schools in the parish. Conformity of behaviour was also achieved by the training of the able-bodied men of the parish in the Guernsey militia. In church, school and militia the governing élite held both the instruments to promote a particular code of cultural values and the sanctions to discipline those who did not conform to social norms. In the terms of sociologists stability and continuity were achieved by cultural reproduction.[3] Samuel Bonamy rejoiced that he and his fellow Guernseymen were 'perfectly united' in their sentiments of religion and government.[4] 'Pluralism' was considered undesirable in the traditional world. Yet already by the early Georgian period some of the agencies of cultural pluralism were being imported.

Although there is very little evidence about the social life of the common people in the early eighteenth century, that of the urban élite can be reconstructed to some extent. By the 1720s and 1730s leading members of the political and economic sectors met regularly together in club and assembly, enjoying a sociability that was in some degree modelled on, and fashioned by, English conventions. Membership of *La Société de la Chambre* was exclusive, being limited to seventeen, and constituted a small clique of the most powerful men in Guernsey. Members included a bailiff, a procureur, a controller, a doctor, a divine, jurats and merchants, the surnames representing a roll-call of the leading insular families of the eighteenth century.[5] The club provided facilities for dining and for recreation (cards and backgammon) but, perhaps most importantly, it subscribed to English magazines and newspapers. A rule stipulated that the newspapers were to be opened *inside* the club and that they were not to be removed from there.[6] It seems reasonable to conjecture that the *Société de la Chambre* was where the St Peter Port 'establishment' exchanged new ideas of fashionability.

Guernsey did not possess a landed gentry in the English sense of the word. An 'estate' of fifty acres was vast by island standards. Nevertheless the letters and journals of wealthy Guernsey families suggest that by George I's reign it was a common practice to spend the summer months in the country and to reside in St Peter Port for the rest of the year. Associations such as the 'Public Assembly for Dancing' – founded in the 1720s or 1730s – met during the winter months.[7] This mirrored the practice of English provincial capitals and shire towns where, as Peter Borsay has shown, most cultural activities were packed into the 'winter season'.[8] Already, then, in the early eighteenth century the traditional patterns of sociability were being modified and the Guernsey gentry were adopting English ways. But the changes were limited; the major transformations came in the second half of the eighteenth century.

The transformation of social life in the late eighteenth century

The social life of St Peter Port was transformed in the second half of the eighteenth century. The extensive development of the entrepôt in the 1740s soon brought considerable wealth to the merchants of St Peter Port and this directly accelerated change in the character of the town's society and culture. There was much surplus money. Some index of the capital accumulation is afforded by the fact that the inhabitants of St Peter Port had 'upwards of two million pounds' invested in the British funds by the early nineteenth century.[9] The upper ranks of St Peter Port society had increasing opportunities to indulge in consumerism in this era of the commercialisation of leisure. There was a greater demand for fashionable goods, for entertainments, for more and better services.

But the development of the entrepôt had a much deeper impact on urban society. By stimulating the retail and service sectors, and by attracting a large number of migrants, it drew St Peter Port more deeply into the British colonial system. Initially this was an economic phenomenon based on the greater volume of trade between St Peter Port and the English ports. However the colonial status of St Peter Port was re-emphasised by the building of a fort and barracks at Fort George, in the 1780s, and the strengthening of the garrison. This brought a large number of British officers to the town with important social consequences. Technically the garrison was in Guernsey not to impose its rule on the islanders but rather to defend the island against the threat of French invasion. Nevertheless, the presence of a large British army contingent was a colonial phenomenon and exercised a considerable impact on the urban culture. As Professor King has observed: 'the life style and cultural behaviour of local populations may be modified as they emulate the ruling colonial élite'.[10]

By the mid-eighteenth century 'most people of fashion' in Guernsey lived in St Peter Port.[11] Urban sociability increased in the second half of the eighteenth century with the establishment of a formal promenade (1760), the founding of masonic lodges and clubs, the introduction of the printing press (c.1775), the building of new assembly rooms (1780-1), the establishment of the Theatre Royal (c.1795) and the opening of academies and circulating libraries. By the late eighteenth century St Peter Port resembled some of the spas and resorts of England, such as Southampton and Weymouth. Indeed, there is some evidence that as early as 1795 a small number of English visitors were coming to the town in the summer season as tourists.[12] During these years St Peter Port was a community undergoing rapid economic and cultural trans-formation. It was a commercial entrepôt developing as a gentry town; its French-speaking community was being assimilated into an English colonial system; and the urban population was increasingly a mixture of native islanders and English migrants. The social life of the period developed amidst these contending pressures. The next paragraphs trace the growth of conspicuous consumption and the quest for fashionability among the wealthy. The élite created arenas of display and spent more of their leisure time in associations. But as St Peter Port became more fashionable it became increasingly the town of the gentry. Cultural and social divides became deeper.

Conspicuous consumption

The patterns of conspicuous consumption and the quest for fashionability were clearly influenced by women, especially merchants' wives. Jack Dobrée joked that as he proposed to remain a bachelor he had money enough to lead a lazy life.[13] The married merchants could find themselves involved in considerable domestic expenses. In April 1766 Peter Lihou wrote to his London suppliers, Messrs. Peter & Peter Perchard, and expressed satisfaction with everything that had been sent 'except the coffee pot which my wife thinks is not fashionable'.[14] In 1771 Lihou wrote to William de Jersey in London requesting that some material be dyed green 'le plus à la mode'. The stuff was to be made into 'un petit veste & culotte à un enfant de 4 à 5 ans' along with a matching 'petite cote'. Lihou's tailor would be able to advise on the type of material 'la plus propre pour l'effet'. The outfit was to be accompanied by a hat 'des plus à la mode' for about a guinea.[15]

These episodes from merchant Lihou's domestic life illustrate the growth of conspicuous consumption in St Peter Port. But more than that, they reveal that costly goods were not in themselves sufficiently prestigious, the coffee pot and child's clothing had to be in *fashionable* styles. Status could be established by projecting an image of affluence and of taste. Expensive items were not ultimately sufficient. *Taste* could bespeak 'the elegant self-assurance of inherited wealth' and create a distance from 'the flashy arrogance of the nouveaux riches'.[16]

The quest for the costly and distinguished manifested itself particularly in the design of houses, the choice of clothing and the selection of food. The wealthy merchant Isaac Dobrée ordered outfits embroidered in gold and silver from Paris, the capital that was the ultimate *arbiter elegantiae*.[17] Later on English fashions prevailed. A nineteenth century commentator felt that the islanders had copied too much from England in their style of living; 'a soirée à la Française would become them more than champagne dinners and suppers, which often partake quite as much of ostentation as of hospitality'.[18] The merchants of St Peter Port not only had the necessary capital for lavish living but were also well placed to secure choice commodities. Several merchant families commissioned dinner sets from England and from China, each plate bearing the family coat of arms.[19]

Arenas of display – the promenade and the assembly

The desire to project an image of wealth and status accelerated the development of locations and situations for display. The promenade at the New Ground was an opportunity 'to see and be seen', a means by which polite society 'could establish and re-inforce its sense of identity'.[20] Elizabeth Ham likened the promenade at the New Ground, St Peter Port, to the Esplanade at Weymouth 'in so far as it was the general resort of the Naval and Military Officers, who were the real magnets, though the bands were the ostensible ones, that drew gaily dressed Belles to the evening Promenade on the New Ground'.[21]

The other principal arena of display was the assembly.[22] In the 1770s this was held weekly in a large room at the bottom of the Pollet.[23] Correspondents wrote of the brilliance and gaiety of the social life and contrasted the 'carelessness and freedom of the Guernsey assemblies' with the 'stiffness and formality' of Jersey society.[24] The assembly was pre-eminently a place for the young and the unmarried. In January 1778 Mrs Dumaresq complained that at the last assembly she 'was the only married person there of both men and women'. The absence of parents and chaperones was, perhaps, an expression of the greater freedom granted to children in the eighteenth century to choose their own marriage partner.[25]

In 1777 the planned construction of a new market provided the opportunity for the building of a spacious upper room to serve as an assembly hall. To this end a sum of one thousand pounds was subscribed by twenty-three members of leading families. These founding members held shares and controlled the running of 'the Rooms'. This enabled them to regulate the membership of the assembly and to exercise the ultimate judgment on the eligibility of newcomers to Guernsey high society. When the application of a Mr Price was turned down, Martha Dobrée explained in a letter: 'there are above a dozen, I might say twenty families, who have at least as much right as him who are only waiting his introduction to propose themselves; the line we have happily kept drawn once broken through, we should not know where to stop'.[26] Membership of the assembly was very select. As the English visitor Berry observed, only first class people were admitted; but he found it difficult to define the criteria: 'ample fortune will not accomplish it and neither business nor lack of noble ancestry is any bar to it'.[27]

The fashionability of the assembly was enhanced by the presence of officers from the British garrison. The assembly served as the setting for balls and suppers given by gentlemen of the island in honour of the garrison; the officers reciprocated by giving a ball on the 4th of June, George III's birthday. The English visitor Elizabeth Ham found that these balls 'always caused great heart-burnings from their exclusiveness'.[28] Among its other functions the assembly was a marriage mart at which eligible bachelors were introduced to the daughters of leading Guernsey families. The entertainments grew increasingly expensive. The cost of throwing a ball for nearly two hundred people amounted to £36 4s 8d in 1786 but thanks to 'senseless extravagance' a similar entertainment cost about £500 twenty-five years later.[29]

Voluntary associations

The growth of affluence and leisure-time produced more complex patterns of sociability. As in England an 'increasingly fashionable way of articulating economic success was through membership of societies'.[30] There was a mushrooming of different types of clubs, associations and societies in St Peter Port. These all shared certain characteristics, convivial eating and drinking in particular. They also represented a social phenomenon that distinguished urban from rural life and made living in town an enjoyable experience. Moreover, they helped to preserve social cohesion during a period of rapid urban expansion. In these respects clubs, associations and societies can be treated under one heading. Nevertheless, there were differences between the associations. Some of the clubs were the preserve of the upper ranks of society, the lower orders being excluded; other associations actively recruited across the boundaries of rank and order. The clubs of local élites were quickly formed and as easily dissolved; the masonic lodges on the other hand belonged to a wider world, with a philosophy, constitution and rule book influenced by practice in London.

Little detailed evidence about the clubs has survived but some indication of club life is furnished by the diaries of Dobrée and Mollet who at various dates attended the Fermain Club (just outside St Peter Port); the Friendly Club; the Port Club; the Pollet Club; the Town Club; and 'Liberty Hall'. Apart from the men's clubs there was a club 'des dames & demoiselles' and Elizabeth Ham visited the Hum-drums, an assembly 'confined entirely to Ladies'. The entertainment consisted of 'Cards, Noyaux, and abundance of rich, sweet cakes'.[31] Some clubs seem to have been frequented by young people and to have been the setting for 'amours'.[32] George Bell, bewitched by Miss Condamine, was forbidden by his parents to go to her club.[33] The clubs entertained one another. In January 1773 Mary Le Mesurier commented: 'It is customary that all clubs give each other suppers at this time of year but we do more we give likewise a dinner.'[34] The members of 'Liberty Hall' owned a boat in which they went on trips to Herm and France[35] but this club also had a political basis. It had been founded by Captain Hellier Gosselin and others who admired Tom Paine and the leaders of the French revolution.[36] This club was possibly the same as the *Société*

Indépendante which in December 1792 solemnly pledged the loyalty of its two
hundred and fifty or so members to King George III. The members asserted
that their club had no subversive intent and that it was devoted to
conversation, literature and amusement.[37]

Club meetings usually took place at taverns, Vinings in the Pollet being
a popular rendez-vous. Frequently there was heavy drinking.[38] One evening
in the winter of 1775 Billy Carey and nine others drank thirty-four bottles of
claret. When Carey wished to leave, his companions took the key from the
locked door. Carey jumped out of the window of the upper chamber and fell
to his death.[39]

The records for masonic bodies are particularly good. The first regular
lodge to be opened in Guernsey was at the Lily Tavern and was constituted by
the Modern Grand Lodge on 10 May 1753.[40] The merchant Thomas Dobrée
was appointed Provincial Grand Master for Guernsey, Jersey, Alderney, Sark
and Herm on 22 December 1753.[41] Two other lodges were constituted by the
Moderns (in 1760 and 1774) but the remaining lodges founded in the
eighteenth and early nineteenth centuries were all Ancients' foundations.[42]

Table 7.1 Masonic lodges founded in St Peter Port, 1760–1810

Name	Style	Foundation No	Meeting Place	Demise
Three Crowns	Moderns	1760 No 256	Three Crowns	1768
?	Ancients	1763 No 116	Three Crowns	soon elapsed
Harmony	Moderns	1774 No 472	Pollet	
Mariners' Lodge	Ancients	1784 No 222	Royal George	
Orange Lodge	Ancients	1789 No 141		1828
Lodge of Harmony	Ancients	1805 No 334	King's Arms	1829
Doyle's Lodge	Ancients	1806 No 336		
Lodge of Unity	Ancients	1806 No 337		1828
Loyalty Lodge	Ancients	1810 No 349		

Source and notes: C. Stonelake, *A History of Freemasonry in the Channel Islands of Guernsey and
Alderney 1753–1951* (Guernsey, 1951). Several of the lodges enjoyed a series of different
numbers. Only the number at foundation is given above. No other lodges were founded until
1849

Members of the lodges came from upper and middling rank
backgrounds. Doyle's lodge had military origins and contained many
members from the army;[43] but it also contained numerous merchants, a
minister, sailmaker, shipwright, musician, stationer and lawyer.[44] In the 1790s
the Orange Lodge included a tavern-keeper, pilot, ship's captain, musician,
carpenter and merchant.[45] Between 1806 and 1810 the Mariners' Lodge
reported initiating fifty-three mariners, three shipwrights, one ropemaker,
one pilot, a ship's captain and nineteen others.[46] These lodges were
'Ancients' and the evidence of their composition, although slight,

corroborates the observation that the 'Ancients' were less élitist than the 'Moderns'.[47] In transcending occupational and national divides the lodges helped to promote cohesion in St Peter Port society at a time when the town was growing rapidly and experiencing social tensions.

Eighteenth century freemasonry consisted of 'pseudo-mysticism and charitable works'[48] but informally it offered more to its members. Brothers travelling abroad had access to an international network of contacts. Captains initiated in Guernsey had entry into the various American lodges.[49] Conversely, foreign merchants and seafarers found hospitality in St Peter Port lodges. In 1808 Mariners' Lodge included members who originated from Sunderland, Bristol, London, Jersey, North Shields, Swansea, Plymouth, Gravesend, Oporto, and Rhode Island.[50] The masonic system particularly reinforced the links between St Peter Port and London. Freemasonry represented one of the exemplars of metropolitan culture exported from England to all quarters of the British Empire. The St Peter Port lodges were in communication with the Grand Lodge in London and this strengthened the influence of English practice. In 1813 Mariners' Lodge resolved 'that any Brother who should speak any other language than the English should pay a fine of sixpence'.[51]

Lodge activities included convivial drinking with guests. On 10 November 1801 the Mariners' Lodge decided to hold a meeting weekly on Fridays for members and friends 'and to pay for cold grog twopence per glass and for warm, ditto, with sugar, threepence. Wine two shillings per bottle, and porter tenpence per glass'. Philanthropy was sometimes combined with entertainment. In 1802 Brother Marshall of the Theatre Royal was given a 'benefit' by the Brethren of Mariners' Lodge. Public parades and church attendance were other features of masonic life. On 20 June 1807 Mariners' Lodge decided that 'the Brethren should walk hand in hand with their Jewels to the Trinity Chapel to hear Bro Isdell preach' and on 13 August 1810 the Worshipful Master and officers of Mariners' 'walked from the Lodge in Town to St Martin's, and enjoyed a Festival at Bro Gore's house' to celebrate the birthday of the Prince of Wales.[52] Public appearances were of value to freemasons because of the enhanced status that could accrue to a member. 'The knowledge that substantial friends, as well as kith and kin, would stand by a tradesman increased his creditworthiness.'[53]

Friendly societies formed another group of clubs. Regular subscription to *La Société des Veuves* (or 'Widows' Society') ensured that on the death of a member of three or more years' standing, the widow received an annual pension of £30 for the duration of her widowhood or until she re-married. This club was started on 26 January 1764 by nineteen merchants, a timber merchant, two clergymen, an advocate, two surgeons, a brewer, a public notary, a sea-officer and a land-officer. Many of these founding members belonged to the highest rank of urban society and were wealthy. A further twenty-nine members were admitted to the society on 8 February 1764 but this second cohort included an innkeeper, mariners, a bricklayer, a cooper, a shopkeeper and a tobacconist along with a gentleman and more merchants. Many of the members admitted in February belonged to a socio-economic rank lower than that of the founder members of January.[54] Far from seeking exclusivity, the society seems intentionally to have been bridging occupational and social divides. Robert Morris has argued that many voluntary societies were founded 'as a response to a specific urban crisis'.[55] It has already been demonstrated that there was some degree of status friction in St Peter Port in the mid-1760s and it is possible that the founders of the 'Widows' Society' were consciously trying to re-establish their authority during a period of rapid social change.[56] Apart from cementing relationships in St Peter Port, the 'Widows' Society' helped to strengthen commercial ties by admitting at least two influential English merchants – Mark Gregory and William Seward.[57] The Society met on the second Wednesday in every month between 8 and 11 p.m., when members and guests dined together.[58]

La Société l'Alliance, founded in August 1774, was essentially a 'box club' for urban wage earners. It paid members when they were indisposed. The society provided a form of health insurance and in return it demanded certain standards of morality. The members dined together once a year.[59]

Cultural differentiation

Cultural differentiation in eighteenth century English towns is a well attested phenomenon and its impact has been seen as powerful and pervasive. However, Peter Borsay has warned that this differentiation should not be overemphasised and Jonathan Barry has recently argued that the cultural/social divides in eighteenth century Bristol should not be exaggerated.[60] The experience of St Peter Port was significantly different from that of English towns. In Guernsey cultural differentiation occurred not just between the élite and the populace but also in the context of two quite different traditions – that of patois-speaking islanders and that of English-speaking immigrants. There were, essentially, four sub-groups in St Peter Port in the second half of the eighteenth century: Guernsey-born élite; Guernsey-born lower orders; immigrant lower orders; 'colonial' élite.

The most obvious divide between the islanders and the immigrants lay in their different languages. English was both the language of commerce and of high society. A lack of fluent English could place the St Peter Port merchant at a disadvantage. The trader Guérin had to throw himself on the goodwill of an English supplier: 'As I am in want of many sorts of goods, of which I donth [*sic*] know the names in English, nor how you sells them, if you can favour me with an explication in English and French'.[61]

The education offered in St Peter Port in the eighteenth century was not adequate for 'the new intercourse which the English brought here on affairs & matters of business'.[62] This encouraged the St Peter Port merchants to send their children to England to be educated. A homesick boy begging to return to Guernsey from a boarding school was advised to remain in England where he would learn to pronounce English with 'that propriety you must unavoidably attain by constantly hearing it spoken by the native'.[63] Closer contact between the islanders and the English 'created a new order of things, and much of the manners and customs began to wear away'.[64] Children sent to England were severed from their cultural roots. W. P. Le Cocq wrote from his boarding school at Chesham: 'I wish somebody would come here who understood Guernsey French as I don't wish to forget it, because it is my native tongue.'[65]

The linguistic collision was accelerated in the late eighteenth century with the establishment of several academies in St Peter Port. The migrants running these schools made a feature of teaching 'good' English. Mr Seager advertised that at his 'Academie Angloise' there would be 'un soin particulier à la prononciation' and that pupils would learn to speak 'sans aucun mauvais accent'.[66] A. B. Fisher stressed ease of pronunciation of English at his school;[67] and R. W. Courtenay taught reading 'according to Sheridan's pronunciation'.[68] Clearly there was not only a cultural divide between islanders and immigrants based on the difference of language but also social differentiation based on pronunciation.

There was a certain amount of bilingualism and language mixing in St Peter Port in the late Georgian period. Elizabeth Ham commented about one resident: 'Poor Mrs Price spoke a funny sort of language, a mixture of Guernsey French and bad English.'[69] Edward Sapir and Benjamin Lee Whorf have hypothesised 'that a speaker's native language sets up a series of categories which act as a kind of grid through which he perceives the world, and which constrain the way in which he categorizes and conceptualizes different phenomena'.[70] The hypothesis is contentious but suggests that linguistic differences can produce cognitive differences and that language can condition a person's view of the environment.[71] Ann Dobrée experienced such a culture shock in the early nineteenth century when some of the St Peter Port streets were re-named in English. She complained: 'The streets are all labelled to my great mortification as it unGuernseyfies us … the profonde rue is promoted to St James Street … ninety-nine steps changed into Constitution Steps et les Cotes to Rosemary Lane.'[72] In St Peter Port, as in British India, English, the language of modernisation, promoted change 'through the transformation of cultural meaning and value'.[73]

Cultural differentiation increased as English became the predominant language of literacy in St Peter Port. By the early nineteenth century there were four circulating libraries in the town, of which one was French, three English. An English visitor found these 'well stocked with the best modern novels and other light popular publications of the day, which, with all the periodical magazines and Reviews, are obtained here almost as soon as they are published in London'.[74] In 1813 Mrs Seager advertised that she had just received from London an extensive circulating library 'consisting of Travels, Voyages, Antiquities, Lives, Memoirs, Romances and Novels; comprising nearly 2000 volumes'.[75]

Between 1791 and 1836 some twenty-two newspapers and magazines were launched in St Peter Port. Many enjoyed only a short existence but it is significant that of the twenty-two titles fourteen were English.[76] Many papers carried material in English and French, but invariably one language predominated. It is possible to detect differential patterns of advertising, the language selected regularly being determined by the group identified as potential consumers.

Theatrical entertainments in the town during the second half of the eighteenth century were usually in English. An argument in favour of encouraging the visit of an English touring company to St Peter Port was that listening to the actors would correct the horrible pronunciation of the youth of the island.[77] The construction in St Peter Port in the 1790s of a purpose-built theatre afforded a permanent venue for dramatic and musical performances. Instead of being an occasional port of call for strolling players, the town became fully incorporated into the circuits of touring companies from the West of England. This bound the island ever closer to English canons of taste and fashionability.[78]

Social and cultural problems

As we saw earlier, with St Peter Port's growth there were increasing social problems in the town. At the same time the old Anglican conformism was challenged by various new denominations. Respect for authority seemed to be on the decline. The local authorities tried to re-affirm the *status quo* by devoting more attention to education and church building. In the latter sphere they were aided by the British government and its representatives. But English culture constituted a threat to traditional insular values and as the nineteenth century wore on the islanders increasingly cherished their Norman heritage. This was partly a nostalgia for a lost world, partly a repudiation of Anglo-Saxon culture.

Religious uniformity came to an end in the last quarter of the eighteenth century, principally because of the arrival in the town of migrants. The first non-Anglican mission arrived in St Peter Port in the 1770s when the Quaker Claude Gay made some converts.[79] The Anglican Dean of Guernsey was tolerant at first; but later became concerned when the Quaker Peter Le Lacheur opened a free school for the labouring poor at five o'clock in the morning. When told to desist Le Lacheur replied that if the Dean, 'or any of his clergy, would undertake to teach his poor neighbor, as he did, without a view of gain' he would desist, and he heard no more of the matter.[80]

There was a sustained effort to win converts to Methodism in the 1780s, some English Methodists seeing the Channel Islands as the key to a mission in France. The islanders' attitude to Methodists was equivocal but the bailiff (William Le Marchant) gave considerable help by selling them land in St Peter Port to build a chapel.[81] Some Methodists provoked hostility by refusing to perform militia drill on Sundays, even during wartime, and the British authorities deplored 'the delinquency of about an hundred Methodistical sectaries' who were 'loose & ill charactered aliens residing on (not natives of) this island'.[82] Despite some friction, Methodism grew steadily and, according to an estimate of 1836, the adult population attending services in the Wesleyan chapels throughout the island amounted to four thousand five hundred.[83]

Dissent in Guernsey was an urban rather than a rural phenomenon. In the ten years from 1821 to 1830 only 5% of the unregistered (i.e. non-Anglican) baptisms in Guernsey were in the nine country parishes, 95% being in St Peter Port.[84] The non-Anglican baptisms in St Peter Port in that decade represented 13.9% of the total number of baptisms in the town, which might suggest that approximately one eighth of the urban population was Nonconformist or Catholic. However, the true figure was almost certainly higher because baptismal rates probably 'lagged' behind conversion rates.

Confronted by a growing range of social and cultural problems, the local authorities re-acted, as in English towns, with a variety of educational and religious responses designed to re-assert control. An Anglican Sunday School was established in 1789 and by 1791 some one hundred and fifty boys and eighty-one girls were receiving instruction in French and English.[85] In 1812 it was amalgamated with the newly opened National School which gave an elementary education combined with Anglican religious instruction. The Reverend Durand reported to the Bishop of Winchester that he thought that by this they had 'effectually counteracted the introduction of the Lancastrian system' into the island.[86] Nevertheless the Nonconformists supplied education. The Wesleyans and French and English Independents founded Sunday schools in the town and by 1827 over six hundred pupils were inscribed on their registers.[87]

In the sector of secondary education the élite, with the co-operation of the Lieutenant-Governor, responded to the challenge of private academies, dissent and 'upward mobility' by re-founding Elizabeth College (1824). Although the Tudor foundation had, by implication, been a free school, the re-founded college charged £12 *per annum* for its education. This was defended on the grounds that free classical instruction 'tended only to excite hopes which could not afterwards be realized'.[88]

The Guernsey establishment campaigned for a new church. In 1815–16 Admiral Sir James Saumarez and others petitioned the English authorities for permission to build another Anglican church in the parish. They claimed that the Town Church could not contain more than one thousand five hundred persons 'while the population of the parish is estimated at more than 12,000, one third of which consists of English residents'.[89] The petitioners noted that English residents were defecting to the Nonconformist chapels 'to the great prejudice & danger of the Established church' and asked permission for a new church to serve 'an increased and increasing English population'. This petition led to the building of St James' Church (1817–18).

In the late Georgian era the élite of St Peter Port found its hegemony challenged. This accelerated the movement of the leading citizens from the town centre to the suburbs. This strategy re-affirmed differentiation in the social hierarchy but there still remained the challenge of English culture. The élite responded to this by resurrecting, in June 1813 and in June 1825, a long discontinued mediaeval ceremony called the *chevauchée*. This was a feudal form of 'beating the bounds' and involved a wealth of pageantry. Jacob described it as 'attended with customs entirely local'.[90] The resurrection of this mediaeval ceremony was a symbolic affirmation of insular traditions. It was accompanied by an increasing antiquarian interest in the heritage of the island. Some of this interest may be attributed to the growing Romantic fashion for the gothic. Even here, however, the St Peter Port gentry in trying to redefine their sense of identity were actually using English cultural language through local cultural artefacts.

Conclusion

Throughout the Georgian era St Peter Port developed new forms of sociability modelled on English practices. It is possible to identify two competing systems. On the one hand clubs and societies offered the opportunity to assert the exclusiveness of status. Membership of the *Société de la Chambre* and the Assembly was prestigious precisely because entry was strictly limited. On the other hand there were several associations which intentionally brought together employers and employees. The *Société des Veuves* and the Masonic lodges bridged occupational and ethnic divides. The stability of St Peter Port during a time of rapid economic change was, in part, secured by these associations. Nevertheless, the entrepôt trade generated a degree of wealth and of immigration that destroyed traditional patterns of urban life. By the early nineteenth century St Peter Port society was riven by deep cultural divides. These were emphasised by the spatial re-organisation of the town. The élite living in their neo-classical villas on the hill above St Peter Port controlled from afar the urban proletariat lodging in ancient slums near the port. The urban morphology is the subject of the next chapter.

8

Physical Transformation

There have been studies of the architecture of St Peter Port but these have focused principally on existing buildings and on styles.[1] Little attention has been paid to the study of the spatial organisation of St Peter Port or to the interaction between geographical, legal, economic, social and political factors in the creation and transformation of the town.

Fundamental to the understanding of the urban geography of St Peter Port are two aspects of insular law. First, the law of succession inside the *barrières* of the town differed from the feudal code that prevailed throughout the rest of the island. Secondly, land transactions in Guernsey shared certain features with the Scottish feuing system. This introduced an inflationary factor into the land market and favoured the building of tall houses.

In the late seventeenth and eighteenth centuries the fabric of St Peter Port was still essentially mediaeval. In 1748 a French commentator saw the town as being 'petite et mal bâtie.'[2] Yet by 1823 Professor Dobrée of Cambridge was able to praise the urban improvements: 'This place is very much improved in its general appearance, besides two or three very glorious things they have done to beautify it'.[3] In analysing this transformation it is convenient to subdivide the period into three phases. First, from 1680 to c.1750, the town hardly grew in size but considerable effort was expended in improving the harbour, building warehouses and constructing a hospital to house the poor. The second phase, c.1750–c.1800, witnessed rapid urban expansion into the fields to the west of the old town. This was accompanied by a new ethic of leisure and civic consciousness. Stone and brick replaced Tudor timber. The mediaeval street market gave way to a handsomely built market-cum-assembly hall; the ancient court-house was abandoned for a fine new complex. The wealthy left the crowded High Street for the privacy of the suburbs. Population pressure led to the construction of new residential areas. Streets were levelled and widened and provision was made for lighting the town. In the third stage, c.1800–c.1830, there was a shift from the concept of individual and parochial responsibility to the idea of collective action at an island level. A series of ambitious schemes – public and private – brought about the demolition of large parts of the mediaeval centre of St Peter Port. Fine new markets and a shopping arcade replaced the vermin-ridden slums of the cramped *venelles* around the church. The physical transformation of St Peter Port was accompanied by a growing concern for the provision of better urban facilities. The government of the town had become increasingly complex.

St Peter Port in 1680

Paintings in the Legge Survey show that in 1680 St Peter Port retained much of its Tudor form and size.[4] The town was still as Camden had described it, 'a little town … long and narrow' bordering on the haven.[5] The Legge Survey draws attention to the location of St Peter Port 'on the side of a steep hill'. This hill constituted what geographers call a fixation line and it exercised an important physical control over the development of the town.[6]

Urban growth was constrained in a second way. From the mediaeval period a ring of *barrière* stones marked the boundary of the town wall. Although royal permission was granted in the fourteenth century for the construction of a wall, Professor Le Patourel doubted whether it was actually built.[7] The existence of such a fortification – designed to protect St Peter Port against French attacks – would certainly have hindered urban growth. But regardless of whether the wall did or did not exist, the *barrière* line was invested with a more potent constraining force: it constituted the demarcation line between town and country, a line of critical importance to the island advocates in settling inheritance matters. The legal system in Guernsey was so arranged that the law of succession inside the town's *barrière* line was a modified version of the feudal code which prevailed throughout the rest of the island.[8]

The area of land inside the *barrières* was limited and consequently expensive. The high cost of land favoured vertical rather than horizontal development. This was one reason why so many town houses were built with narrow frontages and were raised five (and sometimes six) storeys high. A similar phenomenon occurred in Scotland. Richard Rodger has argued that the conferment of burghal status 'fixed highly restrictive boundaries which in the event of commercial development pressurized land availability and forced building operations skywards'.[9]

Dr Rodger has identified a further factor that explains the construction of the high-rise dwellings characteristic of even the smallest of townships in Scotland. He has shown that the Scottish system of 'feuing' combined aspects of freehold and leasehold and that this mixture tended to inflate land prices.[10] Guernsey had a feudal system of land tenure similar in certain respects to the Scottish.[11] In Guernsey the purchase of land could be made by the immediate payment of the price agreed upon; but usually it was 'by the payment of a part only, and the conversion of the remainder into corn rents to be annually paid; or, finally, by converting the whole of the price into such rents'.[12] The Scottish and Guernsey systems shared inflationary elements. In Scotland the mixture of freehold and leasehold in one contract could prompt vendors to impose an onerous feu duty over and above the maximised land value equivalent to the freehold sale. In Guernsey the mixture of part payment and annual corn rent almost certainly exerted a similar influence on land prices. Moreover, in Scotland feu duties were an attractive form of investment, 'competition for which may in itself have forced up the level of feu-duties'.[13] There was comparable investment in *rentes* in Guernsey.[14]

The *barrière* stones were situated in the Pollet, rue des Forges, Berthelot Street, Fountain Street, Beauregard and by the town church.[15] Inside this fixation line there was a compact urban core with relatively small and valuable plot divisions. Outside the line was a 'fringe belt' with a different pattern of land division. In 1680 St Peter Port was still essentially confined by the fixation line and most of the fringe belt consisted of fields (see Plate 1). However, there were two zones where the fixation line had been broken and where development had occurred in the fringe belt. There had been expansion to the west of the town with suburban ribbon development along the valley of Fountain Street; and there had also been building along the sea-shore to the north of the town, linking St Peter Port to the little fishing village known as the 'territoire de Glatigny'.[16]

Much of the fabric of the town was mediaeval and by the late seventeenth century did not impress visitors. In 1677 Charles Trumbull commented: 'Besides the Pier the Town had nothing remarkable in or about it, the houses generally not built for ornament but for present use, without ceilings and with most untoward chimneys.'[17] Even in 1748 a French writer described the town as 'petite et mal bâtie.[18] But a year later Samuel Bonamy presented a more favourable picture of the town. He conceded that the streets were narrow and irregular but boasted that some of the three to four hundred houses were 'very good ones, because most people of fashion live in the town'.[19]

The important buildings were the mediaeval court house (known as the Plaiderie) situated towards the north of the town; and the parish church at the southern end of the town. The Plaiderie and the church represented the juridical and ecclesiastical powers located in St Peter Port. These two buildings were linked by the Pollet and the Grande Rue, the junction of those streets with the Rue des Forges being 'Le Grand Carrefour'. In the early modern period this 'Great Crossways' constituted the geographical centre-point of the town, being almost equi-distant between church and court and also approximately halfway between the northern and southern limits of the *barrière* line. Le Grand Carrefour was where some of the wealthiest merchants lived.[20] They enjoyed a commanding view over the street-market and harbour. Ships' cargoes were unloaded almost directly into the cellars and vaults of the houses; and from the upper windows the merchants kept an eagle eye on port business and any suspicious activities.[21]

Changes between 1680 and c.1750

Between 1680 and 1750 there were three principal areas of improvement in the town – the extensive development of the harbour

(1706–30); the construction of excellent warehousing facilities in the Truchot and Bordage vingtaines (1740s); and the building of the town hospital (1741–3). The warehouses and hospital were built in the fringe belt, outside the *barrières,* where there was space for relatively extensive developments. The hospital site alone covered more than an acre.[22] These projects were costly capital investments of significance in the development of the urban economy. The harbour improvements were financed by voluntary contributions from the town inhabitants and cost about 12,000 livres tournois.[23] Subscriptions and endowments from wealthy merchants and other town dwellers raised about twelve or fourteen thousand livres tournois to erect the town hospital.[24]

It is instructive to notice what the town merchants did *not* do during this period. The Plaiderie was in a poor state of repair and in 1737 the Marquis de Montendre suggested that it would be better to build a handsome new court house than to spend money upon the old. He promised that if the gentlemen of the island would raise about four hundred pounds towards the project he would add one hundred pounds of his own.[25] The Guernsey gentlemen demonstrated their priorities by investing not in a 'creditable new court house … for their honour' but in the unglamorous infra-structure of the economy. The enlargement of the harbour and the construction of the warehouses were vital for the development of the entrepôt. The building of the town hospital was a practical method of controlling poor relief and exacting useful work from the indigent.

Eric Jones and others have demonstrated that between 1660 and 1780 many provincial towns in the south of England were improved, thanks to mounting investment in the public and private urban fabric. Brick replaced timber, thatch gave way to tiles and slates; street-paving, drainage and street-lighting were improved. Georgian towns began to present a more attractive appearance.[26] The stimulus of internal trade and a profitable agricultural sector had already brought about considerable advances by the mid-eighteenth century. St Peter Port slowly imitated the improvements in the English provincial towns.

In the early eighteenth century the streets of St Peter Port were still narrow, poorly repaired and dirty. There was an ancient obligation on householders to repair and keep clean the part of the street in front of their house but this duty was not always honoured.[27] Any cleaning that did take place consisted of sweeping dirt into the open gutter in the centre of the street. The gutters carried away not just rainwater and dirt but also foul domestic water and drainage from the venelles. 'These passages, not more than a foot or a foot and a half in width, received the drainage from the court-yards or small gardens in the rear of the houses, and also the household water and other filth thrown from small windows opening on them.'[28] In 1739 a rate was raised on the householders living in the centre of

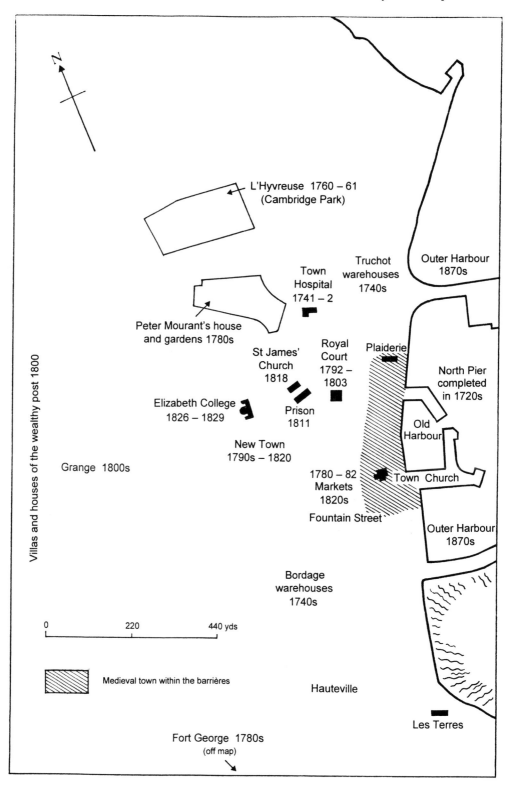

Fig. 8.1: The development of St Peter Port, 1680–1831

the town to pay for the hiring of Simon Reynard as a scavenger. His duties were to include sweeping the streets with a brush and removing domestic dirt, ash and dust three days a week (Tuesday, Thursday and Saturday).[29]

The one sphere in which the town authorities did make consistent efforts was in fire prevention and fire-fighting. St Peter Port was packed with multi-storeyed houses crammed close to one another. Many of the houses had timber frames and thatched roofs and they were not easily accessible. This in itself constituted a fire hazard but the risks of a major conflagration were increased when the merchants stored large quantities of inflammable goods in their cellars. There was also a fire hazard at the harbour when vessels were breamed. St Peter Port was a 'potential firebomb'.[30] At the meeting of Chief Pleas, 1 October 1683, it was proposed that money should be found to buy some leather buckets, ladders and equipment for fire-fighting.[31] The Court found this reasonable and gave instructions for the raising of a tax of 250 livres tournois. Those who owned thatched houses within the *barrières* of the town were ordered to cover their houses with slate ('ardoise') before St Michael's day of the following year; the penalty for failure to comply with this order was set at 500 livres tournois. It was probably this proposal that led to the renewing of the *barrières* stones in 1684.[32] With the boundary clearly marked no householder could plead ignorance.

As the trade of St Peter Port grew, the risk of fire increased. In November 1707 the town constable Nicolas Dobrée paid William Dobrée in London £32 sterling for 'deux engins à eau' and in 1710 a sum of 200 livres tournois was spent on fire buckets from London.[33] The fire-engines of the period were often ineffective but the St Peter Port authorities seem to have been trying to keep up-to-date with the fire-fighting techniques practised in England.[34] When the Sun Fire Insurance Company decided to underwrite insurance policies on properties outside London the Guernsey merchants were swift to respond. Arrangements were usually effected through the agency of Guernsey merchants in London, 'Mr Perchard at the Pewters Corner of Abchurch Lane in Cannon Street,' 'Mr Dobrée on St Mary Hill' and 'Dobrée, Botolph Lane'. The archives of the Sun Fire Insurance Company contain numerous policies taken out by merchants and householders in St Peter Port.[35] Through either luck or vigilance the town seems to have escaped major fires during this period.

Urban improvement c.1750–c.1800

In the second half of the eighteenth century the citizens improved the fabric and amenities of St Peter Port. Population increase led to urban growth; greater prosperity financed architectural fashionability; and new canons of sociability suggested the spatial re-organisation of the town. There was 'infill', with the building of a market hall and assembly room near the town church, on what had previously been the rectory garden. There was replacement; the cramped mediaeval 'Plaiderie' was abandoned in favour of a handsome new courthouse, built at a cost of £7,000 on fringe-belt land (1792–1803).[36] With no room left inside the *barrières* for further development, St Peter Port burst its mediaeval corset and sprawled far beyond the old fixation line. A theatre and chapels were built and new residential areas were developed.[37] Much of the new building was on the hill to the west of the old town. The Le Marchant family released fields and orchards here in the 1780s and 1790s. Further to the west the estate of the 'New Town' was systematically developed by Peter de Havilland from 1792 onwards. There was also residential development in the Hauteville area, in the Canichers, Park Street, Bordage and Poidevin Street.[38]

A certain number of mediaeval and Tudor houses were demolished and replaced by 'more commodious' buildings in hewn stone.[39] The Tudor houses with their narrow timber frontages, jettied structures and carved religious texts had probably exhibited a strong urban consciousness in their day but they were antiquated by the Georgian period.[40] The new fashionability was represented by the town house of the Saumarez family built c.1760. Its three storeys with six bays of dressed granite and a long frontage facing the street expressed 'a certain grandeur new to St Peter Port'.[41]

By the early 1770s there was a move towards the use of brick. Brick houses were more fashionable, offered better protection against fire, harboured fewer rats and were easier to keep clean; the urban habitat became correspondingly healthier.[42] In 1772 quantities of bricks were being shipped from Lymington (Hampshire) to Guernsey by the merchant Priaulx.[43] The Customs records show that in 1775 some 272,000 bricks were shipped from the English outports to Guernsey.[44] As 30,000 were needed for an average fourth grade house, this represents the amount for some nine houses.[45] By the end of the century a brick-kiln had been established in the island; in 1798 an English visitor found that it had 'ample employment'.[46] By the early nineteenth century there were several brickfields in the fringe belt around St Peter Port.[47]

The desire to project an image of wealth and status accelerated the development of locations for display. In 1760 Cambridge Park ('L'Hyvreuse') was levelled to make a drill ground for the militia and to create walks for the fashionable. Before 1760 the gentry of St Peter Port had promenaded along the harbour pier. Cambridge Park, with its commanding views over the town, sea and surrounding islands, proved a more attractive and spacious setting for fashionable walking.[48]

Some inhabitants wished to imitate the metropolitan improvements of fashionable London. There was talk of paving the streets of St Peter Port like those of the English capital.[49] This developing civic consciousness was coupled with a sense of aesthetic propriety. Mrs Dobrée was delighted when, in 1773, she heard that a proper market was to be built to replace the street market of La Grande Rue: 'c'est quelque chose de scandaleux de voir les provisions dans la rue' she commented.[50] Some of the wealthy merchant families were spurred on by a taste for competitive display. 'We have agreed for the two houses in town between your uncle & I, and we propose to pull 'em down next spring, and to build two new houses together, which will be two of the best houses in town' wrote John Le Mesurier to Fred Le Mesurier.[51]

Population pressure was an important agent of change. The numerous migrants flocking into St Peter Port needed accommodation. This created a buoyant housing market in which it paid speculators to build new houses or to convert existing buildings. In 1791 Charles Mollet, a gentleman and sometime merchant, sensed the new market and converted a warehouse in the Profonde Rue into two houses.[52] Population growth prompted other changes. The presence in the town of more consumers stimulated the opening of shops. In 1798 Dobrée grumbled that their cousin Elizabeth Le Marchant (Mrs Andros) had sold her father's house for 96 quarters: 'they have sold it to Mr Naftel the watchmaker who means to make many shops round the house which will dishonour it much'.[53]

As the town was extended outwards, it was simultaneously reorganised internally. In the late eighteenth century the wealthy merchants started to move to the outskirts of St Peter Port;[54] meanwhile the High Street was taken over by retailers. By moving into suburban villas the wealthy escaped the filth, noise and crowds of the streets. The High Street was often blocked and almost impassable. Moreover, life in the High Street lacked privacy; passers looked in at the first families as they ate. 'So homely were the manners and customs of those days that the windows of the sitting rooms would be thrown open that friends would lean over and have a friendly chat through the casements as they passed.'[55] Suburban villas provided the privacy in which the gentry could cultivate 'propriety, discipline and cleanliness'.[56]

The hillside houses enjoyed fine views. Peter Mourant of Candie had 'the sweetest place in Guernsey, about a quarter of a mile from the Town, yet so far above us, losing the view of its irregular pile of buildings, to command the most picturesque scenery of the other islands, the Coast of France, the Frigates in the Roads'.[57] As in similar developments in England, the new villas were surrounded by gardens.[58] Peter Mourant erected a hot-house in his grounds in 1792 or 1793 and within three decades there was scarcely a gentleman's house without one or more of these.[59] Exotic plants were another form of conspicuous consumption. Suburbia was where surplus capital bought status and displayed distinction.

One of the most ambitious developments in the fringe-belt was undertaken by Peter de Havilland, a retired *négociant*.[60] In 1792 he acquired three fields known as La Bataille. Over the course of the next thirty years de Havilland developed this area. By temperament he was cautious and he usually preferred to sell building plots rather than meet the building expenses himself. His son Thomas was bolder and on 7 March 1793 wrote to his father Peter suggesting that 'by building a row of 6 or 8 houses at once, you would not only make the Street regular, but by raising them up as they do in London slightly & leaving a small piece of ground behind each home for a garden etc. it appears to me you might make more money ... you might perhaps get the bricks made on the spot which would avoid a great expense ... I should think you might easily run up ½ doz. of these houses in a year'.[61] The suggestion was rejected by Peter as too rash. As the landowner he was able to work at his own slower pace, controlling the development of the site. He superimposed a grid-iron layout of streets and was able to influence the building styles. Thus, after various vicissitudes, 'New Town' was developed with four streets declared public roads in 1809 (La Rue Havilland, La Rue Allez, La Rue St Jean and La Rue Saumarez). Buildings continued to be constructed for several years after that. The houses in this area were mainly purchased by the middle classes.[62]

Urban improvement c.1800–c.1831

In the Regency period the Grange became the most prestigious residential area of the town. English architects were employed to design handsome houses in classical styles. Such houses constituted 'cultural capital' and helped the owners to gain greater social status and prestige.[63] The development of the Grange was made easier by the levelling of Smith Street. The improvement of the roads leading out of the town was probably both a product of suburban growth and an encouragement to further such growth. A larger population, more trade and increasing traffic were other factors that made street and road improvements essential. In Smith Street there had been a danger 'from the continual passing and repassing of the carts.' Vauvert Road was widened because children were in danger of being crushed to death between the wall and passing carts.[64]

The road improvements involved not just the parochial authorities but also the States of Guernsey. The participation of the insular government in major urban developments was a characteristic of this third phase (1800–31). The States financed the building of a new prison in St Peter Port in 1809 by levying a tax on corn.[65] The next major project undertaken by the States was to improve the public market in St Peter Port. Construction work was delayed by the poor economic position of Guernsey. The States had a debt of £19,137 'and an annual charge for interest and ordinary expenses of £2,390, the revenue of three thousand pounds left only six hundred for unforeseen expenses and improvements'.[66] In 1816 a States committee reported with an imaginative suggestion. It recommended that the expense should be met by the issue of States notes of £1 sterling to the value of £6,000 and that these notes would be available for the payment of the new market in St Peter Port and various other projects elsewhere in the island. The scheme involved the redemption of the bank notes by the income from a duty on spiritous liquors, by rents and by lotteries. A large capital sum was raised without any interest being paid. The project anticipated the idea of 'social credit' and, in some respects, Keynesian economics. Using this scheme the States carried out a series of major works in St Peter Port. The High Street was widened, Smith Street levelled, sewers and pavements were built, the new markets were constructed, the Court House was enlarged, Elizabeth College was rebuilt. The States were proud of their achievement and claimed that their work had 'excited in all classes a similar spirit of improvement'. They noted that in the town parish four hundred and one houses had been built between 1819 and 1829 at an expense of upwards of £207,000.[67]

The new markets were built in the area to the west of the church. Once the heart of the mediaeval town, this had become a slum area by the early nineteenth century. It was an insalubrious place of 'low houses', of 'shops and public houses of an inferior grade', behind which lay 'a labyrinth of narrow alleys and courts which few respectable persons cared to venture into'.[68] This warren of mediaeval slums was systematically demolished. Then the whole area was redeveloped following plans drawn up by the architect John Wilson. The new meat market was opened in 1822 and the fish market in 1830. At least twenty-three houses were demolished on both sides of Fountain Street which was widened from eight to thirty feet.[69]

The development of the market area by the States was rivalled by an amibitious private scheme financed by the businessmen James and George Le Boutillier. They demolished the mediaeval houses in rue Tanquoel, to the north-west of the church, levelled an extensive portion of the hill, and constructed a commercial arcade. The project involved the carting of one hundred and twenty thousand loads of earth or gravel and six thousand loads of stone to the south beach. The scheme bankrupted the Le Boutilliers and as a result the arcade was not covered as had been intended. Nevertheless they succeeded in transforming a mediaeval cul-de-sac into a busy retailing centre.[70]

In 1829 the States claimed that few towns 'present a more animated scenery around them, or one whose ornament and comfort are more generally united'.[71] English visitors were equally impressed. Walmesley wrote of the 'many very excellent houses in the higher part of the town', houses which the Revd Skinner described as 'neat' and 'well arranged'.[72]

The transformation was not just architectural. In the early eighteenth century rates and taxes had been raised irregularly and on an *ad hoc* basis. Parochial problems and improvements had been handled at the parish level. By the early nineteenth century the parish authorities were responsible for a wide range of services and they administered an annual budget. The States helped with some major projects; but that support was bought at the cost of urban autonomy.

Conclusion

The morphology of St Peter Port was initially determined by a variety of topographical and legal factors. Until well into the eighteenth century these forces constrained urban development. However, the entrepôt trade generated the growth of industry, population and wealth. Warehouses were constructed and new houses were built. St Peter Port burst beyond its ancient bounds as the wealthy monopolised the outskirts with their spacious new villas, gardens and walks. The shift to the suburbs accelerated after the collapse of the entrepôt trade and in the context of 'class' friction. The move to the suburbs – and the abandonment of the town centre to the poor – can be seen as the segregation of the wealthy. In fact it was as much a matter of the segregation of the poor. The spatial re-arrangement of the town was a form of social control. The indigent had no reason to frequent the new, high status residential areas; their legitimate social area was around the harbour. The élite increasingly used the States to manage urban affairs. In this way they were able to promote major building developments and impose their plans on the old quarters of St Peter Port. They were also able to block the development of the harbour. *Négociants* with interests in the South American trade had no reason to invest in port developments linked to local shipping and the requirements of shopkeepers.

1. St Peter Port, c. 1678

2. 'Prospect of St Peter's Port & town in the Island of Guernsey taken from Castle Cornet'

3. 'St Peter Port, Guernsey, from Castle Cornet', c.1815

4. A view of 'Guernsey pier', c.1830

COMPAGNIE DES INDES.

LISTE DES MARCHANDISES QUE LA
Compagnie des Indes exposera en vente à Lorient en Bretagne
le premier Septembre 1760, & jours suivans.

SÇAVOIR:

	517000	Livres Caffé de Moka	
	1516200	Livres Caffé de Bourbon	
	46821	Livres Poivre	
	5400	Livres Epipotes	
	537223	Livres Bois rouge	
	5555	Livres Bois de Sapan	
	304888	Livres Cauris	
	1050	Paquets de Rottins	
	200	Ditto avariés	
	16069	Livres Gomme Lacque en bois	
	4283	Livres Raffades	
	12987	Liv. Thé ver d fupérieur	⎫
	6035	Liv. Thé verd Tonkaye	⎬ 31537 L. Thés div.
	12015	Livres Thé Hayfven	⎬
	453	Livres Thé Saotchaon	⎪
	47	Livres Thé Pekao	⎭

	BALLES.			
LCO	553	16590	Piéces Guinées Blanches	
LCOM	2	60	Piéces idem	
LCOV	5	150	Piéces idem	
LCF	51	1830	Piéces idem	
LCM	85	2550	Piéces idem	
LCS	45	1350	Piéces idem	29160 P. Guinées
LCW	104	3120	Piéces idem	blanches.
LCC	107	3210	Piéces idem	
LCCW	3	90	Piéces idem	
LCFW	1	30	Piéces idem	
LCSW	1	30	Piéces idem	
LCMw	4	150	Piéces idem	
SALM	296	23680	Piéces Salempourris , blancs	
SAM	232	18960	Piéces idem	
SAF	17	1700	Piéces idem	44238 P. Salem ,
SAF	2	198	Piéces idem	pourris , blancs.
SAS	1	100	Piéces idem	
MooO	2	200	Piéces Percales	
SRR	3	420	Piéces Mouchoirs communs de 16 à la piéce	
SooRR	2	320	Piéces idem	
SooRB	18	2880	Piéces idem	
ROM	6	700	Piéces Mouchoirs Saffergatis de 16 à la piéce	
		5	Piéces Bazins	
		2	Piéces Baffetas	
		28	Piéces Cravates	
		3	Piéces Mouffelines brodées grandes	
		2	Piéces ditto petites.	
		1	Piéce ditto rayée	
		114	Piéces Mouchoirs de Mouffeline	
		4	Piéces Mouchoirs Organdis	
ADL ⎱ TB ⎰		70	Piéces Stinquerques Organdis	
	1	196	Piéces Organdis & Stinquerques	
	1	196	Piéces idem	
		23	Piéces Organdis	
		139	Piéces Stinquerques, fil d'Organdis	

5. An auction sale at Lorient (1769)

To be SOLD by AUCTION,
At the ISLAND of GUERNSEY,
About the First Week in May next,
(By Commissioners appointed by the High Court of Admiralty of England,)

THE FOLLOWING GOODS:
About 152 Muids of Salt.

Being the Cargo of Le Jeune Auguste, Michel Le Marie, Master, taken on her Passage from Marenne to Havre de Grace, and condemned as Prize.

After the Sale of the Cargo, the Ship, with her Tackle, Apparel, and Furniture, will also be put up to Sale.

*** Catalogues and Particulars of Sale, will be ready to be delivered at Guernsey, by the Commissioners, some Days before the Sale.

To be SOLD by AUCTION,
At the ISLAND of GUERNSEY,
About the First Week in May next,
(By Commissioners appointed by the High Court of Admiralty of England,)

THE FOLLOWING GOODS:
About 98 Muids of Salt.
8 Half Hogsheads of White Vinegar.

Being the entire Cargo of L'Aimable Angelique, Jacques De Visme, Master, taken on her Passage from Miran to Etap, and condemned as Prize.

After the Sale of the Cargo, the Ship, with her Tackle, Apparel, and Furniture, will also be put up to Sale.

*** Catalogues and Particulars of Sale, will be ready to be delivered at Guernsey, by the Commissioners, some Days before the Sale.

To be SOLD by AUCTION,
At the ISLAND of JERSEY,
About the Middle of May next,
(By Commissioners appointed by the High Court of Admiralty of England,)

THE FOLLOWING GOODS:
About

65 Muids	} Salt.
16 Bushels	

Being the entire Cargo of the St. Laurent, Laurens De Boune, Master, taken on her Voyage, from Brouaye to St. Vallery, in France, and condemned as Prize.

After the Sale of the Cargo, the Ship, with her Tackle, Apparel, and Furniture, will also be put up to Sale.

*** Catalogues and Particulars of Sale, will be ready to be delivered at Jersey, by the Commissioners, some Days before the Sale.

To be SOLD by AUCTION,
At the ISLAND of GUERNSEY,
About the First Week in May next,
(By Commissioners appointed by the High Court of Admiralty of England,)

THE FOLLOWING GOODS:
About

2,150 Barrels	Flour
200 Barrels	Salt Pork
19 Hogsheads	Red Wine
3 Tierces and an Half	Olive Oil
207 Firkins	Irish Salt Butter
600 lb.	Mold Candles
252 lb.	Wax Ditto
600 Squares	Plate Glass
17 Bales	Blankets
32 Ditto	} Kerseys and other Woollen Cloths
8 Ditto	Fine Linens
16 Ditto	Coarse Ditto
6 Ditto	Sail Cloth
24 Barrels	Gunpowder
60 Chests	Musquets

And large Quantities of divers other Kinds of Merchandizes, consisting of New Wearing Apparel, Haberdashery and Drapery Goods, Salt, Brandy, Broad Cloth, Hams, Bars of Steel, Iron Hoops, Beans and Pease in Hogsheads, Small Shot, Pewter Basons, Plates, and Spoons, Wool, Knives, Ink, Paper, Wax, and other Stationaries.

Being the entire Cargo of La Belle Rosette, Pierre Montegut, Master, taken on her outward bound Passage from Bourdeaux to Miquelon, and condemned as Prize.

After the Sale of the Cargo, the Ship, with her Tackle, Apparel, and Furniture, will also be put up to Sale.

*** Catalogues and Particulars of Sale, will be ready to be delivered at Guernsey, by the Commissioners, some Days before the Sale.

To be SOLD by AUCTION.
At the ISLAND of GUERNSEY,
About the First Week in May next,
(By Commissioners appointed by the High Court of Admiralty of England,)

THE FOLLOWING GOODS:
200 Hogsheads or upwards of Tobacco
About

102 Casks	} Coffee
2 Hogsheads	
5 Quarter Casks	
219 Bags	Refuse Coffee
10 Quarter Casks	} Shelled Coffee
6 Quarter Casks	
54 Hogsheads	} Sugar
34 Quarter Casks	
51 Hogsheads	Clayed Sugar
130 Hogsheads	Raw Sugar
48 Bales	Cotton
203 Bags	Cocoa
80 Tierces	Rice
1 Barrel and	} Indigo.
2 Quarter Casks	

Being the entire Cargo of Le Grand Terrien, Jean Labadie, Master, taken on her Voyage from Martinico to Bourdeaux, and condemned as Prize.

After the Sale of the Cargo, the Ship, with her Tackle, Apparel, and Furniture, will also be put up to Sale.

*** Catalogues and Particulars of Sale, will be ready to be delivered at Guernsey, by the Commissioners, some Days before the Sale.

To be SOLD by AUCTION,
At the ISLAND of GUERNSEY,
About the First Week in May next,
(By Commissioners appointed by the High Court of Admiralty of England,)

THE FOLLOWING GOODS:
About

19 Hogsheads	} Coffee
3 Tierces	
59 Quarter Casks	
67 Bags	
32 Hogsheads	} Sugar
6 Tierces	
3 Quarter Casks	
60 Bales	Cotton
20 Bags	Cocoa
2 Quarter Casks	} Indigo.
7 Small Barrels	

Being the entire Cargo of La Bonne Amitie, Nicholas Le Febvre, Master, taken on her Voyage from Martinico to Havre-de-Grace, and condemned as Prize.

After the Sale of the Cargo, the Ship, with her Tackle, Apparel, and Furniture, will also be put up to Sale.

*** Catalogues and Particulars of Sale, will be ready to be delivered at Guernsey, by the Commissioners, some Days before the Sale.

To be SOLD by AUCTION,
At the ISLAND of JERSEY,
About the Middle of May next,
(By Commissioners appointed by the High Court of Admiralty of England,)

THE FOLLOWING GOODS:
About

197 Barrels	} Clayed Sugar.
2 Tierces	
6 Quarter Casks	
24 Barrels	White Sugar
59 Barrels	} Coarse Sugar.
4 Tierces	
98 Hogsheads	} Coffee.
12 Barrels	
37 Tierces	
76 Quarter Casks	
303 Bags	} Indigo.
1 Cask	
3 Tierce	
2 Anchors	
2 Quarter Casks	
2 Bales	Cotton.

Being the entire Cargo of Le Florissant, Louis Banos, Master; taken on her Voyage from Cape François to Bourdeaux, condemned as Prize.

After the Sale of the Cargo, the Ship, with her Tackle, Apparel, and Furniture, will also be put up to Sale.

*** Catalogues, and Particulars of Sale, will be ready to be delivered at Jersey, by the Commissioners, some Days before the Sale.

6. Prize goods offered for sale (1779)

7. St Peter Port church (1815)

8. Dutch tiles from houses in St Peter Port

9. Old Fountain Street

COTTAGE,
TEA GARDENS.

Mefs. BERNARD and BARRY, prefent their refpects and beg
leave to inform the Public, that they propofe opening the
Gardens on Monday, July, the 11th, with a

GRAND GALA,
In honour to his
MAJESTY's BIRTH DAY:
To confift of
Mufic-Singing,
Illuminations,
and
FIRE WORKS

The fubfcribers to have twelve Mondays for GALA NIGHTS
and twelve *Saturdays,* for *Promenade Nights.*
Tea, Coffee, Mufic, &c. *for the* 24 *Nights;* one Pound eleven
and *fix-pence:* Mondays, *and Saturdays, the Gardens will be open'd*
to Subfcribers only:
Every Wednefday the gardens will be open'd and
A GRAND GALA
offer'd to the Public in General
Tickets for Tea and Coffee, two Shillings.
Mufic, Singing,
and
FIREWORKS, GRATIS.
The Gardens will be illuminated Mondays and Wednefdays
with 400 BRILLIANT *Lamps,*
of different Sizes, Sorts, and Colours.
N. B. *Cold Suppers* on *moderate terms.*
Tea and Coffee Sunday Evenings;
one Shilling.

The Proprietors affure their Friends and the Public in General
that every effort will be exerted to render the Gardens worthy their
Patronage.
Subcriptions receiv'd at the Cottage from nine till one.

10. Bernard's Vauxhall Gardens, 1796

J. TAYLOR,
PIANO-FORTE MAKER,
From Broadwood's, and late of Brook Street, Bond Street,

Respectfully announces to the Public of Guernsey,
that he is taking a Circuit from London, to repair
and rectify the most intricate imperfections in Pianos
from what cause they may arise; such as a bad tone,
hard touch, defective either in power or brilliancy,
rattling and noise in the keys, not answering the
finger; peddals added to Pianos that have not got
them, additional keys also added, & more particular,
Instruments that have lost their tone, brought to
their former soft and mellow tone; in a word, J. T.
will do any thing on the spot equal to any house in
London.— As his stay will not be long in the
Island, he will be obliged by an early application at
Mr. Charles Marquand's, Haut Ville.

11. Piano-forte maker from London, c.1800

12. The north pier, St Peter Port harbour, c.1740

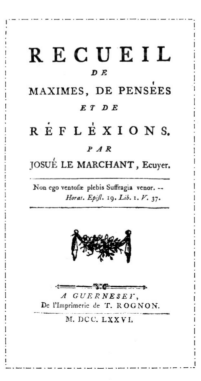

RECUEIL
DE
MAXIMES, DE PENSÉES
ET DE
RÉFLÉXIONS.
PAR
JOSUÉ LE MARCHANT, Ecuyer.

Non ego ventofæ plebis Suffragia venor. --
Horat. Epiſt. 19. *Lib.* 1. *V.* 37.

A GUERNESEI,
De l'Imprimerie de T. ROGNON.
M. DCC. LXXVI.

13. One of the first books printed in St Peter Port

14. Kean plays Hamlet in St Peter Port, 1813

Guernsey Races.

On Thursday 3ᵈ Feb. 1814

At 1 o'Clock,

THE TWO WELL BRED MARES

Jane Driver & Betty Bolter

WILL START FOR

A Stock Purse of Twenty Guineas,

For ONE MILE HEAT, from Rohais House.

CAPTAIN PEARCE . . ⎫
                       ⎬ STEWARDS
LIEUT. GLEDSTANES . ⎭

JUDGE - - - F. P. HUTCHESSON, Esǫ.

Signed,---C. J. Selwyn, Clerk of the Course.

N. B. Should the Weather be unfavourable it will be deferred to the following Day.

There will be a Ball in the Evening at Grover's Hotel.

GREENSLADE, PRINTER.

15. Horse-racing

16. Grover's Hotel (1815)

17. Havelet (1815)

18. Beau Séjour (1815)

19. The Pollet, c.1820

20. A barrière stone

61 GUERNSEY. — *St. Peter Port.* — *Old House in Berthelot Street.*
St-Pierre Port. — *Vieille maison, rue Berthelot.* — *LL.*

21. Berthelot Street

22. Cornet Street

23. The old Carey house, opposite the Town Church

24. The Town Hospital, c.1830

25. The town house of the Saumarez family, built c.1760

26. The French Halles and Assembly Rooms, built 1780-1782

27. William Le Marchant's house, built 1787 (now the Constables' Office)

28. The Royal Court House, built 1792-1807

29. The new prison, built 1811

30. St James' church, built 1818

31. The Arcades and the new Meat Market, built 1822-1830

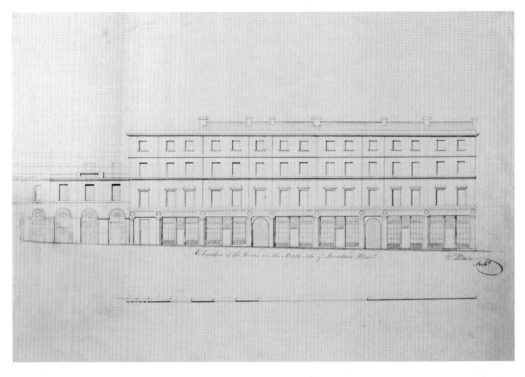

32. Plans for the modernisation of Fountain Street (1828)

33. Le Manoir de Markham – 'a very pretty Gothick villa'

34. Grange Lodge, built by 1830

STRAND BATHS,

COMPRISING Hot, Cold, Vapour, and Shower Baths, are now open for the accommodation of the Public. A book is open for Subscribers and Tickets ready for delivery, at £1 15 0 for twenty Tickets to the Hot, and £1 5 0 to the Cold Baths, napkins included, with every expence for attendance, &c.

Non-Subscribers will pay 2s. 3d. each Hot Bath, and 1s. 9d. the Cold.

N.B. From the very few visitors to the Baths, water will be heated only Wednesdays and Saturdays, from 8 to 4, unless ordered one hour before wanted.

Guernsey, April 24, 1820

New Subscription Baths.

T. GREENSLADE, respectfully informs the Ladies and Gentlemen of the Island, that his NEW BATHS are now completed, and will be open every day next week for their inspection, and to receive subscriptions.

It is presumed they will be found to be fitted up in a style worthy of their patronage and support.

Every further information will be given by Mr. T. Greenslade, or Mr. and Mrs. Bird, who are appointed to take charge of the Baths.

35. An embryonic spa town

LONDON TO THE CHANNEL ISLANDS

Via *POOLE, in TWELVE HOURS*,
WITH A BAG OF LETTERS FROM H. M. POST OFFICE.

Alteration of Time on and after Aug. 1.

Passengers and Baggage via POOLE avoid Dock and Pier Dues.

Goods by this route are free of Dock and Pier Dues.---Freight and Rail Charges same as via Southampton.

THE NEW		SOUTH-WESTERN
STEAM		NAVIGATION
COMPANY'S		UNRIVALLED

STEAM  SHIPS,

Will Leave POOLE HARBOUR,

WITH GOODS AND PASSENGERS, FOR

GUERNSEY & JERSEY

Every MONDAY and THURSDAY Nights, at ELEVEN o'Clock,
Immediately after the arrival of the Up Mail Train from Dorchester:

Returning from JERSEY, every WEDNESDAY Afternoon, at Three o'clock,
and SATURDAY Morning, at Eight o'clock.

The Passage to or from POOLE and GUERNSEY will not exceed **FIVE HOURS AND A HALF,**
THEREBY OFFERING TO THE PUBLIC,---
THE MOST RAPID COMMUNICATION BETWEEN THE CHANNEL ISLANDS AND THE METROPOLIS.

FARES to and from LONDON to GUERNSEY and JERSEY, the same as via SOUTHAMPTON, viz:---

**First Class Rail & Main Cabin, 35s. 6d.—Second Class Rail & Main Cabin, 31s. 6d.
Second Class Rail and Second Cabin, 24s. 6d.—Third Class Rail and
second Cabin, 20s. 8d.**

BETWEEN POOLE AND GUERNSEY AND JERSEY,—

**Main Cabin, 21s.—Fore Cabin, 14s.—Carriages, £3.—Horses, £3.—Dogs, 5s.
STEWARD'S FEES.—Main Cabin, 1s.—Fore Cabin, 6d.**

1 Cwt. of Personal Baggage is allowed each Chief Cabin Passenger, all above that weight will be charged 6d. per cubic foot.

PASSENGERS EMBARK AND DISEMBARK AT POOLE FREE OF CHARGE.

GOODS by the COMPANY'S VESSELS are carried at very REDUCED RATES.
To Merchants and Shippers this route offers peculiar ADVANTAGES OVER EVERY OTHER PORT.
*Merchandize of every description may be Imported or Exported at the low local rate of 3d. per ton only, while the
facilities are equal to any Port in the United Kingdom.*

THE COMPANY'S VESSELS LEAVE

JERSEY FOR ST. MALO,

Every TUESDAY Afternoon, returning every WEDNESDAY Morning,
at Ten o'clock. Also, from

JERSEY TO GRANVILLE,

Every FRIDAY Afternoon, returning every SATURDAY Morning,
ACCORDING TO TIDE.

The SOUTH-WESTERN RAILWAY COMPANY'S TRAINS leave POOLE for DORCHESTER, Five times daily—
from whence Fast Coaches start for BRIDPORT, YEOVIL, TAUNTON, EXETER, &c., &c.

Also, from POOLE first-rate Conveyances for BLANDFORD, SHAFTESBURY, BATH, BRISTOL, &c., &c.

*THE NEW SOUTH-WESTERN STEAM NAVIGATION COMPANY will not be responsible for any damage
or loss of Baggage, nor for Delays, Accidents, or Sea Risks of any kind whatsoever.*

New South-Western Steam Navigation Company's Office,
102, High Street, Poole, July 27th, 1848.

JOHN BROUGHTON, *Agent.*

LANKESTER, PRINTER, 92, HIGH STREET, POOLE.

36. London to the Channel Islands in twelve hours, 1848

37. The quay and harbour, St Peter Port, Victorian era

38. Continuity and change – The Truchot, 1999

Victorian Epilogue

As the nineteenth century progressed, St Peter Port's rôle as a minor entrepôt (serving the South American trade) slowly declined. The free-trade policy pursued by Peel's administration in the 1840s finally undermined its position.

Table 9.1 Alcohol imported into, and exported from, Guernsey, 1833–34, in gallons.

	Imported	Exported
Brandy	196,578	45,216
Geneva	43,766	13,416
Rum	6,432	746
Wine	352,736	207,023

[*Source and notes*: E. C. Barrington, 'The Human Geography of Guernsey' TSG vol. XII, part iii, for 1935 (Guernsey, 1936), p. 370. Contrast with the volume imported into St Peter Port in the late eighteenth century – Chapter Two.]

St Peter Port experienced little growth during the Victorian era, its population hovering between fifteen to eighteen thousand. By 1901 the town inhabitants constituted only 45.2% of the island population, as opposed to 57.1% in 1841. The country parishes prospered and grew thanks to a variety of commercial enterprises. Large quantities of granite were quarried in the northern parishes and were shipped from St Sampson's harbour to England. In many of the parishes horticulture was developed, the fruit and flowers being exported principally to England.

Table 9.2 The population of St Peter Port and Guernsey, 1841–1901

	1841	1851	1861	1871	1881	1891	1901
St Peter Port	15,220	17,070	16,388	16,166	16,658	17,008	18,264
Island, total	26,649	29,757	29,804	30,593	32,607	35,243	40,446
St Peter Port as %	57.1	57.4	55.0	52.8	51.1	48.3	45.2

[*Source and notes*: G. H. Dury, 'The Population of Guernsey: an essay in historical geography', Geography no. 160, vol. XXXIII, part 2, June 1948, pp. 61–69. Town population figures include members of the small military garrison.]

However, it would be wrong to paint too gloomy a picture of St Peter Port's fortunes during the Victorian era. The urban economy re-adjusted to changing circumstances; and the population did not decline. In fact the population figures partly conceal important flows of migrants into, and out of, the town. Islanders who emigrated were in part replaced by immigrant settlers.[1] Hundreds of English families were drawn to the island – principally to the parish of St Peter Port – by the mildness of the climate, the beauty of the scenery and the comparatively low cost of living.[2] Moreover, St Peter Port boasted a large number of genteel dwelling houses, its suburbs being admired for the number of delightful villas and elegant mansions.[3]

The establishment of regular steam packet routes linking Plymouth, Weymouth, Southampton, Jersey, St Malo and Granville to St Peter Port encouraged the growth of tourism. By the 1840s Guernsey was reckoned a place of fashionable resort in the summer season. After the construction of the London – Southampton railway line the travelling time from the capital to St Peter Port was reduced to approximately twelve hours. However, the improvement did not match that of the transport revolution in England. Consequently, St Peter Port was relatively more remote from London in the Victorian era than it had been in the eighteenth century. This in part accounts for the provincialism of the town in the nineteenth century.

St Peter Port survived as a market town, administrative centre and minor 'gentry town'. The class divisions of the 1820s and 1830s continued into the Victorian era. From the 1820s onwards the town traders and shopkeepers lobbied for the improvement of St Peter Port harbour. However their petitions were resisted by some of the élite whose financial

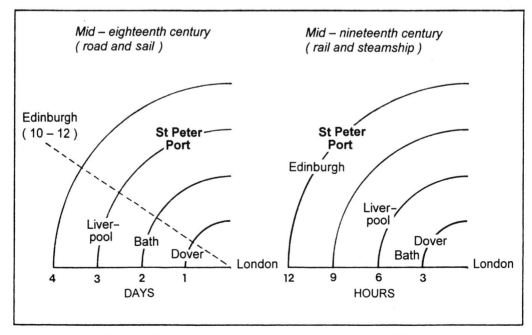

Fig. 9.1: The transport revolution (normal weather conditions)

interests were no longer centred on the port. It was not until the 1870s that St Peter Port harbour was properly enlarged.

There was one last episode in which St Peter Port functioned as an entrepôt. Between 1857 and 1879 a branch of Keiller & Son of Dundee manufactured marmalade in the town. By operating from Guernsey the firm evaded sugar duties. As in the eighteenth century, fruit was imported into St Peter Port from southern Europe. Cheap female labour was employed in the town to process the marmalade, which was then exported to the British Empire. For a few years Guernsey was the world's largest overseas trader in the preserve.[4] The episode represents a remarkable 'echo' of the town's earlier history.

Conclusion

The argument of this study is that during the eighteenth century the merchants of St Peter Port established the town as a major entrepôt in the Atlantic economy. This brought considerable wealth but radically transformed traditional cultural and societal patterns. In the process St Peter Port was converted from a 'French' into an 'English' town.

In the seventeenth century St Peter Port was a relatively poor town of some 3,000 inhabitants. It was in most respects French, the laws, customs and patois of its Guernsey folk being Norman. The nine country parishes sustained the town market and provided the wealthier bourgeoisie with *rentes*. The status titles used in St Peter Port were identical to those of *ancien régime* France. At the summit of the urban hierarchy were a number of merchant families. This mercantile oligarchy organised the insular administration, legislation and economy. The merchants controlled the domestic and foreign trade of the island and operated a putting-out industry which complemented their carrying trade. For a very low wage a large population of peasants and urban poor knitted high quality stockings which the capitalist entrepreneurs exported to France. The power of the merchants was such that the inhabitants of Guernsey and St Peter Port were 'cocooned' from external cultural influences.

In the early eighteenth century the merchants developed St Peter Port as an entrepôt. This was a successful economic strategy that capitalised on the constitutional position of Guernsey in the first British empire. Thanks to their entrepôt the merchants of St Peter Port were no longer constrained by lack of land, labour and capital; the entrepôt offered a commercial service valued by merchants from several countries. In the world of mercantilist legislation the entrepôt was a channel for free trade; and as the entrepôt flourished the St Peter Port merchants became progressively wealthier. St Peter Port rapidly became one of the principal entrepôts in the Atlantic economy in the second half of the eighteenth century. Trade, not privateering, was the fundamental source of the town's prosperity.

The entrepôt trade attracted foreign merchants and migrants to St Peter Port. The town experienced a commercial revolution in which the old economic order was radically altered. The organisation of the new tobacco factories (employing over a thousand workers) was more impersonal than the old putting-out system. Moreover, there were no bonds of kinship between the merchants and the migrant workers as had existed between the merchants and islanders in the hey-day of the knitting industry. By the beginning of the nineteenth century the town was awash with new settlers, migrants and adventurers. This produced cultural pluralism and altered the structure of St Peter Port society. Large flows of immigrants affected the ethnic composition of St Peter Port's population; and differential rates of migration altered the age and gender structure of the community.

Trade linked St Peter Port more closely to London. With its bankers, insurers and agents the metropolis dominated the commercial world of the Atlantic economy. Wherever they traded the St Peter Port merchants depended ultimately upon the financial services provided in London. The Guernsey merchants were aware of metropolitan taste and imitated its fashions. English mores and fashionability were re-emphasised in St Peter Port when the garrison was strengthened at Fort George in the 1780s. By the late eighteenth century the town had acquired many of the amenities characteristic of Peter Borsay's 'English urban renaissance' – a promenade, a theatre, assembly rooms, purpose-built markets and new civic buildings.

When the British government suppressed smuggling during the Napoleonic Wars the St Peter Port merchants were forced to revert to a carrying trade. But the social 'damage' had been done; St Peter Port was a divided community. With the influx of English labourers, artisans and retailers the traditional French system of status designation had broken down. The wealthy merchants fashioned new forms of segregation. The town in turn was divided from the country parishes by deep linguistic and cultural differences. In St Peter Port English was now the language of business and ordinary intercourse; in the country French was in general use.

There are several aspects of St Peter Port's experience that are challenging. Natural increase consistently played a significant rôle in the population growth of the town. More case studies may reveal the extent to which St Peter Port's demographic experience was typical or exceptional for a port. van der Woude's suggestion that higher rates of rural-urban immigration could bring about a rise in urban fertility is compatible with much of the St Peter Port data.[1] However, the principal explanation for natural increase in the town is probably to be found in the combination of positive factors that rendered St Peter Port healthier than many contemporary towns.

As the only town on a small island the experience of St Peter Port was in several respects different from that of towns in neighbouring England and France. In that sense St Peter Port was *sui generis*. But as the solitary town on an island St Peter Port on Guernsey bears a striking similarity to some of the theoretical models beloved by economic theorists. From the point of view of analysis one of the advantages of St Peter Port's location is that there is no difficulty in identifying its rural hinterland; there is no distraction in having to differentiate between the zones serving, and served by, competing towns. This has immediate relevance to the debate about urban parasitism.

Towns have often been viewed as parasitic, 'a centre for consumption, levying a tribute upon production in the countryside'.[2] As Professor Wrigley has observed, the debate about parasitism hinges on the definition of the word. In Sjoberg's terms St Peter Port in the mid-seventeenth century might arguably be judged parasitic. But the development of the entrepôt generated a degree of wealth and industry in the second half of the eighteenth century such that Guernsey was housing a population far larger than the island could sustain by its own agricultural production. 'Functional specialization was the gateway to economic improvement in pre-industrial times.'[3] The entrepôt represented a highly successful form of functional specialization and brought into being a town that was a stimulus to the economic development of the island. A Marxist analysis might conceivably suggest that the prosperity of the urban bourgeoisie was gained through the exploitation of the rural peasantry and town proletariat; and there would be some truth in such an interpretation. But it equally needs to be recognised that had the port not been developed as an entrepôt, many of the poorer islanders would have been forced to emigrate – as, indeed, happened in the nineteenth century when the British government suppressed the smuggling trade.

The St Peter Port data also have relevance to the debate about the rise of the middling classes. It is generally understood that in the early modern period (sixteenth – seventeenth centuries) urban society resembled an inverted T – 'a low podium containing some 95% of the population, while balanced on top of this was a thin skyscraper of more wealthy people'.[4] Dr McInnes and others have argued that change occurred in the eighteenth century because the middle sections of society were growing. This altered the inverted T into a 'pyramidal or conical' shape. This present work on St Peter Port suggests that a certain caution is necessary in discussions about the rise of the middling classes in the eighteenth century. It has been suggested in Chapter Six that it is possible to have simultaneously [a] more occupational diversity; and, [b], an unaltered profile of wealth distribution. The St Peter Port evidence is challenging and seems to support Dr Borsay's observation: 'A larger and more diverse middling stratum would seem to fill the space between rich and poor, and lead to the emergence of a less polarised society. *Whether in reality this was the case is debatable.*'[5]

Archaeologists frequently urge that the Channel Islands should be interpreted in terms of 'centre' and 'periphery'. This model has been employed with success by a number of historians to analyse eras of Ottoman, American and Scandinavian history.[6] The model has some relevance to the study of St Peter Port and is implicit in the discussion about the cultural and hegemonic relationships between Guernsey and London. But it is, at times, too easy to impose paradigms on historical phenomena. In the eighteenth century the urban history of St Peter Port differed in significant ways from that of St Helier in Jersey.[7] The centre-periphery model, when applied to Channel Islands history, can easily mask these urban variables. The distinctive urban history of St Peter Port was the product of a mercantile culture. In the face of changing economic opportunities the entrepreneurs of St Peter Port repeatedly re-adjusted their trading patterns; and as they re-organised the structure of their trade and industry, so they re-fashioned the town as their workplace and home.

APPENDIX 1: Foreign vessels carrying cargoes to St Peter Port, 1746–1762

COUNTRIES OF ORIGIN OF CARGOES

	France	Holland	Portugal	Sicily	Spain
Denmark	wine brandy chestnuts				brandy
Finland			wine oranges lemons		
France	brandy				
Holland	wine	wine brandy merchandise	port	oil wine brandy fruit	fruit wine merchandise
Norway	brandy wine merchandise				brandy
Portugal			wine oranges lemons molasses cork		
Spain					brandy
Sweden		wine			

COUNTRIES OF ORIGIN OF VESSELS

[*Source and notes:* Priaulx 29118/408C, *Dobrée Protest Book.* The number of cases recorded in the Protest Book is too small to allow sound statistical analysis; but the cases do reveal patterns of trading.]

APPENDIX 2:   Guernseymen acting as agents and factors overseas eighteenth – early nineteenth centuries

BRAZIL

Bahia   Le Breton, Lihou & Co [Priaulx library, Priaulx papers; the surnames suggest Guernsey origin].

Rio de Janeiro: P. Bonamy, Miller, Mr G. Collings [Priaulx, Lukis ms. p. 27]; Priaulx, Tupper & Co [Priaulx library, Priaulx papers].

CANADA

Quebec: Mr Brehaut 'went to Quebec, and established there other Guernsey gentlemen' [Priaulx, Lukis ms. p. 27]. Brehaut: see *Dictionary of Canadian Biography* vol 5, 1801–1820, (Toronto, 1982), pp 107–108.

ENGLAND   'As merchant agents in England there were Jacob & Job de la Combe, and Messrs C. Priaulx kept one of the firm in Cornwall. The Messrs Maingy & brothers had Peter Maingy (Fox) in Cornwall. Wm Lukis lived in Devonshire and Cornwall. Between these connections were formed such as the marriage of Peter Maingy to Miss de la Combe, whose two daughters married respectively Mr Thos Bell and the Revd R. Potinger, their brother being Mr Anthony de la Combe Maingy. Mr Uttermark came to Guernsey and married Miss Dobrée' [Priaulx, Lukis ms. p. 27]. Note also the Guernsey banking houses in London [see Chapter Two].

FRANCE

Bordeaux and   'they have been obliged lately to send several of their own people to Bordeaux
Charente: and Charente as factors for the rest, the like having never been practised by them before' [CUL Cholmondeley (Houghton) papers 41/29, c. 1733]. Jean Fiott, a Guernseyman at Bordeaux, 1720s; Jean Martell (born in Jersey, but became interested in the spirits industry in Guernsey) in Cognac and Bordeaux in the 1720s. See A. Bourde de la Rougerie, 'La Famille Martell' in TSG vol. XI, part ii, for 1931 (Guernsey, 1932), p. 260, citing R. Firino, *La Famille Martel*, (Paris, 1924). The Guernsey connections in the Charente are excellently illuminated by Professor L. M. Cullen in *The Brandy Trade under the Ancien Régime Regional Specialisation in the Charente* (Cambridge, 1998).

Bordeaux: William Carey [BL Add Ms. 38389 f 144r, 15 Mar. 1786: Carey resident in Bordeaux for eighteen years, eleven of which in business].

Nantes: Pierre Frédéric Dobrée [Nantes, Archives Municipales, fonds Dobrée; see Chapter Two].

Sète: Peter de Havilland [de Havilland papers; information courtesy of Richard Hocart].

GIBRALTAR

    Thomas Lihou & R. Robinson [Priaulx, Lukis ms., p. 27].

HOLLAND

Rotterdam: Collings, Le Marchant, Maingy, James Bowden [Priaulx, Lukis ms. pp. 25–27]; Mr James Le Marchant of Rotterdam 'who has a house at Amsterdam' [Priaulx, 29109/408C, Lihou letter book, 20 Oct. 1779].

ITALY and TRIESTE

Naples, Trieste: John Maingy, H. Dobrée and others [Priaulx, Lukis ms. p. 27].

Trieste: Métivier, Betts & Carey [Priaulx library, Priaulx papers – headed letters; see also W. W. Carey *et al.*, *The History of the Careys of Guernsey* (Guernsey, 1938), p. 219].

MADEIRA   Thomas Lihou & R. Robinson [Priaulx, Lukis ms. p. 27].

OSTEND   Reserson and Tupper, founded 1781 to facilitate the operation of the house of R & T at Barcelona [Priaulx, Reserson ms].

SPAIN   The 'Careys & Tuppers had their correspondent in Spain – as at Alicant, Barcelona and Valencia' [Priaulx, Lukis ms. p. 25].

Alicante: Carey & Co. [W. W. Carey *et al.*, *The History of the Careys of Guernsey* (Guernsey, 1938), p. 199].

Barcelona: Guille [Priaulx 18459/SR and see Chapter Two].
                Nicolas Reserson and Guillaume De Vic Tupper, house established 1775; house put under the name of George Henri Rollsen, a German employee, in 1778, when France declared war on Britain [Priaulx, Reserson ms]. Métivier, Betts & Carey [W. W. Carey *et al.*, *The History of the Careys of Guernsey* (Guernsey, 1938), p. 219].

SWEDEN

Hälsingbörg: John Le Marchant's eldest son [Priaulx, Lukis ms. p. 27].

WEST INDIES

Antigua: George Betts [Priaulx, Lukis ms. p.27].

Santa Cruz: Abraham John Le Mesurier [Priaulx, Lukis ms. p. 27].

APPENDIX 3: The entrepôt trade

APPENDIX 3.1: Quantities of prohibited East India goods re-exported from England to Guernsey since the peace of Utrecht to Christmas 1716

	1713	1714	1715	1716
Allibanees	–	65	–	–
Anjengos	–	–	30	–
Bafts	–	20	30	240
Chelloes	3	212	–	30
Cheradarees	–	20	–	31
Cherconees	7	57	55	90
Chints	179	1443	435	678
Chuckleas	17	10	–	–
Cloths long blew	–	–	20	–
Culjees	27	–	–	–
Cuttanees	21	72	24	19
Damasks	49	7	–	10
Elatches	–	–	–	51
Gorgoroons	15	4	–	6
Goshees	–	5	6	–
Handkerchiefs	26	–	–	–
Hannos	–	3	–	–
Hawkins	6	–	–	–
Humhums	–	–	110	–
Longeeshera	–	70	–	–
Mackbanees	20	–	–	–
Neganepants	–	–	10	–
Night gowns	–	2	–	–
Nilleas	–	13	–	–
Pallampores	3	39	10	–
Paunches	8	83	–	2
Pelongs	46	–	10	–
Peniasoes	–	38	–	–
Petticoats	4	–	–	–
Persians	–	–	–	2
Photays	12	67	35	–
Quilts	32	65	–	–
Romals	25	575	388	343
Salampores	–	60	–	–
Satins	3	–	–	1
Seersuckers	–	–	–	25
Shalbafts	17	16	–	–
Shawls	–	–	–	1
Silk brocaded	11	3	–	1
Soosays	11	166	33	144
Stuffs Guiney	–	120	1260	24
Taffaties	104	60	4	5
Tapsiels	–	12	–	–
Tepoys	22	10	–	–

[*Source*: PRO CO 390/8 ff 238–240. See H. Yule and A. C. Burnell, *Hobson–Jobson* (London, 1985) for definition of terms.]

APPENDIX 3.2: The quantities of fruit and wine imported into England from Guernsey, 1733–1745.

	PRUNES	RAISINS	LEMONS & ORANGES	WINE
	cwts/qts/lbs	cwts/qts/lbs	number	Tuns/hogsheads/gallons
1733	40.0. 0	62.0.10	2000	228.2.49
1734	142.0. 9	397.1.12	–	224.0.60
1735	514.0. 5	10.0. 0	–	338.3.36
1736	568.0.10	–	–	364.1. 9
1737	290.0.19	–	500	377.1. 3
1738	60.3.26	–	–	420.3.24
1739	203.1.19	–	–	576.1.49
1740	128.3. 4	3565.0. 5	–	1913.0.30
1741	360.0. 7	0.0.27	24250	603.3.41
1742	561.1.16	–	7250	374.1.24
1743	208.2.19	–	10250	787.0.58
1744	62.3.11	297.3.25	16500	847.1.15
1745	–	378.2.17	–	925.0.21

[*Source:* PRO T 64/274, documents 128, 129]

APPENDIX 3.3: 'An account of the quantities of wine imported into England during the last thirty years … from Guernsey and Jersey'

	Port	Spanish	French	Rhenish
		in tuns - hogsheads - gallons		
1755	1044-1-10	151-2-37	21-1-00	–
1756	1381-3-30	253-2-31	23-2-56	2-2-26
1757	687-1-34	315-1-14	126-2-48	0-3-39
1758	1088-3-51	256-2-61	267-1-07	0-3-23
1759	1386-0-36	192-0-59	327-0-51	2-0-37
1760	772-3-40	294-2-19	364-2-61	0-3-45
1761	993-0-42	330-0-48	537-0-13	0-2-27
1762	880-1-19	1093-0-58	296-1-12	–
1763	2589-3-34	675-3-40	140-3-02	2-1-08
1764	748-1-54	111-3-34	32-1-54	–
1765	305-1-54	37-2-49	11-3-45	–
1766	296-2-50	122-2-09	14-2-36	–
1767	295-2-14	38-1-28	31-1-34	–
1768	70-2-04	128-0-13	15-0-00	–
1769	258-0-28	181-1-18	21-0-54	–
1770	472-1-24	229-1-57	16-0-13	0-0-12
1771	642-0-43	188-2-03	19-3-19	0-0-04
1772	515-3-21	42-0-53	16-0-34	0-0-25
1773	677-2-56	213-2-15	18-2-17	–
1774	584-1-06	225-0-08	20-1-05	–
1775	345-3-49	209-2-12	35-3-53	–
1776	386-3-44	194-2-14	13-0-32	–
1777	666-1-14	157-1-29	21-3-19	–
1778	490-2-16	130-3-08	262-2-61	0-0-19
1779	600-3-48	895-2-08	209-0-16	–
1780	836-2-56	1789-1-61	361-3-41	–
1781	784-0-47	1128-3-45	369-0-18	0-2-42
1782	952-1-55	474-3-30	121-1-59	10-1-40
1783	731-3-12	446-1-54	97-1-04	33-1-13
1784	404-2-12	96-2-20	22-0-3	1-1-26

[*Source and notes*: PRO T64/274 document 138.]

This document presents aggregate totals exported from Guernsey and Jersey combined. It should be noted that each year most of the wine was shipped from *Guernsey*. This can be demonstrated by comparison with PRO CUST 3 which distinguishes between exports from Guernsey and exports from Jersey. However, it is clear from merchants' correspondence that the St Peter Port *négociants* organised at least part of the Jersey wine trade and so the aggregate is relevant to the story of the entrepôt.

APPENDIX 3.4: TOBACCO exported from England to Guernsey, lbs weight, 1701–1776

Year	lbs	Year	lbs	Year	lbs
1701	124,930	1731	614,844	1761	–
1702	4,172	1732	372,938	1762	–
1703	–	1733	542,459	1763	353,231
1704	37,846	1734	196,104	1764	348,716
1705	7,338	1735	222,524	1765	579,632
1706	11,009	1736	556,412	1766	755,353
1707	64,671	1737	164,803	1767	369,798
1708	96,686	1738	674,081	1768	317,220
1709	–	1739	1,262,308	1769	326,577
1710	94,179	1740	803,842	1770	91,347
1711	78,663	1741	439,753	1771	94,854
1712	221,915	1742	539,605	1772	391,537
1713	419,877	1743	486,673	1773	562,944
1714	249,003	1744	84,063	1774	515,894
1715	140,233	1745	297,209	1775	316,119
1716	778,351	1746	174,761	1776	32,233
1717	750,300	1747	84,980		
1718	585,414	1748	396,826		
1719	133,622	1749	214,072		
1720	245,231	1750	886,734		
1721	214,962	1751	837,197		
1722	60,689	1752	1,308,956		
1723	229,332	1753	1,361,386		
1724	159,975	1754	942,434		
1725	330,999	1755	219,891		
1726	316,661	1756	354,465		
1727	534,921	1757	388,028		
1728	174,565	1758	47,323		
1729	330,506	1759	159,243		
1730	113,359	1760	421,002		

[*Source and notes*: PRO CUST 3; J. M. Price, 'The Tobacco Trade and the Treasury, 1685–1733: British Mercantilism in its Fiscal Aspects' (Ph.D. thesis, Harvard University, 1954).]

APPENDIX 4: British government estimates of spirits and tobacco handled through the St Peter Port entrepôt

[a] Summary of BL Add Ms 38759 f 105v – f 106r; estimate c. 1802–3

Spirit annually brought into Guernsey and Alderney

	gallons
60 vessels supposed to be employed in bringing geneva into the island from Holland (under licence), calculated @ 150 tuns spirit in each	2,268,000
Brandy 28,000 pipes brought into the island @ 120 gallons each	3,360,000
Rum: 500 puncheons, 100 gallons each	500,000
	6,128,000
The quantity is increased at least 1/6 part by water mixed with the spirits in the island	1,022,000
	7,150,000
The quantity of spirits consumed in the island, what is shipped for other countries, what is lost, cannot exceed	1,000,000
Gallons:	6,150,000

Tobacco

5,000 hogsheads of tobacco annually brought into the island – duty on 1,200 lbs per hogshead @ 1/7 per lb	£475,000

[An alternative calculation of the spirits smuggled]
150 vessels at least employed in smuggling, on average
15 trips annually, bringing 500 tubs; tubs contain
4 – 9 gallons, computation made on 6 gallons .... 6,750,000 gallons

[b] Summary of *An Account, presented to the House of Commons, of the number and names of vessels Cleared out from the Port of Guernsey, in the Months of November and December 1806, and January and February 1807: with the Amount of the excise and custom duties thereon* (London, 1807), p. 10 in Parliamentary Papers, House of Commons, Accounts and Papers, session 27 June – 14 August 1807, iv, <57>, pp. 85–95.

Spirits and tobacco exported from Guernsey, Nov. 1806 – Feb. 1807

[Lost duties]	Customs	Excise
400,560 gallons brandy	29,471 – 15 – 2	302,923 – 10 – 0
49,570 gallons rum	2,244 – 8 – 4	25,714 – 8 – 9
109,395 gallons geneva	7,429 – 14 – 10	82,729 – 19 – 4½
350,300 lbs tobacco	11,165 – 16 – 3	27,732 – 1 – 8

[Pipe of brandy – 120 gallons; pipe of rum – 115 gallons; pipe of geneva – 120 gallons; cask of tobacco – 1000lbs.]

APPENDIX 5: Ships clearing from English and Welsh ports for Guernsey, 1710–17

	1710	1711	1712	1713	1714	1715	1716	1717
London	2	2	3	3	6	5	23	13
Sunderland	2			1		1		1
Newcastle	5	3	3	8	4	5	3	3
Deal							1	
Chichester		4	3	2			1	
Portsmouth		1	4	3	8	5	3	12
Southampton	35	39	48	40	55	52	45	53
Cowes	2	2	2	11	11	8	6	2
Poole	4	14	8	9	4	4	2	1
Weymouth	2	2	6	9	2	4	4	6
Lyme Regis	3	3	4	8	15	7	6	8
Exeter	3	2		1	2		3	1
Dartmouth	3	4	7	2	4	8	11	19
Plymouth	2	4	8	1	5	7	4	14
Looe				1	2	4	1	5
Fowey		3		3	4	10	8	8
Truro							1	
Penryn	1	2	3	6	5	4	2	3
Falmouth		2	1		2	1	1	3
Gweek								1
Penzance				2	1			
St Ives					1			
Padstow			1					1
Bideford		1		1			1	
Minehead								1
Bristol			1	5	3	2	8	8
Neath								1
Swansea	1		3	8	33	35	17	17
Llanelli							1	2
Milford				2	1			

[*Source:* PRO CO 388/18; CO 390/8]

APPENDIX 6: St Peter Port merchants handling wine shipped from the Iberian Peninsula on behalf of English merchants, 1768–1788

	68	69	70	71	72	73	74	75	76	77	78	79	80	...	84	85	86	87	88
W. Bell	+	+	+	+	+	+	+	+	+	+	+	+	+		+	+	+	+	
W. Bell jr																+			
Brock & Co				+															
H. Brock																		+	+
Jean Carey snr		+		+	+	+	+	+	+	+	+								
P. de Carteret															+				
Thos Dobrée												+							
Pierre Frère						+	+		+										+
Jean Guille (jnr & senr)		+	+	+	+	+	+		+	+	+				+				
B. Lageman															+				
J. & T. Le Marchant	+	+	+	+		+													
W. Le Marchant	+	+	+		+	+	+	+	+	+									
E. & J. Le Mesurier		+																	
H. Le Mesurier							+		+										
James Lihou						+													
D. McBride								+											
P. Mourant			+	+												+			
M. de Sausmarez			+																
D. Thomson		+	+	+	+	+	+	+	+	+		+	+		+	+	+	+	
E. Tupper	+	+	+	+	+	+	+	+		+									

[*Source:* Greffe, Livre de Certificats. The wine was shipped in English vessels principally from Oporto, but also from Algarve, Alicante, Barcelona, Cadiz, Canary Islands, Lisbon, Malaga and Seville.]

APPENDIX 7.1: Guernsey-owned vessels arriving in Rio de Janeiro, January
1825 to June 1826.

Vessel's Name	Day Arrived	From	Cargo	Sailed For
	1825			
St. George	Jan. 26	Genoa	19 pipes Olive Oil; 113 Barrels Wheat; 30 cases Tallow Candles; 28 cases and 94 bales Paper; and 105 boxes Steel.	Trieste
Duke of Gloucester	Feb. 3	Guernsey	610 cases Geneva; 227 barrels and 40 bags Wheat; 62 cases, and 100 cheese.	Guernsey
Enterprize	Feb. 10	Bahia	77 pipes, 24 hogsheads, and 44 quarter casks Red Wine; 27 pipes Olive Oil, and 59 barrels Wheat.	Guernsey
Unity	Feb. 14	Ancona	171 barrels and 132 bags Wheat; 54 bales Paper.	Guernsey
Blossom	Feb. 15	Tarragona	20 pipes brandy; 224 pipes, 33 hogsheads, and 19 quarter casks Red Wine; 19 pipes Olive Oil; 150 bales Paper, and 147 boxes Steel.	Guernsey
Collingwood	Feb. 17	Tarragona	146 pipes, 30 hogsheads, and 20 quarter casks Red Wine; 22 pipes Olive Oil; 4 cases Tallow Candles, and 26 bales Paper.	Guernsey
Mercury	Feb. 17	Cette	32 pipes, 6 hogsheads, and 20 quarter casks Brandy; 60 pipes and 20 hogsheads Red Wine; 374 barrels Wheat; 200 strings and bundles Onions; 44 cases and 135 bales Paper; and 114 boxes Steel.	Guernsey
Laura	Apr. 1	Guernsey	109 pipes and 30 quarter casks Red Wine; 22 pipes Vinegar; 14 pipes Geneva; and 207 cases Ale and Porter.	Guernsey
Princess Charlotte	Apr. 5	Tarragona	246 pipes, 48 hogsheads, and 60 quarter casks Red Wine; 19 pipes Olive Oil; and 170 boxes Steel.	Guernsey
Rachel and Mary	Apr. 10	Cette	198 pipes, 40 hhd. and 29 qr. casks Red Wine; and 89 boxes Steel.	Isle of Mayo
Alexander	May 1	Tarragona	291 pipes, 70 hogsheads, and 62 quarter casks Red Wine; and 4 packages Goods (not described).	Boa Pista
Three Sisters	May 21	Tarragona	30 pipes Brandy; 268 pipes and 40 hogsheads Red Wine; 30 cases Macaroni; and 138 boxes Steel.	Trieste
Nancy	July 11	Sicily	4 pipes Brandy; 150 pipes, 40 hogsheads, and 34 quarter casks Red Wine; and 60 pipes Olive Oil.	Trieste
Charles	July 18	Arichat	688 tubs and 833 barrels Codfish.	Antwerp

Dolphin	July	18	Guernsey	32 pipes, 5 quarter casks, and 3 cases Red Wine; 3 pipes Geneva; 16 cases Ale and Porter; 111 cases Soap; and 59 coils Cordage.	Trieste
Two Brothers	July	25	Guernsey	32 pipes and 788 demijohns Geneva; 124 cases Ale and Porter; 1036 bags Wheat; and 20 Hams.	Guernsey
Two Sisters	Aug.	2	Guernsey	In Ballast.	Guernsey
Alexander	Aug.	3	Buenos Ayres	With 4,877 Hides.	Guernsey
Rachel and Mary	Aug.	10	Buenos Ayres	With 4,160 Hides, and 5 packages Goods (not described).	Guernsey
Blossom	Aug.	18	Guernsey	65 pipes Red Wine; 9 pipes Olive Oil; 188 barrels and 29 bags Wheat; 157 Hams; 5 tons Potatoes; and 240 cases of Soap.	Trieste
Venus	Sept.	2	Guernsey	100 cases Ale and Porter.	Buenos Ayres
Alfred	Sept.	16	Antwerp	96 barrels and 667 bags Wheat.	Antwerp
St. George	Sept.	30	Tarragona	20 pipes Brandy; 130 pipes, 16 hogsheads, and 15 quarter casks Red Wine; 20 pipes Olive Oil; 338 cases Tallow Candles; 10 bales Paper; and 118 boxes Steel.	Guernsey
Peace	Oct.	1	Isle Mayo	48 moyos Salt.	Guernsey
Swift	Oct.	7	Tarragona	10 pipes and 30 quarter casks Brandy; and 181 pipes and 47 hogsheads Red Wine.	Guernsey
Collingwood	Oct.	10	Guernsey	13 pipes and 6 hogsheads Red Wine; 4 pipes Geneva; 50 cases Ale and Porter; 60 jars Linseed Oil; 126 cases Soap; 17 coils Cordage; and 9 cases Glass.	Monte Video
Mercury	Oct.	16	Guernsey	32 cases Ale and Porter; 250 bushels Potatoes; and 293 bars Iron.	Trieste
Caroline	Sept. 24 (*sic*)		Isle Mayo	6 pipes Brandy; 6 pipes Geneva; and 60 mayos Salt.	Trieste
Louisa	Nov.	15	Oporto	239 pipes, 36 hogsheads, and 56 quarter casks Port Wine; and 600 strings and bundles Onions.	Trieste
Laura	Nov.	28	Oporto	271 pipes, 36 hogsheads, and 64 quarter casks Port Wine; and 500 strings and bundles Onions.	Guernsey
Hope	Dec.	9	Gibraltar	24 quarter casks Brandy; 86 pipes and 4 hogsheads Red Wine; 3 cases Ale and Porter; 41 pipes Olive Oil; 26 bags Biscuit; 46 cases Paper; 80 boxes Steel; and 1 case Hats.	Monte Video

Union	Dec. 11	Oporto	195 pipes, 28 hogsheads, and 44 quarter casks Port Wine; and 600 strings and bundles Onions.	Trieste
Duke of Gloucester	Dec. 26	Guernsey	59 pipes and 5 hogsheads Brandy; 150 pipes and 6 hogsheads Red Wine; and 46 cases Ale and Porter.	Guernsey

1826

Three Sisters	Feb. 25	Sicily	22 pipes, 14 hogsheads, and 4 quarter casks Brandy; 173 pipes and 26 hogsheads Red Wine; 69 pipes Olive Oil; 86 barrels Wheat; and 169 boxes Steel.	Guernsey
Swift	Feb. 26	Guernsey	152 pipes and 31 hogsheads Red Wine; 5 pipes and 14 hogsheads White Wine; 20 cases Ale and Porter; 16 cases Cider; and 75 coils Cordage.	Trieste
St. George	Mar. 1	Guernsey	1 pipe and 1 hogshead Brandy; 155 pipes and 12 hogsheads Red Wine; 20 pipes and 111 demi-johns Geneva; 220 jars Linseed Oil; and 1½ tons Potatoes.	Guernsey
Reward	Mar. 5	Oporto	307 pipes, 20 hogsheads, and 188 quarter casks Port Wine; and 24 cases Ale and Porter.	Guernsey
Two Brothers	Mar. 12	Tarragona	30 pipes and 24 quarter casks Brandy; 195 pipes and 30 hogsheads Red Wine.	Gibraltar
Dolphin	Mar. 18	Trieste	30 pipes Olive Oil; 149 barrels and 352 bags Wheat.	Guernsey
Blossom	Apr. 12	Tarragona	30 pipes Brandy; 215 pipes, 28 hogsheads, and 20 quarter casks Red Wine; 20 pipes Olive Oil; 26 cases Currants; 308 cases Tallow Candles; and 160 boxes Steel.	Trieste
Charles	May 5	Tarragona	15 pipes and 10 hogsheads Brandy; 202 pipes, 20 hogsheads, and 50 quarter casks Red Wine.	Trieste
Alexander	May 24	Tarragona	60 pipes Brandy; 277 pipes and 35 hogsheads Red Wine.	Guernsey
Collingwood	June 17	Guernsey	258 barrels and 59 bags Wheat; 8 cases Soap; 1 case Tallow Candles; and 18 dozen Brooms.	Hamburg

[*Source: The Star,* 6 Feb. 1827, captains, passage and sailing dates omitted. Full details are available from the author.]

APPENDIX 7.2: Details of the Guernsey vessels arriving in Rio de Janeiro, Jan. 1825 – June 1826, are as follows:

Vessel	owners	type	tonnage	date launched
Alexander *	Mansell & Price	Ship	250	1815
Alfred *	Jones and Lidstone	Cutter	61	1822
Blossom *	Bonamy & Co.	Brig	149	1821
Caroline *	Boucaut & Co.	Brig	152	1820
Charles *	Le Nouri & Co.	Cutter	28	1820
Collingwood	C. Priaulx & Co.	Brig	114	
Dolphin	C. Priaulx & Co.	Brig	168	
Duke of Gloucester *	Mess Collings	Brig	113	1817
Enterprize	C. Priaulx	Schooner	118	
Hope *				
Laura *	Mellish & Co.	Brig	204	1820
Louisa *	Bonamy & Co.	Brig	169	1824
Mercury	J. Le Quesne	Ship	250	
Nancy *	Han. Sheppard	Brig	159	1819
Peace	Thoume & Co.	Brig	130	
Princess Charlotte	W. Le Lievre	Brig	174	
Rachel and Mary	Thoume & Co.	Brig	141	
Reward	H. Sheppard & Co.	Ship	206	
St George *	Vidamour & Co.	Brig	111	1819
Swift	Bienvenu & Co.	Brig	163	
Three Sisters *	J. Le Quesne	Brig	220	1820
Two Brothers				
Two Sisters *	De Putron & Co.	Brig	158	1819
Union *	Mitchel & Co.	Brig	116	1819
Unity	Thoume & Co.	Brig	131	
Venus	N. Le Page & Co.	Schooner	111	

* built in Guernsey

[*Sources*: J. Jacob, *Annals of the British Norman Isles* (Paris, 1830), pp. 456–460. *The Star*, 6 Feb. 1827, p2 c-e; and contemporary almanacks and papers. There were two cutters called *Hope*, and two vessels called *Two Brothers* – a brig and a cutter.]

APPENDIX 8: The trade of Priaulx, Tupper & Co., Rio de Janeiro

Major cargoes shipped by Priaulx, Tupper & Co. of Rio de Janeiro, 1827–31

		1827	1828	1829	1830	1831
Coffee:	bags	28322	27265	47326	39350	47805
	barrels			321	233	
Sugar:	cases	529	1314	472	2175	1950
	boxes				5	
	bags	567	1414	560	751	929
	barrels		65			9
Hides		1296	573	5728	3399	13026
Horns				2000		21708
Tobacco in rolls					114	

Source: Priaulx Library, Priaulx papers

The firm sent cargoes (various) in 1831 to Antwerp, Cowes, Guernsey, Hamburg, Leghorn, London, Rotterdam and Trieste.

APPENDIX 9: Inventory of the goods in stock of Peter Mourant & Co., 'the old partnership, supplied to present partnership, 1 Jan. 1785'. This inventory gives a valuable glimpse into the world of the *négociant* and his cargoes, equipment, ships, utensils, office.

			£	s	d
8	pipes	Cette spirit	147 –	4 –	4
84	pipes	Cette Brandy	1193 –	6 –	6
70	pipes	Geneva	846 –	1 –	9
90	veltes	Jamaica Rum	31 –	10 –	0
47	veltes	Shrub	16 –	9 –	0
10	pipes	Brandy wash	50 –	0 –	0
12	pipes	Rum in the Tuns	178 –	1 –	5 ½
22	pipes	Brandy in the Tuns	248 –	17 –	7
38	pipes	Salou brandy ⎫	406 –	10 –	6
7	half hogsheads	" ⎭			
6	pipes	Cognac Brandy (Common)	76 –	17 –	7
26	pipes	Cognac Brandy (London)	362 –	9 –	4 ½
11	puncheons	Rum in the cellars	118 –	8 –	4
164	puncheons	" at Candie ⎫	1898 –	1 –	10
11.25	hogsheads	⎭			
10	hogsheads of	St Drezeny wine	45 –	0 –	0
1	pipe	⎫			
6	hogsheads	⎬ Claret	65 –	0 –	0
2	tierces	⎭			
16	dozens of	St Drezeny wine	4 –	0 –	0
2	pipes	Sea Stock wine	12 –	12 –	0
11	dozens	" " "	2 –	4 –	0
2375	lbs	sling stuff	19 –	0 –	0
2319	lbs	made slings	20 –	5 –	10
1340	lbs	spunyarn	10 –	14 –	5
60	dozens	bottles	5 –	0 –	0
15	pieces of	cloth for bags	63 –	7 –	6
15	ditto	oil case	3 –	4 –	9
28	double	½ hundred bags	3 –	10 –	0
85	double	¼ ditto	5 –	6 –	3
90	lbs	lead in sheets		10 –	9 ½
19		cave bottles		19 –	0
6		juggs		6 –	0
20		empty puncheons	5 –	0 –	0
24		empty hogsheads	1 –	16 –	0
60		" "	4 –	10 –	0
65		" ½ "	6 –	10 –	0
566		ankers	56 –	12 –	0
109		half ankers	9 –	10 –	9
120		four gallon kegs	8 –	5 –	0
70		flaggins [sic]	3 –	10 –	0
32		six pound dollop bags		10 –	8
6		twelve pound " "		3 –	0
5/8 of the ship Hope valued at £3,000			1875 –	0 –	0
1/2 of the ship Pomona valued at £2,600			1300 –	0 –	0

30 pipes of Cette Brandy sent to Madeira which are not comprehended in the Inventory and as we make the owners of ship Hope. Drs for the amount of the invoice we make this partnership Drs for them at the price as we charge the other Brandy Viz. 4231½ gallons @ 2/=   423 – 3 – 0

20 pipes	Cognac brandy sent to Madeira with the other 30 pipes Cette Brandy as above 2277½ gallons at 2/3		256 – 4 – 4 ½	
	1/4 of schooner Fly valued at £360		90 – 0 – 0	
	5/8 of £98 – 14 – 6 premium &c of insurance on ship Hope which has been charged to the old partnership		61 – 13 – 9	

£9,937 – 7 – 4

UTENSILS IN TRADE

8 tuns valued at	£70 – 0 – 0
Sundry coopers tools	3 – 7 – 0
A large new beam	6 – 0 – 0
A large ditto & scale	2 – 2 – 0
A small beam & scales	6 – 0
Sundry weights	5 – 0 – 0
Candle sticks & scoops	5 – 0
Notes & bills of exchange	5 – 0
A standard gold weight & scales	15 – 0
2 pairs of hand scales	1 – 0 – 0
A set of avoirdupois weight	7 – 6
Salmon's Gazetteer	6 – 0
Osnabrey's Foreign Exchanges	10 – 0
A standard pair of candlesticks	18 – 0
A mahogany desk	2 – 0 – 0
6 chairs	12 – 0
Baldwin's Survey of the Customs	1 – 1 – 0
Lex Mercatoria	1 – 7 – 0
150 quills	6 – 0
300 paper bags	4 – 0
5½ reams of white packing paper	1 – 2 – 0
6 lbs thread	6 – 0
28 lbs twine	1 – 5 – 0
16 papers of Powder for ink	8 – 0
13 quires of writing paper	6 – 0
2 " of post "	1 – 0
2 reams of common "	1 – 4 – 0
4 reams of French "	1 – 0 – 0
A tackle & double blocks	1 – 5 – 0
2 Falls of cordage weighing 65 lbs at 42/= per 100w	1 – 7 – 4
2 spoons for lead	5 – 0
4 moulds for ditto	12 – 0
2 hand barrows	8 – 0
78 sticks of sealing wax	6 – 6

106 – 07 – 4

£10,043 – 14 – 8

[*Source*: Priaulx Library, 37383 Ms of Mourant & Co. 1783. Unit costs – per gallon etc. – omitted.]

APPENDIX 10: Summary of population figures for St Peter Port and Guernsey, 1680–1831

	St Peter Port	Guernsey	
1680	2,865		Estimate based on militia figures.
1727	4,350	10,500	Corn calculations – food shortage.
1735	6,000		Church estimate – exaggerated (?).
1756		12,000	Royal Court letter book.
1765	5,370		Corn calculation – food shortage.
1781	8,000		Royal Court letter book.
1789		18,000 +	Report to Home Office.
1794		20,000	Report to Home Office.
1800	10,950	18,655	Stiles' estimate.
1807		20,000 +	Report to Home Office.
1814	11,000	19,293	+ 2,000 sailors and strangers. W. Berry, *History of the Island of Guernsey* (London, 1815), p. 23.
1821	11,173	20,302	Census: *Gazette de Guernesey*, 4 Aug. 1821.
1827	12,132	22,116	Census; COf B44.
1831	13,893	24,349	Census: *Actes*, vol. VI (1829–35) pp. 162–163. G. H. Dury, 'The Population of Guernsey: an essay in historical geography', *Geography*, no. 160, vol. XXXIII, part 2, June 1948, pp. 61–69, discusses the nineteenth century population figures.

[For population sources and discussions see Chapter Four.]

APPENDIX 11: The population of Guernsey, 1727 and 1800

		1727				**1800**		
[a] Parish	[b] Sq kil	[c] Pop	[d] % of total	[e] Density	[f] Pop	[g] % of total	[h] Density	[i] 1800/ 1727
St Peter Port	6.5	4350	42.5	669	10950	58.7	1685	2.5
St Martin	7.3	993	9.7	136	1132	6.1	155	1.1
Câtel	10.1	937	9.1	93	1453	7.8	144	1.6
St Peter/Wood	6.2	849	8.3	137	1130	6.1	182	1.3
St Saviour	6.2	794	7.7	128	933	5.0	150	1.2
Vale	8.2	602	5.9	73	842	4.5	103	1.4
St Andrew	4.4	561	5.5	128	675	3.6	153	1.2
Forest	4.2	485	4.7	115	552	3.0	131	1.1
Torteval	3.1	347	3.4	112	336	1.8	108	1.0
St Sampson	5.4	328	3.2	61	652	3.5	121	2.0
	61.6	**10246**	**100.0**	**166**	**18655**	**100.1**	**303**	**1.8**
9 Country parishes	55.1	5896	57.5	107	7705	41.3	140	1.3

[*Notes and sources*: The population, percentage of total population, and density of population per square kilometre, of the ten Guernsey parishes in 1727 [c] – [e] and in 1800 [f] – [h]. Column [i]: population 1800/population 1727. Areas have been adjusted to allow for the land reclamation at the Braye in the early 19th century. For population sources see Chapter Four.]

APPENDIX 12: Guernsey militia returns, 1621, 1656, 1680

Parish	1621 [a] no	[b] %	1656 [c] no	[d] %	1680 [e] no	[f] %	[g] %
St Peter Port	312	27.0	340	24.0	521	27.4	[28.9%]
St Martin	136	11.8	180	12.7	198	10.4	[11.0]
Catel	120	10.4	160	11.3	182	9.6	[10.1]
St Peter/Wood	120	10.4	140	9.9	183	9.6	[10.2]
St Saviour	130	11.2	160	11.3	202	10.6	[11.2]
Vale	114	9.9	140	9.9	119	6.3	[6.6]
St Andrew	63	5.4	90	6.3	105	5.5	[5.8]
Forest	60	5.2	100	7.1	120	6.3	[6.7]
Torteval	45	3.9	48	3.4	169 [?]	8.9	[3.8]
St Sampson	57	4.9	60	4.2	103	5.4	[5.7]
	1157	100.1	1418	100.1	1902	100.0	[100.0]

[*Notes and sources*: The number of men serving in the Guernsey militia, by parish, and the percentage of the total number, in 1621 [a] – [b], 1656 [c] – [d] and 1680 [e] – [f]. The figure for Torteval, 1680, looks erroneous and the percentages are reworked in [g] on the assumption that the Torteval figure should read 69 (Guernsey total 1802). G. E. Lee (ed.), *Note-book of Pierre Le Roy* (Guernsey, 1893), p. 15; F. Tupper, *The History of Guernsey* (Guernsey, 1854), pp. 463, 465, 467.]

APPENDIX 13: Food shortages and crises in St Peter Port and Guernsey, 1659 – 1775

1659 July	Great loss of corn because of a storm; Le Roy p. 21.
1662	'a great scarcity of corn in this Island, such as no man living had ever seen, barley being worth 4 livres the bushel, and wheat 5 livres tournois' Le Roy, p. 33.
1697 June	'Grande disette' affecting island and town; supplies from Southampton delayed. *Actes*, vol. 2, p. 53.
1725 July	'Grande disette'. Failure of island crop. *Actes*, vol. 2, pp. 147–148; COf A67 p. 60; Priaulx 29122/408C, Watkins Ms vol. 4, 23 June 1725.
1727 Jan./Feb.	See Chapter Four, endnote 2.
1729 Apr.	Disette. Corn obtained from Holland and Hamburg. COf A67 Taxes p. 123, p. 28 (at end); Priaulx 29122/408C, Watkins Ms vol. 4, 19 Apr. 1729.
1751 Nov.	Mediocre island crop. *Actes*, vol. 2, p. 199.
1752 May	Possible need to import wheat and barley. *Actes*, vol. 2, pp. 200–203.
1756 June	Large supply of cereal expected from abroad. *Actes*, vol. 2, p. 214.
1757 Feb./May	Concern in February. Supplies bought from English vessel and sold at subsidised price to town poor: 9 l.t. per quarter to poor, 9–18 l.t. to others, depending on their means. TC DdCdF pp. 109, 110, 112; *Actes*, vol. 2, pp. 214–216; COf A22 Taxes 21 Nov. 1757, p. 289.
1758 Feb./May	Two hundred quarters of wheat needed for town poor and those taxed at less than 20 quarters. Corn from England. TC DdCdF p. 116; *Actes*, vol. 2, pp. 220–221.
1765 May	3,580 quarters of corn required to feed town population from 19 May until Michaelmas. TC DdCdF p. 143.
1766 Jul./Aug	'Grande disette'. Vessel laden with corn for Brest arrested in harbour, July; available to poor at 9 l.t. per quarter. TC DdCdF pp. 147, 148.
1767 April	Six hundred quarters of wheat required by town. Duc de Choiseul permitted two or three thousand bushels of grain to be exported from Cherbourg to Guernsey. TC DdCdF p. 151; Dupont vol. 4, p. 534.
1768 April	Five hundred quarters of wheat and one hundred quarters of barley needed for St Peter Port. Some supplies from Southampton. TC DdCdF p. 155.
1772 Nov.	Three thousand l.t. voted for import of corn for town poor. TC DdCdF p. 172.
1773 March	Town decision to import 1,000–1,200 quarters of wheat from Quebec and 300 quarters of barley from Danzig. August: wheat sold at subsidised price to poor. TC DdCdF pp. 177–178; COf B2 pp. 56–63.
1774 March	News sought from James Le Marchant at Rotterdam about corn prices at Danzig; flour to be imported to the town from Southampton. December: Town constables authorised to import wheat from America. TC DdCdF pp. 188, 197; COf B2 pp. 71–72, 82–87.
1775 Jan.	Barley to be imported to St Peter Port from Wells (Norfolk). Feb. – August: price of wheat, barley, flour fixed. TC DdCdF pp. 199, 200; COf B2 p. 90.

APPENDIX 14: Corn shipped from England to Guernsey, 1744–1763

Quantities in quarters and bushels

Year ending Christmas	Barley	Malt	Oatmeal	Rye	Wheat
1744	353/4	612/3			775/1
1745	6/	356/			291/6
1746		586/4			166/7
1747	240/	901			525/7
1748	10/	825/4	7/4		406/7
1749		830/4			260/
1750	250/	884/4			540/
1751	353/	1213/		6/	653/7
1752	912/2	1022/			771/4
1753	178/	494/7			153/6
1754	137/4	722/6			463/1
1755	405/1	506/3			564/3
1756	447/	1037/4			683/
1757	302/2	1255/1			433/2
1758	278	1168/5			1227/
1759	168	381/2			1059/3
1760	18/6	1155/2			1780/7
1761	299	512/1	6		1691/4
1762	179/3	1167/6			2105/2
1763	214/	918/			1659/7

[*Source:* BL Add Ms 38387 f 32v – f 52r]

APPENDIX 15.1: Census of St Peter Port, 1827, population divided into: A: natives, B: settled migrants, C: recent migrants

Vingtaines	Natives		Migrants, settled		Migrants, recent	
	Male	Female	Male	Female	Male	Female
01 Grande-Rue	154	213	20	19	41	37
02 Pollet et rue Forêt	142	229	94	123	49	30
03 Rue des Forges	50	98	16	28	10	13
04 Rue Berthelot	26	38	21	11	37	17
05 Rue de l'Eglise	32	44	25	18	37	19
06 Rue du Marché	55	92	21	41	22	20
07 Rue de la Fontaine	84	148	8	9	52	37
08 Rue du Bordage	81	135	13	12	39	24
09 Rue des Cornets et Beauregard	189	263	44	52	117	90
10 La Tour	55	96	6	7	14	6
11 Haute-Ville et Fort-George	189	314	57	85	54	39
12 Haut Pavé et Ruette Brulée	120	151	5	9	23	16
13 Contrée-Mansell	205	288	21	31	27	16
14 Rue Poidevin	91	108	7	8	12	9
15 Rue du Parc et Charroterie	99	117	9	12	11	9
16 Grand et Petit Marché	39	76	9	15	0	0
17 Vauquiedor et Havilland	34	35	4	6	8	2
18 Mont Durand	185	209	23	48	27	20
19 Vauvert et Cordiers	75	139	28	46	36	24
20 Grange et Vaudinerie etc	87	115	26	52	2	1
21 Rohais et Foulon	64	63	19	28	0	0
22 St Jacques	75	116	8	12	15	0
23 L'Hyvreuse	86	111	46	76	12	12
24 Doyle-Road	19	21	15	17	1	0
25 Ville-Neuve	221	377	108	145	79	58
26 Truchot	135	166	6	7	16	12
27 Canichers &c	139	196	62	76	25	27
28 Glategny	137	213	25	25	64	46
29 Salters' Street et Piette	173	222	36	42	53	31
30 Rue de Paris et Amballes	122	154	46	54	32	15
31 Bouët	165	150	16	25	14	3
32 Couture et Ramée	117	140	20	23	11	6
33 Terres, Hubits, Herm &c	50	69	22	31	52	21
	3495	4906	886	1193	992	660
	28.8	40.4	7.3	9.8	8.2	5.4]

[*Source*: COf B44, census August 1827; *Gazette de Guernesey*, 12 Jan. 1828]

APPENDIX 15.2: Population of St Peter Port, 1827: indices of dissimilarity

		a	b	c	d	e	f
a	Natives, males	x	7	29	31	28	30
b	" females		x	27	28	24	25
c	Migrants, settled, males			x	8	31	31
d	" settled, females				x	36	35
e	" recent, males					x	10
f	" recent, females						x

[*Source and notes*: as for Appendix 15.1. The original definitions of the three categories were as follows: [Native] *Natifs ou mariés à des natifs, ou ayant acquis un établissement permanent.* [Settled migrant] *Etrangers qui ont intention de rester, et ayant maison ou logement à eux.* [Recent migrant] *Etrangers sur passage ou demeurant en cabaret, ou autre maison de réception pour les étrangers.* It should be noted that the 'native' category contained an immigrant element.]

The index of dissimilarity 'allows the distribution of a subgroup of the population to be compared to the distribution of other subgroups' [J. R. Short, *Urban Data Sources* (London, 1980), p. 82]. The ID values can range from 0 to 100; values close to 0 imply that the two subgroups have similar spatial distribution, whereas values close to 100 indicate that the spatial distributions are dissimilar. The analysis above shows the correspondence between spatial distance for different origin/gender groups. The highest indices of dissimilarity – 36 and 35 – are to be found between the settled migrant females and the recent migrant arrivals in St Peter Port [male and female].

A second analytical approach which throws further light on residential patterns is the index of segregation. This is considered in Appendix 15.3.

APPENDIX 15.3: Population of St Peter Port, 1827: indices of segregation

NATIVE		males	13
		females	10
MIGRANTS	Settled,	males	24
	Settled,	females	27
	Recent,	males	24
	Recent,	females	24

[*Source*: as for Appendix 15.1]

Notes: The index of segregation 'facilitates the comparison of a subgroup distribution with that of the whole population,' (J. R. Short, *op. cit.*, p. 82). The index of segregation values can range from 0 to 100, the values closer to 100 denoting a greater degree of residential segregation. The table shows the extent to which the migrant groups [c,d,e,f,] did not exhibit a similar spatial distribution to the distribution of the total population. The category of 'settled migrant females' [IS 27] exhibited the greatest degree of residential segregation.

The indices of dissimilarity and segregation 'provide a measure of the degree of association between the spatial distribution of different groups of the population' but they measure the whole subgroup across the town. A third technique employs the calculation of the location quotient which measures the degree of concentration of particular groups, area by area. This analysis is considered in Appendix 15.4 below.

APPENDIX 15.4: Population of St Peter Port, 1827: location quotients

Street	Natives		Settled Migrants		Recent Migrants	
	males	females	males	females	males	females
01 Grande-Rue	1.1	1.1	0.6	0.4	1.0	*1.4*
02 Pollet et rue Forêt	0.7	0.8	*1.9*	*1.9*	0.9	0.8
03 Rue des Forges	0.8	1.1	*1.0*	*1.3*	0.6	*1.1*
04 Rue Berthelot	0.6	0.6	*1.9*	0.7	*3.0*	*2.1*
05 Rue de l'Eglise	0.6	0.6	*2.0*	*1.0*	*2.6*	*2.0*
06 Rue du Marché	0.8	0.9	*1.1*	*1.7*	*1.1*	*1.5*
07 Rue de la Fontaine	0.9	1.1	0.3	0.3	*1.9*	*2.0*
08 Rue du Bordage	0.9	1.1	0.6	0.4	*1.6*	*1.5*
09 Rue des Cornets et Beauregard	0.9	0.9	0.8	0.7	*1.9*	*2.2*
10 La Tour	1.0	1.3	0.4	0.4	0.9	0.6
11 Haute-Ville et Fort-George	0.9	1.1	*1.1*	*1.2*	0.9	1.0
12 Haut Pavé et Ruette Brulée	1.3	1.2	0.2	0.3	0.9	0.9
13 Contrée-Mansell	1.2	1.2	0.5	0.5	0.6	0.6
14 Rue Poidevin	1.3	1.1	0.4	0.3	0.6	0.7
15 Rue du Parc et Charroterie	1.3	1.1	0.5	0.5	0.5	0.6
16 Grand et Petit Marché	1.0	1.4	0.9	*1.1*	0	0
17 Vauquiedor et Havilland	1.3	1.0	0.6	0.7	*1.1*	0.4
18 Mont Durand	1.3	1.0	0.6	1.0	0.6	0.7
19 Vauvert et Cordiers	0.7	1.0	*1.1*	*1.3*	*1.3*	*1.3*
20 Grange et Vaudinerie etc	1.1	1.0	*1.3*	*1.9*	0.1	0.1
21 Rohais et Foulon	1.3	0.9	*1.5*	*1.6*	0	0
22 St Jacques	1.2	1.3	0.5	0.5	0.8	0
23 L'Hyvreuse	0.9	0.8	*1.8*	*2.3*	0.4	0.6
24 Doyle-Road	0.9	0.7	*2.8*	*2.4*	0.2	0
25 Ville-Neuve	0.8	0.9	*1.5*	*1.5*	1.0	*1.1*
26 Truchot	1.4	1.2	0.2	0.2	0.6	0.6
27 Canichers &c	0.9	0.9	*1.6*	*1.5*	0.6	0.9
28 Glategny	0.9	1.0	0.7	0.5	*1.5*	*1.7*
29 Salters' Street et Piette	1.1	1.0	0.9	0.8	*1.2*	1.0
30 Rue de Paris et Amballes	1.0	0.9	*1.5*	*1.3*	0.9	0.7
31 Bouët	1.5	1.0	0.6	0.7	0.5	0.1
32 Couture et Ramée	1.3	1.1	0.9	0.7	0.4	0.3
33 Terres, Hubits, Herm &c	0.7	0.7	*1.2*	*1.3*	*2.6*	*1.6*

[*Source:* as for Appendix 15.1.]

Notes: The location quotient measures the degree of concentration of particular groups. If a subgroup in an area has a location quotient less than 1 the subgroup is under-represented in that area; if the location quotient is greater than 1, the subgroup is over-represented. Concentrations of migrants are indicated by bold italics.

APPENDIX 15.5

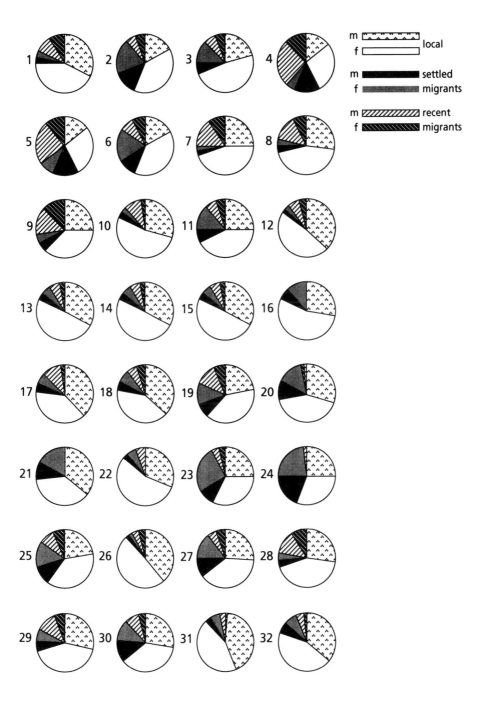

Pie charts to illustrate the population composition of the streets of St Peter Port, 1827.
See Appendix 15.4 (opposite) for the identification of the streets. The pies are constructed
of uniform size to allow easier comparison of the ratios. No. 33 omitted
(not wholly St Peter Port)

APPENDIX 16: 'Foreign' male migrants in St Peter Port (arriving in 1830 and still resident in the town in December of that year. N = 192)

MIGRANTS	
Number of single male migrants:	77.6%
Number of male migrants with dependents:	22.4%
DEPENDANTS	
Mean no. of dependants per accompanying male migrant:	2.8
Median	2
Mode	1
Standard deviation	1.98
AGE of migrant males	
Mean:	31 years
Median:	28
Mode:	22
Standard deviation:	11.3
ORIGIN	
England	79.0%
France:	8.4
Ireland:	8.4
Scotland:	3.7
Elsewhere:	0.5

[*Source:* COf B44, Census of migrants, 1830.]

APPENDIX 17: Occupations of 1009 migrants, St Peter Port, 1830

(The classification of occupations is a somewhat arbitrary affair. For example, inn-keepers are sometimes seen as belonging to the service sector, sometimes to the food and drink sector. For that reason the full analysis is given.)

LABOURERS: 25.5%

CONSTRUCTION: 20.5%
[Carpenters 47, masons and stonemasons 25, sawyers 21, painters 19, plasterers 18, shipwrights 15, joiners 11, cabinet-makers 10, stone-cutters 9, wheelwrights 8, brickmakers 5, bricklayers 4, turners 4, coachmakers 2, builder 1, stone dresser 1, thatcher 1, moulder 1, chairmaker 1, gilder 1, lath-maker 1, millwright 1, upholsterer 1, varnish maker 1]

PENSIONERS, GENTLEMEN & PROFESSIONS: 13.8%
[Pensioners 68, gentlemen 45, merchants 12, clerks 4, shipowners 2, schoolmasters 2, professor of languages 1, attorney 1, surgeon 1, officer 1, engineer 1, student 1]

SERVICES & MISCELLANEOUS: 11.8%
[Servants 32, gardeners 21, shopkeepers 15, miners 9, printers 5, auctioneers 3, chimney sweeps 3, gas-workers 3, rope-makers 3, musicians 2, agent 1, artist 1, bandboxmaker 1, billiard-table keeper 1, butler 1, cattle-dealer 1, chandler 1, chemist 1, cigar-maker 1, coal-meter 1, grave-digger 1, rag merchant 1, razor-grinder 1, grinder 1, rigger 1, soapmaker 1, shopman 1, signalman 1, stationer 1, tobacconist 1, trunkman 1, trussmaker 1, ware-merchant 1]

FOOD & DRINK: 8.0%
[Bakers 22, butchers 18, innkeepers 12, brewers 9, millers 7, distillers 5, maltsters 3, confectioners 2, cider merchant 1, curer of hams 1, publican 1]

LEATHER TRADES: 7.8%
[Shoemakers 51, cordwainers 13, boot & shoemakers 4, saddlers 6, dyers 3, curriers 2]

METALWORK: 5.1%
[Blacksmiths 14, smiths 10, plumbers 4, founders 4, watchmakers 4, braziers 3, iron-founders 2, nailors 2, tinmen 2, brassfounder 1, gunsmith 1, hardwareman 1, locksmith 1, plater 1, whitesmith 1]

CARRYING/TRANSPORT: 3.4%
[Carters 11, coachmen 4, livery-stable keepers 4, seamen 3, stable-keepers 2, grooms 2, sailors 2, gigsman 1, master mariner 1, pilot 1, boatman 1, porter 1, waggoner 1]

TEXTILES: 3.1%
[Tailors 30, hatter 1]

AGRICULTURE AND FISHERY: 1.0%
[Farmers 4, husbandmen 2, oystermen 2, fisherman 1, nurseryman 1]

[*Source:* COf B44 Census of migrants, 1830]

APPENDIX 18: Alien merchants residing in St Peter Port, eighteenth century

John Taylor, vintner, TC burial 9 Nov. 1742.

Richard Keyt, vintner, TC burial 9 Feb. 1743.

Andrew Affleck, vintner, from Hampstead, Middlesex; will proved 19 Jan. 1743; EC Wills (1738–54), p. 91.

Abraham Frecker, vintner, from Gosport, Isle of Wight; will proved 19 Sept. 1761; EC Wills (1754–62), p. 208.

James Stewart, wine merchant; BL Lansdowne Ms 657, f 24r – f 25r 1 Feb. 1752 Harris to Ligonier. Harris saw Stewart in St Peter Port c.1748 and considered him responsible for the scheme whereby St Peter Port merchants imported wine into Guernsey for British colleagues who thus evaded duty payable to the king. Harris described Stewart as being 'just then broke from being Lord Provost of Edinburgh' but 'at this day the greatest wine merchant in Europe'.

William Bell, wine merchant, see Chapter Five.

James Campbell, merchant, PRO CUST 62/66, p. 184, 1 Feb. 1747/1748, Southampton customs to London.

David Thomson, merchant, probably from Montrose, Scotland; will proved 8 Feb. 1796; EC Wills (1795–1803), pp. 44–46. (Sometimes spelt Thompson.)

Daniel Vardon, merchant, from Atis, Normandy; will proved 25 July 1793; EC Wills (1780–95), pp. 302–308.

Louis Dunière, privateering agent (and merchant?), from Quebec; see P. L. Wickins, 'The Economics of Privateering: Capital Dispersal in the American War of Independence', Journal of European Economic History, vol. 13, no. 2 – Fall 1984, p. 389. Dunière: see *Dictionary of Canadian Biography* vol 5, 1801–1820, (Toronto, 1982), pp 283–284.

John Harvey, merchant, from Cornwall (? Falmouth); Stevens-Cox collection, Harvey papers.

Mr Lagerman, merchant; PRO WO 34/108 f 31r, 5 Jan. 1782 Irving to Amherst: 'German merchant who has resided here some years'; PRO WO 34/108 f 39r, Irving to Hill: 'from Morlaix'. (Sometimes spelt Lageman.)

Mr Adam, merchant, German; PRO WO 34/108, 14 Jan. 1782 Irving to Hillsborough.

Isaac Crousaz de Prelaz, wine merchant, Swiss, resident by 1783 (family papers belonging to Mrs Grant).

Ninian Douglas, merchant, 'in the island of Guernsey', mentioned in the will of Benjamin Douglas, s. of George Douglas of Jedburgh; will proved 30 Dec. 1796; EC Wills (1795–1803), pp. 70–72.

There are others whose surnames suggest that they were of foreign origin (e.g. John Cornelius).

APPENDIX 19: The work of porters and coopers

Charges on 1 pipe of wine:	
Duty	2/5
Landing & stowing	1/3
Shipping & putting out	1/3
Cooper to receive in cellar	3d
Candles & bung cloth	3d
Cooperage, hoops &c from 2/ to 2/6 or 6/6 if trimm'd entirely new according to what is done on it.	
Warehouse room	6d. per month
Commission	2/6
If forced or rack'd	[*variable*]

[*Source:* Priaulx, Guille letter book, 4 Oct. 1792, Guille to Shuffield.]

APPENDIX 20: Inhabitants of St Peter Port insuring with the *Sun Fire Insurance Company*, London, 1718–31

Abbreviations: d.h. = dwelling house

MERCHANTS

Samuel BONAMY: for goods and merchandise in his appartment belonging to Mr Dobrée at the lower end of Cornet St.; and for goods and merchandise in his cellar under the d.h. of Mr Nicholas Naftell, the upper end of Cornet Street [12/212, 213/19679, 19680].

Nicholas CAREY, gentleman: d.h. in High St., goods and merchandise in d.h. [12/228/19737, 19738].

Peter CAREY Esq.: house, late the d.h. of Peter Martin Esq in the Great Street. Peter Carey Esq for his goods and merchandise in his warehouse near his brewhouse [11/3/16815, 16816].

Peter Anthony COUTART merchant: Elisha Le Marchant & Peter Anthony Coutart – goods and merchandise in their warehouse by itself in the upper end of 'la profonde rue' near Mr de Havilland's gardens – not exceeding £500 [22/148/38530].

Henry DE JERSEY, merchant: for his goods and merchandise in his d.h., Fountain St [10/212/15593; see also 10/421/12230].

Nicholas DE SAUSMAREZ, merchant, for his house being the d.h. only of Carterette Rougett, High St. [10/128/15191]; d.h., High St. [12/440/20800].

Elisha DOBREE senior, merchant: for his d.h. and for his goods and merchandise in his d.h. [10/283/15940, 15941].

John DOBREE: d.h. and house adjoining to his dwelling house, Pollet [9/126/13465, 13466].

Nicholas DOBREE, merchant: d.h. and warehouse adjoining to d.h.: goods and merchandise in warehouse adjoining d.h., Forge St. [10/105/15083, 15084; 14/287/26038. See also 22/132 for house and barns at Portsea].

Thomas DOBREE, merchant: d.h. situate between the houses of Aaron Guillaume & the heirs of Elisha Saumarez [10/421/–].

John GRANGERAU, merchant: for his household goods and stock in trade in his d.h., lower end of Fountain St. [23/361/40729].

Mathew GUERIN, merchant: d.h. at the top of Fountain St. insured for £500 [22/148/38531].

John JERSEY, merchant: for his goods in trade only in his shop in the house of Mr Daniel Naftel called Newhouse – £500 [23/420/41047].

John LE MESURIER, merchant: for his d.h., Fountain St. [9/84/13262]; stoned and tiled d.h. £500; his goods and stock in trade therein £500 [30/200/50249]. Briard House, Great St., in possession of Simon Reviere, house only, £1000 [14/385/26478].

John LE ROY, merchant: d.h. Fountain St. [10/35/14763].

Thomas MASSEY, merchant: d.h. only, £500 [14/390/26503].

Charles MAUGER, merchant: house called the Grand Boscq now empty [10/201/15538]; goods and merchandise in house called Bosse [10/436/16680].

Elias MAUGER, merchant, d.h. High St. [13/56/22374].

Peter STEPHEN, merchant: goods and merchandise value of £1000 [10/355/16274, 16275. *Vide* also 12/395/20565 and 26/230/44851].

GENTLEMEN AND OTHERS

John BOWDEN, brewer: house at Mont Chibell, brewhouse and house next door [9/60/13146, 13147; 9/126/13467].

James CAREY: d.h. Fountain St. [10/128/15190].

Eleazar LE MARCHANT, gentleman: d.h. [9/297/14307].

Thomas LE MARCHANT, gentleman: house at Great Crossway, High St. insured for £1000 [16/174/30382].

Daniel MAUGER, mariner: d.h. High St. [11/365/18615].

Rachel MAUGER, widow: d.h. Market Place [11/58/17056].

Capt Daniel NAFTELL: d.h. near the church [9/112/12221].

Capt Nicholas NAFTELL: mariner [9/343/–].

Elizabeth PERCHARD, widow: d.h. Fountain St., goods in d.h. [12/103/19128, 19129].

[*Source:* London, Guildhall Library, 11936; references to vol/page/policy number.]

APPENDIX 21: Vessels built in Guernsey, 1812–27

[Numbers; aggregate tonnage in brackets]

	Ship	Brig	Schooner	Cutter
1812				1 [16]
1813				
1814				1 [32]
1815	1 [250]	1 [140]		3 [118]
1816				3 [61]
1817	1 [208]	1 [113]		1 [22]
1818		1 [204]		
1819	1 [232]	4 [544]	2 [199]	
1820		4 [716]		1 [28]
1821		5 [1110]		1 [112]
1822				1 [61]
1823		2 [395]		5 [109]
1824	1 [225]	2 [409]		11 [264]
1825			1 [146]	7 [280]
1826		2 [354]		
1827		4 [698]		

[*Source and notes*: J. Jacob, *Annals of the British Norman Isles* (Paris, 1830), pp. 456–457. A few of these vessels were built at St Sampson's or in Sark; the vast majority were constructed at yards in the town or parish of St Peter Port.]

APPENDIX 22: Commercial establishments in St Peter Port, 1834

PROFESSIONS: academies and schools, 27; advocates, 7; law agents, 14; notaries, 7; professors and teachers, 16; surgeons, 19; surveyors, 2; veterinary surgeon, 1.

SERVICES & MISCELLANEOUS: auctioneers, 6; banks, 2; baths, 2; bed-feather dealers, 3; booksellers and stationers, 10; china, glass and earthenware dealers, 10; chemists and druggists, 9; coal merchants, 9; coopers, 6; fire insurance agents, 13; inns and hotels, 8; libraries, circulating, 1; lottery office, 1; merchants, general & commission, 20; newspapers, 4; optician, 1; perfumers and hairdressers, 7; piano forte tuners, 2; printers, 5; public reading room, 1; rope makers, 2; ship and general agents, 14; soap and candle manufacturers, 4; taverns and public houses, 29; tobacco and snuff manufacturers, 8; umbrella makers, 3; watch makers and jewellers, 13; furniture polisher, 1; commission agent, 1; surgical instrument maker, 1; brush and sieve dealer, 1; furniture broker, 1; lath rendr., 1; stationer, 1; optician & mathematical instrument maker, 1; religious tract depository, 1; trunk maker, 1; brush, bellows & last maker, 1; musical instrument dealer, 1; Guernsey Bible Society.

CONSTRUCTION: block and pump makers, 3; boat builders, 2; brick makers & lime burners, 6; cabinet makers, 13; carpenters, painters, glaziers, builders, 29; carvers and gilders, 2; coach makers & wheelwrights, 3; machine ruler, 1; painters, house, sign and ornamental, 8; plasterers, 12; sawyers, 7; ship builders, 5; stone and marble masons, 3; timber merchants, 6; turners, 5; wheelwrights, 3; slate merchant, 1; millwright, 1.

FOOD & DRINK: bakers, 27; brewers, 7; butchers, 36; confectioners, 2; corn merchants, 9; distillers, 2; grocers, 16; grocers, wine and spirit merchants and dealers, 33; millers 6; wine and spirit merchants, 17; wine merchants, 6; spirit dealer, 1; chocolate manufacturer, 1; eating house, 1.

LEATHER TRADES: boot and shoe makers, 49; dyers & scourers, 7; saddlers &c., 4; tanners, 3.

METALWORK: blacksmiths, 13; brass founders, 2; braziers and tin-plate workers, 7; ironmongers, braziers &c., 8; plumbers, 4; white smiths & bell hangers, 13; nail manufacturer, 1.

TEXTILES: clothes salesmen, 4; fancy repositories, 7; hat manufacturers, 3; linen and woollen drapers, 17; milliners & straw bonnet makers, 12; pelisse and dressmakers, 3; sail makers, 3; silk manufacturer, 1; straw bonnet makers, 4; tailors, 8; stay maker, 2; truss maker & furrier, 1; silk mercers, 1.

TRANSPORT/CARRYING: livery stable keepers, 10.

AGRICULTURE: nursery & seedsmen & florists, 5; seedsman, 1.

[*Source:* J. Stevens Cox (ed.), *Guernsey Commercial Directory for 1834* (Guernsey, 1980).]

APPENDIX 23: Residential patterns and wealth by vingtaine, 1727

Vingtaine	quarters	% of total	rank	mean *per caput*	rank
Carrefour	5060	20.7	1	99.2	1
Grande Rue	4115	16.9	2	82.3	3
Berthelot	1020	4.2	10	53.7	6
Pilori	2875	11.8	3	89.8	2
Eglise	1225	5.0	8	51.0	8
Cimetière +	2275	9.3	5	47.4	9
Fontaine	2695	11.0	4	51.8	7
Contrée Mansell +	1065	4.4	9	32.3	10
de Putron	150	0.6	12	15.0	12
St Jacques +	2000	8.2	6	54.1	5
Truchot	1390	5.7	7	69.5	4
Pollet	545	2.2	11	28.7	11
	24415	100.0		62.0	

The highest tax assessments in St Peter Port, 1727

Name	Quarters	Vingtaine
Thomas Le Marchant snr	700	Carrefour
Nicolas Dobrée snr	600	"
Josué Le Marchant	600	Berthelot
Pierre Estienne	600	Pilori
Pierre Careye	550	Cimetière/Beauregard
Veuve Mr Nicolas Le Pelley*	510	Carrefour
Madame de Havilland*	500	Grande Rue
Jean Mauger	450	Grande Rue
James de Beauvoir	425	St Jacques
Nicolas Careye	400	Grande Rue
Daniel de Lisle senr	400	Carrefour
Samuel Bonamy	400	Eglise
Eleazar Le Marchant	400	Truchot

* & children

[*Source:* COf A67]

Notes: + *vingtaines aggregated in the original assessments:*

   Cimetière with Beauregard;

   Contrée Mansell with Hauteville and Mont Durand;

   St Jacques with Couture and Bouet.

In the following analyses the tax payers are classified with regard to their tax assessment:

LOW: assessment of tax payer less than 20 quarters;

MIDDLE: assessment of tax payer between 20 and 99 quarters;

HIGH: assessment of tax payer 100 quarters and above.

LOCATION QUOTIENTS, 1727

'The Location Quotient is calculated by dividing the percentage of the subgroup of the population in an area by the percentage of the total population in the same area … If an area has an LQ value greater than 1 then that subgroup of the population is over-represented in that particular area.' [J. R. Short, *Urban Data Sources* (London, 1980), p. 81.] In St Peter Port in 1727 the highly assessed tax payers were over-represented in the vingtaines of Carrefour, Grande Rue, Pilori (and *marginally* in St Jacques).

	Low	Middle	High
Carrefour	0.8	0.9	*1.7*
Grande Rue	0.8	1.0	*1.4*
Berthelot	1.3	0.8	0.9
Pilori	0.9	0.7	*1.9*
Eglise	0.8	1.2	0.9
Cimetière +	0.9	1.4	0.3
Fontaine	0.9	1.2	0.7
Contrée Mansell +	1.4	0.9	0.5
de Putron	2.0	0.5	0.0
St Jacques +	1.2	0.8	*1.1*
Truchot	1.0	1.1	0.8
Pollet	1.4	0.9	0.3

THE INDEX OF DISSIMILARITY, 1727

The Index of Dissimilarity 'provides a measure of the similarity in the spatial distribution of two socio-economic and/or birthplace groups. The ID value ranges from 0 to 100. When the ID value is close to 0 this implies that the two populations have similar spatial distributions. Conversely, the closer the calculated value is to 100 the more dissimilar are the two spatial distributions and hence the greater the degree of residential segregation.' [J. R. Short, *op. cit.*, pp. 76–77.] In St Peter Port in 1727 there was greatest dissimilarity in the spatial distribution of the highly and lowly assessed tax payers (ID 31).

	Low	Middle	High
Low	x	19	31
Middle		x	29
High			x

THE INDEX OF SEGREGATION, 1727

The Index of Segregation 'measures the extent to which a specified subgroup has a similar spatial distribution to the distribution of the total population … The IS value ranges from 0 to 100 with values closer to 100 indicating a greater degree of residential segregation.' [J. R. Short, *op. cit.*, pp. 78–79].

Low	19
Middle	17
High	29

APPENDIX 24: Residential patterns and wealth by vingtaine, 1800

Vingtaine	quarters	% of total	rank	mean *per caput*	rank
Carrefour	15665	16.6	1	198.3	3
Pollet	11060	11.7	3	175.6	4
Grande Rue	9510	10.1	5	257.0	2
Berthelot	13080	13.8	2	319.0	1
Eglise	3475	3.7	10	93.9	8
Cimetière +	7095	7.5	8	168.9	5
Fontaine	8265	8.8	6	87.9	9
Contrée Mansell +	5420	5.7	9	80.9	10
Hauteville +	9540	10.1	4	99.4	7
St Jacques +	3200	3.4	11	47.8	11
Truchot +	8145	8.6	7	121.6	6
	94455	100.0		135.7	

The highest tax assessments in St Peter Port, 1800

Name	Quarters	Vingtaine
Elizee Tupper	2450	Cimetière/Beauregard
Jean Carey senr. fils Jean	1550	Carrefour
Pierre Mourant	1530	"
Thomas Le Marchant fils James	1500	"
Osmond de Beauvoir	1500	Grande Rue
Henry Brock	1410	Berthelot
Jean Lukis	1300	"
Dame veuve Richard de Beauvoir	1210	Grande Rue
William de Jersey	1200	Berthelot
Nicolas Maingy jr.	1200	"
Thomas Mansell	1200	Contrée Mansell
Nicolas Maingy snr.	1080	"

[*Source*: COf A66]

Notes: + *vingtaines aggregated in the original recording:*

> *Cimetière aggregated with Beauregard;*
>
> *Contrée Mansell with Mont Durand;*
>
> *Hauteville with de Putron;*
>
> *St Jacques with Couture and Bouet;*
>
> *Truchot with Glateny;*
>
> *Eglise with Pilori.*

In the following analyses the same definitions of LOW, MIDDLE and HIGH are used as in the analyses for 1727 (see Appendix 23, which also provides definitions of Location Quotient, Index of Dissimilarity and Index of Segregation).

LOCATION QUOTIENTS, 1800

	Low	Middle	High
Carrefour	0.8	0.8	*1.5*
Pollet	0.7	0.9	*1.3*
Grande Rue	0.7	0.7	*1.7*
Berthelot	0.8	0.5	*1.9*
Eglise	0.7	1.2	0.7
Cimetière	1.1	1.0	1.0
Fontaine	0.6	1.2	0.8
Contrée Mansell	1.9	1.0	0.6
Hauteville	0.9	1.2	0.8
St Jacques	1.8	1.2	0.4
Truchot	0.9	1.0	*1.1*

THE INDEX OF DISSIMILARITY, 1800

	Low	Middle	High
Low	x	17	30
Middle		x	27
High			x

THE INDEX OF SEGREGATION, 1800

Low	17
Middle	9
High	18

APPENDIX 25: Residential patterns and wealth by vingtaine, 1831

Vingtaine	quarters	% of total	rank	mean *per caput*	rank
Rue des Forges	17850	12.5	3	238	3
Pollet	11520	8.1	6	122.6	6
Marché	5635	3.9	9	86.7	9
Eglise	4075	2.8	10	72.8	10
Vauvert	15790	11.0	5	135.0	5
Grange	30285	21.2	1	426.5	1
Ville-Neuve	16865	11.8	4	219.0	4
Hauteville	25360	17.7	2	253.6	2
St Jacques	6885	4.8	8	91.8	8
Glatney	8760	6.1	7	93.2	7
	143025	99.9		173.6	

The highest tax assessments in St Peter Port, 1831

Name	Quarters	Vingtaine
Jean Allaire senr	5250	Vauvert
Thomas Priaulx senr	3500	Hauteville
Hellier Rougier	2000	Ville Neuve
Jean Carey fils Jean	1900	Grange
Joseph Collings	1730	”
William Collings	1700	”
Jean Collings	1670	Rue des Forges
Jean Maingy	1475	Grange
Marie & Rachel Le Marchant	1420	Pollet
Thomas Maingy	1400	Hauteville
Jean Carey fils Isaac	1400	Rue des Forges

[*Source:* COf A51]

Notes:

1   *Rue des Forges* included *L'Hyvreuse, Rue St Jacques, Cour, Rue Neuve*
2   *Pollet* included *Carrefour, Grande Rue, Rue Berthelot*
3   *Marché* included *Rue du Moulin, Bordage, Rue de la Fontaine*
4   *Eglise* included *Rue des Cornets, Rue Poidevin, Falaise*
5   *Vauvert* included *Contrée Mansell, Mont Durand*
6   *Grange*
7   *Ville Neuve*
8   *Hauteville* included *de Putron*
9   *St Jacques* included *Couture, Bouet*
10   *Glatney* included *Canichers*

LOCATION QUOTIENTS, 1831

[For definitions see Appendix 23.]

	Low	Middle	High
Rue des Forges	0.4	0.9	*1.3*
Pollet	1.4	1.1	0.7
Marché	1.2	0.8	0.5
Eglise	0.4	1.5	0.6
Vauvert	1.2	1.2	0.7
Grange	0.2	0.5	*1.8*
Ville-Neuve	0.5	0.7	*1.5*
Hauteville	0.6	0.7	*1.4*
St Jacques	1.7	1.0	0.7
Glatney	1.7	1.0	0.7

THE INDEX OF DISSIMILARITY, 1831

	Low	Middle	High
Low	x	15	37
Middle		x	28
High			x

THE INDEX OF SEGREGATION, 1831

Low	28
Middle	21
High	33

APPENDIX 26: Census of St Peter Port, 31 May 1831

1.	Inhabited houses	1728	
	Families	2864	
2.	Houses building	77	
3.	Houses uninhabited	82	
4.	Families – employed in agriculture	172	
	– in trade, manufacture, etc.	1275	2,864
	– all other families	1417	
5.	Males (French – 164)	5969	13,893
	Females (French – 141)	7924	
6.	Males upwards of 20 years	2874	
7.	Agriculture – occupiers 1st class	44	
	– 2nd class	21	
	– labourers in agriculture	120	
8.	Manufacturers	9	
	[3 cement, 3 tobacco, 1 brick & lime,		
	1 soap, 1 gas]		2,874
9.	Retail trade & handicraft	1348	
10.	Wholesale and capitalists, clergy, office-		
	clerks, professional and other educated men	581	
11.	Labourers, not agricultural	423	
	[Quarry men 2, miners 12, fishermen 10]		
12.	All other males of 20 years	263	
13.	Male servants – upwards of 20 years	65	
	– under 20 years	9	
	All female servants	917	

[*Source:* COf B44]

APPENDIX 27: The Theatre in St Peter Port

1740s

For the Benefit of Mr Salmon on Wednesday Evening will be acted a play call'd *The Inconstant or the way to win him* with several new songs by Miss Cale. To which will be added a pantomime entertainment never perform'd here before call'd *Harlequin Doctor Faustus* the character of Harlequin by Mr Salmon [Priaulx, 31469/20H, accounts book of Nathaniel Carey, sheet pinned in (– for printing as a poster?); apparently referring to St Peter Port]

1748

18 Nov 1748: receu de Mr. Sivile, comedien, pour autr. qu il receu hier, jour que les comediens donnerent pour le benefice de l'Hopital £26.12.0 tos. [Island Archives Service, DC/HX–117–1, St Peter Port Hospital journal, reference by courtesy of H Lenfestey Esq]

1774–1775

An English troupe in St Peter Port. Performances included: *4 Nov* The London Merchant; The Padlock; *23 Nov* The Fop's Fortune; The Author; *28 Nov* The Strategem; The Contrivance; *5 Dec* Rule a wife and have a wife; The Citizen; *14 Dec* The Wonder a woman keeps a secret; The Jubilee *21 Dec* Alonzo; The Jubilee; *28 Dec* The West Indian; The Golden Pippin; *1775 13 Jan* The Conscious Lovers; The Irish Widow; *20 Jan* A Word to the Wise; A Trip to Scotland; *25 Jan* Cymon; Catharine and Petruchio; *27 Jan* The Clandestine Marriage; High Life below stairs; *13 Feb* The Fair Penitent [Priaulx, Charles Mollet journal]

1783–1784

An English troupe in St Peter Port; performances from December through to May [J. P. Warren, (ed.) 'Extracts from the Journal of Elisha Dobrée'. TSG vol. X, part iv, for 1929 (Guernsey, 1930), pp. 493–551.]

Performance for the benefit of Mr Hamilton, Monday **3 May** 1784: 'new comic opera / THE CASTLE OF ANDALUSIA / Address to the Ladies and Gentlemen of Guernsey by Hamilton / THE IRISH WIDOW (farce)/ Boxes 3s. Upper Boxes 2–6 / Pit 2s Doors open 5 begin exactly at 6.' [Priaulx, Edith Carey scrapbook, playbill]

Performance for the benefit of Mrs Cooper, Monday **10 May** 1784: 'a Musical Piece / of one act Auld Robin Gray / Comedy: THE ENGLISH MERCHANT / end of the play the celebrated CRUTCH DANCE / Musical Entertainment of THE WATERMAN [Priaulx, Edith Carey scrapbook, damaged playbill]

1787–1788

Theatre constructed behind 'the Rooms' (i.e. behind the Assembly Rooms) for the visit of a troupe of French actors (16 players); the theatre was heralded as the best ever seen in the island and was capable of holding an audience of over six hundred [Nantes, archives municipales, fonds Dobrée, Dobrée to Dobrée 17 Oct 1787]

The season lasted from October 1787 until March 1788. Performances included: *29 Oct* le Père de famille; les trois frères rivaux; *7 Nov* le mechant et l'amant auteur & valet; *17 Nov* le Joueur & l'avocat Patelin; *24 Nov* la Matromanie & le médicin malgré lui [J. P. Warren (ed.) 'Extracts from the Journal of Elisha Dobrée' TSG vol. XI, part i, for 1930 (Guernsey, 1931), pp. 106–123. Priaulx: Charles Mollet journal.]

On 3 March 1788 there was a 'riot' at the playhouse 'which caused the house to be shut up & the players prevented from acting any more' (Warren, *op. cit.*). The reason for this was a dispute between Vatar, a French printer working in St Peter Port, and Madame Desroches, allegedly because she would not hold a benefit performance for some of the actors, in particular for an actress whom Vatar protected. [*Gazette de l'île de Jersey*, vol. 2, 23 mars 1788 pp. 142–143; 29 mars 1788 pp. 147–148; 5 avril 1788 pp. 155–156.]

1793

Recommendation from Durell (of Jersey) to de Sausmarez (Guernsey), 4 Nov. 1793, vouching for the good behaviour of Fisher's company of players. Evidently Fisher had been playing in Jersey and wished to have a season in Guernsey [Sausmarez Manor: de Sausmarez papers]

At about this time John Bernard sent a company, 'wardrobe, and some scenery to Guernsey, where a theatre had been reared during the past summer, for which I supplied the entire funds, and had occasionally inspected in flying visits from Plymouth'. Bernard's leave to perform 'was but once in two years; and at the fall of the curtain, I let the house to a tobacconist, to be employed *ad interim* as a warehouse' [J. Bernard, *Retrospections of the Stage* (London, 1830), vol. 2, pp. 251–252]

1795

Bernard returned to Guernsey, armed with a letter from the Duke of Clarence [*Op. cit.*, pp. 304–308]. Thenceforth the theatre in St Peter Port was often styled the Theatre Royal. From 1795 onwards there appear to have been regular seasons. For many years Mr Hughes was the lessee. The Theatre Royal stood on what is now the site of the Magistrate's Court. It was small but boasted boxes, a pit, a gallery, stalls and upper circle.

There are some interesting anecdotes about the theatre in E. Gillett (ed.), *Elizabeth Ham by herself 1783–1820* (London, 1945). The general context of the Georgian theatre in the West Country is considered by G. Hare, *The Georgian Theatre in Wessex* (London, 1958), which has a few references to the Channel Islands. John Middlebrook considers the site of the early theatre in St Peter Port in his important essay 'La Comédie', The Review of The Guernsey Society, vol. XLVIII, No. 2, pp. 49–51.

APPENDIX 28

MAPS

Map 1:   Guernsey and its parishes

Map 2:   The east coast of Guernsey as depicted in 'A New and Exact Chart of the Islands of Guernsey, Sercq, Herm & Jethou'. This was executed from a survey made by Nicholas Dobrée; engraved by Emanuel Bowen; and published in 1746. It was issued with an accompanying pamphlet of navigational observations – *Observations sur les cartes des Isles de Guernesey* with a text in French and English [BL Maps 30.b.80]. This Dobrée map helped to establish St Peter Port as a major entrepôt. It was published again in 1779, 1786 and 1794

Map 3:   St Peter Port, 1787, as depicted in 'An Accurate Survey and Measurement of the Island of Guernsey. Surveyed by Order of His Grace the Duke of Richmond'

Map 4:   St Peter Port, c.1800. St Peter Port harbour could accommodate forty or fifty vessels but was not sufficiently large for the booming entrepôt trade. This map envisaged the construction of a new harbour to the north of the town. The suppression of smuggling in the early 19th century and the development of St Sampson's harbour relieved the pressure on St Peter Port. [Priaulx, de Magnac ms.]

Map 5:   St Peter Port, early 19th century. A few details appear to have been added after the original drafting of the map. [Priaulx, de Magnac ms.]

Map 6:   St Peter Port, early 19th century. A few details appear to have been added after the original drafting of the map. [Priaulx, de Magnac ms.]

Map 7:   St Peter Port, 1814. Part of a map executed by the architect John Wilson, published in William Berry's *History of the Island of Guernsey* (London, 1815). The map shows clearly the military barracks in and around St Peter Port

Map 8:   St Peter Port – the Grange. Part of the map entitled *The Town of St Peter Port and its Environs*. Surveyed by John Wood, 34 Paul Street, Exeter and published by Turner & Co. of Edinburgh, 1843

Map 9:   St Peter Port in the late nineteenth century

For a fuller treatment of the cartography of Guernsey the reader should consult J. P. Warren 'Evolution of the map of Guernsey' TSG vol. XVII part ii, for 1961 (Guernsey, 1962), pp. 125–172.

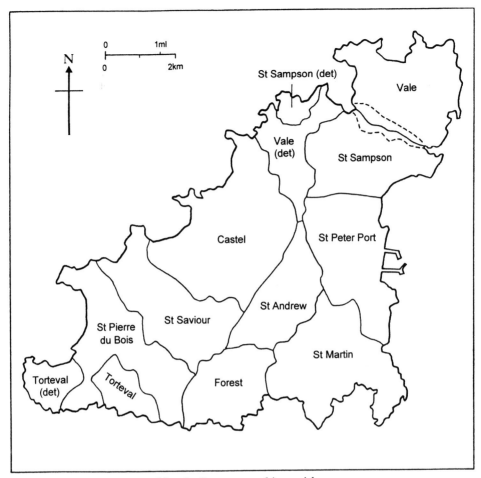

Map 1: Guernsey and its parishes

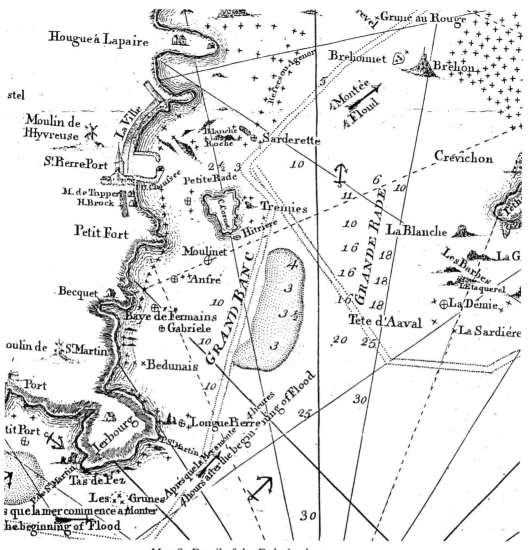

Map 2: Detail of the Dobrée chart

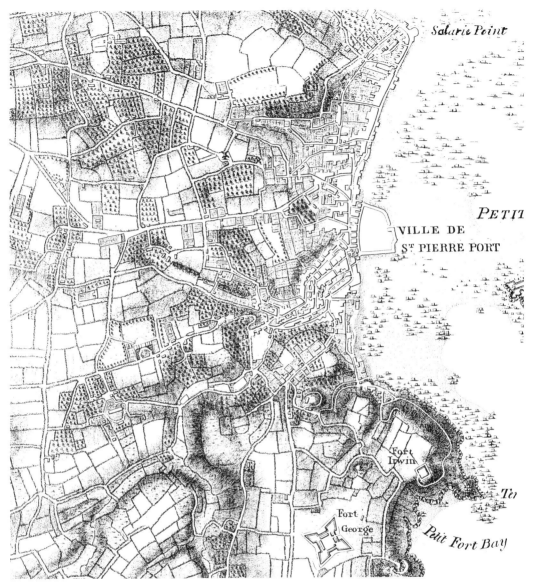

Map 3: St Peter Port, 1787

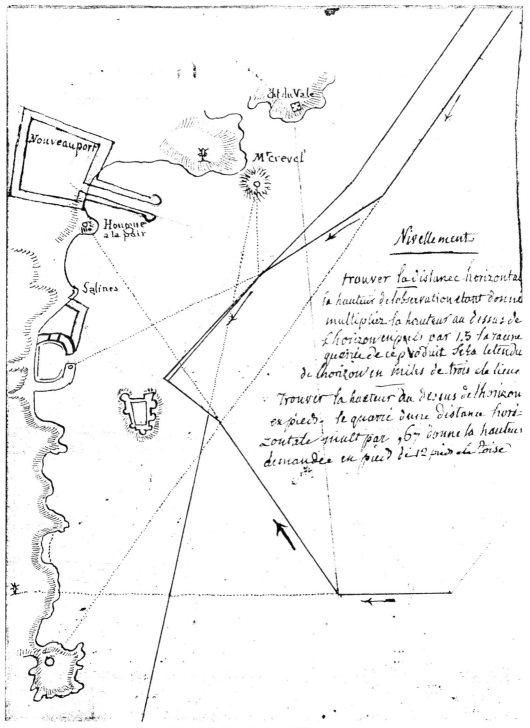

Map 4: St Peter Port, c.1800

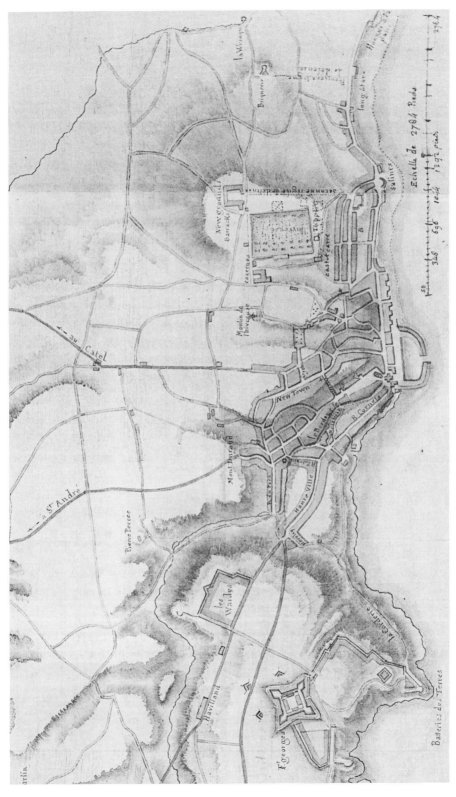

Map 5: St Peter Port, early nineteenth century

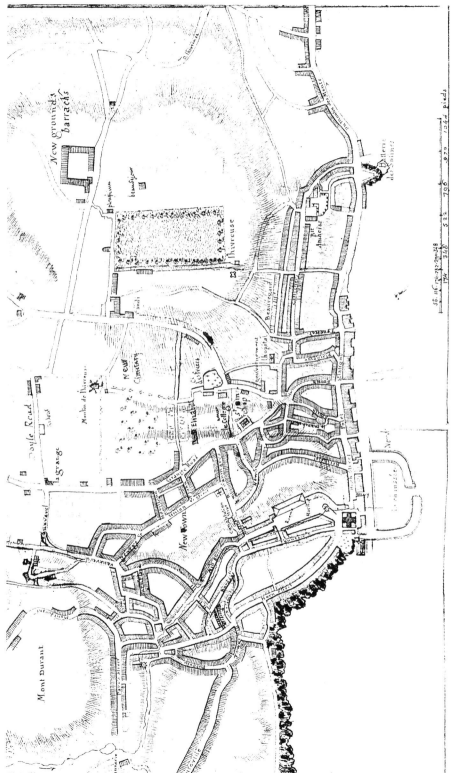

Map 6: St Peter Port, early nineteenth century

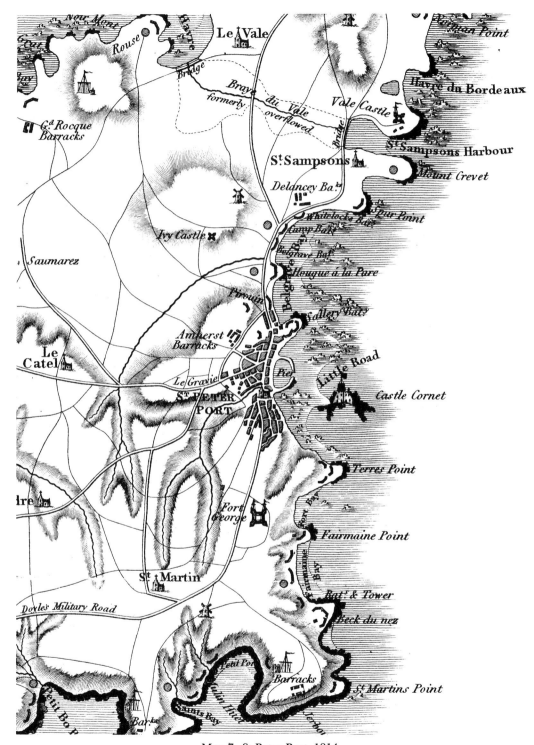

Map 7: St Peter Port, 1814

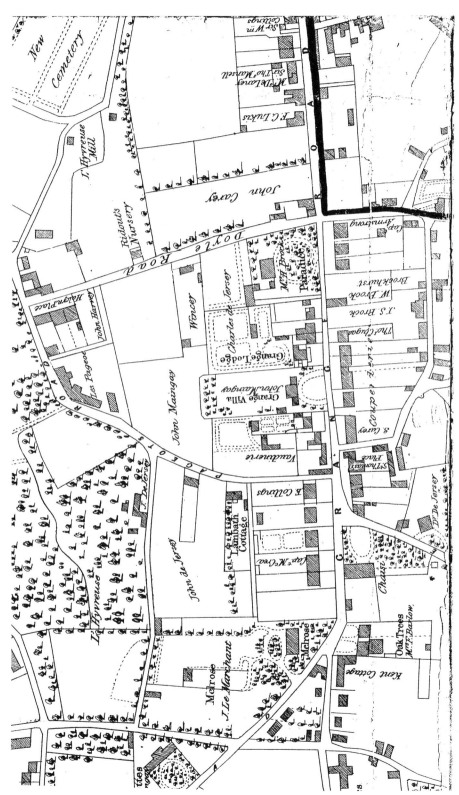

Map 8: St Peter Port – The Grange

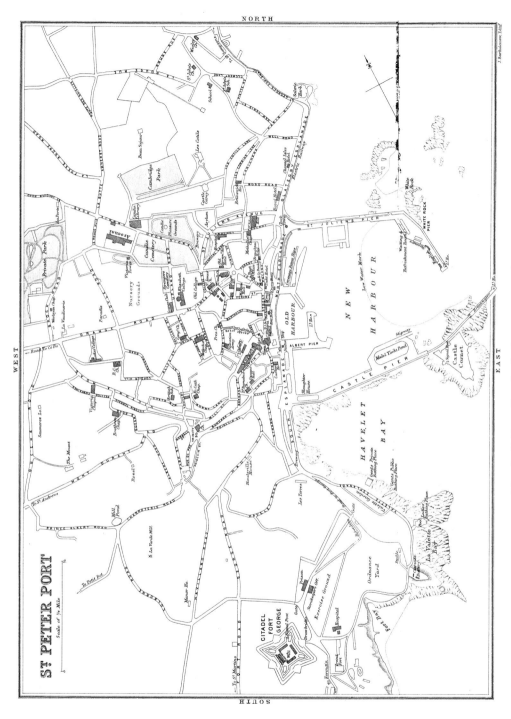

Map 9: St Peter Port in the late nineteenth century

NOTES

CHAPTER 1

1. J. H. Le Patourel, 'The Early History of St Peter Port', TSG vol XII, part ii, for 1934 (Guernsey, 1935), pp. 171–209.
2. E. F. Carey, 'The growth of St Peter Port in the early nineteenth century from the MS. of the late F. C. Lukis, Esq.', TSG vol. XII part ii, for 1934 (Guernsey, 1935), pp. 151–170.
3. C. E. B. Brett, *Buildings in the Town and Parish of St Peter Port* (Guernsey, 1975).
4. J. McCormack, *The Guernsey House* (Chichester, 1980).
5. G. Lenfestey (ed.), *Hôpital de St Pierre Port, Délibérations "A" (1726) 1741–1801*, typescript (Guernsey, 1991), p. i.
6. Information from Mr Videlo, sometime Greffier.
7. A. G. Jamieson (ed.), *A People of the Sea* (London, 1986), privateering: pp. 109–194; entrepôt: p. 372; one chapter on smuggling (pp 195–219).
8. P. Raban, 'War and Trade in the Mid-Eighteenth Century', TSG vol. XXII, part i, for 1986 (Guernsey, 1987), pp. 131–163, touches on the entrepôt trade with some quantification, pp. 152–153 in particular.
9. S. Fisher, 'Lisbon as a Port Town in the Eighteenth Century' in S. Fisher (ed.), *Lisbon as a Port Town, the British Seaman and other Maritime Themes* (Exeter, 1988), pp. 3,8,9. Fisher cites as models Ruth Pike's work on Seville; and the studies of W. G. Hoskins, W. E. Minchinton, F. E. Hyde and G. Jackson on Exeter, Bristol, Liverpool and Hull respectively, *op. cit.* p. 8.
10. P. Borsay (ed.), *The Eighteenth-Century Town* (Harlow, 1990), p. 3.
11. P. Abrams, 'Towns and Economic Growth: Some Theories and Problems' in P. Abrams and E. A. Wrigley (eds.), *Towns in Societies* (Cambridge, 1980), p. 27.
12. P. Abrams, 'Towns and Economic Growth: Some Theories and Problems' in P. Abrams and E. A. Wrigley (eds.), *Towns in Societies* (Cambridge, 1980), pp. 27–31.
13. M. J. Daunton, 'Towns and Economic Growth in Eighteenth-Century England' in P. Abrams and E. A. Wrigley (eds.), *Towns in Society* (Cambridge, 1980), pp. 274–276.
14. S. Chapman, *Merchant Enterprise in Britain* (Cambridge, 1992), p. 11.
15. P. Borsay (ed.), *The Eighteenth-Century Town* (Harlow, 1990), pp. 2–3.
16. J. de Vries, *European Urbanization 1500–1800* (London, 1984).
17. I. Wallerstein, *The Modern World-system: Capitalist Agriculture and the Origins of the European World Economy in the Sixteenth Century* (New York, 1973).
18. P. M. Hohenberg and L. H. Lees, *The Making of Urban Europe 1000–1950* (Cambridge, Massachusetts, 1985), p. 65.
19. P. Corfield, *The Impact of English Towns 1700–1800* (Oxford, 1982), p. 16.
20. P. Borsay (ed.), *The Eighteenth-Century Town* (Harlow, 1990), p. 5.
21. P. Clark (ed.), *The Transformation of English Provincial Towns* (London, 1984), p. 17.
22. *Ibid.*, p. 16 (Exeter, Nottingham and Leeds).
23. J. de Vries, *European Urbanization 1500–1800* (London, 1984), pp. 179–200 summarises, and offers a critique of, the van der Woude and Sharlin theories.
24. P. Clark, 'Migration in England during the late seventeenth and early eighteenth centuries' in P. Clark and D. Souden (eds.), *Migration and Society in Early-Modern England* (London, 1987), pp. 213–252, explores motivation and determining factors. See also C. G. Pooley and I. D. Whyte (eds.), *Migrants, Emigrants and Immigrants* (London, 1991), pp. 1–15 for observations about research trends and techniques.
25. P. Clark, 'Migrants in the city: the process of social adaptation in English towns, 1500–1800' in P. Clark and D. Souden (eds.), *Migration and Society in Early-Modern England* (London, 1987).
26. P. Borsay (ed.), *The Eighteenth-Century Town* (Harlow, 1990), p. 10.
27. *Vide supra.*
28. P. Borsay, *The English Urban Renaissance* (Oxford, 1989) explores culture and society in English provincial towns between 1660 and 1770 in these terms.
29. P. Borsay (ed.), *The Eighteenth-Century Town* (Harlow, 1990), p. 35.
30. *Ibid.*, p. 35.
31. P. Clark, *Sociability and Urbanity: Clubs and Societies in the Eighteenth Century City* (Leicester, 1986), p. 22.
32. A. D. King, *Urbanism, Colonialism, and the World-Economy* (London, 1990), p. 23.
33. P. Kriedte, *Peasants, Landlords and Merchant Capitalists* (Oxford, 1990), p. 126.
34. G. Jackson, 'The ports' in D. H. Aldcroft and M. J. Freeman (eds.), *Transport in the Industrial Revolution* (Manchester, 1983), p. 188.
35. D. Swann, 'The pace and progress of port investment in England, 1660–1830', *Yorkshire Bulletin of Economic and Social Research*, xii, 1960, pp. 32–44.

36. P. J. Corfield, *The Impact of English Towns 1700–1800* (Oxford, 1982), p. 39.
37. W. E. Minchinton, 'Bristol – metropolis of the west in the eighteenth century' in P. Clark (ed.), *The Early Modern Town* (London, 1976), pp. 297–313.
38. S. Chapman, *Merchant enterprise in Britain* (Cambridge, 1992), p. 25, *passim*.
39. M. Rediker, *Between the Devil and the Deep Blue Sea* (Cambridge, 1987), p. 27; P. J. Corfield, *The Impact of English Towns 1700–1800* (Oxford, 1982), pp. 46–47.
40. M. Rediker, *Between the Devil and the Deep Blue Sea* (Cambridge, 1987), p. 42.
41. W. E. Minchinton, 'Bristol-metropolis of the west in the eighteenth century' in P. Clark (ed.), *The Early Modern Town* (London, 1976), p. 306.
42. A. T. Patterson, *A History of Southampton 1700–1914*, vol. 1, Southampton Record Ser., xi (Southampton, 1966), pp. 41–58. E. M. Sandele 'Georgian Southampton: A Watering-Place and Spa' in J. B. Morgan and P. Peberdy (eds.), *Collected essays on Southampton* (Southampton, 1958), pp. 79–87.
43. S. McIntyre, 'Towns as Health and Pleasure Resorts: Bath, Scarborough, and Weymouth 1700–1815' D. Phil. thesis (Oxford, 1973).
44. The papers include *A Catalogue of Baker's Circulating Library, In the High Street, And in the Summer Season, Adjoining to Mr. Martin's Rooms, Southampton* (Southampton, 1776).
45. See Chapter Six.
46. J.-P. Poussou, 'The Population Increase of French Towns Between 1750 and 1914, and its Demographic Consequences' in R. Lawton and R. Lee (eds.), *Urban Population Development in Western Europe from the Late-Eighteenth to the Early Twentieth Century* (Liverpool, 1989), pp. 70–71.
47. P. Kriedte, *Peasants, Landlords and Merchant Capitalists* (Oxford, 1990), p. 127.
48. J.-P. Poussou, 'The Population Increase of French Towns Between 1750 and 1914, and its Demographic Consequences' in R. Lawton and R. Lee (eds.), *Urban Population Development in Western Europe from the Late-Eighteenth to the Early-Twentieth Century* (Liverpool, 1989), p. 71.
49. E. Le Roy Ladurie, *La ville classique*, vol. 3 of G. Duby (ed.), *Histoire de la France urbaine* (Paris, 1981), pp. 366–369.
50. E. Le Roy Ladurie, *ibid.*, p. 369.
51. J. G. Clark, *La Rochelle and the Atlantic Economy during the Eighteenth Century* (Baltimore, 1981), p. 41. P. Haudrères, 'La Compagnie Française des Indes (1719–1795)' (Thesis, University of Paris IV, 1987), analyses the volume and value of trade at Lorient.
52. F. Braudel, *The Identity of France*, vol. 2 (London, 1990), pp. 565–576.
53. J. G. Clark, *La Rochelle and the Atlantic Economy during the Eighteenth Century* (Baltimore, 1981), pp. 25–26.
54. A. Cabantous, *La Mer et les Hommes pêcheurs et matelots dunkerquois de Louis XIV à la Révolution* (Dunkirk, 1980), pp. 34–36, 295–296; A. Cabantous, *Histoire de Dunkerque* (Toulouse, 1983), pp. 87–89.
55. J. G. Clark, *La Rochelle and the Atlantic Economy during the Eighteenth Century* (Baltimore, 1981), p. 23.
56. BL Add Ms 38228 f 4r, 5 Aug 1792 Gregory to Lord Hawkesbury.
57. G. B. Nash, *The Urban Crucible* (Cambridge, Mass., 1979) p. 4.
58. *Ibid.*, p. 4.
59. P. Clark, *Sociability and Urbanity: Clubs and Societies in the Eighteenth Century City* (Leicester, 1986), p. 12; A. D. King, *Urbanism, Colonialism and the World-Economy* (London, 1991), pp. 25–26.
60. Some Sun Fire Insurance policies listed Guernsey thus.
61. D. K. Fieldhouse, *The Colonial Empires* (Basingstoke, 1992), p. 60.
62. *Ibid.*, pp. 68–69.
63. PRO WO 34/106, f147r–f147v, 17 Aug 1780 Irving to Amherst.
64. R. H. Hilton, *English and French towns in feudal society* (Cambridge, 1992), pp. 6–7.
65. J. Le Patourel, 'The Early History of St Peter Port', TSG vol XII, part ii, for 1934 (Guernsey, 1935), pp. 171–209.
66. *Ibid.*, p. 193.
67. W. Camden, *Britannia* (Amsterdam, 1639), p. 455.
68. P. Heylyn, *A Full Relation of two Journeys* (London, 1656), p. 299.
69. F. B. Tupper, *The History of Guernsey* (Guernsey, 1854), pp. 311–315.
70. A. J. Eagleston, *The Channel Islands under Tudor Government, 1485–1642* (Cambridge, 1949), p. 155.
71. *Ibid.*, p. 156. BL Lansdowne Ms 657 f17v, 25 Sept 1750 Strahan to Governor: great connection between the jurats and the merchants and consequent difficulty of obtaining justice.
72. See Chapter Seven.
73. Priaulx 31458, Jean Guille ms. p. 355.
74. A. J. Eagleston, *The Channel Islands under Tudor Government* (Cambridge, 1949), p. 155. The above account of the constitution is based principally on T. Dicey, *An Historical Account of Guernsey* (London, 1751); BL King's Ms 48; BL Add Ms 6253. For the Tudor background see now Dr D. M. Ogier's very readable account of *Reformation and Society in Guernsey* (Woodbridge, 1996).
   Bibliographical note: there has recently been extensive research, mainly by French scholars, into the history of the Atlantic world and allied themes. Those keen to read more deeply in this area should

see the works of the following authors, details of which have been added to the Bibliography: Acerra and Meyer (1990), Boulaire (1989), de Wismes (1998), Duffy *et al.* (1992, 1994), Festa (1991), Hancock (1995), Hilaire-Perez (1997), Le Bouedec (1997), Martinière (1997), Morgan (1993), Nières (1988), Petre-Grenouilleau (1997), Poussou *et al.* (1998), Price (1995), Richard (1997), Starkey *et al.* (1997), Tracy (1997), Walvin (1997).

CHAPTER 2

1. *Gazette de l'Ile de Jersey,* 3 mars 1787, p. 126, report of speech of the bailiff to the States of Guernsey 20 Jan. 1787.
2. P. M. Hohenberg and L. H. Lees, *The Making of Urban Europe 1000–1950* (Cambridge, Mass., 1985), p. 65, for town types.
3. W. W. Carey *et al.*, *The History of the Careys of Guernsey* (London, 1938), p. 102.
4. M. Mollat, *Histoire des pêches maritimes en France* (Paris, 1987), pp. 90, 113.
5. R. Ommer, 'The Cod Trade in the New World' in A. G. Jamieson (ed.), *A People of the Sea* (London, 1986), pp. 245–268. Knitting industry: see Chapter Three below.
6. A. L. Simon, *The History of the Wine Trade in England* (London, 1907), vol. 2, pp. 39–42.
7. F. B. Tupper, *The History of Guernsey* (Guernsey, 1854), p. 312, citing petition to Cromwell: 'The inhabitants ... have lost their ships, their traffic, and their trading.'
8. See Chapter One, above; and J. Walvin, *Fruits of Empire* (Basingstoke, 1997).
9. I. K. Steele, *The English Atlantic 1675–1740* (Oxford, 1986), p. 23.
10. *The Case of the Inhabitants of the Island of Guernsey, in Relation to several Orders of Council obtained by the Commissioners of the Customs, for setting Custom-House-Officers in the Island, and subjecting the Inhabitants to the Laws relating to the Customs in Great Britain.* [n.d., Priaulx copy marked c.1708/1709].
11. BL Add Ms. 38463 f 208v, 17 Aug. 1764, Southampton Customs board to London Customs House.
12. C. M. Andrews, *The Colonial Period of American History* (New Haven, 1943), vol. 4, pp. 66–67. However, a copy of an Order-in-Council, 20 March 1675, permitted trade between Guernsey (and Jersey) and British plantations in America, without ships having to journey via an English port. Island Archives Service, Price Collection, AQ49/1. It is not surprising that the English customs felt confused at times.
13. C. M. Andrews, *op.cit.,* vol. 4, p. 68.
14. Priaulx 18459 p. 18, 7 June 1777, Guille to Knowsley (of Hull).
15. Greffe, Original Correspondence, vol. 1, no. 99, 18 Nov. 1667, Atkins to Andros.
16. Northampton Record Office, Finch Hatton papers, 278.
17. F. Braudel, *Civilization and Capitalism* (London, 1984), vol. 3 (*The Perspective of the World*), p. 346. A. Lespagnol, *Messieurs de Saint-Malo* (St Malo, 1990), pp. 403–494.
18. A. Croix, *La Bretagne aux 16e et 17e siècles* (Paris, 1981), vol. 1, p. 62. A. Lespagnol, *op. cit.*, p. 192.
19. J. Delumeau, *Le Mouvement du port de Saint Malo, 1681–1720* (Paris, 1966), p. x. A. Lespagnol, *op. cit.*, p. 192.
20. P. Bonnassieux (ed.), *Archives Nationales, Conseil de Commerce et Bureau du Commerce 1700–1791* (Paris, 1900), p. 26, 27 Jan. 1702.
21. C. M. Andrews, *op. cit.*, vol. 4, p. 68: 'This traffic was carried on in defiance partly of the acts of trade and navigation and partly of the acts passed in 1678, 1689, 1693 and 1704 prohibiting trade with France.'
22. PRO SP 47/3, copy of extract of letter 29 Sept. 1712 from Mr John Sherwood.
23. Greffe, Depositions, 23 June 1713.
24. C. M. Andrews, *op. cit.*, vol. 4, p. 67. See also Priaulx 31468, pp. 6–7: Guille engaging crew in the St Malo – Dinard region, Nov.–Dec. 1713.
25. BL Sloane Ms 4053 f 239 r, 1 July 1734, Carey to Sloane [' ... about 18 years ago ...']. A. Lespagnol, *op. cit.*, pp. 541–646 for trade of St Malo with the South Seas.
26. *Vide infra.*
27. J. Duncan, *The History of Guernsey* (London, 1841), pp. 232–233.
28. PRO CUST 62/59, 10 Sept. 1719, Eyre to Southampton Customs board.
29. Cambridge U L, Cholmondeley (Houghton) Papers, 41/29.
30. BL Lansdowne Ms 657 f 17r, 25 Sept. 1750, Strahan to Governor.
31. T. Dicey, *An Historical Account of Guernsey* (London, 1751) p. 33.
32. Royal Court, Legge survey.
33. *Actes*, vol. 1 pp. 145, 165.
34. *The Case of the Town Parish versus the Nine Country Parishes ... 1759* (Guernsey, 1843), p. 19. E. W. Sharp, 'The Evolution of St Peter Port Harbour' TSG XVIII, part iii, for 1967 (Guernsey, 1968), pp. 226–255. R. Hocart, *An Island Assembly The Development of the States of Guernsey 1700–1949* (Guernsey, 1988), p. 5.
35. W. Le Marchant, *Histoire de l'Erection Originelle de l'avancement & Augmentation du Havre de la Ville de St. Pierre Port à Guernesey* (Oxford, c. 1755), Appendice pp. 4-5.

36. T. Dicey, *An Historical Account of Guernsey* (London, 1751), pp. 195–196. There are copies of the sailing directions in the Priaulx Library, Guernsey, and the British Library. The significance of Dobrée's charts is underlined by Dicey's comment that all the others 'in any of the Books of Charts' were 'extremely erroneous and not to be depended on' (Dicey, *op. cit.* pp. 195–196).
Nicholas Dobrée (1678–1751) was one of the leading merchants in St Peter Port in the first half of the 18th century. A monument in the Town Church records that he devoted himself to the security of navigation, the improvement of the harbour and the establishment of the town hospital; text in W. Berry, *The History of the Island of Guernsey* (London, 1815), p. 148. For further details of his life see R. Hocart, 'A Guernsey Merchant and his Family in the Reign of George II' TSG vol. XXI, part iii, for 1983 (Guernsey, 1984), pp. 360–378; and C. Aptel *et al.*, *Thomas Dobrée Un Homme Un Musée* (Nantes, 1997), pp. 26–28.

37. L. M. Cullen, *Anglo-Irish Trade 1660–1800* (New York, 1968), p. 148: the importance of Guernsey as a smuggling entrepôt was 'greatly enhanced' in 1765.

38. G. Dupont, *Histoire du Cotentin et de ses Iles* (Caen, 1885), vol. 4 pp. 447, 471–473 (citing memorandum by the Marquis de Crenay, 1748, referring to the Channel Islands).

39. 'Entrepôt: 1. Temporary deposit of goods, provisions, etc.; chiefly *concr.* a storehouse or assemblage of storehouses for temporary deposit. 2. A commercial centre; a place to which goods are brought for distribution to various parts of the world. 3. A mart or place where goods are received and deposited, free of duty, for exportation to another part or country.' L. Dudley Stamp (ed.), *A Glossary of Geographical Terms* (London, 1963), p. 177.

40. *Vide infra*, Chapter Three, for these port-related industries.

41. BL Add Ms 38463 f 199v – f 200r, 13 Aug. 1764, Poole Customs report.

42. *Ibid.* f 200r.

43. Information from Dr N. A. M. Rodger. See also PRO T1 381/9, 4 Oct. 1758, Cleveland to West: requesting permission for 46,250 gallons of wine to be shipped from Guernsey to navy at Spithead (wartime).

44. PRO HO 98/30, 5 Feb. 1807 Doyle to Treasury.

45. PRO T1 445 f 215v, 24 Nov. 1766, Lutwidge: proposal to prevent 'the fraud which arises from entering French wines under the denomination of Portugal or Spanish Wines in order to evade the payment of the French duty'. See also F. Wilkins, *Strathclyde's Smuggling Story* (Kidderminster, 1992), p. 39: claret to be shipped from Guernsey 'under the denomination of Spanish Galicia'.

46. BL Add Ms 38463 f 214v, 25 Aug. 1764, Weymouth Customs board to London.

47. Priaulx, Lukis ms. See Fig. 2.4 and Appendix 2. F. Mauro 'Merchant Communities, 1350–1750' in J. D. Tracy (ed.), *The Rise of Merchant Empires* (Cambridge, 1990), pp. 255–286, discusses the significance of merchant networks.

48. Nantes, Archives Municipales, fonds Dobrée. J. Meyer, *L'Armement nantais dans la deuxième moitié du XVIIIe siècle* (Paris, 1969) p. 185. C. Aptel *et al.*, *Thomas Dobrée, Un Homme Un Musée*, (Nantes, 1997), pp. 32–35.

49. *Vide supra.*

50. Priaulx 18459 contains copies of several letters from Guille to such foreign agents. 'Fabritius & Wever earned considerable commission … by lending name and nationality to illicit British trade direct from England or via Copenhagen and Ostend', O. Feldbaek, *India trade under the Danish Flag 1772–1808* (Denmark, 1963), p. 141.

51. A. G. Jamieson, 'Channel Island Shipowners and Seamen, 1700–1900' in A. G. Jamieson, ed., *A People of the Sea* (London, 1986), pp. 312–313.

52. Priaulx, Le Mesurier papers [SR], articles of agreement.

53. *Gazette de l'Ile de Jersey*, 3 mars 1787, p. 127: 'M. Paul Le Mesurier … qui s'est montré fort actif pour nos intérêts toutes les fois qu'il en a eu l'occasion'. See Sir L. Namier and J. Brooke, *The House of Commons 1754–1790* (London, 1964), vol. 3 pp. 33–34 for outline of his career. W. R. Meyer, 'Paul Le Mesurier, Lord Mayor of London' TSG vol. XXI, part v, for 1985 (Guernsey, 1986), pp. 701–704.

54. Priaulx 18459 contains copies of letters from Guille to Gregory; *Gazette de l'Ile de Jersey*, 3 mars 1787, p. 127, mentions Gregory's defence of Channel Islands' interests.

55. Guildhall Library, Lloyd's lists, 1780s.

56. Sir L. Namier and J. Brooke, *The House of Commons 1754–1790* (London, 1964), vol. 2 p. 536, (Gregory was MP for Newtown, I of W). Priaulx 18459 for Gregory & Guille business in Spain.

57. BL Add Ms 38463 f 208v, 17 Aug. 1764 Southampton Customs board report; f 201r, 13 Aug. 1764 Exeter Customs board report; f 218 r, 13 Sept. 1764, Portsmouth Customs board report.

58. Greffe, Amirauté. Priaulx, 29118/408C.

59. See Appendix 1.

60. Priaulx 18459 p. 110, 14 Aug. 1778 Guille to Ekman. Gothenburg Landsarkivet, Ekman & Co papers contain some references to the Guernsey trade (e.g. B1:10 letter book 1782–1784, pp. 35, 129–130).

61. BL Add Ms 38463 f 208v, 17 Aug. 1764 Southampton Customs report.

62. R. Davis, *The Rise of the English Shipping Industry in the Seventeenth and Eighteenth Centuries* (London, 1962), p. 60.

63. *Vide infra*, Tables 2.2 and 2.3.

64. Royal Court, Legge survey (= BL King's Ms 48). R. Ommer, 'The Cod Trade in the New World' in A. G. Jamieson (ed.), *A People of the Sea* (London, 1986), pp. 245–268, surveys the topic.

65. J. Duncan, *History of Guernsey* (London, 1841) p. 259.

66. Greffe, Amirauté vol. 11: 8 Nov. 1740.

67. Greffe, Amirauté vol. 11: 28 Aug. 1742 (the weight suggests approximately one hundred elephant tusks).

68. Greffe, Amirauté vol. 11: 13, 19, 20 Feb. 1741/42; 15, 18, 22 May 1742; 14, 19 June 1742; 10 July 1742. Seaborn and Ebsworthy captained slave ships from Bristol. See D. Richardson *Bristol, Africa and the Eighteenth-Century Slave Trade to America* (Bristol, 1987), vol. 2 pp. 15, 45, 86, 99, 115; vol. 3 (1991), p. 18.

69. F. B. Tupper, *The History of Guernsey* (Guernsey, 1854), p. 366.

70. Other references to Guernsey vessels planning to voyage to Africa, mid-18th century: PRO ADM 7/135, pass 434; pass 1366 [ship *African*]; ADM 7/136, pass 2693. *Guernsey Evening Press* 18 Apr. 1930: document *re* sale of 105 slaves from *African* in Barbados, 1750. In the sale 22 men and 5 women were bought by William Le Mesurier for £702 and an old man was purchased for £15 by Dan Tupper. Le Mesurier and Tupper appear to be Guernsey settlers.

71. L. M. Cullen, 'The Early Brandy Trade (1600–1760)' in E. Aerts *et al.* (eds), *Production, Marketing and Consumption of Alcoholic Beverages since the Late Middle Ages* (Leuven, 1990), p. 25.

72. Greffe, Amirauté, vol. 10: 19 Dec. 1730, pp. 42, 43 (13,799 gallons of rum from Antigua to Guernsey, shipped in *la Marie*).

73. PRO CUST 62/65, p. 251, 13 Sept. 1744 London Customs House to Southampton board. PRO T1/445 f 214r, 24 Nov. 1766 Lutwidge *re* Manx traders.

74. Priaulx 20763, 21 Sept. 1796 Guille to Yates.

75. BL Add Ms 38759, f 105v – f 106r.

76. *An Account presented to the House of Commons, of the number and names of vessels Cleared out from the Port of Guernsey, in the Months of November and December 1806, and January and February 1807: with the Amount of the excise and custom duties thereon.* 21st July, 1807, p. 10, in Parliamentary Papers, House of Commons, session 27 June – 14 August 1807, iv <57>, pp. 85–95. See Appendix 4 of this book.

77. H. E. S. Fisher, *The Portugal Trade* (London, 1971), p. 26.

78. PRO SP 89/55, f 255r, 6 Apr. 1762 Consul and Committee to Egremont.

79. PRO CUST 3/63.

80. BL Add Ms 38463, f 211v, 20 Aug. 1764 Warren Lisle report to London Customs board.

81. S. Baldwin, *A Survey of the British Customs* (London, 1770) p. 182, summarising the Acts 4 Geo III chap. 13 sect. 11; 8 Geo III chap. 23 sect. 2, 3.

82. PRO CUST 3/64 – 3/88.

83. *Vide infra*, trade with Ireland. French merchants lodged their wine in Guernsey to evade occasional taxes imposed in France: PRO T1/445, f 216r, 24 Nov. 1766, Lutwidge report.

84. BL Add Ms 38463, f 61r, 23 Mar. 1693/1694 Council report.

85. J. M. Price, *France and the Chesapeake* (Ann Arbor, 1973), vol. 1 p. 130.

86. J. M. Price, *op. cit.*, vol. 1, p. 131; and see Appendix 3.4 of this work.

87. See Appendix 3.4.

88. *Ibid.*

89. PRO CUST 3.

90. *Vide infra*, trade with Scotland.

91. J. M. Price, *op. cit.*, vol. 2, pp. 796–797.

92. PRO HO 98/23, 23 Aug. 1791 Brown to Amherst; 25 Aug. 1791 Le Marchant to Amherst.

93. BL Add Ms 38759 f 105v.

94. See Appendix 4.

95. PRO CO 390/8, ff 238–240. See Appendix 3.1.

96. F. Braudel, *Civilization and Capitalism 15th – 18th Century* (London 1988), vol. 1 (*The Structures of Everyday Life*), p. 251.

97. PRO SP 47/3, 22 July 1732, Mauger and de Sausmarez to Duke of Newcastle.

98. PRO SP 47/4, 18 Sept. 1734 Henry Mauger report. Compare Cambridge U L Cholmondeley (Houghton) Papers, 41/30 (c.1733?) 80 'toneaux de thee' (= 320 'barriques') imported in one year from Nantes.

99. PRO CUST 62/63, 15 Dec. 1737 London Customs House to Southampton board. Similarly CUST 62/63, 24 Dec. 1737; CUST 62/64, 10 Feb. 1740/1741; CUST 62/65, 26 Apr. 1744, 9 Aug. 1744, 14 Sept. 1744; CUST 62/66, 17 Sept. 1747, 19 Mar. 1747/1748.

100. PRO CUST 62/63, 12 May 1737 London Customs House to Southampton.

101. PRO CUST 3/44.

102. BL Add Ms 38463, f 196v, 9 Aug. 1764, Portsmouth board to London Customs House.

103. BL Add Ms 38463, f 199v, 13 Aug. 1764, Poole board to London Customs House.

104. BL Add Ms 38463, f 196v, 9 Aug. 1764, Portsmouth board to London Customs House.

105. BL Add Ms 38463, f 218r, 13 Sept. 1764, Portsmouth board to London Customs House.

106. *The Times*, 26 Oct. 1790, p. 2b.

107. A. Crawford, *Bristol and the Wine Trade* (Bristol, 1984), p. 21.
108. 12,353 tuns of Portuguese wine were imported into England in 1763: E. B. Schumpeter, *English Overseas Trade Statistics 1697–1808* (Oxford, 1960), Table XVI, p. 55.
109. F. B. Tupper, *The History of Guernsey* (Guernsey, 1854), p. 439.
110. E. B. Schumpeter, *op. cit.*, Table XVII, p. 59; and *vide supra* for Guernsey figures.
111. T. M. Devine, *The Tobacco Lords* (Edinburgh, 1990), pp. 108, 160.
112. See Appendix 5.
113. A. Anderson, 'Trade between the Channel Islands and Southampton in the Mid-Eighteenth Century' BSJ, vol. XVIII (1964), pp. 445–451. PRO HO 98/30, 5 Feb. 1807 Doyle report.
114. F. Crouzet, *Britain Ascendant: comparative studies in Franco-British economic history* (Cambridge, 1990), p. 414.
115. PRO CUST 3.
116. G. N. Clark, *Guide to English Commercial Statistics 1696–1782* (London, 1938), pp. 37–39.
117. James Watson, merchant, Greenock, 1738–1750: Scottish Record Office CS. 96/1919 (renumbered). Other information kindly supplied by Dr K. Marshall.
118. PRO CUST 14/2, f 6r – f 6v (microfilm numbers).
119. PRO CUST 14/13B, 3 f 12r (microfilm numbers).
120. PRO CUST 14/1B, f 282v (microfilm numbering); CUST 14/8 f 96v (microfilm numbering). For Scottish trading links with Guernsey in the late eighteenth and early nineteenth centuries see also: Scottish Record Office GD.1/306 (Alexander Oliphant Letter Book, correspondence with Mr Thomas Barry of Guernsey about wine, 1767–1768); CS. 96/3231, Sederunt book 1803–1804, p. 33: Hugh Mathie bankrupt, stock of wine in Guernsey.
121. W. Le Marchant, *The Rights and Immunities of the Island of Guernsey* (London, 1805), Appendix p. 57.
122. PRO HO 98/23, 14 Feb. 1782 Budd to Irving; 15 Feb. 1782 Irving to Hillsborough. See L. Vignols, 'L'Importation en France au XVIIIe siècle du boeuf d'Irlande' in *Revue Historique* part 159 pp. 79–95 (1928) for the context of this trade.
123. PRO CUST 15/86 onwards lists Guernsey trade separately.
124. PRO CUST 15/91: 1395 yards of linen, year ending 25 Mar. 1788.
125. PRO CUST 15/99.
126. A. G. Jamieson, 'Voyage Patterns and Trades of Channel Island Vessels, 1700–1900' in A. G. Jamieson (ed.), *A People of the Sea* (London, 1986), p. 378.
127. PRO CUST 105/102, 27 Jan. 1810 Guernsey Customs to Commissioners.
128. *Star* 6 Feb. 1827 p. 2 c-e; *Star*, 18 Oct. 1825, p. 3b. See Appendices 7 and 8.
129. R. Davis, *The Rise of the English Shipping Industry* (London, 1962), pp. 62, 65.
130. PRO ADM 1/3863, 187627 (dated 1702; refers to 1701). See also the Introduction; and P. Corfield, *The Impact of English Towns 1700–1800* (Oxford, 1982), pp. 36–37, for 1709 data.
131. BL Add Ms 38376 f 85r – f 88r.
132. A. G. Jamieson, 'Island Shipowners and Seamen' in A. G. Jamieson (ed.), *A People of the Sea* (London, 1986), p. 323.
133. See Chapter 1, Table 1.2: and R. Davis, *The Rise of the English Shipping Industry* (London, 1962), p. 35.
134. See Chapter Three below for Guernsey shipbuilding.
135. Priaulx 18459 p. 103, 25 July 1778 Guille to Tonkin (offering a share in a Bermudan built vessel, mounting sixteen guns, purchased at Bristol).
136. Priaulx 18459 p. 122, 11 Oct. 1778 Guille to Perkins.
137. BL Add Ms 38376 f 85r – f 88r.
138. J. Marshall, A Digest of all the Accounts (London, 1833), Part 2, pp. 226, 234. J. Jacob, *Annals of Some of the British Norman Isles* (Paris, 1830), pp. 459–461. A. G. Jamieson, 'Channel Island Shipowners and Seamen, 1700–1900' in A. G. Jamieson (ed.), *A People of the Sea* (London, 1986), pp. 312–366.
139. C. E. B. Brett, *Buildings in the Town and Parish of St Peter Port* (Guernsey, 1975), p. 10.
140. J. S. Bromley, 'A New Vocation: Privateering in the Wars of 1689–97 and 1702–13' in A. G. Jamieson (ed.), *A People of the Sea* (London, 1986), p. 112.
141. A. G. Jamieson, 'The Return to Privateering: Channel Island Privateers, 1739–83' in A. G. Jamieson (ed.), *A People of the Sea* (London, 1986), p. 168; and see note 139 above.
142. P. L. Wickins: 'The Economics of Privateering: Capital Dispersal in the American War of Independence' in *Journal of European Economic History*, vol. 13, no. 2 – Fall 1984, p. 377, *passim*.
143. P. L. Wickins, *op. cit.*, pp. 377, 387–389.
144. J. S. Bromley, *op. cit.*, p. 116.
145. A. G. Jamieson, *op. cit.*, p. 172.
146. P. L. Wickins, *op. cit.*, p. 382; A. G. Jamieson, *op. cit.*, p. 161.
147. A. G. Jamieson, *op. cit.*, p. 161.
148. PRO SP 47/4, 9 Nov. 1739 Carey to Duke of Newcastle.
149. *The Case of the Town Parish versus the Nine Country Parishes … 1759* (Guernsey, 1843), p. 27.
150. Greffe, de Sausmarez papers (D.I.15.21), list of prizes. *Lloyd's Evening Post*, 31 Mar. – 2 Apr. 1779, vol. XLIV, no. 3397, p. 316. (Plate 6).
151. Priaulx 18459 p. 122, 11 Oct. 1778 Guille to Perkins.

152. *The Case of the Town Parish versus the Nine Country Parishes … 1759* p. 60. The tax assessments are considered in more detail later (Chapter Six below).
153. F. Tupper, *The History of Guernsey* (Guernsey, 1854), p. 456.
154. Priaulx 18459 p. 123, 12 Oct. 1778 Guille to Menais Robert frères: 'il ne nous est point defendu de faire commerce avec la France par le moyen des neutres, il faut faire des expéditions simulés, soit pour Hollande, Espagne ou Portugal ou se servir d'un négociant d'Hollande'.
155. Priaulx 18459 p. 119, 18 Sept. 1778, Guille to Brillantais Marion (St Malo).
156. *Ibid.*
157. D. Starkey, 'British Privateering against the Dutch in the American Revolutionary War, 1780–1783' in S. Fisher (ed.) *Studies in British Privateering, Trading Enterprise and Seamen's Welfare, 1775–1900* (Exeter, 1987), pp. 12–13.
158. Henry De Sausmarez was educated in Holland 'to learn commerce': De Sausmarez, *An Account of the Proceedings of Henry De Sausmarez, of the Island of Guernsey, Gent.* (London, 1717), p. 3. Many merchants' sons were sent to England in the eighteenth century for the same purpose.
159. W. Le Marchant, *The Rights and Immunities of the Island of Guernsey* (London, 1805), Additional Appendix, pp. 13–15.
160. See Appendix 4 for estimates of lost revenue.

CHAPTER 3

1. P. M. Hohenberg and L. Lees, *The Making of Urban Europe 1000–1950* (Cambridge, Mass., 1985), p. 65, for town types.
2. J. H. Le Patourel, 'The Early History of St Peter Port' TSG vol. XII part ii, for 1934 (Guernsey, 1935), p. 187. By the eighteenth century produce was sold in St Peter Port streets every day of the week, Sundays excepted, *The Case of The Town Parish versus the Nine Country Parishes … 1759* (Guernsey, 1843), p. 9.
3. P. Sawyer, 'Early fairs and markets in England and Scandinavia' in B. L. Anderson and A. J. H. Latham (eds.), *The Market in History* (London, 1986), p. 67.
4. [Anonymous] 'Sketches of Guernsey and Guernseymen Fifty Years Ago – High Street' *Elizabeth College Magazine,* July 1842, vol. 1 no. 3 pp. 49–52.
5. Sir Edgar MacCulloch, *Guernsey Folk Lore* (London, 1903), pp. 32–33.
6. *The Case of the Town Parish versus the Nine Country Parishes … 1759* (Guernsey, 1843), pp. 23–24.
7. R. L. Stein, *The French Slave Trade in the Eighteenth Century* (Wisconsin, 1979), p. 152.
8. *Actes* vol. 1 pp. 121–122: list of those who contributed to the harbour developments.
9. Greffe, Amirauté records provide information about the ownership of shipping pre-1750 (*pace* A. G. Jamieson, 'Channel Island shipowners and seamen, 1700–1900' in A. G. Jamieson (ed.), *A People of the Sea* (London, 1988), p. 312.
10. F. B. Tupper, *The History of Guernsey* (Guernsey, 1854), p. 366. 'In Guernsey the number of Advocates was limited in 1777 to the two Law Officers (H.M. Procureur and H.M. Comptroller) and six others'. M. Morley (ed.), *The Gallienne Letters 1835–1895* (Guernsey, n.d.), p vi, (in Foreword by de V. G. Carey, Q.C.)
11. Greffe (uncatalogued manuscript).
12. R. H. Mayne, *Old Channel Islands Silver* (Jersey, 1969); C. Woolmer and C. Arkwright, *Pewter of the Channel Islands* (Edinburgh, 1973); G. J. C. Bois, *An Introduction to Channel Islands Pewter* (Jersey, 1993).
13. PRO ADM 1/3863 'An abstract of the number of vessells …'
14. *Ordonnances,* vol. 1 pp. 67–68.
15. J. de L. Mann, 'A Guernsey Merchant of the Commonwealth Period' TSG vol. XXI part ii, for 1982 (Guernsey, 1983), pp. 222–223.
16. G. E. Lee (ed.), *Note-book of Pierre Le Roy Guernsey* (Guernsey, 1893), p. 20.
17. e.g. Priaulx 29121/408C, Watkins Mss, vol. 3, 31 Oct. 1727.
18. Priaulx 31469, Nathaniel Carey's account book.
19. *Elizabeth College Magazine,* vol. 1 no. 2 June 1842 p. 27.
20. *Actes,* vol. 1 pp. 121-122 (1711) lists several female merchants and *négociants.* There are also frequent references to 'femmes marchandes' in the early 18th century volumes of the Cour d'Amirauté records (Greffe). For working women in England: J. Rendall, *Women in industrialising society: England 1750–1880* (Oxford, 1990), p. 27. D. Souden, 'Migrants and the population structure of later seventeenth century provincial cities and market towns' in P. Clark (ed.), *The transformation of English provincial towns 1600–1800* (London, 1984), pp. 133–168.
21. Priaulx, Tupper papers.
22. *The Case of the Town Parish versus the Nine Country Parishes … 1759* (Guernsey, 1843), p. 9 ('hundreds of the common people in town, who have no other way of getting their livelihood but by knitting hose or stockings'). Cp. L. A. Clarkson, *Proto-Industrialization: The First Phase of Industrialisation?* (Basingstoke, 1991), p. 54.

23. P. Kriedte, H. Medick and J. Schlumbohm, *Industrialization before Industrialization* (Cambridge, 1981), especially pp. 98–107.

24. R. Hocart, 'The Journal of Charles Trumbull' TSG vol. XXI part iv, for 1984 (Guernsey, 1985), p. 571.

25. BL Add Ms 38463 f 144r, May 1716 Petition from Jersey and Guernsey.

26. Priaulx 18459, Guille letters to Crew and Tatham.

27. BL Add Ms 29561 f 37r, 26 Jan. 1684/5 Major to Hatton.

28. *Statutes of the Realm* 12 Car II cap. 32.

29. P. J. Bowden, *The Wool Trade in Tudor and Stuart England* (London, 1962), p. 212. S. Carey Curtis, 'The Thirty-first Annual Report of the Antiquarian Section' TSG vol. XIII part vi, for 1942 (Guernsey, 1943), p. 363.

30. Greffe, Amirauté vol. 3, f 26v, 18 Oct., 1687.

31. A. G. Jamieson, 'The Channel Islands and smuggling, 1680–1850' in A. G. Jamieson (ed.), *A People of the Sea* (London, 1988), pp. 199–200.

32. PRO CUST 3/3.

33. J. Thirsk, 'The fantastical folly of fashion' in *The Rural Economy of England* (London, 1984), p. 248.

34. S. Carey Curtis, *op. cit.*, p. 363.

35. J. Thirsk, *op. cit.*, pp. 248–249.

36. *The Case of the Inhabitants of the Island of Guernsey, in Relation to several Orders of Council obtained by the Commissioners of the Customs, for settling Custom-House-Officers in the Island, and subjecting the Inhabitants to the Laws relating to the Customs in Great Britain* [c. 1708/9].

37. *The Case of the Town Parish versus the Nine Country Parishes … 1759* (Guernsey, 1843), p. 9.

38. R. Hocart, 'The Journal of Charles Trumbull' TSG vol. XXI part iv, for 1984 (Guernsey, 1985), p. 571.

39. J. de Vries, *European Urbanization* (London, 1984), p. 220.

40. J. de L. Mann, 'A Guernsey Merchant of the Commonwealth Period' TSG vol. XXI, part ii, for 1982 (Guernsey, 1983), p. 220 – agents in Paris. T. F. Priaulx and R. de Sausmarez, 'The Guernsey stocking export trade in the seventeenth century' TSG vol. XVII, part ii, for 1961 (Guernsey, 1962), pp. 210–223.

41. [W Le Marchant]: *The Rights and Immunities of the Island of Guernsey* (London, 1771), p. 38.

42. Greffe, Amirauté vol. 10, p. 19, 15 Aug. 1730 (Jacob Bart *vers* Margueritte femme du Sieur James Hubert *re* work on brigantine – a typical case).

43. Greffe, Amirauté vol. 13, 24 Aug. 1751 (Pierre Ougier to collect for le Sr James Le Ray a vessel built to specification in Virginia).

44. PRO CO 33/16, part 2 f 64r (pencil diamond): the sloop *Two Brothers*, Henry Lambert master, cleared Barbados 22 April 1747 with 8,170 gallons of rum bound for Falmouth. PRO CO 33/16, part 2 f 75r: the snow *Charming Nancy*, master Thos. Roberts, 4 guns, 18 men, registered Liverpool 1749, Richard Barret owner, entered Barbados 18 Dec. 1752 with 149 slaves from Africa; both vessels identified as built in Guernsey. See also P. Raban, 'War and Trade in the Mid-Eighteenth Century' TSG vol. XXII, part i, for 1986 (Guernsey, 1987), p. 142 (*Fox*, 15 tons, built Guernsey Jan. 1745; *Lottery*, 100 tons, built Guernsey Dec. 1757); and P. Raban, 'Clandestine Trade in the Mid-Eighteenth Century' TSG vol. XXII, part ii for 1987 (Guernsey, 1988), p. 322 (*Speedwell* built Guernsey 1732).

45. E. F. Carey (ed.), 'A Trip to Guernsey in 1798 by W. T. Money' TSG vol. XI, part ii, for 1931 (Guernsey, 1933), pp. 249–250.

46. A. G. Jamieson, 'Shipbuilding in the Channel Islands' in A. G. Jamieson (ed.), *A People of the Sea* (London, 1986), p. 293.

47. PRO HO 98/23, 20 Feb. 1788 Browne to Lord Sydney ('nine manufactories of tobacco'); HO 98/23, 23 Aug. 1791 Browne to Lord Amherst; HO 98/23, 25 Aug. 1791 Le Marchant to Lord Amherst (eleven or twelve hundred men, women and children employed).

48. F. B. Tupper, *The History of Guernsey* (Guernsey, 1854), p. 387.

49. See Chapter Five, endnote 23; J. Price, *France and the Chesapeake* (Ann Arbor, 1973), vol. 2, p. 987, note 63 for Watson.

50. G. Dupont, *Histoire du Cotentin et de ses Iles* (Caen, 1885), vol. 4 pp. 436–437.

51. PRO HO 98/30, 5 Feb. 1807 Doyle report.

52. J. G. Jenkins and R. A. Salaman, 'A Note on Coopering' in C. Singer *et al.* (eds.), *A History of Technology* (Oxford, 1957), vol. 3, p. 129.

53. Scottish RO, GD.1/306/1, Oliphant letter book f 57v, 20 Jul. 1768 Oliphant to Barry.

54. J. Geraint Jenkins and R. A. Salaman, *op. cit.*, pp. 130-133.

55. Priaulx 20763, 4 Oct. 1792 Guille to Shuffield.

56. T. Unwin, *Wine and the Vine* (London, 1991), p. 56.

57. F. B. Tupper, *The History of Guernsey* (Guernsey, 1854), pp. 454–456.

58. R. G. Lipsey, *An Introduction to Positive Economics* (London, 1987), p. 557 for concept of induced imports.

59. N. McKendrick, J. Brewer and J. H. Plumb, *The Birth of a Consumer Society* (London, 1982). H. Carter

and C. Roy Lewis, *An Urban Geography of England and Wales in the Nineteenth Century* (London, 1990), p. 92, for criticism.

60. J. Rule, *The Vital Century* (Harlow, 1992), p. 257.
61. *Gazette de Guernesey*, 14 June 1794.
62. Plate IV 'St Peter's Port, Guernsey' by Gosselin (BL K top LV 63.b).
63. *Gazette de Guernesey*, 23 July 1796.
64. *Gazette de Guernesey*, 7 Nov. 1796; 19 Nov. 1796; 4 Feb. 1797.
65. *Gazette de Guernesey*, 6 Aug. 1808, p. 127c.
66. *Gazette de Guernesey*, 16 July 1796.
67. *Gazette de Guernesey*, 7 July 1810 p. 106a (quotation in text); 30 Nov. 1811 p. 191b.
68. *Gazette de Guernesey*, 17 Aug. 1793 p. 142; 2 Apr. 1808 p. 55a; 12 Oct. 1811 p. 163a; 1 May 1813 p. 72c; 31 July 1813 p. 124b.
69. *Gazette de Guernesey*, 5 Nov. 1796, supplement.
70. All references are to the *Gazette de Guernesey*:
    Hairdressers and wigmakers:
       M. White, 242 High Street, 'from London' 30 Jan. 1808, p. 19b;
       J. Wheadon, 140 Pollet Street, 2 Jan. 1808, p. 4b;
       E. Norman, 2 Sept. 1809, p. 138b, from No. 28 London St., Fitzroy Square, London, recommended 'by Ladies of quality and of the first distinction in that City, to many ladies of rank in this Island', visiting for ten days.
    Fencing master:
       Mr Siordet, 13 July 1811, p. 112c.
    Dancing masters:
       Octavius Devall from London, 29 Sept. 1798; p. 172;
       Mr Smart from London, 28 Jan. 1804, p. 16;
       F. St Laurent 'Professor of Modern, Scenic and Grotesque Dancing', 6 July 1811, p. 106a.
    Music master:
       Mr Williams, professor of music, 8 June 1811, p. 91a.
    Art masters:
       J. Jeremie, 14 Feb. 1795, p. 27;
       A Frenchman offering to teach drawing, 2 Jan. 1796, p. 4;
       Mr Caza-Nova, 4 March 1797, pp. 35–36.
    Artists:
       Hunt, profile painter, 23 Dec. 1797, p. 23b;
       G. Emdin, from London, 13 July 1811, p. 111c.
    Architect:
       W. Damerum, ?/?/1802, p. 168 (newspaper fragment).
71. J. Bernard, *Retrospections of the Stage* (London, 1830), vol. 2, pp. 317–320. See Appendix 27 for theatre in St Peter Port.
72. See Chapter Seven, subsection on *Cultural Differentiation*.
73. J. Jacob, *Annals of Some of the British Norman Isles* (Paris, 1830), pp. 456–460.
74. *The Sarnian Monthly Magazine*, 1 July 1815, 'Peregrinus' citing acts of 4 Oct. 1574, 11 Apr. 1575, 3 Oct. 1631.
75. See Appendix 26.
76. Sir George Head, *A Home Tour through various parts of the United Kingdom* (London, 1837), pp. 168–169.
77. R. Davis, *The Rise of the English Shipping Industry* (London, 1962), p. 390. G. Rudé, *Hanoverian London 1714–1808* (London, 1971), pp. 7, 28–32.
78. A. Cabantous, *La Mer et les Hommes pêcheurs et matelots dunkerquois de Louis XIV à la Révolution* (Dunkirk, 1980), pp. 34–36.
79. P. Butel, 'La construction navale et les industries annexes dans les ports de commerce au sud de la Loire <La Rochelle, Bordeaux et Bayonne> aux xviie et xviie siècles' in *I porti come impresa economica* (Florence, 1988), pp. 698–699.
80. G. N. von Tunzelmann, 'Technological and organizational change in industry during the Industrial Revolution' in P. K. O'Brien and R. Quinault (eds.), *The Industrial Revolution and British Society* (Cambridge, 1993), pp. 266–273.

CHAPTER 4

1. F. B. Tupper, *The History of Guernsey* (Guernsey, 1854), p. 386.
2. Priaulx 19H, Letters of Pierre Careye (typescript); F. B. Tupper, *The History of Guernsey* (Guernsey, 1854), p. 362 (figures rounded up to 10,500 and 4,500). 'Four bushel of wheat, which compose their

quarter, exactly equal three Winchester bushel' T. Quayle, *General View of the Agriculture ... of the Islands* (London, 1815), p. 314.

3. TC DdCdF, 19 May 1765.
4. PRO HO 98/23, 28 Nov. 1789, Brown to Grenville.
5. PRO HO 98/24, 2 July 1794, Small report; HO 98/30, 5 Feb. 1807, Doyle report to Treasury.
6. F. B. Tupper, *The History of Guernsey* (Guernsey, 1854), p. 465.
7. *Ibid.*, pp. 466–467.
8. M. Drake (ed) *Population Studies from Parish Registers* (Matlock, 1982), pp. xxix – xxx.
9. A. Whiteman, *The Compton Census of 1676* (Oxford, 1986), p. 72.
10. Priaulx 29121/408C, 23 June 1735 de Fresne to Bishop of Winchester.
11. Greffe, General Letter Books, first series, vol. 1 p. 94, 3 July 1756 Royal Court to Privy Council; vol. 1 p. 217, 4 Aug. 1781 Royal Court to Committee of Council.
12. See Appendix 10 for summary of population figures.
13. See Appendix 11.
14. P. Jeremie, *On Parochial and States Taxation in Guernsey* (Guernsey, 1856), p. 10. See fig. 4.2 for population shift.
15. Housed in the Greffe.
16. Winchester, Diocesan Records, A/4/A bundle 5 item A, 7 Apr. 1809 Durand to the Bishop of Winchester.
17. P. Corfield, *The Impact of English Towns 1700–1800* (Oxford, 1982), p. 106.
18. E. A. Wrigley and R. S. Schofield, *The Population History of England 1541–1871*, (Cambridge, 1989), p. 174.
19. *Ibid.*, p. 174, footnote 24.
20. *Ibid.*, p. 181.
21. J. de Vries, 'The Population and Economy of the Preindustrial Netherlands' in R. I. Rotberg and T. K. Rabb (eds), *Population and Economy* (Cambridge, 1986), p. 108.
22. PRO HO 98/28, 3 Oct. 1805 Doyle to Lord Hawkesbury.
23. Priaulx 16D, letter book, 17 Dec. 1770; Priaulx 18459/SR, Guille letter book p.82, 18 Apr. 1778, Guille to Wise.
24. Greffe, scrapbook of Guillaume Guille (1748). This is confirmed by an analysis of the Town Church burial records.
25. Greffe, Original letters vol. 1 f 27, 19 Oct. 1661 de Quetteville to Andros.
26. J. Jeremie, Account of Guernsey (Guernsey, 1821), p. 100.
27. TC DdCdF, p. 102, 22 July 1755.
28. J. Jeremie, *Account of Guernsey* (Guernsey, 1820), p. 100.
29. J. P. Warren (ed.), 'Extracts from the Diary of Elisha Dobrée', TSG vol. X part 4, for 1929 (Guernsey, 1930), p. 507, footnote. The notebook of Nicholas is in the Priaulx Library.
30. COf A24 Taxes, 1780–1788: 9 Dec. 1786. Nantes, archives municipales, fonds Dobrée, 15 Jan. 1787 Dobrée to Dobrée.
31. Stevens-Cox: Harvey ms., 30 July 1805, Ann Grut to Peter Grut.
32. *Gazette de Guernesey*, 2 April 1808.
33. *Ordonnances*, vol. 2, p. 66.
34. *Ibid.*, vol. 2, pp. 315–316.
35. *The Monthly Selection* (Guernsey, 1824–1825), pp. 421, 464.
36. *Ibid.*, pp. 95, 128.
37. Dr S. K. Kellett-Smith, 'The Guernsey Cholera Epidemic of 1832' TSG vol. XX, part 5, for 1980 (Guernsey, 1981), pp. 654–655.
38. Dr S. K. Kellett-Smith, *op. cit.*, pp. 651, 655.
39. J. Dupâquier, 'Demographic crises and subsistence crises in France, 1650–1789' in J. Walters and R. Schofield (eds.), *Famine, disease and the social order in early modern society* (Cambridge, 1989) pp. 189–199.
40. G. Cabourdin *et al.* 'Les crises demographiques' in J. Dupâquier (ed.) *Histoire de la population française* (Paris, 1988) vol. 2, p. 203–206.
41. *Ibid.*, pp. 213–215, fig. 76, p. 215.
42. E. A. Wrigley and R. S. Schofield, *The Population History of England, 1541–1871* (Cambridge, 1989), p. 683.
43. *Vide supra.*
44. PRO SP 47/4, 25 July 1733, Petition of bailiff and jurats.
45. PRO SP 47/4, 25 July 1733 Petition of bailiff and jurats. See also J. M. David 'Some Notes on 18th Century Local Shipping' TSG vol. XVI, part iii, for 1957 (Guernsey, 1958), p. 275.
46. Greffe, Ordres du Conseil et Actes du Parlement.
47. P. Chaunu, *La civilisation de l'Europe classique* (Paris, 1966), p. 229.
48. J. Duncan, *The History of Guernsey* (London, 1841), p. 284.
49. F. Braudel, *Civilization and Capitalism* (London, 1988), vol. 1 (*The Structures of Everyday Life*) p. 61.
50. F. Braudel, 'Pre-modern towns' in Clark, P. (ed.), *The Early Modern Town A Reader* (London, 1976), p. 56.

51. T. Dicey, *An Historical Account of Guernsey* (London, 1751), pp. 23, 25 (fish-eating). T. Quayle, *General View of the Agriculture and present state of the islands on the coast of Normandy* (London, 1815), pp. 233–296 describes the agriculture of Guernsey.

52. P. Heylyn, *A Full Relation of two Journeys* (London, 1656), p. 301.

53. P. Falle, *An Account of the Isle of Jersey* (London, 1694), pp. 62–63.

54. PRO WO 34/105, f 145r – 145v Memorial of Earl of Seaforth.

55. T. Quayle, *General View of the Agriculture and present state of the islands on the coast of Normandy* (London, 1815), pp. 247, 326. *Ordonnances*, vol. 1, pp. 414–421; vol. 2, p. 568.

56. M. Livi-Bacci, *Population and Nutrition* (Cambridge, 1990), p. 119.

57. See Appendix 13: *Actes* vol. 2, pp. 245–247.

58. See Appendix 13: 1773 – wheat from Quebec, barley from Danzig.

59. See Appendix 13: 1757, 1773.

60. See Appendix 13: 1757.

61. L. Sinel, *Jersey through the Centuries* (Jersey, 1984), p. 31.

62. P. Goubert, *The French Peasantry in the Seventeenth Century* (Cambridge, 1989), p. 96.

63. *Ordonnances*, vol. 1 p. 289: 7 Apr. 1766, town inhabitants forbidden to keep free-flying pigeons (which fouled roofs 'et par ce moyen corrompent l'eau des citernes').

64. P. E. Razzell, 'Population change in eighteenth-century England' in M. Drake (ed.), *Population in Industrialization* (London, 1969), pp. 128–156.

65. See Chapter Five.

66. T. Dicey, *An Historical Account of Guernsey* (London, 1751), p. 191. Island Archives Service, Town Hospital, Delibérations 'A' pp. 325–327, 341.

67. A. Lespagnol, *Messieurs de Saint-Malo* (St Malo, 1990), pp. 187–189.

68. A. Cabantous, *La Mer et les Hommes, pêcheurs et matelots dunkerquois de Louis XIV à la Révolution* (Dunkirk, 1980) pp. 7, 27–29, 38–39. A. Cabantous, *Histoire de Dunkerque* (Toulouse, 1983), pp. 7, 89, 95. [The patterns of corn shortage and epidemics at Dunkirk were as follows: corn shortages in 1684, 1694, 1709–1710, 1740–1741, 1760, 1763, 1765–1766, 1767, 1769, 1775, 1779, 1793, An III; epidemics: 1666–1669, 1711–1712, 1743–1744, 1752, 1757, 1759, 1771, 1780–1782, 1794. A. Cabantous (1980), p. 30].

CHAPTER 5

1. C. G. Pooley and I. D. Whyte (eds.), *Migrants, Emigrants and Immigrants* (London, 1991), p. 4.

2. *Ibid.*, p. 12.

3. PRO SP 47/4, 9 Nov. 1739 Carey to Duke of Newcastle.

4. E. Le Roy Ladurie, 'Family structures and inheritance customs in sixteenth century France' in J. Goody et al. (eds.), *Family and Inheritance* (Cambridge, 1979), p. 53.

5. J. Duncan, *The History of Guernsey* (London, 1841), pp. 288–289.

6. T. Quayle, *General View of the Agriculture and present state of the Islands on the coast of Normandy* (London, 1815), p. 249.

7. J. Duncan, *The History of Guernsey* (London, 1841), p. 288.

8. W. Berry, *The History of the Island of Guernsey* (London, 1815), p. 285. J. Jacob, *Annals of Some of the British Norman Isles* (Paris, 1830), p. 166.

9. T. Quayle, *General View of the Agriculture and present state of the Islands on the coast of Normandy* (London, 1815), p. 283.

10. N. Naftel, *Memoirs of Nicholas Naftel* (*sine loco*, America, 1888), p. 6. E. Carey, 'The Beginnings of Quakerism in Guernsey' TSG vol. VIII, part ii, for 1918 (Guernsey, 1919), pp. 115–117.

11. *The Case of the Town Parish versus the Nine Country Parishes … 1759* (Guernsey, 1843), p. 19.

12. See Chapter Three for a fuller discussion of this putting-out industry.

13. M. de Garis, 'The Parish of St. Pierre du Bois and some of its inhabitants in the 18th and early 19th centuries' TSG vol. XIV, part iv, for 1949 (Guernsey, 1950), pp. 480–481.

14. Greffe, Contrats pour Lire et pour Date, vol. 38, pp. 263–265.

15. D. V. Glass, 'Socio-economic status and occupations in the City of London at the end of the seventeenth century' in P. Clark (ed.), *The Early Modern Town* (London, 1976), pp. 229, 232 note 12 for typical examples.

16. *Vide infra*: Urban Attitudes to Immigration.

17. J. G. Williamson, *Inequality, Poverty, and History* (Oxford, 1991), pp. 56–57.

18. COf A67 Taxes 1715–1740, pp. 150–151, 6 July 1727 (Aldridge). Jacob Bart, shipbuilder, TC burial 22 May 1748 (wife, 31 Oct. 1743); William Baker, cooper, TC burial (daughter) 3 Nov. 1745; Willington, sailmaker, COf A67 Livre de Taxe (1724, Eglise); *et alii* in registers and family files (Priaulx Library).

19. Sausmarez Manor 68K, 18 May 1738 Durrell to de Sausmarez.

20. See Appendix 18.

21. Priaulx, family files: Le Marchant (E. Carey ms notebook).
22. PRO WO 34/105, f 3r, 15 Dec. 1778 Irving to Amherst: Bell one of the most considerable merchants in the wine trade in St Peter Port.
23. Greffe, Amirauté, vol. 7, f 65r, 30 Mar. 1717 (le Sr Louis de Solignac, French, forbidden to manufacture tobacco in the island).
24. Greffe, Amirauté, vol. 12, f 124v, 20 July 1748 (Dobrée representing Stewart in action brought by Cornelius).
25. e.g.:

Nathanael Scammel	butcher (TCR baptism, godfather, 31 March 1740);
James Downer	butcher, from Whitechapel, London (EC Wills 1754–62, pp. 57–60; 17 June 1757);
John Lawrence	baker (TCR burial, 23 March 1765);
Joseph Fulford	tailor (TCR burial, 6 March 1755);
John Toms	tailor (EC Wills 1754–62, pp. 134–139, 28 June 1759);
Richard Matherell	shoemaker (TCR baptism of dau., 28 Dec. 1742);
Elizabeth Sevry	seamstress (TCR burial, 27 Mar. 1744);
Robert Pyle	joiner (Newport, I. of W.; EC Wills 1704–1737, pp. 364–365; 17 Dec. 1737);
John Hoybeen	glazier (TCR burial, 21 Feb. 1740).

26. William Wardin, staymaker, TCR baptism of son, 8 July 1740.
27. See below and Chapter Eight.
28. *Ordonnances*, vol. 1, p. 220.
29. *Ordonnances*, vol. 1, pp. 251–253.
30. COf A5 Comptes Courants 1779–1808, ff 1–89 (at end of volume).
31. *Ordonnances*, vol. 1, pp. 347–349, 5 Oct. 1767.
32. *Ibid.* pp. 321–322, 11 Aug. 1781.
33. *Ibid.* pp. 330–331, 4 Apr. 1785.
34. *Ibid.* p. 302, 6 Oct. 1777.
35. *Ibid.* pp. 295–296, 27 Apr. 1772.
36. *Ibid.* p. 298, 4 Oct. 1773.
37. *Ordonnances*, vol. 1, pp. 335–336, 23 May 1786. See COf A58 and COf B5 for 'Cautions pour les étrangers.'
38. C. W. Baird, *Histoire des Réfugiés Huguenots en Amérique* (Toulouse, 1886), p. 236.
39. Ecclesiastical Court registers, Actes vols. 1 and 2. See Fig. 8.
40. Priaulx 31468, Jean Guille journal, p. 51.
41. D. C. A. Agnew, *Protestant Exiles from France, chiefly in the Reign of Louis XIV* (London, 1871), vol. 2, p. 285.
42. A. Grant and R. Gwynn, 'The Huguenots of Devon' in Report and Transactions of the Devon Association for the Advancement of Science, Literature and Art, vol. 117, 1985, pp. 170–171.
43. Town church registers:
Maître Pierre de Boinay, surgeon, from Quintin, m. Demlle Marie Fautrart du Bo, 1 Feb. 1683. le Sr Pierre Carriere, apothecary, 'réfugié françois' buried 22 Nov. 1703. Sebastien du Bocage, surgeon, buried 4 Mar. 1706. Isaac Cholet de Saintonge 'maître d'école' buried 20 June 1684. LeSr Adrian Viel 'protestant français de Caen et agent de la petite école' buried 8 May 1715.
44. J. S. Bromley, 'A New Vocation: privateering in the wars of 1689–1697 and 1702–1713' in A. G. Jamieson (ed.), *A People of the Sea* (London 1986), pp. 115–116. Greffe, Amirauté, vol. 4, f 109r, 13 Dec. 1704: Jean Capon adopted the name 'Jean Chyperd pour n'être reconnu des français'.
45. COf A67 Livre de Taxes 1715–1740 for domicile. Huguenot origins can be demonstrated by family files (Priaulx Library), Ecclesiastical Court registers and wills.
46. EC Wills 1704–1737: p. 71 William Chaillou (26 Feb. 1713); p. 139 François Germe (19 Sept. 1720); p. 335 Louis Dollon (24 June 1735).
47. *Gazette de Guernesey*, 17 Sept. 1791, pp. 148–149.
48. Thirty-four of the priests were from Normandy, ninety-four from Brittany: PRO HO 98/25, ff 36–39.
49. C. Hettier, *Relations de la Normandie et de la Bretagne avec les Îles de la Manche pendant l'émigration* (Caen, 1885), pp. 84–86, J. Bernard, *Retrospections of the Stage* (London, 1830), vol. 2, pp. 310–311. PRO HO 98/25 f 70v, émigré keeping a billiard table.
50. PRO HO 98/28, 7 Sept. 1805 Doyle to King, with accompanying lists.
51. C. E. Brett conjectured that the émigrés 'no doubt brought with them metropolitan tastes which put both the island vieux-riches and nouveaux-riches on their mettle' *Buildings in the town and parish of St Peter Port* (Guernsey, 1975), p. 10; but he cited no evidence. There is, on the other hand, evidence of the British military garrison influencing urban fashionability from the 1780s onwards; see Chapter Seven.
52. O. and J. Grubiak, *The Guernsey Experiment* (Hawthorne, California, 1963), p. 21.
53. F. B. Tupper, *The History of Guernsey* (Guernsey, 1854), p. 456.
54. J. Duncan, *The History of Guernsey* (London, 1841), p. 534: the salty air was 'of benefit to consumptive patients … an insular watering place offers great advantage.'

55. COf B44, census of migrants 1830, entry 511 John Morris, gasworker, from London; entry 651 John Currie, gasworker, from Scotland.

56. Priaulx, newsclipping of obituary of Le Boutillier [n.d.].

57. A. G. Jamieson, 'The coming of steam: cross-channel services and island steamers' in A. G. Jamieson (ed.), *A People of the Sea* (London, 1986), esp. pp. 444–450.

58. BL Add Ms 33699 f 211r (newsclipping). COf B31 lists the large numbers of passengers who landed in Guernsey, 1828–1832.

59. See Fig. 5.3; G. Duby *et al.*(ed.) *Histoire de la France rurale* (Paris 1975–6), vol. 3 pp. 65, 81, 82 (for demographic pressures in Normandy). *Vide infra* for English conditions.

60. COf B44, Census of migrants 1830; see Appendixes 16 and 17 and Fig. 5.3.

61. COf B44, Census of migrants 1830; entries 541 (Wyatt); 523, 524, 525 (Pikes); 684 (Avery); 806 (Prout).

62. COf B44, Census of migrants 1830: entries 319, 549, 566, 574, 673.

63. COf B44, entries 478, 481, 482, 484, 487, 488.

64. Census returns and Cof B44..

65. *Gazette de Guernesey*, 4 August 1821. See Fig. 5.4.

66. Cited by P. J. Corfield, *The impact of English towns 1700–1800* (Oxford, 1982), p. 105.

67. Ecclesiastical Court, Register 1799–1863, pp. 64–65. In 1827 settled migrants and 'recently arrived' migrants constituted 30.8% of the town population of 12132 [Source: COf B44].

CHAPTER 6

1. F. B. Tupper, *The History of Guernsey* (Guernsey, 1854), p. 456.

2. *Ibid.*, p. 456.

3. COf A67.

4. See Chapter Three for wages of knitters. J. Rule, *Albion's People* (Harlow, 1992), pp. 116–117.

5. COf A67, Livre de Taxe (1715–1740), pp. 148–149.

6. T. Dicey, *An Historical Account of Guernsey* (London, 1751), p. 191.

7. J. Rule, *op. cit.*, pp. 116–117.

8. See Table 6.4.

9. See Appendix 13, details for 1758.

10. H. P. Brown, *Egalitarianism and the Generation of Inequality* (Oxford, 1991), p. 312.

11. P. Clark and P. Slack, *English Towns in Transition, 1500–1700* (Oxford, 1976), p. 111.

12. See W. D. Rubinstein, *Wealth and Inequality in Britain* (London, 1986), p. 60, Fig. 1, for Lorenz Curve of British Income inequality, 1688–1963.

13. N. Currer-Briggs and R. Gambier, *Huguenot Ancestry* (Chichester, 1985), p. 112.

14. E. Le Roy Ladurie, *La Ville Classique* (Paris, 1981), pp. 408–426 (vol. 3 in G. Duby (ed.), *Histoire de la France Urbaine* (Paris, 1981).

15. See Appendix 20.

16. L. D. Schwarz, 'Social class and social geography: the middle classes in London at the end of the eighteenth century' in P. Borsay (ed.), *The Eighteenth-Century Town* (Harlow, 1990), pp. 315–337; Peter Borsay's comment, *op. cit.*, p. 315, (my emphasis).

17. W. G. Hoskins, *Industry, Trade and People in Exeter 1688–1800* (Manchester, 1935), pp. 119–120.

18. S. Chapman, *Merchant Enterprise in Britain* (Cambridge, 1992), p. 47.

19. R. H. Mayne, *Old Channel Islands Silver* (Jersey, 1969), pp. 64–65, for silver work of Henri.

20. Guildhall Library, Dobrée bank ledger.

21. COf A22 pp. 251, 382 (Guérin); 239, 383 (De Lisle). (Jean Guérin and Delisle both in Fontaine vingtaine).

22. Priaulx 31458, pp. 343–359, 'Observations against an act of the Royal Court ordering the Douzainiers to give the Title of Esquire to Jurats & the Procureur and Comptroller'.

23. *Ordonnances*, vol. 1, p. 288.

24. J. F. Bosher, *The French Revolution* (London, 1989), p. 31. For dichotomous classification in England see P. J. Corfield, 'Class in eighteenth-century Britain' in P. J. Corfield (ed.), *Language, History and Class* (Oxford, 1991), pp. 117–119.

25. Greffe, Livre de Crime vol. 16, pp. 48–49, 14 Nov. 1780, Henry Potbury, butcher; vol. 16 pp. 216–218, 12 Oct. 1782, James Skinner Esq., ensign 96th regiment; vol. 16, pp. 272–273, 2 May 1783, Andrew Williamson of Helston.

26. *Gazette de Guernesey*, 23 Dec. 1797.

27. Greffe, Livre de Crime, vol. 15 f 43r –43v, 10 Sept. 1774, Libra Reynolds, from Pembrokeshire; vol. 16 p.181, 9 March 1782, Elizabeth Anley sent back to England; vol. 17, p. 266, 16 Dec. 1786, George Taylor from Armagh, Ireland, (claiming to have establishment in Old Street, London) and Bridget Lacky; vol. 19, p. 49, 19 Apr. 1794 William Woody, Derby; vol. 19, pp. 247–248, 20 Aug. 1796, Margueritte Morton, wife of Alexander Fraser of Inverness; vol. 19, p. 248, 20 Aug. 1796, James

Martin from Kingsbridge, Devon; vol. 19, p. 364, 18 July 1797, Ann Hoskins, wife of Christopher Dixon, from Boston, America.

28. BL Add Ms 45928 (i) f 270r, Memorial: increase in crime because of strangers and soldiers in the island; need for more court sittings. Greffe, Livre de Crime, vol. 15, f 126r, 20 Nov. 1779, William Lee from Polperrow, Cornwall, stealing from prize vessel; vol. 19, pp. 289–290, 3 Jan. 1797, Rachel Drasdale, wife of William Kerby (soldier in Dumbartonshire Fencibles) stole chintz, linen, silk etc.

29. Greffe, Livre de Crime, vol. 19, p. 254, 10 Oct. 1796, Alexander Thomson, officer in the Dumbartonshire Fencibles, challenged François James Scott, Esq., major in the Dumbartonshire Fencibles, to a duel; vol. 19, pp. 256–258, 18 Oct. 1796, Mons Louis Florent Victurnier, one of the Chasseurs nobles of the regiment of Mons le Duc de Mortemar, found dead and another officer seriously wounded.

30. Priaulx Library: a manuscript note by W. W. Carey records that Russian troops (stationed in Guernsey in 1799) drank oil from the lamps. [Note in H. Ross-Lewin, *With 'The Thirty Second' In the Peninsular and other Campaigns* (Dublin, 1904), p. 43]. There had been no lamps in 1798: W. T. Money, 'A Trip to Guernsey in 1798', ed. E. Carey, TSG vol. XI, part ii, for 1931 (Guernsey, 1932), p. 250.

31. *Vide supra.*

32. See Fig. 2.13.

33. T. Dicey, *An Historical Account of Guernsey* (London, 1751), pp. 186–187. See Appendix 13 for subsidised corn.

34. TC DdCdF, p. 13, 4 March 1730.

35. G. Taylor, *The Problem of Poverty 1660–1834* (London, 1969), pp. 29, 104 for badging in England. Taylor comments that the provision of the English Act of 1697 signified 'the harsh attitudes which stemmed from mercantilist needs to utilise the labour force'.

36. T. Dicey, *An Historical Account of Guernsey* (London, 1751), p. 187.

37. *Ibid.*, p. 193.

38. *Ibid.*, p. 191.

39. Island Archives Service, DC/HX-79-01, Délibérations 'A' (1726) 1741–1801; see also typescript ed. G. Lenfestey, pp. iii-v.

40. Island Archives Service, DC/HX-117-2, Journal, pp. 504–509.

41. Island Archives Service, DC/HX-118-1, Journal, p. 7, 21 Mar. 1752.

42. W. Berry, *The History of the Island of Guernsey* (London, 1815), p. 159. In 1811 – during the trade recession – the number admitted to the Hospital rose to 250; in 1812–15 on average 230 were admitted (*Ibid.*, p. 159).

43. COf A22 pp. 1–34; A25 (not paginated).

44. T. Dicey, *An Historical Account of Guernsey* (London, 1751), p. 185.

45. T. Quayle, *General View of the Agriculture and Present State of the Islands on the Coast of Normandy* (London, 1815), pp. 291–296.

46. See Appendix 24.

47. W. Berry, *The History of the Island of Guernsey* (London, 1815), p. 299.

48. A. de Tocqueville, *Democracy in America*, translated by H. Reeve, (London, 1840), vol. 4, p. 14 (Part the Second, Chapter 2).

49. *The Star*, 9 Feb. 1830.

50. See Chapter Eight.

51. E. Baigent, 'Economy and society in eighteenth-century English towns: Bristol in the 1770s' in D. Denecke and G. Shaw (eds.), *Urban Historical Geography Recent progress in Britain and Germany* (Cambridge, 1988), pp. 109–124.

52. A. McInnes, *The English Town, 1660–1760* (London, 1980), pp. 24–25.

53. P. Borsay (ed.), *The Eighteenth-Century Town* (Harlow, 1990), p. 15 (my italics).

CHAPTER 7

1. There were instances of power conflict between individuals; and of conflict involving extra-urban agents; this does not vitiate the substantive point.

2. BL Add Ms 6253, Bonamy ms. f 24 v.

3. A. Giddens, *Sociology* (Cambridge, 1991), p. 429.

4. BL Add Ms 6253 Bonamy ms. f 25 r; compare T. Dicey, *An Historical Account of Guernsey* (London, 1751), p. 112.

5. Greffe, de Sausmarez collection, Account book of Société de la Chambre.

6. *Ibid.*, Jean Cornelius fined, April 1752.

7. Sausmarez Manor, letter book of Mathieu de Sausmarez, p. 309, 14 Sept. 1733, de Sausmarez to Slowley, 14 Sept. 1733.

8. P. Borsay, *The English Urban Renaissance* (Oxford, 1989), p. 139.

9. PRO HO 98/30, 5 Feb. 1807 Doyle to Treasury.
10. A. D. King, *Urbanism, Colonialism, and the World Economy* (London, 1991), p. 59.
11. BL Add Ms 6253, Bonamy ms. f 20r.
12. *Gazette de Guernesey*, 28 Nov. 1795, letter *re* theatre.
13. Priaulx, Le Mesurier papers, 2 Oct. 1779, John Le Mesurier to Frederick Le Mesurier.
14. Priaulx, 29109/408C Lihou letter book, Lihou to Perchard, n.d. Apr. 1766.
15. Priaulx, 29109/408C Lihou letter book, 16 Feb. 1771, Lihou to de Jersey.
16. P. Bourdieu, *Distinction* (London, 1989), p. 77.
17. Greffe, Amirauté vol. 13: 15 Dec. 1750 (Dobrée actioned by Mr Jean Pierre Beuselin for 2647 livres – 14s – 6d [French currency] for 'deux habits, vestes & cullottes brodez, l'un en or, & l'autre en argt que l'acteur lui a fait faire à Paris').
18. F. B. Tupper, *The History of Guernsey* (Guernsey, 1854), p. 433.
19. H. H. P. Le Mesurier, 'Notes on the Armorial China of some of the Guernsey families' TSG vol. XII, part iii (Guernsey, 1936), pp. 285–297.
20. M. Girouard, 'The Georgian Promenade' in P. Corfield *et al.*, *Life in the Georgian Town* (London, 1985), p. 26.
21. E. Gillett (ed.), *Elizabeth Ham by herself 1783–1820* (London, 1945), p. 66.
22. P. Borsay, *The English Urban Renaissance* (Oxford, 1989), pp. 150–162.
23. F. B. Tupper, *The History of Guernsey* (Guernsey, 1854), p. 367.
24. Priaulx, Le Mesurier mss., 20 Aug. 1777 Le Mesurier to Le Mesurier.
25. Priaulx, Le Mesurier mss., 14 Jan. 1778 Mrs Dumaresq (née Le Mesurier) to Le Mesurier. See L. Stone, *The Family, Sex, and Marriage in England 1500–1800* (Harmondsworth, 1979), chaps. 7–8.
26. J. de L. Mann, 'The Sixties and the Forties', QRGS vol. XVII, no. 1, Spring 1961, p. 11.
27. W. Berry, *The History of the Island of Guernsey* (London, 1815), p. 158.
28. E. Gillett (ed.), *Elizabeth Ham by herself* (London, 1945), p. 169.
29. F. B. Tupper, *The History of Guernsey* (Guernsey, 1854), p. 368.
30. P. Clark, *Sociability and Urbanity: Clubs and Societies in the Eighteenth Century City* (Leicester, 1986), p. 13.
31. J. P. Warren (ed.), 'Extracts from the Journal of Elisha Dobrée' in TSG vol. X, part iv, for 1929 (Guernsey, 1930), pp. 493–551; cont'd in vol. XI, part i, for 1930 (Guernsey, 1931), pp. 106–123. Priaulx, Mollet journals. E. Gillett (ed.), *Elizabeth Ham by herself 1783–1820* (London, 1945), p. 70.
32. Priaulx, Le Mesurier mss, 30 Oct. 1775 Dumaresq to Le Mesurier.
33. Priaulx, Le Mesurier mss, 14 Jan. 1778 Dumaresq to Le Mesurier.
34. Priaulx, Le Mesurier mss, 9 Jan. 1773 Le Mesurier to Le Mesurier.
35. J. P. Warren, *op. cit. supra* TSG vol. X, part iv, p. 528.
36. J. P. Warren, *op. cit. supra* TSG vol. X, part iv, p. 525.
37. *Gazette de Guernesey*, 29 Dec. 1792, pp. 40–42.
38. F. B. Tupper, *The History of Guernsey* (Guernsey, 1854), p. 367.
39. Nantes, Archives Municipales, Fonds Dobrée, 2-A-19, 13 Dec. 1775, Dobrée to Dobrée.
40. C. Stonelake, *A History of Freemasonry in the Channel Islands of Guernsey and Alderney 1753–1951* (Guernsey, 1951), p. 11.
41. A. C. F. Jackson, 'Freemasonry in Jersey', *Ars Quatuor Coronatorum*, vol. 86 (1973), pp. 177–220.
42. C. Stonelake, *op. cit.*, sketches the history of many of the lodges.
43. W. T. Kinnersly, *History of Doyle's Lodge of Fellowship Guernsey* (Guernsey, 1872), p. 16.
44. United Grand Lodge, London, archives, SN 1473.
45. United Grand Lodge, London, archives, SN 1141.
46. United Grand Lodge, London, archives, A 50 COC fol: K. Cochrane, *A Collection of Histories of Lodges with a nautical connection* (typescript, 1989).
47. P. Clark, *Sociability and Urbanity: Clubs and Societies in the Eighteenth Century* (Leicester, 1986), p. 10.
48. *Ibid.* p. 10.
49. Stonelake, *op. cit.*, p. 16.
50. United Grand Lodge, London, A 50 COC fol, K. Cochrane, *op. cit.*
51. Stonelake, *op. cit.*, p. 27.
52. *Ibid., passim.*
53. J. Brewer, 'Commercialization and Politics' in N. McKendrick, J. Brewer, J. H. Plumb, *The Birth of a Consumer Society* (London, 1982), p. 220.
54. *Articles of the Friendly Society, of the Island of Guernsey* (Salisbury, 1764), pp. 15–18.
55. R. J. Morris, 'Voluntary societies and British urban élites 1780–1850: an analysis' in P. Borsay (ed.), *The Eighteenth-Century Town* (Harlow, 1990), p. 341.
56. See Chapter Six for friction, R. J. Morris, *op. cit.*, p. 340.
57. *An Additional Article, of the Friendly Society in Guernsey* (Southampton, n.d., 1769?), p. 9, entries 88 and 90. See Chapter Two, endnote 54 for Mark Gregory. William Seward of Southampton is frequently mentioned in the correspondence of the Guernsey merchants.
58. *Articles of the Friendly Society, of the Island of Guernsey* (Salisbury, 1764), p. 5.
59. *Articles et Reglements d'une Société d'Amis* (Guernsey, 1775).

60. P. Borsay (ed.), *The Eighteenth-Century Town* (Harlow, 1990), pp. 34–36.
61. Island Archives Service, AQ P002/05U Guérin ledgers, 13 Feb. 1788, Guérin to John Clark & Co.
62. Priaulx, Lukis ms., E. Carey transcript.
63. Priaulx, 37282/16D Letter book, 19 Apr. 1771 (identities uncertain).
64. Priaulx, Lukis ms., E. Carey transcript.
65. Priaulx, Le Cocq letters/SR, 4 Feb. 1800, W.P. Le Cocq to parents.
66. *Gazette de Guernesey*, 13 Dec. 1794.
67. *Gazette de Guernesey*, 17 Nov. 1798.
68. *Gazette de Guernesey*, 5 Nov. 1796.
69. E. Gillett (ed.), *Elizabeth Ham by herself 1783–1820* (London, 1945), p. 170.
70. P. Trudgill, *Sociolinguistics*, (Harmondsworth, 1983), p. 24.
71. *Ibid.*, p. 26.
72. Priaulx, Dobrée family file, 1 Aug. 1818 Dobrée to Routh.
73. D. Washbrook, 'To each a language of his own: language, culture, and society in colonial India' in P. Corfield (ed.), *Language, History and Class* (Oxford, 1991), p. 188.
74. [Anon] *A Summer Stroll Through the Islands of Jersey and Guernsey* (Jersey, 1809), p. 31. Cf. P. Borsay, *The English Urban Renaissance* (Oxford, 1989), p. 287: 'Simply by purchasing a newspaper or borrowing a periodical or book from the local circulating library or club, a country dweller could be put in contact with national and international news and fashion.'
75. *Gazette de Guernesey*, 24 Apr. 1813, p. 67c.
76. J. C. Palmer and J. E. C. Palmer, *A Classified List of Books and Pamphlets published 1647–1953 relating to the Island of Guernsey* (Harpenden, 1987), pp. 23–24 lists many of these.
77. *Gazette de Guernesey*, 28 Nov. 1795.
78. See Appendix 27.
79. E. Carey, 'The beginnings of Quakerism in Guernsey', TSG vol. VIII, part ii, for 1918 (Guernsey, 1919), pp. 115–126.
80. J. F. Naftel (ed.), *Memoirs of Nicholas Naftel* (America, 1888), p. 28.
81. M. Le Lievre, *Histoire du Méthodisme dans les Iles de la Manche* (Paris, London, 1885), pp. 313–314.
82. PRO HO 98/24, 22 July 1794 Small to Amherst; 29 July 1794 Small to Amherst.
83. J. Duncan (ed.), *The Guernsey and Jersey Magazine* (Guernsey, 1836), vol. 2, p. 184.
84. *Actes* (1829–1835), p. 164.
85. J. P. Warren (ed.), 'Extracts from the Diary of Elisha Dobrée', TSG vol. X, part iv, p. 547, footnote 2. *Gazette de Guernesey*, 15 Jan. 1791.
86. Winchester, Diocesan records, 21 M65 J1/5, 25 June 1812 Durand to Bishop of Winchester.
87. J. Jacob, *Annals of the British Norman Isles* (Paris, 1830), p. 408.
88. *Ibid.*, p. 357.
89. Greffe, Ecclesiastical Court Register, 1799–1863, pp. 64–65.
90. J. Jacob, *Annals of the British Norman Isles* (Paris, 1830), p. 336. See E. W. Sharp, 'La Chevauchée de sa Majesté' in *The Channel Islands Anthology*, no. 2 (Guernsey, 1975), pp. 18–22.

CHAPTER 8

1.   B. Little, *St Peter Port, its story and buildings* (Guernsey, 1963). C. E. B. Brett, *Buildings in the town and parish of St Peter Port* (Guernsey, 1975). J. McCormack, *The Guernsey House* (Chichester, 1980), pp. 112-131.
2.   G. Dupont, *Histoire du Cotentin et de ses Iles* (Caen, 1885), vol. 4, p. 473.
3.   C. R. Fay, 'Peter Paul Dobrée of Guernsey and Cambridge' QRGS vol. XII, no. 3, Autumn 1956, p. 51.
4.   The original of the Legge Survey is in the National Maritime Museum, Greenwich. There are copies in the British Library [King's Ms 48]; and in the Royal Court Library, St Peter Port.
5.   W. Camden, *Britannia* (Amsterdam, 1639), p. 455.
6.   H. Carter and C. R. Lewis, *An Urban Geography of England and Wales in the Nineteenth Century* (London, 1990), pp. 110–111.
7.   J. H. Le Patourel, 'The Early History of St Peter Port', TSG vol. XII, part ii, for 1934 (Guernsey, 1935), p. 191. There is still doubt. J. McCormack, *The Guernsey House* (Chichester, 1980), pp. 114–115.
8.   Outside the *barrières* the eldest son automatically inherited a *vingtième* (twentieth part of the whole) and *préciput* (the house and its appurtenances). The urban exemption can be traced back to the sixteenth century and may have been made in the mediaeval period.
9.   R. Rodger, 'The Invisible Hand' in D. Fraser and A. Sutcliffe (eds.), *The Pursuit of Urban History* (London, 1983), p. 192.
10. *Ibid.*
11. It is worth noting in this context that both Scottish and Guernsey law are ultimately based on Roman Law.

12. J. Duncan, *The History of Guernsey* (London, 1841), pp. 284–285.
13. R. Rodger, *op. cit.*, p. 202.
14. Cp. T. Quayle, *General View of the Agriculture and Present State of the Islands on the coast of Normandy* (London, 1815), p. 42, for similar speculation in neighbouring Jersey.
15. E. Carey, 'Social Life in Guernsey in the sixteenth century', TSG vol. VIII, part iv, for 1920 (Guernsey, 1921), pp. 244–247.
16. *Ibid.*, p. 247.
17. R. Hocart, 'The Journal of Charles Trumbull', TSG vol. XXI, part iv, for 1984 (Guernsey, 1985), p. 571.
18. G. Dupont, *Histoire du Cotentin et de ses Iles* (Caen, 1885), vol. 4, p. 473.
19. BL Add Ms 6253 Bonamy ms f 20r.
20. See Chapter Six above.
21. Greffe, Deposition, 20 Oct. 1709: from his window the merchant le Sieur Pierre Estienne saw suspicious activity aboard a hoy from Gosport.
22. J. Jacob, *Annals of the British Norman Isles* (Paris, 1830), p. 145.
23. *The case of the Town Parish versus the nine country parishes ... 1759* (Guernsey, 1843), p. 19.
24. *Ibid.*, p. 18.
25. Sausmarez Manor, 68 K, 22 Oct. 1737 Durell to de Sausmarez.
26. E. L. Jones and M. E. Falkus, 'Urban improvements and the English economy in the seventeenth and eighteenth centuries' in P. Borsay (ed.), *The Eighteenth-Century Town* (Harlow, 1990), pp. 116–158.
27. *Ordonnances*, vol. 1, pp. 109–111 (regulations, 1611).
28. Priaulx, Lukis ms.
29. COf A67, Livre de Taxe 1715–1740, pp. 277–286.
30. E. L. Jones and M. E. Falkus, 'Urban improvement and the English economy in the seventeenth and eighteenth centuries' in P. Borsay (ed.), *The Eighteenth-Century Town* (Harlow, 1990), pp. 116–158, esp pp. 121–127 for background to fire-fighting in England.
31. Priaulx, Lukis ms.
32. *Ordonnances*, vol. 1, p. 217.
33. COf A67, Livre de Taxe (1715–1740), pp. 7–10 (at back of volume).
34. J. P. Warren, 'Fire Marks and Early Fire-fighting in Guernsey', TSG vol. XVI, part i, for 1955 (Guernsey, 1956), pp. 35–46 for later story of fire-fighting.
35. See Appendix 20.
36. C. E. B. Brett, *Buildings in the town and parish of St Peter Port* (Guernsey, 1975), p. 36.
37. See Maps, Appendix 28.
38. R. Hocart, 'The Building of the New Town', TSG vol. XXIII, part ii, for 1992 (Guernsey, 1993), pp. 342–377.
39. Priaulx, Lukis ms.
40. *Ibid.* An inscribed lintel from a house in the Grande Rue is preserved at the Guille Allès [LA PAIX DE DIEU SOIT CEANS. FAIT LE 16 OCTOBRE 1578 DE PAR ANDRE MONAMY]. Lukis also recorded 'EN DIEU J'AI MIS MON APPUI ET SA PROVIDENCE M'A CONDUI'.
41. C. E. B. Brett, *Buildings in the town and parish of St Peter Port* (Guernsey, 1975), p. 29, plate 88.
42. E. L. Jones and M. E. Falkus, 'Urban Improvement and the English economy in the seventeenth and eighteenth centuries' in P. Borsay (ed.), *The Eighteenth-Century Town* (Harlow, 1990), p. 127.
43. Sausmarez Manor 68K, 3 Mar. 1772, Burrard to de Sausmarez 'when Priaulx comes here for bricks, which he often does'.
44. PRO CUST 3.
45. L. Clarke, *Building Capitalism* (London, 1992), p. 101.
46. W. T. Money, 'A Trip to Guernsey in 1798',(ed. E. Carey), TSG vol. XI, part ii, for 1931 (Guernsey, 1932), p. 249.
47. Brickfields advertising in the *Gazette de Guernesey*: Sarchet's Brick-kiln, 30 Jan. 1808, p. 18c; Joseph Gullick by New-Ground Barracks, 24 Jun. 1809, p. 88c; brick and lime manufactory at Mares-Pirouin near the Long-Store, 30 Sept. 1809 p. 154c; N. Torode & Co 'au Bouet, proche le Fort Arrive', 28 Sep. 1811, p. 155c.
48. A. Brice, *The Grand Gazetteer* (Exeter, 1759), p. 665: the pier 'is used as the chief Place of Rendezvous, on Parties of Pleasure, by the fashionable Part of the Town'. See Plate 12.
49. Nantes, Archives Municipales, fonds Dobrée, 23 Oct. 1772 Mother to Dobrée: 'on a bien parlé ici de paver les rues comme ceux de Londres'.
50. Nantes, Archives Municipales, fonds Dobrée, 6 Feb. 1773 Dobrée to son. Cf. *Actes* vol. 1, p. 331.
51. Priaulx, Le Mesurier mss., 22 Nov. 1773 Le Mesurier to Le Mesurier (almost certainly a reference to St Peter Port).
52. Priaulx, Mollet journals, 15 June 1791 (houses insured 24 November).
53. Nantes, Archives Municipales, fonds Dobrée, 16 July 1798, Dobrée to Dobrée.
54. Peter Mourant, who had Candie House built in the 1780s, was one of the first to move to the suburbs; see Chapter Six, Conclusion.

55. Priaulx, Lukis ms.
56. L. Davidoff and C. Hall, *Family Fortunes: Men and Women of the English Middle Class 1780–1850* (London, 1987), p. 180. Cp. R. Rodger, *Housing in Urban Britain 1780–1914: Class, Capitalism and Construction* (Basingstoke, 1989), p. 40.
57. W. T. Money, 'A Trip to Guernsey in 1798' (ed. E. Carey), TSG vol. XI, part ii, for 1931 (Guernsey, 1932), p. 239–240.
58. R. Rodger, *Housing in Urban Britain 1780–1914: Class, Capitalism and Construction* (Basingstoke, 1989), p. 41.
59. J. Jacob, *Annals of Some of the British Norman Isles* (Paris, 1830), pp. 199, 208.
60. R. Hocart, 'The Building of the New Town', TSG vol. XXIII, part ii, for 1992 (Guernsey, 1993), pp. 342–377.
61. Information kindly supplied by R. Hocart Esq.
62. See Appendix 25.
63. P. Bourdieu, *Distinction* (London, 1989), p. 12, *passim.*
64. Priaulx, Lukis ms.; Dobrée family file, transcript of letter of 15 Aug. 1812, Dobrée to Routh; *Actes*, vol. 3, pp. 373–376.
65. R. Hocart, *An Island Assembly* (Guernsey, 1988), p. 23.
66. O. and J. Grubiak, *The Guernsey Experiment* (Hawthorne, 1963), p. 21.
67. *Ibid.*, p. 24.
68. Priaulx, Lukis ms.
69. See H. Colvin, *A Biographical Dictionary of British Architects 1600–1840* (London, 1978), pp. 899–900 for details of Wilson's career. Fountain Street: see Priaulx, Lukis ms., transcript of letter from La Serre, 12 Apr. 1827. The plans are in the Candie Museum.
70. Priaulx, obituary of Le Boutillier, unidentified newsclipping.
71. O. and J. Grubiak, *The Guernsey Experiment* (Hawthorne, 1963), p. 24.
72. W. Walmesley, *A Pedestrian Tour through the Islands of Guernsey and Jersey*, K. C. Renault ed., (Chichester, 1992), p. 37. Add. Ms. 33699 f 8r (Skinner's tour in 1827).

VICTORIAN EPILOGUE

1. For emigration see D. W. Kreckeler, *Guernsey Emigrants to Australia, 1828–1899* (Guernsey, 1995). M. Turk, *The Quiet Adventurers in Canada* (Detroit, 1979).
2. *Barbet's Guide for the Island of Guernsey* (Guernsey, 1844), p. 4.
3. C. E. B. Brett, *Buildings in the town and parish of St Peter Port* (Guernsey, 1975) lists and illustrates some of these.
4. The full story of this remarkable episode is discussed by Dr William Mathew in his recent monograph *The Secret History of Guernsey Marmalade: James Keiller & Son Offshore, 1857–1879* (Guernsey, 1998).

CONCLUSION

1. See Chapter One and Chapter Four.
2. E. A. Wrigley, 'Parasite or Stimulus: The Town in a Pre-industrial Economy' in P. Abrams and E. A. Wrigley (eds.), *Towns in Societies* (Cambridge, 1980), p. 307.
3. *Ibid.*, p. 308.
4. A. McInnes, *The English Town, 1660–1760* (London, 1980), p. 25.
5. P. Borsay (ed.), *The Eighteenth-Century Town* (Harlow, 1990), p. 15. (My emphasis, GSC).
6. P. Burke, *History and Social Theory* (Cambridge, 1992), 79-84.
7. There is still much scope for research into the history of St Helier. Provisionally the present writer would draw attention to the following features. First, the Jersey merchants were not concentrated in St Helier at an early date in the manner in which the Guernsey merchants were all to be found in St Peter Port. Secondly, the Jersey merchants were more involved in trade with France, and less with England, in the eighteenth century. Thirdly, the Jersey merchants kept more to the knitting industry and Newfoundland fishing than their Guernsey counterparts. Fourthly, the St Peter Port merchants enjoyed a better reputation in international trade than the Jersey merchants. Fifthly, Jersey boys tended to be sent to France for their education, while Guernsey sons went to England. Sixthly, in the late eighteenth century St Helier was not as affluent a town as St Peter Port. These impressions need to be tested against more evidence. Provisionally I would suggest that while the St Peter Port

merchants became *négociants* engaging wholeheartedly in international trade, the Jersey merchants clung rather conservatively to a mixed economy of 'putting-out', Newfoundland fishing, *petit cabotage* and some *grand commerce*. It is difficult to escape the conclusion that there was a difference in the culture of the two islands. The centre-periphery model seems inadequate as an analytical tool in this context.

Bibliography

Manuscript sources

Printed original sources

      A.   Acts and Orders

      B.   Newspapers and contemporary journals

      C.   Contemporary writings

Printed secondary sources

Unpublished theses

MANUSCRIPT SOURCES

ENGLAND

Cambridgeshire

Cambridge University Library

    Cholmondeley (Houghton) papers

Hampshire

Winchester, Hampshire Record Office

    Diocesan Archives: the manuscripts cited in this monograph are in the course of being re-catalogued and are now to be found under 21M65/J1/5.

London

British Library

Add Mss	6253	'The State of Guernsey' by Christopher Lord Hatton; and 'A Short Account of the Island of Guernsey AD 1749' by Samuel Bonamy
	29561	Finch-Hatton family correspondence
	33699	Skinner, Rev John, Journal of a tour to the Channel Islands 1827
	38228	Liverpool papers, vol. XXXIX
	38376	Liverpool papers, vol. CLXXXVII
	38387	Liverpool papers, vol. CXCVIII
	38389	Liverpool papers, vol. CC
	38463	Liverpool papers, vol. CCLXXIV
	38759	Huskisson papers, vol. XXVI
	45928(i)	Keppel Papers

    King's Ms 48 G. Legge 'Present State of Guernsey'

    Lansdowne Ms 657 Miscellaneous collection relating to Guernsey and Jersey

    Sloane Ms 4053 Correspondence to Sir Hans Sloane

Customs and Excise, New Beam House

    Excise statistics, England, 1684–1867

Guildhall Library

    3291/1, 3291/2 Dobrée ledgers

    11936 Sun Fire Insurance Company

Public Record Office

ADM	1	Admiralty and Secretariat papers
ADM	7	Admiralty and Secretariat
CO	33	Barbados miscellanea
CO	388	Board of Trade Original Correspondence
CO	390	Board of Trade Miscellanea
CUST	3	Ledgers of imports and exports, England
CUST	14	Ledgers of imports and exports, Scotland
CUST	15	Ledgers of imports and exports, Ireland
CUST	59	Outport records: Weymouth
CUST	60	Outport records: Poole

CUST	62	Outport records: Southampton
CUST	105	Outport records, Channel Islands
HO	98	Home Office: Channel Islands, Isle of Man and Isles of Scilly: correspondence and papers.
HO	99	Home Office: Channel Islands, Isle of Man and Isles of Scilly: entry books.
SP	47	Secretaries of State: State Papers Channel Islands: correspondence
SP	89	State Papers Foreign Portugal
T	1	Treasury Board Papers
T	64	Treasury, various
WO	34	Amherst Papers

United Grand Lodge of England, Freemasons' Hall

SN 1141; 1473; A 50 COC;

Northamptonshire

Northamptonshire Record Office

Finch-Hatton papers (278)

FRANCE

Nantes

Archives municipales

Fonds Dobrée

GUERNSEY

Constables' Office, St Peter Port

A	5	Comptes courants 1779–1808
A	22	Livre de Taxes, 1740–1762
A	23	Livre de Taxes, 1762–1780
A	24	Livre de Taxes, 1780–1788
A	25	Livre de Taxes, 1789–1797
A	50	Compte courant, 1794–1814
A	51	Livre de Taxes, 1823–1839
A	58	Cautions pour les étrangers, 1766–1807
A	65	Livre de Taxes, 1810–1823
A	66	Livre de Taxes, 1797–1803
A	67	Livre de Taxes, 1715–1740
A	69	Livre de Taxes, 1803–1810
B	2	Délibérations de la Douzaine, 1732–1783
B	5	Cautions pour les étrangers, 1785–1786
B	31	Passengers landed, 1828–1832
B	32	Délibérations de la Douzaine, 1783–1815
B	44	Census of St Peter Port, 1827; summary of 1831 census; census of migrants 1830.

Ecclesiastical Court Archives [housed in the Greffe]

> Registers ['Actes']
>
> Wills ['Testaments']

Greffe, St Peter Port

> [References to the catalogue published by the List and Index Society – *List of Records in the Greffe, Guernsey, volume 1* (Special Series volume 2, London, 1969) are given in parentheses].
>
> Amirauté, 1653–1934 (I.23, p. 32)
>
> Commonplace book (IV.76. 113, p. 56)
>
> Contrats pour Lire et pour la Date, 1567–1772 (I.1, p. 30)
>
> Crimes, 1563–1957 (I.26, p. 32)
>
> Depositions, 1699–1715 (I.36.10, p. 35)
>
> Garrison register
>
> General Letter Books, first series (II.46, p. 40)
>
> Guille, scrapbook of Guillaume Guille, 1748 (IV.76.65, p. 52)
>
> Uncatalogued ms., octavo, 17th–18th century, listing *cabaretiers* etc. [discovered by Mr Beale]
>
> Livre de Certificats 1768–1788 (II.50.14, p. 41)
>
> Ordres du Conseil et Actes du Parlement (II.39, p. 40)
>
> de Sausmarez papers (Greffe): account book of Société de la Chambre, 1737–1766, (D.I.15.20, p. 121)
>
> de Sausmarez papers (Greffe): Prize lists (D.I.15.21, p. 121)

Island Archives Service, Victoria Road, St Peter Port

> AQ 005/12-01, Guérin ledger
>
> AQ 49/1, Price papers, copy of Order in Council
>
> DC/HX-79-01, Délibérations "A" (1726) 1741–1801 (also typescript copy edited by G. Lenfestey)
>
> DC/HX-117-1, Journal I
>
> DC/HX-117-2, Journal II
>
> DC/HX-118-1, Journal III

Priaulx Library, St Peter Port

[Items marked with an asterisk are from the Guille-Allès Library and are currently housed at the Priaulx Library]

> 19H, Letters of Pierre Careye (typed transcripts)
>
> 18459/SR   Guille letter book
>
> 19548/907D   de Magnac ms. (SR)
>
> 20763/SR   Guille letter book
>
> 29109/408C   Lihou letter book *
>
> 29118/408C   Dobrée protest book *
>
> 29121/408C   Watkins ms. vol. 3 *
>
> 29122/408C   Watkins ms. vol 4 *
>
> 31458/80D   Guille ms., Recueil d'Ordres en Conseil

31468/20H   Guille memorandum book

31469/20H   N Careye accounts book

37282/16D   letter book, Le Cocq

37383   Ms of Mourant & Co. 1783

Family files: de Garis; Dobrée; Guille; Le Marchant

Le Cocq letters (SR)

919-B & F Le Mesurier papers (SR)

Lukis ms (SR)

Mollet journals (SR)

Reserson ms. (account of ill-fated partnership) (SR)

Edith Carey scrapbook

Private collections

Mrs Grant: de Crousaz papers

Sausmarez Manor: Letter Book of Mathieu de Sausmarez, the elder, 1733–1735 [*List of Records in the Greffe, Guernsey*, vol. 1 (London, 1969), IV.11.7, p. 114]; family archives

Stevens-Cox: Harvey papers; Warren papers; paintings, photographs and ephemera

Royal Court Library

Legge Survey, 1680 (ms copy of BL King's Ms 48)

Original Letters [*List of Records in the Greffe, Guernsey*, vol. 1 (London, 1969) IV.77.3, p. 59]

St Peter Port church vestry ['Town Church']

Délibérations des Chefs de Famille

Registers of baptisms, marriages and burials

SCOTLAND

Scottish Record Office, Edinburgh

CS. 96/1919 *re* James Watson

CS. 96/3231 *re* Hugh Mathie

GD. 1/306 Alexander Oliphant letter book

SWEDEN

Landsarkivet – Gothenburg

Ekman archives

PRINTED ORIGINAL SOURCES

A: Acts and Orders

Statutes of the Realm:

Acts 12 Car II cap 32; 4 Geo III chap. 13 sect. 11; 8 Geo III chap 23 sect. 2, 3.

Parliamentary Papers:

An Account presented to the House of Commons, of the number and names of vessels Cleared out from the Port of Guernsey, in the Months of November and December 1806, and January and February 1807, with the Amount of the excise and customs duties thereon. 21st July, 1807, p. 10, in

Parliamentary Papers, House of Commons, session 27 June – 14 August 1807, iv <57>, pp. 85–95.

Guernsey *Actes* and *Ordonnances*:

Actes des Etats de l' Île de Guernesey, 1605–1845, vols. 1–8 (Guernsey, 1851–1938).

Recueil d' Ordonnances de la Cour Royale de l' Isle de Guernesey, 1533–1840, 2 vols (Guernsey, 1852–1856)

B: Newspapers and contemporary journals

Elizabeth College Magazine (Guernsey)

Gazette de Guernesey (Guernesey)

Gazette de l' Île de Jersey (Jersey)

The Guernsey and Jersey Magazine (London)

The Guernsey Evening Press (Guernsey)

Lloyd's Evening Post (London)

Lloyd's List (London)

The Monthly Selection (Guernsey)

The Sarnian Monthly Magazine (Guernsey)

The Star (Guernsey)

The Times (London)

C: Contemporary Writings

[Anon.] 'Sketches of Guernsey and Guernseymen Fifty Years Ago – High Street' in *Elizabeth College Magazine*, July 1842, vol. 1, no. 3, pp. 49–52.

[Anon.] *A Summer Stroll Through the Islands of Jersey and Guernsey* (Jersey, 1809).

Articles et Règlements d' une Société d' Amis (Guernsey, 1775).

Articles of the Friendly Society, of the Island of Guernsey (Salisbury, 1764); *An Additional Article, of the Friendly Society in Guernsey* (Southampton, n.d.).

The Case of the Inhabitants of the Island of Guernsey, in Relation to several Orders of Council obtained by the Commissioners of the Customs, for setting Custom-House-Officers in the Island, and subjecting the Inhabitants to the Laws relating to the Customs in Great Britain (n.d., c. 1708/9).

The Case of the Town Parish versus the Nine Country Parishes, respecting a change in the rates and representation, appointed to be heard before the Committee of the Privy Council, at eleven o'clock, on Thursday, April 26, 1759. (Guernsey, 1846).

Baldwin, S., *A Survey of the British Customs* (London, 1770).

Barbet's Guide for the Island of Guernsey (Guernsey, 1844).

Bernard, J., *Retrospections of the Stage*, 2 vols (London, 1830).

Berry, W., *History of the Island of Guernsey* (London, 1815).

Bonnassieux, P., (ed.) *Archives Nationales, Conseil de Commerce et Bureau du Commerce 1700–1791* (Paris, 1900).

Brice, A., *The Grand Gazetteer* (Exeter, 1759).

Camden, W., *Britannia* (Amsterdam, 1639).

Carey, E. (ed.), 'A Trip to Guernsey in 1798 by W. T. Money' TSG vol. XI, part ii, for 1931 (Guernsey, 1932), pp. 237–258.

De Sausmarez, H., *An Account of the Proceedings of Henry De Sausmarez, of the Island of Guernesey, Gent.* (London, 1717).

Dicey, T., *An Historical Account of Guernsey, from its first settlement before the Norman Conquest to the present time* (London, 1751).

Falle, P., *An Account of the Isle of Jersey* (London, 1694).

Gillett, E. (ed.), *Elizabeth Ham by herself 1783–1820* (London, 1945).

Head, Sir George, *A Home Tour through various parts of the United Kingdom* (London, 1837).

Heylyn, P., *A Full Relation of two Journeys* (London, 1656).

Hocart, R., 'The Journal of Charles Trumbull' TSG vol. XXI, part iv, for 1984 (Guernsey, 1985), pp. 566–585.

Inglis, H. D. , *The Channel Islands* (London, 1834).

Jacob, J., *Annals of the British Norman Isles* (Paris, 1830).

Lee, G. E. (ed.), *Notebook of Pierre Le Roy* (Guernsey, 1893).

Le Marchant, W., *Histoire de l'Erection Originelle de l'Avancement & Augmentation du Havre de la VIlle de St Pierre Port à Guernesey* (Oxford, c.1755).

[Le Marchant, W.], *The Rights and Immunities of the Island of Guernsey* (London, 1771; reprinted with additional material, London, 1805).

Marshall, J., *A Digest of all the Accounts* (London, 1833).

Naftel, J. F., (ed.), *Memoirs of Nicholas Naftel* (*sine loco*, America, 1888).

Quayle, T., *General View of the Agriculture and present state of the Islands on the coast of Normandy* (London, 1815).

Stevens-Cox, J., (ed.), *Guernsey Commercial Directory for 1834* (Guernsey, 1980).

Walmesley, W., *A Pedestrian Tour through the Islands of Guernsey and Jersey* (K. C. Renault ed.) (Chichester, 1992).

Warren, J. P. (ed.), 'Extracts from the Journal of Elisha Dobrée' TSG vol. X, part iv, for 1929 (Guernsey, 1930), pp. 493–551; vol. XI, part i, for 1930 (Guernsey, 1931), pp. 106–123.

PRINTED SECONDARY SOURCES

Abrams, P., 'Towns and Economic Growth: Some Theories and Problems' in P. Abrams and E. A. Wrigley (eds.), *Towns in Societies* (Cambridge, 1980), pp. 9–33.

Acerra, M., and Meyer, J., *L'Empire des mers des Galions aux Clippers* (Paris, 1990).

Agnew, D. C. A., *Protestant Exiles from France, chiefly in the Reign of Louis XIV* (London, 1871).

Anderson, A., 'Trade between the Channel Islands and Southampton in the Mid-Eighteenth Century' BSJ vol. XVIII (1964), pp. 445–451.

Andrews, C. M., *The Colonial Period of American History*, 4 vols (New Haven, 1943).

Aptel, C., Biotteau N., Richard M., Santrot, J. *Thomas Dobrée 1810–1895 un homme un musée* (Paris – Nantes, 1997).

Arnold, D., *The Georgian Villa* (Stroud, 1998).

Baigent, E., 'Economy and society in eighteenth-century English towns: Bristol in the 1770s' in D. Denecke and G. Shaw (eds.), *Urban Historical Geography. Recent progress in Britain and Germany* (Cambridge, 1988), pp. 109–124.

Baird, C. W., *Histoire des Réfugiés Huguenots en Amérique* (Toulouse, 1886).

Barrington, E. C., 'The Human Geography of Guernsey' TSG vol. XII, part iii, for 1935 (Guernsey, 1936), pp. 351–426.

Bois, G. J. C., *An Introduction to Channel Islands Pewter* (Jersey, 1993).

Borsay, P., *The English Urban Renaissance* (Oxford, 1989).

Borsay, P. (ed.), *The Eighteenth-Century Town, A Reader in English Urban History 1688–1820* (Harlow, 1990).

Bosher, J. F., *The French Revolution* (London, 1989).

Boulaire, A., *Voiles et Voiliers au temps de Louis XV et Louis XVI* (Paris, 1992).

Bourde de la Rogerie, A., 'La Famille Martell' TSG vol. XI, part ii, for 1931 (Guernsey, 1932), pp. 259–262.

Bourdieu, P., *Distinction* (London, 1989).

Bowden, P. J., *The Wool Trade in Tudor and Stuart England* (London, 1962).

Braudel, F., 'Pre-Modern towns' in P. Clark (ed.), *The Early Modern Town, A Reader* (London, 1976), pp. 53–90.

Braudel, F., *Civilization and Capitalism*, 3 vols. (London, 1984).

Braudel, F., *The Identity of France*, 2 vols. (London, 1990).

Brett, C. E. B., *Buildings in the town and parish of St Peter Port* (Guernsey, 1975).

Brewer, J., 'Commercialization and Politics' in N. McKendrick, J. Brewer, J. H. Plumb, *The Birth of a Consumer Society* (London, 1982), pp. 195–262.

Brewer, J., *The Pleasures of the Imagination English culture in the eighteenth century* (London, 1997).

Bromley, J. S., 'A New Vocation: privateering in the wars of 1689–1697 and 1702–1713' in A. G. Jamieson (ed.), *A People of the Sea* (London, 1986), pp. 109–147.

Brown, H. P., *Egalitarianism and the Generation of Inequality* (Oxford, 1991).

Burke, P., *History and Social Theory* (Cambridge, 1992).

Butel, P., 'La construction navale et les industries annexes dans les ports de commerce au sud de la Loire <La Rochelle, Bordeaux et Bayonne> aux XVIIe et XVIIIe siècles' in *I porti come impresa economica* (Florence, 1988), pp. 689–702.

Butel, P., *Européens et espaces maritimes (vers 1690–1790)* (Bordeaux, 1997).

Cabantous, A., *La Mer et les Hommes pêcheurs et matelots dunkerquois de Louis XIV à la Révolution* (Dunkirk, 1980).

Cabantous, A., *Histoire de Dunkerque* (Toulouse, 1983).

Cabourdin, G., Biraben, J.-N., and Blum, A., 'Les crises démographiques' in J. Dupâquier, *et al.* (eds.), *Histoire de la population française* (Paris, 1988), vol. 2, pp. 175–219.

Carey, E., 'The beginnings of Quakerism in Guernsey' TSG vol. VIII, part ii, for 1918 (Guernsey, 1919), pp. 115–126.

Carey, E., 'Social Life in Guernsey in the sixteenth century' TSG vol. VIII, part iv, for 1920 (Guernsey, 1921), pp. 243–273.

Carey, E., (ed.) 'A Trip to Guernsey in 1798 by W. T. Money' TSG vol. XI, part ii, for 1931 (Guernsey, 1932), pp. 237–258.

Carey, E., 'The growth of St Peter Port in the early 19th century from the MS of the late F. C. Lukis, Esq.' TSG vol. XII, part ii, for 1934 (Guernsey, 1935), pp. 151–170.

Carey, W. W., *et al.*, *The History of the Careys of Guernsey* (London, 1938).

Carey-Curtis, S., 'The Thirty-first Annual Report of the Antiquarian Section' TSG vol. XIII, part vi, for 1942 (Guernsey, 1943), pp. 360–363.

Carter, H., and Lewis, C. R., *An Urban Geography of England and Wales in the Nineteenth Century* (London, 1990).

Chapman, S., *Merchant Enterprise in Britain* (Cambridge, 1992).

Charbonnel, N., *Commerce et course sous la Révolution et le Consulat à la Rochelle* (Paris, 1977).

Chaunu, P., *La civilisation de l'Europe classique* (Paris, 1966).

Clark, G. N., *Guide to English Commercial Statistics 1696–1782* (London, 1938).

Clark, J. G., *La Rochelle and the Atlantic Economy during the Eighteenth Century* (Baltimore, 1981).

Clark, P., *Sociability and Urbanity: Clubs and Societies in the Eighteenth Century City* (Leicester, 1986).

Clark, P., 'Migration in England during the late seventeenth and early eighteenth centuries' in P. Clark and D. Souden (eds.), *Migration and Society in Early-Modern England* (London, 1987), pp. 213–252.

Clark, P., (ed.), *The Early Modern Town* (London, 1976).

Clark, P., (ed.), *The Transformation of English Provincial Towns 1600–1800* (London, 1984).

Clark, P., and Slack, P., *English Towns in Transition 1500–1700* (London, 1976).

Clark, P., and Souden, D. (eds.), *Migration and Society in Early-Modern England* (London, 1987).

Clarke, L., *Building Capitalism* (London, 1992).

Clarkson, L. A., *Proto-Industrialization: The First Phase of Industrialization?* (Basingstoke, 1991).

Colvin, H., *A Biographical Dictionary of British Architects 1600–1840* (London, 1978).

Corfield, P., *The Impact of English Towns 1700–1800* (Oxford, 1982).

Corfield, P., 'Class in eighteenth-century Britain' in P. J. Corfield (ed.), *Language, History and Class* (Oxford, 1991).

Cowan, A., *Urban Europe 1500–1700* (London, 1998).

Crawford, A., *Bristol and the Wine Trade* (Bristol, 1984).

Croix, A., *La Bretagne aux 16e et 17e siècles* (Paris, 1981).

Crouzet, F., *Britain Ascendant: comparative studies in Franco-British economic history* (Cambridge, 1990).

Cullen, L. M., *Anglo-Irish Trade 1660–1800* (New York, 1968).

Cullen, L. M., 'The Early Brandy Trade' in E. Aerts, *et al.* (eds.), *Production, Marketing and Consumption of Alcoholic Beverages since the Late Middle Ages* (Session B-14, Proceedings of the Tenth International Economic History Congress, Leuven, 1990), pp. 20–30.

Cullen, L. M., *The Brandy Trade under the Ancien Régime – Regional Specialisation in the Charente* (Cambridge, 1998).

Currer-Briggs, N., and Gambier, R., *Huguenot Ancestry* (Chichester, 1985).

Daunton, M. J., 'Towns and Economic Growth in Eighteenth-Century England' in P. Abrams and E. A. Wrigley (eds.), *Towns in Societies* (Cambridge, 1980), pp. 245–277.

David, J. M., 'Some Notes on 18th Century Local Shipping', TSG vol. XVI, part iii, for 1957 (Guernsey, 1958), pp. 268–276.

Davidoff, L. and Hall, C., *Family Fortunes: Men and Women of the English Middle Class 1780–1850* (London, 1987).

Davis, R., *The Rise of the English Shipping Industry in the Seventeenth and Eighteenth Centuries* (London, 1962).

Davis, R., *The Rise of the Atlantic Economies* (London, 1982).

de Garis, M., 'The Parish of St. Pierre du Bois and some of its inhabitants in the 18th and early 19th centuries', TSG vol. XIV, part iv, for 1949 (Guernsey, 1950), pp. 479–488.

de la Morandière, C., *Histoire de la pêche française de la morue dans l'Amérique septentrionale*, 3 vols. (Paris 1962–66).

Delumeau, J., *Le Mouvement du port de Saint Malo, 1681–1720* (Paris, 1966).

de Tocqueville, A., (Reeve, H., trans.), *Democracy in America*, 4 vols. (London, 1840).

Deveau, J.-M., *Le Commerce rochelais face à la Révolution Correspondance de Jean-Baptiste Nairac (1789–1790)* (La Rochelle, 1989).

Devine, T. M., *The Tobacco Lords* (Edinburgh, 1990).

de Vries, J., *European Urbanization 1500–1800* (London, 1984).

de Vries, J., 'The Population and Economy of the Preindustrial Netherlands' in R. I. Rotberg and T. K. Rabb (eds.), *Population and Economy* (Cambridge, 1986), pp. 101–122.

de Wismes, A., *Les Ports de Bretagne au temps de la grande marine à voiles* ([Paris?], 1998).

Drake, M., *Population Studies from Parish Registers* (Matlock, 1982).

Duby, G., *et al.* (eds.), *Histoire de la France rurale*, 4 vols. (Paris, 1975–76).

Duffy, M., *et al.*, *The New Maritime History of Devon, Volume 1: From Early Times to the Late Eighteenth Century* (London, 1992). *Volume II: From the Late Eighteenth Century to the Present Day* (London, 1994).

Duncan, J., *The History of Guernsey* (London, 1841).

Dupâquier, J., 'Demographic crises and subsistence crises in France, 1650–1725' in J. Walter and R. Schofield (eds.), *Famine, disease and the social order in early modern society* (Cambridge, 1989), pp. 189–199.

Dupont, G., *Histoire du Cotentin et de ses Îles*, 4 vols. (Caen, 1885).

Dury, G. H., 'The Population of Guernsey: an essay in historical geography', *Geography* no. 160, vol. XXXIII, part 2, June 1948, pp. 61–69.

Eagleston, A. J., *The Channel Islands under Tudor Government, 1485–1642* (Cambridge, 1949).

Falvey, J., and Brooks, W. (eds.), *The Channel in the eighteenth century: bridge, barrier and gateway. Transactions of the Anglo-French Colloquium held at the University of Southampton, 20-23 September 1988. [Studies on Voltaire and the eighteenth century 292]* (Oxford, 1991).

Fay, C. R., 'Peter Paul Dobrée of Guernsey and Cambridge', QRGS, vol. XII, no. 3, Autumn 1956, pp. 46–52.

Feldbaek, O., *India trade under the Danish Flag 1772–1808* (Copenhagen, 1963).

Festa, G., 'Manche et permanence historique: les îles anglo-normandes dans la conscience des Lumières' in J. Falvey and W. Brooks (eds.), *The Channel in the eighteenth century* (Oxford, 1991), pp. 81–95.

Fieldhouse, D. K., *The Colonial Empires* (Basingstoke, 1992).

Fisher, H. E. S., *The Portugal Trade* (London, 1971).

Fisher, S., 'Lisbon as a Port Town in the Eighteenth Century' in S. Fisher (ed.), *Lisbon as a Port Town, the British Seaman and other Maritime Themes* (Exeter, 1988), pp. 9–36.

Fraser, D. and Sutcliffe, A. (eds.), *The Pursuit of Urban History* (London, 1983).

Giddens, A., *Sociology* (Cambridge, 1991).

Girouard, M., 'The Georgian Promenade' in P. Corfield *et. al.*, *Life in the Georgian Town* (London, 1985), pp. 26–33.

Glass, D. V., 'Socio-economic status and occupations in the City of London at the end of the seventeenth century' in P. Clark (ed.), *The Early Modern Town* (London, 1976).

Goubert, P., *The French Peasantry in the Seventeenth Century* (Cambridge, 1989).

Grant, A., and Gwynn, R., 'The Huguenots of Devon' in *Report and Transactions of the Devon Association for the Advancement of Science, Literature and Art*, vol. 117, 1985 (Exeter, 1985), pp. 161–194.

Grubiak, O. and J., *The Guernsey Experiment* (Hawthorne, California, 1963, 1980).

Hancock, D., *Citizens of the World* (Cambridge, 1995).

Hare, G., *The Georgian Theatre in Wessex* (London, 1958).

Hettier, C., *Rélations de la Normandie et de la Bretagne avec les Îles de la Manche pendant l'émigration* (Caen, 1885).

Hilaire-Perez, L., *L'expérience de la mer. Les Européens et les espaces maritimes au XVIIIe siècle* (Paris, 1997).

Hilton, R. H., *English and French towns in Feudal Society* (Cambridge, 1992).

Hocart, R., 'A Guernsey Merchant and his Family in the Reign of George II', TSG vol. XXI, part iii, for 1983 (Guernsey, 1984), pp. 360–378.

Hocart, R., 'The Journal of Charles Trumbull', TSG vol. XXI, part iv, for 1984 (Guernsey, 1985), pp. 566–585.

Hocart, R., *An Island Assembly – The Development of the States of Guernsey 1700–1949* (Guernsey, 1988).

Hocart, R., 'The Building of the New Town', TSG vol. XXIII, part ii, for 1992 (Guernsey, 1993), pp. 342–377.

Hocart, R., *Peter de Havilland: Bailiff of Guernsey* (Guernsey, 1997).

Hohenberg, P. M., and Lees, L., *The Making of Urban Europe 1000–1950* (Cambridge, Mass., and London, 1985).

Hoskins, W. G., *Industry, Trade and People in Exeter 1688–1800* (Manchester, 1935).

Jackson, A. C. F., 'Freemasonry in Jersey' in *Ars Quatuor Coronatorum*, vol. 86 (1973), pp. 177–220.

Jackson, G., 'The ports' in D. H. Aldcroft and M. J. Freeman (eds.), *Transport in the Industrial Revolution* (Manchester, 1983), pp. 177–209.

Jamieson, A. G. (ed.), *A People of the Sea* (London, 1986).

Jamieson, A. G., 'The Return to Privateering: Channel Island Privateers, 1739–83' in A. G. Jamieson (ed.), *A People of the Sea* (London, 1986), pp. 148–172.

Jamieson, A. G., 'Channel Island Shipowners and Seamen, 1700–1900' in A. G. Jamieson (ed.), *A People of the Sea* (London, 1986), pp. 312–366.

Jamieson, A. G., 'The Coming of Steam: Cross-Channel Services and Island Steamers' in A. G. Jamieson (ed.), *A People of the Sea* (London, 1986), pp. 444–476.

Jenkins, J. G., and Salaman, R. A., 'A Note on Coopering' in C. Singer *et al.* (eds.), *A History of Technology*, vol. 3 (Oxford, 1957).

Jeremie, J., *Historical Account of Guernsey* (Guernsey, 1821).

Jeremie, P., *On Parochial and States Taxation in Guernsey* (Guernsey, 1856).

Jones, E. L. and Falkus, M. E., 'Urban improvement and the English economy in the seventeenth and eighteenth centuries' in P. Borsay (ed.), *The Eighteenth-Century Town* (Harlow, 1990), pp. 116–158.

Kellett-Smith, S. K., 'The Guernsey Cholera Epidemic of 1832', TSG vol. XX, part v, for 1980 (Guernsey, 1981), pp. 643–655.

Kindleberger, C. P., *Mariners and Markets* (Hemel Hempstead, 1992).

King, A. D., *Urbanism, Colonialism, and the World-Economy* (London, 1990).

Kinnersly, W. T., *History of Doyle's Lodge of Fellowship Guernsey* (Guernsey, 1872).

Kriedte, P., *Peasants, Landlords and Merchant Capitalists* (Providence R. I. and Oxford, 1990).

Kriedte, P., Medick, H., and Schlumbohm, J., *Industrialization before Industrialization* (Cambridge, 1981).

Langton, J., 'Residential patterns in pre-industrial cities: Some case studies from seventeenth-century Britain' in J. Barry (ed.), *The Tudor and Stuart Town A Reader in English Urban History 1530–1688* (Harlow, 1990), pp. 166–205.

Law, C. M., 'Some notes on the urban population of England and Wales in the eighteenth century', *Local Historian*, 10, no. 1 (1972), pp. 13–26.

Lawton, R., and Lee, R. (eds.), *Urban Population Development in Western Europe from the Late-Eighteenth to the Early-Twentieth Century* (Liverpool, 1989).

Le Bouedec, G., *Activités maritimes et sociétés littorales de l'Europe atlantique* (Paris, 1997).

Le Lievre, M., *Histoire du Méthodisme dans les Îles de la Manche* (Paris, London, 1885).

Le Mesurier, H. P., 'Notes on the Armorial China of some of the Guernsey families', TSG vol. XII, part iii, for 1935 (Guernsey, 1936), pp. 285–297.

Le Patourel, J., 'The Early History of St Peter Port', TSG vol. XII, part ii, for 1934 (Guernsey, 1935), pp. 171–209.

Le Patourel, J., *Medieval Administration of the Channel Islands* (Oxford, 1937).

Lepetit, B., *Les villes dans la France moderne (1740–1840)* (Paris, 1988).

Le Roy Ladurie, E., 'Family structures and inheritance customs in sixteenth century France' in J. Goody *et al.* (eds.), *Family and Inheritance* (Cambridge, 1979), pp. 37–70.

Le Roy Ladurie, E., (ed.), *La Ville Classique* (Paris, 1981), vol. 3 of G. Duby (ed.), *Histoire de la France urbaine* (Paris, 1980–1985).

Lespagnol, A., *Messieurs de Saint-Malo* (St Malo, 1990).

Lipsey, R. G., *An Introduction to Positive Economics* (London, 1987).

Little, B., *St Peter Port, its story and buildings* (Guernsey, 1963).

Livi-Bacci, M., *Population and Nutrition* (Cambridge, 1990).

McCormack, J., *The Guernsey House* (Chichester, 1980).

MacCulloch, Sir Edgar, *Guernsey Folk Lore* (London, 1903).

McInnes, A., *The English Town 1660–1760* (London, 1980).

McKendrick, N., Brewer, J., and Plumb, J. H., *The Birth of a Consumer Society* (London, 1982).

Mann, J. de L., 'The Sixties and the Forties', QRGS vol. XVII, no. 1, Spring 1961, pp. 10–11.

Mann, J. de L., 'A Guernsey Merchant of the Commonwealth Period', TSG vol. XXI, part ii, for 1982 (Guernsey, 1983), pp. 217–225.

Marquand, Captain H., *Memoirs of a Victorian Master Mariner* (ed. E. B. Marquand) (Cardiff, 1996).

Marr, L. J., *Guernsey People* (Chichester, 1984).

Martinière, G., and Vidal, L., *Les Européens et la mer au XVIIIe siècle* (Paris, 1997).

Mathew, W. M., *The Secret History of Guernsey Marmalade: James Keiller & Son Offshore, 1857–1879* (Guernsey, 1998).

Mauro, F., 'Merchant Communities, 1350–1750' in J. D. Tracy (ed.), *The Rise of Merchant Empires* (Cambridge, 1990), pp. 255–286.

Mayne, R. H., *Old Channel Islands Silver* (Jersey, 1969).

Meyer, J., *L'Armement nantais dans la deuxième moitié du XVIIIe siècle* (Paris, 1969).

Meyer, W. R., 'Paul Le Mesurier, Lord Mayor of London', TSG vol. XXI, part v, for 1985 (Guernsey, 1986), pp. 701–714.

Minchinton, W. E., *The Trade of Bristol in the Eighteenth Century* (Bristol, 1957).

Minchinton, W. E., 'Bristol – metropolis of the west in the eighteenth century', in P. Clark (ed.), *The Early Modern Town* (London, 1976), pp. 297–313.

Minchinton, W. E., *The Port of Bristol in the Eighteenth Century* (Bristol, 1983).

Mollat, M., *Histoire des pêches maritimes en France* (Paris, 1987).

Mollat, M., *Europe and the Sea* (Oxford, 1993).

Morgan, K., *Bristol and the Atlantic trade in the eighteenth century* (Cambridge, 1993).

Morley, M. (ed.), *The Gallienne Letters 1835–1895* (Guernsey, n.d. c.1992).

Morris, R. J., 'Voluntary societies and British urban elites' in P. Borsay (ed.), *The Eighteenth-Century Town* (Harlow, 1990), pp. 338–366.

Namier, Sir L., and Brooke, J., *The House of Commons 1754–1790*, 3 vols. (London, 1964).

Nash, G. B., *The Urban Crucible* (Cambridge, Mass., and London, 1979).

Nières, C., *Histoire de Lorient* (Lorient, 1988).

Ogier, D. M., *Reformation and Society in Guernsey* (Woodbridge, 1996).

Ommer, R., 'The Cod Trade in the New World' in A. G. Jamieson (ed.), *A People of the Sea* (London, 1986), pp. 245–268.

Palmer, J. C. and Palmer, J. E. C., *A Classified List of Books and Pamphlets published 1647–1953 relating to the Island of Guernsey (revised)* (Harpenden, 1987).

Patterson, A. T., *A History of Southampton 1700–1914* (Southampton, 1966).

Petre-Grenouilleau, O., *Les négoces maritimes français XVIIe–XXe siècle* (Paris, 1997).

Pooley, C. G., and Whyte, I. D. (eds.), *Migrants, Emigrants and Immigrants* (London, 1991).

Porter, R., and Roberts, M. M., *Pleasure in the Eighteenth Century* (Basingstoke, 1996).

Poussou, J.–P., 'The Population Increase of French Towns between 1750 and 1950 and its Demographic Consequences' in R. Lawton and R. Lees (eds.), *Urban Population Development in Western Europe from the Late-Eighteenth to the Early-Twentieth Century* (Liverpool, 1989), pp. 68–92.

Poussou, J.–P., Bonnichon, P., Huetz de Lemps, X. *Espaces coloniaux et espaces maritimes au XVIIIe siècle* (Paris, 1998).

Priaulx, T. F., and de Sausmarez, R., 'The Guernsey stocking export trade in the seventeenth century' TSG vol. XVII, part ii, for 1961 (Guernsey, 1962), pp. 210–223.

Price, J. M., *France and the Chesapeake*, 2 vols. (Ann Arbor, 1973).

Price, J. M., *Tobacco in Atlantic Trade, The Chesapeake, London and Glasgow 1675–1775* (Aldershot, 1995).

Raban, P., 'War and Trade in the Mid-Eighteenth Century', TSG vol. XXII, part i, for 1986 (Guernsey, 1987), pp. 131–163.

Raban, P., 'Clandestine Trade in the Mid-Eighteenth Century', TSG vol. XXII, part ii, for 1987 (Guernsey, 1988).

Razzell, P. E., 'Population change in eighteenth-century England' in M. M. Drake (ed.), *Population in Industrialization* (London, 1969), pp. 128–156.

Rediker, M., *Between the Devil and the Deep Blue Sea* (Cambridge, 1990).

Rendall, J., *Women in industrialising society: England 1750–1880* (Oxford, 1990).

Richard, G., *Européens et Espaces Maritimes au XVIIIe siècle* (Paris, 1997).

Richardson, D., *Bristol, Africa and the Eighteenth-Century Slave Trade to America*, 3 vols. (Bristol, 1987–1991).

Rodger, R. G., 'The Invisible Hand' – market forces, housing and the urban form in Victorian cities' in D. Fraser, and A. Sutcliffe (eds.), *The Pursuit of Urban History* (London, 1983), pp. 190–211.

Rodger, R. G., *Housing in Urban Britain 1780–1914: Class, Capitalism and Construction* (Basingstoke, 1989).

Rodger, R. G. (ed.), *European Urban History* (Leicester, 1993).

Rotberg, R. I., and Rabb, T. K. (eds.), *Population and Economy* (Cambridge, 1986).

Rubinstein, W. D., *Wealth and Inequality in Britain* (London, 1986).

Rude, G., *Hanoverian London 1714–1808* (London, 1971).

Rule, J., *Albion's People* (Harlow, 1992).

Rule, J., *The Vital Century* (Harlow, 1992).

Sandele, E. M., 'Georgian Southampton: A Watering-Place and Spa' in J. B. Morgan, and P. Peberdy (eds.), *Collected essays on Southampton* (Southampton, 1958), pp. 79–87.

Sawyer, P., 'Early fairs and markets in England and Scandinavia' in B. L. Anderson and A. J. H. Latham (eds.), *The Market in History* (London, 1986).

Schumpeter, E. B., *English Overseas Trade Statistics 1697–1808* (Oxford, 1960).

Schwarz, L. D., 'Social class and social geography: the middle classes in London at the end of the eighteenth century' in P. Borsay (ed.), *The Eighteenth-Century Town* (Harlow, 1990), pp. 315–337.

Sharp, E. W., 'La Chevauchée de sa Majesté' in *The Channel Islands Anthology*, no. 2 (Guernsey, 1975), pp. 18–22.

Sharp, E. W., 'The Evolution of St Peter Port Harbour', TSG vol. XVIII, part iii, for 1967 (Guernsey, 1968), pp. 226–255.

Short, J. R., *Urban Data Sources* (London, 1980).

Simon, A. L., *The History of the Wine Trade in England* (London, 1906).

Sinel, L., *Jersey through the Centuries* (Jersey, 1984).

Sjoberg, G., *The pre-industrial city, past and present* (Glencoe, Ill., 1960).

Stamp, L., *A Glossary of Geographical Terms* (London, 1963).

Starkey, D. J., 'British Privateering against the Dutch in the American Revolutionary War, 1780–1783' in H. E. S. Fisher (ed.), *Studies in British Privateering, Trading Enterprise and Seamen's Welfare, 1775–1900* (Exeter, 1987), pp. 1–17.

Starkey, D. J., van Eyck van Heslinga, E. S., and de Moor, J. A., *Pirates and Privateers New Perspectives on the War on Trade in the Eighteenth and Nineteenth Centuries* (Exeter, 1997).

Steele, K., *The English Atlantic 1675–1740* (Oxford, 1986).

Stein, R. L., *The French Slave Trade in the Eighteenth Century* (Wisconsin, 1979).

Stone, L., *The Family, Sex and Marriage in England 1500–1800* (Harmondsworth, 1979).

Stonelake, C., *A History of Freemasonry in the Channel Islands of Guernsey and Alderney 1753–1951* (Guernsey, 1951).

Swann, D., 'The pace and progress of port investment in England, 1660–1830' *Yorkshire Bulletin of Economic and Social Research*, XII 1960, pp. 32–44.

Taylor, G., *The Problem of Poverty 1660–1834* (London, 1969).

Thirsk, J., *The Rural Economy of England* (London, 1984).

Tracy, J. D., *The Rise of Merchant Empires* (Cambridge, 1990).

Tracy, J. D., *The Political Economy of Merchant Empires* (Cambridge, 1997).

Trudgill, P., *Sociolinguistics* (Harmondsworth, 1983).

Tunzelmann, G. N. von, 'Technological and organizational change in industry during the Industrial Revolution' in P. K. O'Brien and R. Quinault (eds.), *The Industrial Revolution and British society* (Cambridge, 1993).

Tupper, F. B., *The History of Guernsey* (Guernsey, 1854).

Unwin, T., *Wine and The Vine – an historical Geography of Viticulture and the Wine Trade* (London, 1991).

Vance, J. E., 'Land assignment in pre-capitalist, capitalist and post-capitalist cities', *Economic Geography 47* (1971), pp. 101–120.

Vignols, L., 'L'Importation en France au XVIIIe siècle du boeuf salé d'Irlande' in *Revue Historique* part 159, pp. 79–95 (1928).

Wallerstein, I., *The Modern World-system: Capitalist Agriculture and the Origins of the European World Economy in the Sixteenth Century* (New York, 1973).

Walter, J., and Schofield, R., *Famine, disease and the social order in early modern society* (Cambridge, 1989).

Walvin, J., *English Urban Life 1776–1851* (London, 1984).

Walvin, J., *Fruits of Empire Exotic Produce and British Taste 1660–1800* (Basingstoke, 1997).

Warren, J. P., 'Fire Marks and Early Fire-fighting in Guernsey', TSG vol. XVI, part i, for 1955 (Guernsey, 1956), pp. 35–46.

Washbrook, D., 'To each a language of his own: language, culture, and society in India' in P. Corfield (ed.), *Language, History and Class* (Oxford, 1991), pp. 179–203.

Weatherill, L., *Consumer behaviour and material culture in Britain 1660–1760* (London, 1996).

Whiteman, A., *The Compton Census of 1676* (Oxford, 1986).

Wickins, P. L., 'The Economics of Privateering: Capital Dispersal in the American War of Independence' in *Journal of European Economic History*, vol. 13, no. 2 – Fall 1984, pp. 375–395.

Wilkins, F., *Strathclyde's Smuggling Story* (Kidderminster, 1992).

Williamson, J. G., *Inequality, Poverty, and History* (Oxford, 1991).

Woolmer, C., and Arkwright, C., *Pewter of the Channel Islands* (Edinburgh, 1973).

Wrigley, E. A., 'Parasite or Stimulus: The Town in a Pre-industrial Economy' in P. Abrams and E. A. Wrigley (eds.), *Towns in Societies* (Cambridge, 1980), pp. 295–309.

Wrigley, E. A., and Schofield, R. S., *The Population History of England 1541–1871* (Cambridge, 1989).

UNPUBLISHED THESES

Haudrères, P., 'La Compagnie Française des Indes (1719–1795)' (University of Paris IV, 1987).

McIntyre, S., 'Towns as Health and Pleasure Resorts: Bath, Scarborough, and Weymouth 1700–1815', D. Phil. thesis (Oxford, 1973).

Price, J. M., 'The Tobacco Trade and the Treasury, 1685–1733: British Mercantilism in its Fiscal Aspects' Ph.D. thesis (Harvard, 1954).

INDEX NOMINUM

(See also Appendixes 6, 18 and 20 for lists of merchants)

INDEX LOCORUM

(For St Peter Port locations see p. 238)

St Peter Port

(See also *Index Rerum* under *assembly, church, hospital, taverns*)

INDEX RERUM

TABULA GRATULATORIA

Office of the Lieutenant-Governor
Channel Islands Interest Group, New Zealand Society of Genealogists Inc.
Guernsey Customs & Excise Department
Features Department, Guernsey Evening Press, Braye Road, Vale
Le Conte and Wright Limited
Société Jersiaise Library

S. J. Ainsworth
Richard T. Allan
Mr and Mrs D. N. Allison
Miss J. F. Arthur
Mrs E. Ashton
Mrs L. Ashton, Guernsey Museums and Galleries
Mr and Mrs J. Atkinson
C. N. Aubin

J. R. Barrows
Mr and Mrs P. W. Baudains
D. M. Bertrand
C. R. W. Best
Mr and Mrs M. E. Best
Miss J. Bichard
Catherine Bienvenu
Martin Bienvenu
Miss M. N. Bienvenu
Advocate A. R. Binnington
K. C. Birch
Dr W. A. Blanpied
Mrs J. M. Blondel
M. P. Blondel
A. G. F. Bodman
Mr and Mrs P. M. Bodman
Mr J. and Mrs B. M. Bougourd
J. J. Bougourd
M. H. Bougourd
Advocate C. J. Bound
Roger Bowns
L. Bradshaw
R. N. Brehaut
Mrs J. A. Brook
Captain I. F. Brouard
Mrs S. Brouard
R .W. Brown
J. P. Brun

Major General F. G. Caldwell
J. and K. Cann
Colonel M. J. Capper
Mr and Mrs W. J. Carman
D. A. Carter
Mr and Mrs P. R. Castle
Y. F. Cataroche
Professor K. J. Cathcart
M. G. Cave
Mrs E. T. R. Cevat
Sam Clapp
Mrs M. A. Clarke
Mr and Mrs B. A. Clegg
R. W. Clegg
Mr and Mrs D. Codville
Canon V. J. Collas
Mr and Mrs R. L. Collenette
Mrs A. J. S. Collins
Mrs J. Compton-Williams
C. D. Cook
Mrs J. B. Cook
Simon Coombe
J. P. Cooper
Christopher Cormack
Cynthia Cormack
Dr P. D. M. Costen
H. G. Coutanche
P. V. Creasey
J. A. Crocker
Mrs F. A. Crump
B. L. Cumner

B. G. de Carteret
John N. de Garis
Dr S. T. de Garis
J. A. de Havilland
Mr and Mrs B. R. de Jersey
Dr P. E. de Jersey

T. J. de Putron
Seigneur P. W. D. St. V. de Sausmarez
Jurat P. J. de Veulle
P. M. du Port
Miss Daisy Darby
Mr and Mrs C. C. Davey
M. Davies
M. J. Day
Mrs S. R. Dean
Mrs G. K. Deane
W. J. Denning
R. B. Dobrée
J. G. Doggart
J. A. B. Dorrien Smith
Mrs J. P. Down
Mrs M. A. Drew
D. A. W. Dunn, I.S.O., B.A., M.Sc.
Phil Dupré
A. B. Dyke

Mrs A. F. D. Ede-Golightly
Mrs L. D. Edge
Mrs J. H. E. Edwards
Miss K. Edwards
Mrs C. L. Elliott
Mr and Mrs J. D. Ellis
R. A. Ellis
Mrs P. E. England

Mrs J. A. Falla
M. A. Falla
Mr and Mrs N. J. Falla
S. J. Falla
J. Fallaize
M. J. Fattorini
Advocate J. R. Finch
Mrs M. M. S. Fisken and N. R. A. Burnell
S. G. Foote
Mrs M. J. Foster
Mrs G. F. Freeman

Douzaine Representative Brian Gabriel
Mrs S. G. Gammie
Mrs N. Gardiner
Professor V. Gardiner
Mrs N. M. Gartell
Mrs C. M. Gavey
G. P. Gavey
J. A. Gavey

M. E. Gavey
Mr G. N. and Mrs J. M. Georgano
K. A. Gibbs
M. P. Gill
S. L. Gill
Alex Glendinning
David Godfrey
Deputy J. A. B. Gollop
Mr and Mrs R. E. Gould
A. S. Green, M.B.E.
M. A. Green
Mrs D. F. Gregg
Mr and Mrs J. G. L. Griffith-Jones
I. C. Griffiths
Mrs R. J. Grigg
E. J. Grimsley
G. Guilbert
David Gurney

Mrs C. J. Hall
C. P. M. Harris
S. A. Harris
D. N. Hawkins
J. A. Hawkins
Elizabeth and Geoffrey Head
R. L. Heaume
R. L. Hedger
Tim and Eleanor Henderson
Canon G. Hetherington, K.H.S.
D. P. B. Hibbs
J. J. Hickman
Mrs F. A. Higgs
Mr W. C. and Mrs H. M. Hill
P. J. Hobday
Mr and Mrs P. R. Hocart
R. P. Hocart
Mrs M. E. Holland
Mr and Mrs J. G. Hooley
B. G. Hopper
Ted Hotton
J. D. Huddleston
J. G. Hughes
C. H. and J. Hunt
Mr and Mrs M. D. Hutchings
T. G. Hutt
Major and Mrs C. A. Hynes

Mrs R. E. Jagger
Mr and Mrs N. Jee

Dr David Jeffs
Jurat S. W. J. Jehan
Mr and Mrs G. P. Jenkinson
P. Johnston
T. W. Jones

Miss C. M. M. Kamphuis
Mrs S. A. Keighley
C. Kelleher
Advocate J. D. Kelleher

André and Sylvia La Joie
R. E. Le Bargy
M. H. Le Boutillier
Mr and Mrs D. O. Le Conte
Dr A. Le Lievre
R. Le Maitre
Mrs D. K. Le Page
J. P. F. Le Page
Dr K. E. Le Page
P. R. Le Pelley
Jurat S. E. F. Le Poidevin
Sir Martin Le Quesne
C. W. Le Tissier
D. J. Le Tissier
H. N. Le Tissier
L. C. Le Tocq
E. H. Lainé
Mr and Mrs S. Lainé
Advocate C. G. P. Lakeman
Mr and Mrs R. J. Leaman
R. Lemprière
Mrs B. M. Lesley
The Honourable Mrs V. Llewellen Palmer
M. I. Lloyd
P. Lockwood
Mrs M. K. Logan
Mrs M. L. Long
A. A. Lopes
T. A. Loveridge

Miss M. E. MacDonald
R. MacDonald
K. M. McAuliffe
David McClintock
John McCormack, F.S.A.
R. R. Machon
G. R. Mahy
Mr and Mrs G. W. Mahy

Harry Maingay
James W. Maingay
Captain James Major
Peter Mansell
Miss S. P. Marquand
R. J. Marquis
James Marr
Dr S. Marsh
Mrs R. C. Martel
Mrs M. H. Martin
R. P. Martin
Mrs D. E. Maslin
P. E. Mason
Mrs E. A. Mather
Mrs M.-L. Mendham (née Robin)
K. Miles
Mr and Mrs R. L. Millard
I. R. Monins
B. Moullin
Dr M. Mowbray
Mrs T. Munro
Dr M. T. Myres

B. E. Naftel
The Revd D. Nash and Mrs J. Nash
Alistair Neilson
P. J. Newbould
Patricia Nichols
Mrs A. Nicolle
Dr D. C. Nicolle
Mr and Mrs J. R. Nicolle
Mrs M. F. Nightingale
M. R. Norman

T. P. O'Leary
S. J. Ogier
G. L. Oke
Ms C. M. Osborne
Mr and Mrs B. R. Owen
Denise Ozanne
D. J. Ozanne
Mrs J. M. Ozanne
N. M. Ozanne
The Misses N. and H. Ozanne
Mrs Y. M. Ozanne

A. P. Payne
R. C. Payne
Mrs M. L. Perkins

Mrs C. A. Perrot
M. W. Peters
Marion Piercey
Captain B. Pill
M. K. Pipe
R. Plumley
R. J. Prevel
J. A. Prout
D. L. Purdy

C. J. Rabey
Mrs A. Radford
John Razzak
Dr S. E. Rebstein
C. P. Renouf
Miss E. Renouf
J. D. Renouf
David Roberts
Mrs A. L. Robilliard
Mr and Mrs D. J. Robilliard
K. L. J. Robilliard
St. J. A. Robilliard
J. P. Robinson
M. E. Robson-Huff-Gallienne
Dr W. J. Rodwell
Deputy John Roper
P. G. Roussel
T. C. B. Roussel
G. R. Rowland
C. J. G. Russell
J. S. Rutter
Mrs Patience Ryan

J. and D. Salmon
Mr G. and Mrs J. Sampson
Mr and Mrs R. E. Schemel
D. Scholes
Mrs I. K. Scott-Slawther
M. F. Seabrook
Mrs A. Seebeck
Mrs A. B. Setters

D. W. F. Smith
Pauline Smith
Mrs R. M. Z. Smith
Mr and Mrs J. C. S. F. Smithies
D. A. Somerville
Duncan Spence
M. Spillman
Mrs M. Spooner
Mrs H. M. Stanford
Mrs J. M. Steel
Miss S. L. Stevens
Ern Stranger
Mr H. R. and Mrs S. K. Stranger
John G. Stranger
Mrs M. C. Swift

Mr and Mrs S. M. Taylor
P. R. Thatcher
D. L. Theisen
Mrs P. V. Tickner
Mrs B. U. Tippett
Mrs M. M. Todd
Mrs M. Torné-Moore
The Reverend B. Torode
S. C. G. Torode
N. R. Tostevin
C. P. G. Tracy
Dr G. D. C. Tytler

C. Van Vessem
Mrs S. M. Veillard
Mrs M. G. Vidamour

Miss E. D. Ward
Miss E. J. Ward
M. A. Ward
Mr and Mrs I. A. Way
Mr and Mrs J. Webb
Miss M. M. White
F. Wilkins
Mr and Mrs M. J. Wilson